FROMMER'S
EasyGuide
TO
CHICAGO

By
Kate Silver

Easy Guides are ✦ Quick To Read   ✦ Light To Carry
✦ For Expert Advice   ✦ In All Price Ranges

FrommerMedia LLC

Published by
FROMMER MEDIA LLC

ISBN 978-1-62887-122-7 (paper), 978-1-62887-123-4 (ebk)

Editorial Director: Pauline Frommer
Editor: Elizabeth Heath
Production Editor: Erin Geile
Cartographer: Andrew Dolan
Cover Design: Howard Grossman

For information on our other products or services, see www.frommers.com.

FrommerMedia LLC also publishes its books in a variety of electronic formats. Some content that appears
in print may not be available in electronic formats.

Manufactured in the United States of America

5 4 3 2 1

CONTENTS

ABOUT THE AUTHOR

Kate Silver's ties to Chicago go back generations, to her great grandfather, followed by her grandparents, who lived here when she was young. She remembers the urban adventures Chicago offered her as a child—taking the train, visiting the Chicago Board of Trade, looking up at skyscrapers—and moved to the city in 2009 to be a part of the action. As a 5-plus-year resident, Silver, who is a journalist and freelance travel writer, brings to this book the perspective of a newer resident coupled with the context of Midwestern roots. Silver has contributed to a number of guidebooks in the past, all of which centered on Las Vegas, her previous home. Her work regularly appears in the *Washington Post, Chicago Tribune, Chicago Sun-Times*, and other publications.

The author would like to thank her boyfriend, Neil, for his patience during the writing of this book and his continued willingness to eat a double dinner in the name of research.

ABOUT THE FROMMER'S TRAVEL GUIDES

For most of the past 50 years, Frommer's has been the leading series of travel guides in North America, accounting for as many as 24% of all guidebooks sold. I think I know why.

Though we hope our books are entertaining, we nevertheless deal with travel in a serious fashion. Our guidebooks have never looked on such journeys as a mere recreation, but as a far more important human function, a time of learning and introspection, an essential part of a civilized life. We stress the culture, lifestyle, history, and beliefs of the destinations we cover, and urge our readers to seek out people and new ideas as the chief rewards of travel.

We have never shied from controversy. We have, from the beginning, encouraged our authors to be intensely judgmental, critical—both pro and con—in their comments, and wholly independent. Our only clients are our readers, and we have triggered the ire of countless prominent sorts, from a tourist newspaper we called "practically worthless" (it unsuccessfully sued us) to the many rip-offs we've condemned.

And because we believe that travel should be available to everyone regardless of their incomes, we have always been cost-conscious at every level of expenditure. Though we have broadened our recommendations beyond the budget category, we insist that every lodging we include be sensibly priced. We use every form of media to assist our readers, and are particularly proud of our feisty daily website, the award-winning Frommers.com.

I have high hopes for the future of Frommer's. May these guidebooks, in all the years ahead, continue to reflect the joy of travel and the freedom that travel represents. May they always pursue a cost-conscious path, so that people of all incomes can enjoy the rewards of travel. And may they create, for both the traveler and the persons among whom we travel, a community of friends, where all human beings live in harmony and peace.

Arthur Frommer

THE BEST OF CHICAGO

C hicago is, indeed, my kind of town, and after your visit to the country's third largest city, I hope it will be yours, too. Chicago has it all: world-class culture, incredible food, vibrant green park spaces, a great lake, and miles and miles of sandy beaches. Plus, it's all wrapped up in a bundle of Midwestern friendliness and served without a whiff of pretension.

The name "Chicago" actually comes from a Native American word referring to a stinky onion that flourished in the wild here, more than 200 years ago. Today, I like to think of that stinky onion more figuratively: when you pull the first layer of Chicago back, you begin to realize just how many layers still remain. The "Windy City," nicknamed not for its gusty breezes, but for its hot-air-filled politicians, has a fascinating history, much of which is kept alive through its museums, architecture, and locals who love to spin a good yarn, often with a pint in hand. From **Grant Park,** the skyline is awe-inspiring, while the attractions of the nearby **Museum Campus** draw visitors and locals alike. Serious shoppers head for the high-fashion boutiques and multilevel malls along the **Magnificent Mile,** but the tree-lined streets of the **Gold Coast** and walking trails along the **Lake Michigan** shoreline offer a respite from the crowds. A rattling **El** ride through the heart of the **Loop** brings the city's booming business district up close and personal, allowing for in-depth exploration of the area, car free.

Although it's impossible to cover everything notable in Chicago in just one book—much less one "best of" chapter—I've attempted to scratch the surface and help jumpstart a path of exploration. Because Chicago has so many noteworthy restaurants, hotels, bars and overall experiences, I've included my "best of" list below, but I have no doubt that if we were to poll 300 Chicagoans, we'd get 300 entirely different lists. One of the best parts of exploring Chicago is that you get to make it your own. I challenge you to use this list as a guide, but don't be afraid to stray from it and find your own favorites, as well.

CHICAGO'S best AUTHENTIC EXPERIENCES

o **Ride the rails:** Find out why the Loop is so named by hopping a Brown Line elevated train (or "the El," for short). Watch the city unfold as the train crosses the Chicago River and screeches past downtown high-rises. Half the fun is peeping into the windows of offices and homes as you speed by. Don't worry, even us locals can't resist. See "Getting Around," p. 226.

○ **Escape downtown:** Stay on the Brown Line, or transfer to another train and escape downtown. Chicago is known as "a city of neighborhoods" for good reason. Each neighborhood feels like its own small town with its own distinct identity, from the gentrifying-yet-still-grunge-filled Logan Square to the multi-million dollar brownstones of Old Town and Lincoln Park. See "Neighborhoods in Brief," p. 36.

○ **Pedal with the people:** See those powder blue bikes around town? Those are Divvy bikes, and they've been a huge hit with locals and visitors alike since Chicago unveiled its Divvy bike share program in 2013, dispersing 4,000 bikes to 400 stations throughout the city. With Chicago's infamous traffic, it generally takes the same amount of time to bike from A to B as it does to drive or take public transportation. Plus, with Divvy, it's easier to justify that extra piece of Chicago-style pizza. See the "biking" section in chapter 6, page 161.

○ **Chill out on the lakefront:** It really is cooler by the lake (both literally and figuratively), and we Chicagoans treat the Lake Michigan waterfront as our personal playground. Miles of parkland hug the shoreline; walk to Monroe Harbor for picture-perfect views of the city or join active Lincoln Park singles for biking or jogging farther north. For an even better look at the city, get out on the water. At Navy Pier, you can board a vessel that's just your speed, from a water taxi to a tall-mast schooner. See "Exploring Chicago" chapter, p. 160.

○ **Stroll through a street fest:** There are more than 400 to choose from throughout the year, peaking in the summer, with fests that pay tribute to heritage, arts, food, music, and more. See street fest sidebar (p. 127) in the "Exploring Chicago" chapter.

○ **Raise a glass:** There's no doubt you'll find long lines and high heels waiting to get into the clubs in River North, but the preferred Chicago nightlife is in bars, lounges, and taverns around town. Just a few years ago, it seemed that the more neighborhood-like, the darker the corners, the colder the Guinness, the better. But today, cocktail enthusiasts from their 20s to their 80s are enjoying the craft cocktail revolution, whether they're savoring effervescent, on-tap bourbon elixirs at **Billy Sunday** in Logan Square (p. 219), an Italian sorbet cocktail in the West Loop's **Lone Wolf** (p. 213), or a fresh-fruit-filled Painkiller No. 3 at Chicago's newest tiki bar, **Three Dots and a Dash.** See p. 214.

CHICAGO'S best OVERALL EXPERIENCES

○ **Take it all in:** You can see four states on a clear day from the **Skydeck at Willis Tower** (some still call it Sears): Indiana, Michigan, Wisconsin, and Illinois. Plus, with the recent addition of the **Ledge,** you can feel your palms moisten as you stare straight down 1,353 feet, 103 stories to the ground. See p. 113.

○ **Explore the architecture:** The first skyscraper was built in Chicago, and the architecture here continues to be a tradition of one-upmanship. Just by taking a walk through the Loop, you'll see incredible, towering structures (see Loop walking tour, p. 183). But I strongly encourage you to sign up for an architecture tour with the Chicago Architecture Foundation. You'll walk away with a better understanding of Chicago history and the stories behind our skyline. Although all of the tours are outstanding, the architecture river cruise is a standout. See p. 155.

- **Picnic in the park:** Millennium Park, that is. Or at the closest beach. Or just grab a spot of grass along the lake. Whatever you do, find some food, sit down and gaze at the towering skyline, then the peaceful lake, and understand why we Chicagoans love our city so much—enough to put up with those nasty winters.
- **Take in a game:** Chicago is a huge sports town, so if you really want to be one with the locals, hit the stands. You have a whole lot to choose from—baseball, basketball, football, hockey, soccer, we've got 'em all. See the "Exploring Chicago" chapter, p. 164.

CHICAGO'S best DINING EXPERIENCES

- **Best diner: Little Goat.** At Little Goat, by Stephanie Izard, of *Top Chef*/Girl and the Goat fame, you almost expect to see "Lurlene" embroidered on the servers' purple diner dresses at this reinvented diner, as they dole out goat burgers, paratha breakfast burritos, and fish tostadas to the hungry masses who gladly wait an hour in line for a table. See p. 107.
- **Best sushi: Kai Zan.** It's a bit of a hike to get to Kai Zan, on the edge of Humboldt Park, but you can thank me for it later. Each small fish dish is handled like a work of art here, and your entire plate comes alive by picking and choosing additions like tempura flakes and ginger. See p. 107.
- **Best restaurant for ethnic food you didn't realize existed: Fat Rice.** Okay, so there's only one Macanese restaurant I've ever eaten at, and it's Fat Rice in Logan Square. In my research for this book, this was the singular place that I would have gone back to every night if I could, just for another bowl of squid fried rice. See p. 108.
- **Best cheap eats: Nhu Lan.** At this tiny Vietnamese spot, a $3 to $4 banh mi sandwich is a meal in itself. Add some vitamins with a fresh fruit smoothie with boba. At $3.50, the drink is actually pricier than some of the sandwiches. See p. 105.
- **Best spots for kids:** My boyfriend still smiles at memories of childhood trips to **Ed Debevic's**, where today, sassy servers still sling burgers and Green River soda to kids, who get a kick out of their snark. See p. 83. And then, of course, there's the kid-friendly deep-dish pizza experience, which you'll want to do at least once (don't arrive starving; the pizzas take at least a half hour to cook). **Gino's East** and **Lou Malnati's** have been around for decades, and they're still serving up authentic versions of the city's gooey, gut-busting specialty. For something different from the usual fast food, try **Wishbone** in the West Loop, a family-owned spot specializing in Southern food with a casual vibe and plenty of mix-and-match menu options for fussy eaters. See p. 94, 88, and 83, respectively.
- **Best pizza deal: La Madia.** You won't find Chicago-style pie at La Madia, but you will find light, fresh, and delectably thin crust, which two can share, along with a salad and cookies for $19 ($31 if you add two glasses of wine). See p. 95.
- **Most romantic spot: L2O.** Low lighting, cozy booths, and spacious tables invite in a little Love Potion No. 9 at L20. Lovers bat eyes at one another over favorites like avocado-wrapped ahi tuna, or bond over their surprise at boundary-pushing courses like pigeon and geoduck. See p. 100.
- **Best restaurant for a celebratory splurge: Boka.** The dining room decor is sophisticated yet playful and the menu is creative yet approachable at Boka. It feels like

every diner is celebrating at this Lincoln Park spot, where jubilance and eclectic American cuisine come together for a perfect evening. It's a refreshing change from the stiff hush that many fine-dining establishments summon. See p. 96.

CHICAGO'S best FREE THINGS TO DO

o **Explore Millennium Park:** This downtown park, carved out of the northwest corner of Grant Park, is one of the city's best spots for strolling, hanging out, and people-watching, and it's an easy walk from downtown hotels. While the Jay Pritzker Pavilion, designed by Frank Gehry, is the highest-profile attraction, the park's two main sculptures have quickly become local favorites. *Cloud Gate,* by British sculptor Anish Kapoor, looks like a giant silver kidney bean; watch your reflection bend and distort as you walk around and underneath. The *Crown Fountain,* designed by Spanish sculptor Jaume Plensa, is framed by two giant video screens that project faces of ordinary Chicagoans. It looks a little creepy at first, but watch the kids splashing in the shallow water and you'll soon realize that this is public art at its best. See p. 116.

o **Go wild at Lincoln Park Zoo:** You have no excuse not to visit: Lincoln Park Zoo is open 365 days a year and, astonishingly, remains completely free, despite many recent upgrades. Occupying a prime spot of Lincoln Park close to the lakefront, the zoo is small enough to explore in an afternoon and varied enough to make you feel as though you've traveled around the world. For families, this is a don't-miss stop. See p. 134.

o **Listen to music under the stars:** Summer is prime time for live music—and often you won't have to pay a dime. The Grant Park Music Festival presents free classical concerts from June through August in Millennium Park. A few blocks south, you'll find the outdoor dance floor that's home to Chicago SummerDance, where you can learn new dance moves and swing to a variety of live acts on Thursday through Sunday nights. The summer also brings a range of large-scale music festivals—from Blues Fest to a rock-'n'-roll-themed Fourth of July concert—but the Grant Park classical concerts are considerably less crowded and perhaps a whiff more civilized. See p. 200.

o **Visit a museum or other attraction:** A number of museums and attractions here are free year-round, like the Chicago Botanic Garden, Chicago Cultural Center, Garfield Park Conservatory, David and Alfred Smart Museum of Art, Museum of Contemporary Photography, National Museum of Mexican Art, and others. Some of the others offer free days. DuSable Museum of African American History is free on Sunday, and kids younger than 15 get in free to the Chicago Children's Museum on Navy Pier the first Sunday of each month. See box p. 123.

o **Watch the skies light up with Navy Pier fireworks:** Grab some grass or sand along the lakefront and behold the colorful fire in the sky. Twice a week, Wednesdays at 9:30pm and Saturdays at 10:15pm, from late May until the end of August, Navy Pier blasts a fireworks show that rivals just about any Fourth of July, aside from Dubai, that is. See p. 132.

o **Take a free tour with a local guide:** The Chicago Greeter program offers complimentary tours, ranging from 1 to 4 hours. Tours can be tailored to your language and interests, and are a quick, easy, and free way to discover the real Chicago. See p. 118.

HOG Butcher for the World,
Tool Maker, Stacker of Wheat,
Player with Railroads and the Nation's Freight Handler;
Stormy, husky, brawling,
City of the Big Shoulders.

– from "Chicago," by Carl Sandburg

best UNEXPECTED CHICAGO

○ **Neighborhood flavor:** You can eat some amazing food in the Loop, but if you venture further out, you'll feel like you've crossed into a different city. Head north to sample the wonderful lunch buffets of "Little India" on Devon Avenue (p. 105); travel to the Pilsen neighborhood, where it's well worth the wait for delicious enchiladas and gorditas at Nuevo Leon (p. 79); all eyes are on the noodle artisan as he pulls your ramen at Chinatown's Hing Kee (p. 79); and nothing says Greektown like an order of flaming cheese at Athena or its Mediterranean neighbors (p. 79).

○ **Beercades:** Leave the pricey craft cocktails of the Loop behind, and head to your closest barcade, aka beercade, a brilliant combination of bar and arcade. Chicago has a number of them to choose from, with locations in Lakeview, Wicker Park, Logan Square, and Boystown (p. 218).

○ **Bring your own booze policies:** Many of the restaurants in Chicago allow diners to bring their own beer and wine (see p. 82 for tips on a few places to go). If you land at a spot with this policy, you can rest assured that you're dining with locals and not tourists.

○ **Beaches:** If you haven't spent much time in Chicago, "sandy beaches" probably aren't your first association with the city. But "The Third Coast" is actually one of Chicago's nicknames, thanks to our beachfront location on Lake Michigan. Throughout the summer, the area's beaches remained packed, with families grilling, twenty-somethings playing beach volleyball, and love birds snuggling in the sand. See p. 160 for overviews of some of our gorgeous beaches.

CHICAGO'S best FAMILY EXPERIENCES

○ **Lincoln Park Zoo:** With a carousel, a farm, a train to ride, and hundreds of animals, the Lincoln Park Zoo is a kid's paradise—and a parent's, too: it's free! See p. 134.

○ **Museum of Science and Industry:** Whether you're crawling through a heart valve, chasing a miniature train, or stirring up your own tornado, this science-filled playroom is entertaining for all ages. See p. 139.

○ **Chicago Children's Museum:** If it has the power to lure locals to touristy Navy Pier, you know this museum has got to be good. Kids can build buildings, climb treehouses, drive a firetruck, create art, and more. Plus, if you've made it this far, your kids will love the Ferris wheel on Navy Pier. See p. 154.

○ **Shedd Aquarium:** With sea lions, dolphins, beluga whales, and more, the sea is truly your oyster at Shedd Aquarium. After getting eye-to-eye with the underwater creatures, kids can splash and play in the Polar Play Zone, made just for them. See p. 127.

CHICAGO'S best HOTELS

o **Best luxury hotel for the old-money set: The Langham.** The team of eight butlers sets this new luxury property apart from any hotel in town. They'll draw your bath, unpack your clothes, help you get show tickets, and more. And then there are the rooms. When I first saw the large, beautifully designed rooms here, surrounded by floor to ceiling windows in the former IBM building, I wanted to move in and never leave. See p. 65.

o **Best luxury hotel for the new money set: Trump International Hotel & Tower.** Want to make-believe you've got your own pied-à-terre in the heart of downtown? This is the place to live out your fantasy—the contemporary-cool rooms are actually studio apartments with full kitchens, plenty of space to lounge, and killer views of the skyline. See p. 65.

o **Best moderately priced hotel: Hotel Monaco.** Its prime Loop location and stylish decor set Hotel Monaco apart, and the window seats in every room are a lovely spot for taking in the city. Plus, with the most pet-friendly policy in town, you can bring along Fluffy or borrow a goldfish for the night. See p. 52.

o **Best inexpensive hotel: Acme Hotel Company.** "Character-filled" is an understatement for the Acme Hotel, a small, locally owned property where staff wear jeans and the artsy vibe is a refreshing change from beige, cookie-cutter properties in this River North spot. See p. 67.

o **Best room service: The Thompson and The James.** Gone are the days when a generic kitchen served boring, overpriced room service. In Chicago, many hotels have tasked their on-site, high-profile restaurants with this amenity, to great response. This category is a tie. The Thompson Hotel's (p. 70) fresh seafood/Italian–focused restaurant, Nico Osteria, has been a huge hit with guests. And at The James Hotel (p. 68), visitors can have succulent Chateaubriand from David Burke's Primehouse served on their own timetable.

o **Best hotel pool:** With its floor-to-ceiling windows overlooking Michigan Avenue, the pool at the **Peninsula Chicago** is a bright, stylish oasis flooded with natural light. But for historic charm, it's hard to beat the Spanish-styled junior Olympic-size pool at the **InterContinental Chicago.** Considered an engineering marvel when it was constructed in 1929, it was a favorite training spot for Olympic gold-medal swimmer (and later *Tarzan* star) Johnny Weissmuller. See p. 58 and 61, respectively.

o **Best Off-the-Beaten-Path Hotels:** The **Guest House Hotel**, the **Majestic Hotel,** and the **Best Western Hawthorne Terrace,** located in residential areas on the North Side, have a more personal feel than many downtown hotels. They're also convenient to public transportation and less expensive than most of what you'll find in the Loop. See p. 45, 72, and 71, respectively.

o **Best Service:** The attention to detail, regal pampering, and well-connected concierges at the **Waldorf Astoria** (p. 69), **Ritz-Carlton** (p. 59), and the **Four Seasons** (p. 58) make them the hotels of choice for travelers who want to feel like royalty. But the team of butlers at **The Langham** (p. 65) truly takes the service-centric cake.

CHICAGO'S most overrated EXPERIENCES

- **Navy Pier:** Here's a little secret: we locals rarely go to Navy Pier. In fact, we're shocked every time we hear that it's the No. 1 tourist and leisure destination in the Midwest. It's overpriced, crowded, and a pain to get to. Yes, you get incredible views of the city and the lake, but you can get those same views from any of Chicago's beaches, minus the crowds, the parking prices, and the $7 ice cream cone. If we locals do go to the Pier, it's because a) We have visitors from out of town who have requested it; or b) We're visiting the Children's Museum, Shakespeare Theater, or taking a boat cruise, all of which require us to set foot here.

- **Taste of Chicago:** They say it's the largest food festival in the world, drawing in 3 million people over 5 days. Most locals I know have been once—if that—and that's enough. Food is overpriced, lines are insanely long, and we just don't understand why you'd go to this massive festival for a mediocre meal when you can visit any of the participating restaurants for a far better experience.

- **Billy Goat Tavern:** Here's the thing. Billy Goat earned its reputation decades ago for having a surly staff and mediocre service. The Goat became famous when *Saturday Night Live* picked up on its foibles, broadcasting it to the world. Today, the self-titled "World Famous Billy Goat" has nine locations in the city and in the 'burbs. And yet, its burgers are mediocre at best, it still doesn't serve fries ("No fries, cheeps!"), and I still don't get the appeal. If you are going to go to a Billy Goat, make sure it's the original, on the lower level of Michigan (430 N. Michigan). The dive bar is a great place to get a drink and, quite likely, rub elbows with some of the journalists who have helped make this place famous.

- **Chicago-style pizza:** If you haven't tried our deep dish, you should. But don't expect it to change your life. The pizza, in which the crust alone can weigh two pounds or more, is as thick as a bicycle tire. It's topped with gooey cheese and then tomato sauce, and is a force to be reckoned with. Locals actually tend to prefer thin-crust pizza, which is far less nap inducing, and you don't get heart palpitations just looking at it.

CHICAGO'S best NIGHTLIFE EXPERIENCES

- **Get the blues:** Here in the world capital of the blues, you've got your pick of places to feel them, from the touristy but lively atmosphere of Kingston Mines in Lincoln Park, where musicians perform continuously on two stages, to the roadhouse feel of Buddy Guy's Legends, where musicians in town while on tour have been known to play impromptu sets. See "The Live Music Scene," p. 206.

- **Take in a show:** The stage lights rarely go dark on one of the country's busiest theater scenes. Chicago is home to a downtown Broadway-style district anchored by beautifully restored historic theaters, the nationally known Goodman Theatre, and the city's resident Shakespeare troupe. Beyond downtown, you'll find a number of innovative independent companies, where future stars get their big breaks and the pure love of theater makes up for the low budgets. See the "Chicago After Dark" chapter, p. 197.

HOW TO BLEND WITH THE locals

o **Walk through the revolving door.** Why? Because it's more energy efficient, keeping either cool or warm air in, depending on the season. Most of our buildings downtown have a number of door options, and generally, we can pick out the tourists because they're either the ones avoiding the revolving door or trying to fit into *our* small section of revolving door, along with us. Grab your own wedge of the door and push your way in like the rest of us.

o **Consider putting mustard on that hot dog.** Between you and me, I like ketchup on a hot dog. But many Chicagoans have a thing about it. They won't burn you at the stake, but you may get a raised eyebrow, or at worst, end up at a hot dog shop that refuses to provide ketchup on principle. Try the mustard. It's not bad.

o **Buy a tamal from the tamale guy.** You'll have to get out of the Loop and into a neighborhood tavern for this Chicago-est of Chicago experiences. A number of tamale guys actually roam the neighborhood pubs, and their M.O. is the same: They carry a small, portable cooler filled with hot, fresh tamales and salsa, usually charging $5 for six. In sobriety, it may seem like a risky endeavor. After a few pints of Half Acre's Daisy Cutter (a local brew) however, it's a brilliant investment. Where can you find him? No idea. He's

like a super hero, showing up where he's needed most. You can try and track him on Twitter (@tamaletracker) but he may be gone in the time it takes to say "Tamales, por favor!"

o **Get your car towed or ticketed.** If you opted to drive here or rent a car, be very careful of where you park. Parking signs are both ubiquitous and tricky, sometimes contradicting one another. Some areas of town require permits, others close parking lanes during certain hours, and in winter, snow routes go into effect. Many of us law-abiding citizens have gotten ticketed and towed in Chicago, victims of the overzealous, highly profitable, shockingly vigilant machine.

o **Be friendly.** Chicago is in the Midwest, after all, and the Midwest is known for its pleasant attitude and friendliness. When I first moved here from Las Vegas, it actually took a while to get used to how genuinely kind perfect strangers were. I used to make a game of it: "Flirting with me, or just Midwestern?" Usually, the answer was the latter.

o **Walk.** We walk a lot in Chicago. A mile is nothing to us. Two miles, on a nice day, isn't so bad either. In a city with horrible traffic and high density, walking is often quicker than public transportation and certainly faster than driving around and then trying to find a parking space. Plus, there's so much to see!

o **Bask in cool jazz at the Green Mill:** This atmospheric uptown jazz club is the place to go to soak up smooth sounds from some of the hottest up-and-coming performers on the jazz scene, while the club itself is a living museum of 1930s Chicago. See p. 205.

o **Deepen your laugh lines at an improv show:** Chicago is a comedy breeding ground, having launched the careers of John Belushi, Bill Murray, Mike Myers, and Tina Fey through improv hot spots such as Second City. We Chicagoans are a funny people, let us prove it to ya at a comedy club or two. See p. 203.

THE best CHICAGO WEBSITES

o **Metromix** (www.chicago.metromix.com): Operated by the *Chicago Tribune*, this site features expanded versions of the newspaper's entertainment and restaurant coverage. It's a good place to check reviews and get an early look at new bars and nightclubs.

o **The Chicago Reader** (www.chicagoreader.com): The site of the city's alternative weekly paper is the place to find extensive coverage of the local music scene and reviews of smaller theater productions.

o **Time Out Chicago** (www.timeout.com/chicago): This online entertainment magazine covers food, music, the art scene, and shopping with a slightly irreverent attitude. Scroll through the site's extensive event listings, and you'll find more than enough cool happenings to keep you busy while you're here.

o **Choose Chicago** (www.choosechicago.com): This official Chicago visitors' site gives a good overview of festivals, parades, and other upcoming events in town.

o **Chicagoist** (www.chicagoist.com): Want to see what issues have Chicagoans riled up? Check out this sounding board for local news (an offshoot of the New York–centric site Gothamist.com), which covers everything from government corruption scandals to the latest celebrity sightings. You'll find a similar roundup of news, local gossip, and opinion pieces at the online magazine *Gapers Block* (www.gapersblock.com).

o **LTH Forum** (www.lthforum.com): Local foodies come to this bulletin board to get the scoop on hot new restaurant openings. The site also keeps a running list of "Great Neighborhood Restaurants," if you're looking for places with character rather than buzz.

o **League of Chicago Theatres** (www.chicagoplays.com): If you're planning to catch a show while in town, visit this comprehensive theater site, where you can search specific dates to see what's playing.

CHICAGO IN CONTEXT

2

Chicago has spent the last few years in the national media spotlight, for reasons both inspiring and embarrassing. On the one hand, it's the adopted hometown of President Barack Obama, the place he got his start in politics and where he still maintains his Hyde Park home. His victory rally in downtown's Grant Park signaled Chicago's vitality and influence to the whole world (many of his top presidential advisors were local business and philanthropic leaders before they moved to Washington).

Unfortunately, Chicago must also lay claim to politicians such as former Illinois state governor Rod Blagojevich. "Blago," a product of the city's shady Democratic political machine, stunned even cynical Chicagoans with his blatant moneygrubbing and attempts to sell Obama's former Senate seat to the highest bidder. Obama's talk about a new era of hope in politics turned out to be short-lived, with his ties to Chicago wheeler-dealers a liability. Blagojevich proved that the old ways of doing business aren't so easily erased.

It's easy to be cynical about Chicago politics—the miracle is that such cynicism doesn't pervade the way Chicagoans feel about their city. We're proud of our gorgeous skyline and love nothing better than hearing visitors compare our hometown favorably to New York. (You'll make friends for life if you tell us you'd rather live here than the Big Apple.) As the retail, financial, and legal center of the Midwest, Chicago has a thriving, diverse business community and an active arts scene, attracting everyone from thrifty wannabe hipsters to ambitious future CEOs. The one thing they've got in common? A certain humility that comes with living in the Second City. Being down-to-earth is a highly rated local virtue.

In this chapter, you'll get an overview of the issues facing the city today, as well as a quick primer on Chicago's history. Because architecture plays such an important role in the look of the city—and so many influential architects have worked here—you'll also find a guide to the major styles of buildings you'll pass by during your visit. But you won't get a full sense of the city's spirit unless you understand the city's role in popular culture, too. Chicago has been home to many great writers and has served as a setting for dozens of films, so this chapter includes a section on recommended books and movies. Check out a few before your trip to put you in a Chicago state of mind.

CHICAGO TODAY

Like other major American cities, Chicago has benefited from a renewed interest in urban living over the past 2 decades, as former suburbanites flock to the neighborhoods that are a walk, bus-, bike- or El-ride from downtown and fall in love with all of the perks that come with city living: a theater scene, dining scene, nightlife, shopping, and endless people watching. Massive new condo buildings have sprung up along the lakefront south of the Loop, while the West Loop—once a no-man's-land of industrial buildings—has become another hot residential neighborhood.

In many ways, this building boom has erased the physical legacy of Chicago's past. The stockyards that built the city's fortune have disappeared; the industrial factories that pumped smoke into the sky south of the city now sit vacant. Although no one misses the stench of the stockyards or the pollution that came with being an industrial center, the city's character has become muted along the way. Living here no longer requires the toughness that was once a hallmark of the native Chicagoan.

And yet a certain brashness remains. Although some people may still have a "Second City" chip on their shoulders, we've gotten more confident about our ability to compete with New York or Los Angeles. We know our museums, restaurants, and entertainment options are as good as those of any other city in the country; we just wish everyone else knew it, too.

Relatively affordable compared to New York, Chicago is a popular post-college destination for ambitious young people from throughout the Midwest. The city also draws immigrants from other countries (as it has for more than 100 years). Hispanics (mostly of Mexican origin) now make up nearly one-third of the city's population. Immigration from Eastern Europe is also common, especially from countries such as Poland, Russia, and Romania. This constant influx of new blood keeps the city vibrant.

This is not to say the city doesn't have problems. Despite roughly 2.8 million people total and a large African-American population, Chicago's residential districts continue to be some of the most segregated in the country. The South Side is overwhelmingly black; the North Side remains mostly white. As in other major cities, the public school system seems to constantly teeter on the edge of disaster. Although fine schools are scattered throughout the city, competition to get into them seems to surpass that of Ivy League colleges. Because of that, many families are forced to send their children to substandard local schools with high dropout rates or opt to move to the suburbs.

However, the waves of gentrification sweeping the city have transformed many neighborhoods for the better. For years, the city's public housing was a particular disgrace, epitomized by decrepit 1960s high-rises that had degenerated into isolated bastions of violence and hopelessness. The largest and worst complexes have been torn down during the last decade, replaced with low-rise, mixed-income housing. Some streets I used to avoid after dark are now lined with brand-new supermarkets, parks, and—inevitably—a Starbucks or two.

The city's crime problem has been more intractable. Despite a murder rate that's one of the highest in the country, Chicago doesn't strike visitors as a dangerous place, because most of the violence is contained within neighborhoods where gangs congregate and tourists rarely go. But gang-instigated shootings are still shockingly common on the South Side and West Side, and children are often innocent victims caught in the crossfire. It's something we've gotten far too blasé about, and it continues to be a blot on Chicago's reputation.

Another continuing embarrassment is our local politics. Time and again, our aldermen and other city officials reward our cynicism with yet another scandal involving insider payoffs and corrupt city contracts. For more than 20 years under Mayor Richard M. Daley (himself the son of another longtime mayor, Richard J. Daley), Chicagoans accepted a certain level of shady behavior—after all, there was no denying that the city blossomed under the Daleys' leadership.

When the younger Daley stepped aside in the spring of 2011, his potential successors were quick to serve up the usual campaign promises about wiping out corruption. Now we're left wondering: Is it possible? Our newest mayor, Rahm Emanuel, is no stranger to political fights: He worked in the Clinton White House, served as a member of the U.S. House of Representatives, and survived 2 years as President Obama's chief of staff. Emanuel, a dance- and theater-lover, has also pledged his strong support to the city's sometimes cash-strapped cultural institutions, which is good news for residents and visitors alike. But the city at large scoffed in 2013, when the Board of Education passed his plan to close 50 of our public schools, mostly in poor, black areas. In spite of the local politicians, we Chicagoans passionately defend and boast about our city. Ever since the stockyards were our main source of wealth, we've become masters of overlooking the unsavory. As long as Chicago thrives, we don't seem to really care how it happens.

LOOKING BACK: CHICAGO HISTORY

First Settlement

Chicago owes its existence to its strategic position: The patch of land where it stands straddles a key point along an inland water route linking Canada to the Gulf of Mexico.

In 1673, Jacques Marquette, a French Jesuit missionary, and Louis Joliet, an explorer, found a short portage between two critically placed rivers, one connected to the Mississippi, and the other (via the Chicago River) to Lake Michigan. Although Native Americans had blazed this trail centuries beforehand, its discovery by the French was the first step in Chicago's founding—although no permanent settlement was built there for another 100 years.

By then, the British controlled the territory, having defeated the French over 70 years of intermittent warfare. After the Revolutionary War, the land around the mouth of the Chicago River passed to the United States. The Native American inhabitants, however, wouldn't give up their land without a fight, which is why the first building erected here—between 1803 and 1808—was the military outpost Fort Dearborn. (It sat on the south side of what is now the Michigan Avenue Bridge, on the site of the current McCormick Bridgehouse & Chicago River Museum; p. 119.) Skirmishes with local Native American tribes continued until 1832. A year later, the settlement of 300-plus inhabitants was officially incorporated under the name "Chicago." (A French version of a Native American word believed to mean "wild onion," it may also have referred to the equally non-aromatic local skunks.)

Speaking of Chicago . . .

Chicago is a facade of skyscrapers facing a lake, and behind the facade every type of dubiousness.

–E. M. Forster, British author

Gateway to the West

Land speculation began immediately, and Chicago was carved piecemeal and sold off to finance the Illinois and Michigan Canal, which eliminated the narrow land portage and fulfilled the long-standing vision of connecting the two great waterways. Commercial activity quickly followed. Chicago grew in size and wealth, shipping grain and livestock to the eastern markets and lumber to the prairies of the West. Ironically, by the time the Illinois and Michigan Canal was completed in 1848, the railroad had arrived, and the water route that gave Chicago its *raison d'être* was rapidly becoming obsolete. Boxcars, not boats, became the principal mode of transportation throughout the region. The combination of the railroad, the emergence of local manufacturing, and, later, the Civil War caused Chicago to grow wildly.

The most revolutionary product of the era sprang from the mind of Chicago inventor Cyrus McCormick, whose reaper filled in for the farmhands who had been sent off to the nation's battlefields. Local merchants not only thrived on the contraband trade in cotton during the war, but also secured lucrative contracts from the federal government to provide the army with tents, uniforms, saddles, harnesses, lumber, bread, and meat. By 1870, Chicago's population had grown to 300,000, a thousand times greater than its original population, in just 37 years since incorporation.

The Great Fire

A year later, the city lay in ashes. The Great Chicago Fire of 1871 began on the southwest side of the city on October 8. Legend places its exact origin in the O'Leary shed on DeKoven Street, although most historians have exonerated the poor cow that supposedly started the blaze by kicking over a lantern. The fire jumped the river and continued north through the night and the following day, fizzling out only when it started to rain. The fire took 300 lives—a relatively low number, considering its size—but destroyed 18,000 buildings and left 90,000 people homeless.

The city began to rebuild as soon as the rubble was cleared. By 1873, the city's downtown business and financial district was up and running again, and 2 decades later Chicago had sufficiently recovered to stage the 1893 World's Columbian Exposition commemorating the 400th anniversary of the discovery of America. The Exposition was, in effect, Chicago's grand coming-out party, a chance to show millions of visitors that this was a modern, progressive city. Chicago already had a reputation as a brash business center; now it proved it could also be beautiful. *Harper's Magazine* described the "White City," the collection of formal buildings constructed for the Exposition, as "a Venus that arose from Lake Michigan."

The Great Fire gave an unprecedented boost to the professional and artistic development of the nation's architects. Drawn by the unlimited opportunities to build, they gravitated to the city in droves, and the city raised a homegrown crop of architects. Chicago's reputation as an American Athens, packed with monumental and decorative buildings, is a direct byproduct of the disastrous fire that nearly brought the city to ruin.

In the meantime, the city's labor pool continued to grow, as many immigrants decided to stay rather than head for the prairie. Chicago still shipped meat and agricultural commodities around the nation and the world, and the city was rapidly becoming

Looking Back at Chicago

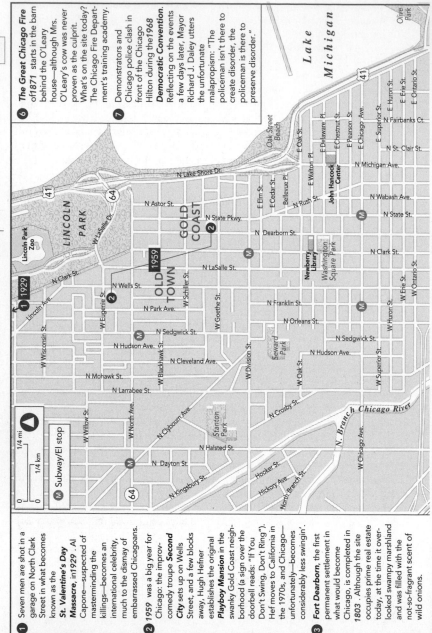

6 **The Great Chicago Fire** of *1871* starts in the barn behind the O'Leary house—although Mrs. O'Leary's cow was never proven as the culprit. What's on the site today? The Chicago Fire Department's training academy.

7 Demonstrators and Chicago police clash in front of the Chicago Hilton during the *1968 Democratic Convention.* Reflecting on the events a few days later, Mayor Richard J. Daley utters the unfortunate malapropism: "The policeman isn't there to create disorder, the policeman is there to preserve disorder."

1 Seven men are shot in a garage on North Clark Street in what becomes known as the *St. Valentine's Day Massacre,* in *1929* . Al Capone—suspected of masterminding the killings—becomes an international celebrity, much to the dismay of embarrassed Chicagoans.

2 *1959* was a big year for Chicago: the improv-comedy troupe *Second City* sets up on Wells Street, and a few blocks away, Hugh Hefner establishes the original *Playboy Mansion* in the swanky Gold Coast neighborhood (a sign over the doorbell reads: "If You Don't Swing, Don't Ring"). Hef moves to California in the 1970s, and Chicago—unfortunately—becomes considerably less swingin'.

3 *Fort Dearborn,* the first permanent settlement in what would become Chicago, is completed in *1803* . Although the site occupies prime real estate today, at the time it overlooked swampy marshland and was filled with the not-so-fragrant scent of wild onions.

Lake Michigan

Olive Park

Oak Street Beach

LINCOLN PARK

GOLD COAST

OLD TOWN

N. Branch Chicago River

John Hancock Center

Newberry Library

Washington Square Park

Seward Park

Stanton Park

Lincoln Park Zoo

M Subway/El stop

1/4 mi
1/4 km

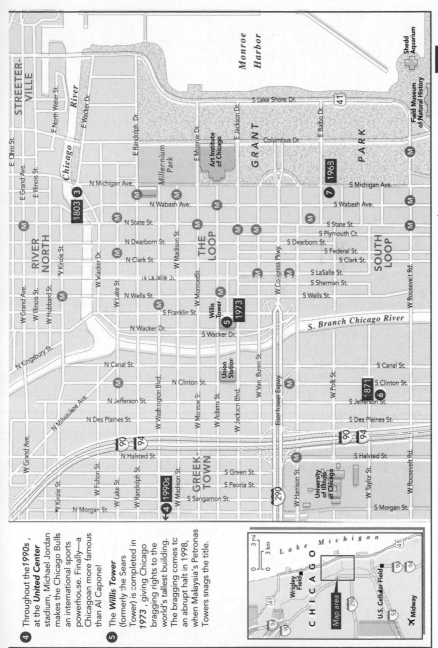

4 Throughout the1990s, at the **United Center** stadium, Michael Jordan makes the Chicago Bulls an international sports powerhouse. Finally—a Chicagoan more famous than Al Capone!

5 The **Willis Tower** (formerly the Sears Tower) is completed in 1973, giving Chicago bragging rights to the world's tallest building. The bragging comes to an abrupt halt in 1998, when Malaysia's Petronas Towers snags the title.

Speaking of Chicago . . .

Loving Chicago is like loving a woman with a broken nose. You may find lovelier lovelies, but never a lovely so real.

–Nelson Algren, Chicago novelist

a mighty industrial center, creating finished goods, particularly for the markets of the ever-expanding western settlements.

The Cradle of Organized Labor

Chicago never seemed to outgrow its frontier rawness. Greed, profiteering, exploitation, and corruption were as critical to its growth as hard work, ingenuity, and civic pride. The spirit of reform arose most powerfully from the working classes, people whose lives were plagued by poverty and disease despite the city's prosperity. When the labor movement awoke in Chicago, it did so with a militancy and commitment that would inspire unions throughout the nation.

The fear and mistrust between workers and the local captains of industry came to a head during the Haymarket Riot in 1886. On May 1, tens of thousands of workers went on strike to demand an 8-hour workday. (Eventually, that date would be immortalized as a national workers' holiday around the world—although never, ironically, in the United States.) A few days later, toward the end of a rally held by a group of anarchist labor activists in Haymarket Square, a bomb exploded near the line of policemen standing guard. The police fired into the crowd, and seven policemen and four workers were killed.

Although the 5-minute incident was in no sense a riot, it seemed to justify fears about the radicalism of the labor movement, and eight rally leaders were soon arrested. After a speedy and by no means impartial trial, five of the men—none of whom were ever proven to have a connection to the bombing—were sentenced to death. The bomber was never found. Haymarket Square itself no longer exists, but a plaque commemorates the spot, on a fairly desolate stretch of Des Plaines Street, just north of Randolph Street.

The city's labor movement fought on. By the 1890s, many of Chicago's workers were organized into the American Federation of Labor. The Pullman Strike of 1894 united black and white railway workers for the first time in a common struggle for higher wages and workplace rights. The Industrial Workers of the World, or the Wobblies, which embraced for a time so many great voices of American labor—Eugene V. Debs, Big Bill Haywood, and Helen Gurley Flynn—was founded in Chicago in 1905.

The Gangster Era

During the 1920s, the combination of Prohibition and a corrupt city administration happy to accept kickbacks from mobsters allowed organized crime to thrive. The most notorious local gangster of the era was a New York transplant named Al Capone, who muscled his way into control of the so-called Chicago Outfit. During his heyday in the mid-1920s, Capone's operations included bootlegging, speakeasies, gambling joints, brothels, and pretty much every other unsavory-but-profitable business; the Outfit's take was reportedly $100 million a year.

Capone liked to promote himself as a humble, selfless businessman—and he did set up soup kitchens at the start of the Great Depression—but he was also a ruthless thug who orchestrated gangland killings while always giving himself an alibi. The most notorious of these hits was the Valentine's Day Massacre of 1929, when four of Capone's men killed seven members of a rival gang in a North Side garage. To gain access to the building, two of Capone's gang dressed as policemen. Thinking it was a raid, the intended victims dropped their guns and put their hands up against the wall, only to be gunned down. The execution-style murder became national news, reinforcing Chicago's already bloody reputation.

In the end, Capone and the Outfit were brought down by a combination of growing public outrage and federal government intervention. With the repeal of Prohibition, the gangsters' main source of income was erased. At around the same time, an agent of the Internal Revenue Service put together evidence that Capone—who had never filed a tax return and claimed to have no income—was, in fact, earning plenty of cash. He was found guilty of tax evasion and served 7 years in prison, including a stint at Alcatraz in San Francisco. After his release, he retired to Florida and died of a heart attack in 1947, at the age of 48. Although the Chicago Outfit continued its shady dealings after Capone's fall—using Las Vegas casinos for massive money-laundering operations—the city was no longer the site of vicious turf battles.

The Chicago Machine

While Chicago was becoming a center of industry, transportation, and finance and a beacon of labor reform, it was also becoming a powerhouse in national politics. Between 1860 and 1968, Chicago was the site of 14 Republican and 10 Democratic presidential nominating conventions. (Some even point to the conventions as the source of Chicago's "Windy City" nickname, laying the blame on politicians who were full of hot air.) The first of the conventions gave the country Abraham Lincoln; the 1968 convention saw the so-called Days of Rage, a series of increasingly violent confrontations between demonstrators protesting the Vietnam War and Chicago police officers. The simmering tension culminated in a riot in Grant Park, outside what's now the Chicago Hilton; as police began beating protestors and bystanders with clubs and fists, TV cameras rolled, and demonstrators chanted, "The whole world is watching."

And it was. The strong-arm tactics of Mayor Richard J. Daley—a supporter of eventual nominee Hubert Humphrey—made Humphrey look bad by association and may have contributed to Humphrey's defeat in the general election. (Maybe it was a wash; some also say that Daley stole the 1960 election for Kennedy.) A national inquiry later declared the event a police-instigated riot, while the city's own mayor-approved investigation blamed out-of-town extremists and provocateurs.

The supposed ringleaders of the uprising included Black Panther leader Bobby Seale; Tom Hayden, co-founder of Students for a Democratic Society; and Abbie Hoffman and Jerry Rubin, founders of the Youth International Party, or Yippies. They were charged with conspiracy and incitement to riot in the trial of the so-called Chicago 8 (later the Chicago 7, after charges in one case were dropped). Five were sentenced to prison terms, but their sentences were soon reversed after it was revealed that the FBI had bugged the offices of the defense lawyers.

The reversal was a setback for Mayor Daley, but his local power base held firm. The Democratic machine that he put in place during his years in office, from 1955 to 1976, was based on a practical sharing of the spoils: As long as the leaders of every ethnic and special interest group in town were guaranteed a certain number of government jobs, their leaders would bring in the votes.

chicago stories: THE GREAT MIGRATION

From 1915 to 1960, hundreds of thousands of black Southerners poured into Chicago, trying to escape segregation and seeking economic freedom and opportunity. The "Great Migration" radically transformed Chicago, both politically and culturally, from an Irish-run city of recent European immigrants into one in which no group had a majority and no politician—white or black—could ever take the black vote for granted. Unfortunately, the sudden change gave rise to many of the disparities that still plague the city, but it also promoted an environment in which many black men and women could rise from poverty to prominence.

Although jobs in the factories, steel mills, and stockyards paid much better than those in the cotton fields, Chicago was not the paradise that many blacks envisioned. Segregation was almost as bad here as it was down South, and most blacks were confined to a narrow "Black Belt" of overcrowded apartment buildings on the South Side. But the new migrants made the best of their situation, and for a time in the 1930s and

'40s, the Black Belt—dubbed "Bronzeville" or the "Black Metropolis" by the community's boosters—thrived as a cultural, musical, religious, and educational mecca. As journalist Nicholas Lemann writes in *The Promised Land: The Great Black Migration and How It Changed America* (Vintage, 1992), "Chicago was a city where a black person could be somebody."

Some of the Southern migrants who made names for themselves in Chicago included black separatist and Nation of Islam founder Elijah Muhammad; Robert S. Abbott, publisher of the powerful Chicago Defender newspaper, who launched a "Great Northern Drive" to bring blacks to the city in 1917; Ida B. Wells, the crusading journalist who headed an anti-lynching campaign; William Dawson, for many years the only black congressman; New Orleans–born jazz pioneers "Jelly Roll" Morton, King Oliver, and Louis Armstrong; Native Son author Richard Wright; John H. Johnson, publisher of Ebony and Jet magazines and one of Chicago's wealthiest residents; blues musicians Willie Dixon,

His reach extended well beyond Chicago's borders; he controlled members of Congress, and every 4 years he delivered a solid Democratic vote in the November elections. But he also helped build Chicago into a modern business powerhouse, promoting the construction of O'Hare Airport, the McCormick Place Convention Center, and the Sears Tower, as well as expanding the city's highway and subway systems. Since his death in 1976, the machine has never wielded such national power, but it still remains almost impossible for a Republican to be voted into local office.

CHICAGO'S ARCHITECTURE

Although the Great Chicago Fire leveled almost three square miles of the downtown area in 1871, it did clear the stage for Chicago's emergence as a breeding ground for innovative architecture. Some of the field's biggest names—Frank Lloyd Wright, Louis Sullivan, and Ludwig Mies van der Rohe—made their mark on the city. And today Chicago's skyline is home to iconic buildings, including the John Hancock Center and the Willis Tower (nee Sears).

Muddy Waters, and Howlin' Wolf; Thomas A. Dorsey, the "father of gospel music," and his greatest disciple, singer Mahalia Jackson; and Ralph Metcalfe, the Olympic gold medalist sprinter who turned to politics once he got to Chicago, eventually succeeding Dawson in Congress.

When a 1948 Supreme Court decision declared it unconstitutional to restrict blacks to certain neighborhoods, the flight of many Bronzeville residents to less crowded areas took a toll on the community. Through the 1950s, almost a third of the housing became vacant, and by the 1960s, the great social experiment of urban renewal through wholesale land clearance and the creation of large tracts of public housing gutted the once-thriving neighborhood.

Community and civic leaders now appear committed to restoring the neighborhood to a semblance of its former glory. Landmark status has been secured for several historic buildings in Bronzeville, including the Liberty Life/Supreme Insurance Company, 3501 S. King Dr., the first African-American–

owned insurance company in the northern United States; and the Eighth Regiment Armory, which, when completed in 1915, was the only armory in the U.S. controlled by an African-American regiment. The former home of the legendary Chess Records at 2120 S. Michigan Ave.—where Howlin' Wolf, Chuck Berry, and Bo Diddley gave birth to the blues and helped define rock 'n' roll—is now home to Willie Dixon's Blues Heaven Foundation (www.bluesheaven.com; ✆ 312/808-1286), which was set up by his widow, Marie Dixon, with financial assistance from rock musician John Mellencamp. Along Dr. Martin Luther King, Jr. Drive, between 24th and 35th streets, several public art installations celebrate Bronzeville's heritage. The most poignant is sculptor Alison Saar's Monument to the Great Northern Migration, at King Drive and 26th Street, depicting a suitcase-toting African-American traveler standing atop a mound of worn shoe soles.

For information about tours of Bronzeville, see "Neighborhood Tours" in chapter 6 (p. 159).

Early Skyscrapers (1880–1920)

In the late 19th century, important technical innovations—including safety elevators, fireproofing, and telecommunications—combined with advances in skeletal construction to create a new building type: the skyscraper. These buildings were spacious, cost-effective, efficient, and quick to build—in short, the perfect architectural solution for Chicago's growing downtown. Architect Louis Sullivan (1865–1924) was the first to formalize a vision of a tall building based on the parts of a classical column. His theories inspired the Chicago School of Architecture, examples of which still fill the city's downtown. Features of Chicago School buildings include a rectangular shape with a flat roof; large windows (made possible by the development of load-bearing interior skeletons); and the use of terra cotta, a light, fireproof material that could be cast in any shape and attached to the exterior, often for decoration.

A good example of the development of the skyscraper is the **Monadnock Building,** 53 W. Jackson Blvd. (Holabird & Root, 1889–91; Holabird & Roche, 1893). The northern section has 6-foot-thick walls at its base to support the building's 17 stories; the newer, southern half has a steel frame clad in terra cotta (allowing the walls to be

Chicago's Most Important Buildings

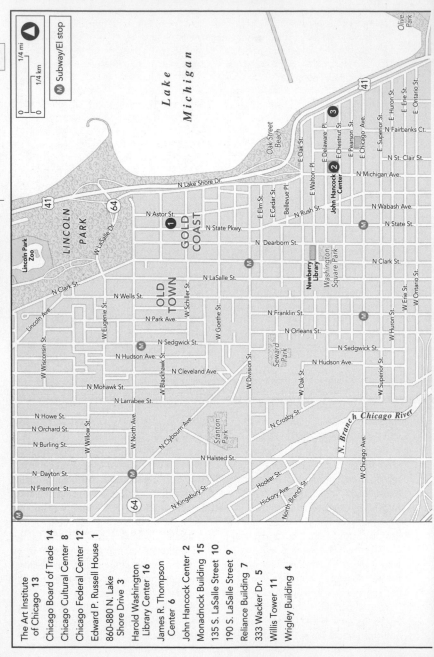

Subway/El stop

The Art Institute
of Chicago **13**

Chicago Board of Trade **14**

Chicago Cultural Center **8**

Chicago Federal Center **12**

Edward P. Russell House **1**

860-880 N. Lake
Shore Drive **3**

Harold Washington
Library Center **16**

James R. Thompson
Center **6**

John Hancock Center **2**

Monadnock Building **15**

135 S. LaSalle Street **10**

190 S. LaSalle Street **9**

Reliance Building **7**

333 Wacker Dr. **5**

Willis Tower **11**

Wrigley Building **4**

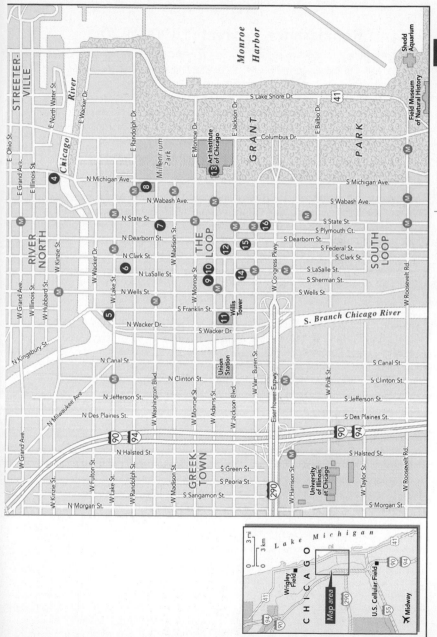

STREETER-
VILLE

*Monroe
Harbor*

Shedd
Aquarium

E Ohio St.

E Grand Ave.

E Illinois St.

E North Water St.

E Wacker Dr.

Chicago River

E Randolph Dr.

Millennium
Park

E Monroe Dr.

E Jackson Dr.

S Lake Shore Dr.

41

Field Museum
of Natural History

N Michigan Ave.

Art Institute
of Chicago

E Monroe Dr.

13

Columbus Dr.

E Balbo Dr.

GRANT

PARK

4

8

N Wabash Ave.

S Michigan Ave.

S Wabash Ave.

RIVER
NORTH

N State St.

7

N Dearborn St.

N Clark St.

6

N LaSalle St.

N Wells St.

THE LOOP

W Madison St.

W Monroe St.

9 10

12

15

14

16

S State St.

S Plymouth Ct.

S Dearborn St.

S Federal St.

S Clark St.

S LaSalle St.

S Sherman St.

S Wells St.

SOUTH
LOOP

S Roosevelt Rd.

N Kinzie St.

W Kinzie St.

W Grand Ave.

W Illinois St.

W Hubbard St.

N Wacker Dr.

W Lake St.

S Franklin St.

Willis
Tower

11

W Congress Pkwy.

S. Branch Chicago River

5

N Wacker Dr.

S Wacker Dr.

N Kingsbury St.

N Canal St.

Union
Station

N Clinton St.

N Jefferson St.

N Des Plaines St.

N Washington Blvd.

W Monroe St.

W Adams St.

W Jackson Blvd.

W Van Buren St.

Eisenhower Expwy.

S Canal St.

S Clinton St.

S Jefferson St.

S Des Plaines St.

W Polk St.

N Milwaukee Ave.

90 94

W Grand Ave.

N Halsted St.

GREEK-
TOWN

S Green St.

S Peoria St.

S Sangamon St.

90 94

S Halsted St.

W Taylor St.

W Roosevelt Rd.

W Kinzie St.

W Fulton St.

W Lake St.

N Randolph St.

W Madison St.

W Harrison St.

University
of Illinois
at Chicago

290

N Morgan St.

S Morgan St.

Lake Michigan

3 mi

3 km

0

0

CHICAGO

Wrigley
Field

Map area

U.S. Cellular Field

90 94

41

290

94

41

55

Midway

much thinner). The **Reliance Building,** now the Hotel Burnham (p. 52), 1 W. Washington St. (Burnham & Root and Burnham & Co., 1891–95), was influential for its use of large glass windows and decorative spandrels (the horizontal panel below a window).

Second Renaissance Revival (1890–1920)

The grand buildings of the Second Renaissance Revival, with their textural richness, suited the tastes of the wealthy Gilded Age. Typical features include a cubelike structure with a massive, imposing look; a symmetrical facade, including distinct horizontal divisions; and a different stylistic treatment for each floor, with different column capitals, finishes, and window treatments on each level. A fine example of this style is the **Chicago Cultural Center,** 78 E. Washington St. (Shepley, Rutan & Coolidge, 1897), originally built as a public library. This tasteful edifice, with its sumptuous decor, was constructed in part to help secure Chicago's reputation as a culture-conscious city.

Beaux Arts (1890–1920)

This style takes its name from the Ecole des Beaux-Arts in Paris, where a number of prominent American architects received their training, beginning around the mid–19th century. In 1893, Chicago played host to the World's Columbian Exposition, attended by 21 million people at a time when Chicago's population was just over 1 million. Overseen by Chicagoan Daniel H. Burnham (1846–1912), the fairgrounds in Hyde Park were laid out in Beaux Arts style, with broad boulevards, fountains, and temporary ornate white buildings, mostly by New York–based architects. (One of the few permanent structures is now the Museum of Science and Industry, p. 139.)

Grandiose compositions, exuberance of detail, and a variety of stone finishes typify most Beaux Arts structures. Chicago has several Beaux Arts buildings that exhibit the style's main features. The oldest part of the **Art Institute of Chicago,** Michigan Avenue at Adams Street (Shepley, Rutan & Coolidge, 1893), was built for the World's Columbian Exposition. A later example of yet another skyscraper is the gleaming white **Wrigley Building,** 400-410 N. Michigan Ave. (Graham, Anderson, Probst & White, 1919–24), which serves as a gateway to North Michigan Avenue.

Art Deco (1925–33)

Art Deco buildings are characterized by a linear, hard edge or angular composition, often with a vertical emphasis and highlighted with stylized decoration. The **Chicago Board of Trade,** 141 W. Jackson Blvd. (Holabird & Root, 1930), punctuates LaSalle Street with its dramatic Art Deco facade. High atop the pyramidal roof, an aluminum statue of Ceres, the Roman goddess of agriculture, gazes down over the building. The last major construction project in Chicago before the Great Depression, **135 S. LaSalle St.** (originally the Field Building; Graham, Anderson, Probst & White, 1934), has a magnificent Art Deco lobby. A fine example of an Art Deco townhouse is the **Edward P. Russell House,** 1444 N. Astor St. (Holabird & Root, 1929), in the city's Gold Coast.

International Style (1932–45)

The International Style was popularized in the United States through the teachings and designs of **Ludwig Mies van der Rohe** (1886–1969), a German émigré who taught and practiced architecture in Chicago after leaving Germany's influential Bauhaus school of design. In the 1950s, erecting a "Miesian" office building made companies appear progressive. Features of the style include a rectangular shape; the frequent use of glass; an absence of ornamentation; and a clear expression of the building's form and function. (The interior structure of stacked office floors is clearly visible, as are the locations of mechanical systems, such as elevator shafts and air-conditioning units.)

Some famous Mies van der Rohe designs are the **Chicago Federal Center,** Dearborn Street between Adams Street and Jackson Boulevard (1959–74), and **860-880 N. Lake Shore Dr.** (1949–51). Interesting interpretations of the style by **Skidmore, Owings & Merrill,** a Chicago firm that helped make the International Style a corporate staple, are the **Willis Tower** (1968–74) and the **John Hancock Center** (1969)— impressive engineering feats that rise 110 and 100 stories, respectively.

Postmodern (1975–90)

As a reaction against the stark International Style, postmodernists began to incorporate classical details and recognizable forms into their designs—often applied in outrageous proportions. One example, **190 S. LaSalle St.** (John Burgee Architects with Philip Johnson, 1987), brings the shape of a famous Chicago building back to the skyline. The overall design is that of the 1892 Masonic Temple (now razed), complete with the tripartite divisions of the Chicago school. Another amalgam of historical precedents is the **Harold Washington Library Center,** 400 S. State St. (Hammond, Beeby & Babka, 1991). An extremely modern interpretation of a three-part skyscraper—but you have to look for the divisions to find them—is **333 Wacker Dr.** (Kohn Pedersen Fox, 1979–83), an elegant green-glass structure that curves along a bend in the Chicago River. Unlike this harmonious juxtaposition, the **James R. Thompson Center,** 100 W. Randolph St. (Murphy/Jahn, 1979–85), inventively clashes with everything around it.

CHICAGO IN POPULAR CULTURE

Art

Chicago may have thrived as a business center and transportation hub, but it's also a gathering spot for artists from throughout the Midwest. In part, that's due to the presence of the School of the Art Institute of Chicago, considered one of the best fine arts colleges in the country. The school produces a steady stream of arts-minded graduates, many of whom stay in town to work at local art galleries or fashion boutiques. Notable Art Institute alumni include painters Georgia O'Keefe and Grant Wood; iconic '70s fashion designer Halston; sculptors Claes Oldenburg, Jeff Koons, and Richard Hunt; alternative cartoonist and illustrator Chris Ware; and humorists Sarah Vowell and David Sedaris. Another downtown academic institution, Columbia College Chicago, also fosters an environment of creativity: The largest private arts and media college in the country, it offers undergraduate and graduate programs in film, arts management, creative writing, journalism, dance, and photography.

Books

So many great American writers have come from Chicago, lived here, or set their work in the city that it's impossible to recommend a single book that says all there is to say about the city. But here are a few to get you started.

Upton Sinclair's enormously influential *The Jungle* tells the tale of a young immigrant encountering the brutal, filthy city (see box, "Jungle Fever," below). James T.

Farrell's trilogy *Studs Lonigan,* published in the 1930s, explores the power of ethnic and neighborhood identity in Chicago. Other novels set in Chicago include Saul Bellow's *The Adventures of Augie March* and *Humboldt's Gift,* and Richard Wright's *Native Son. The Time Traveler's Wife,* by local author Audrey Niffenegger, unfolds amid recognizable Chicago backdrops such as the Newberry Library. (The movie version, alas, filmed only a few scenes here.)

For an entertaining overview of the city's history, read *City of the Century* by Donald Miller (an excellent PBS special based on the book is also available on DVD). Erik Larson's *Devil in the White City,* a history book that reads like a thriller, tells the engrossing story of the 1893 World's Columbian Exposition and the serial killer who preyed on young women who visited from out of town. For another look at the seamy underside of Chicago's history, try *Sin in the Second City* by Karen Abbott, which focuses on the city's most notorious—and expensive—brothel.

Two books give a human face to the city's shameful public housing history: Daniel Coyle's *Hardball: A Season in the Projects,* the true story of youngsters on a Little League baseball team; and Alex Kotlowitz's *There Are No Children Here,* a portrait of children growing up in one of the city's most dangerous projects. Kotlowitz also wrote *Never a City So Real: A Walk in Chicago,* which tells the stories of everyday Chicagoans, from a retired steelworker to a public defender to the owner of a soul-food restaurant.

But no one has given a voice to the people of Chicago like Studs Terkel, whose books *Division Street: America, Working,* and *Chicago* are based on interviews with Chicagoans from every neighborhood and income level; and the late newspaper columnist Mike Royko, author of perhaps the definitive account of Chicago machine politics, *Boss.* His columns have been collected in *One More Time: The Best of Mike Royko* and *For the Love of Mike: More of the Best of Mike Royko.*

Film

Chicago became a popular setting for feature films in the 1980s and '90s. For a look at Chicago on the silver screen, check out *Ferris Bueller's Day Off* (1985), the ultimate

jungle FEVER

It's hard to get a man to understand something if his salary depends on him not understanding it.

—Upton Sinclair

The most influential work of Chicago-based literature may also be the most disturbing. Upton Sinclair's *The Jungle,* an exposé of the city's meatpacking industry, caused a sensation when it was published in 1906. Although the book is a novel, following the tragic life of a poorly paid Lithuanian immigrant, it was based on Sinclair's firsthand observations at the Union Stockyards; many of its most gruesome scenes, such as when a man falls into a processing tank and is ground up along with the rest of the meat, were based on fact. After *The Jungle* became an international bestseller, U.S. meat exports plummeted and panicked meat-packing companies practically begged for government inspections to prove their products were safe. A Food and Drug Act was passed soon after, which made it a crime to sell food that had been adulterated or produced using "decomposed or putrid" substances; eventually, that led to the founding of the Food and Drug Administration (FDA).

teenage wish-fulfillment fantasy, which includes scenes filmed at Wrigley Field and the city's annual St. Patrick's Day Parade; *The Fugitive* (1993), which used the city's El trains as an effective backdrop; and *My Best Friend's Wedding* (1996). For many Chicagoans, the quintessential hometown movie scene is the finale of *The Blues Brothers* (1979), which features a multicar pileup in the center of downtown Daley Plaza.

Sometimes locally born actors choose to shoot movies in their hometown. A film that fueled a thousand paparazzi photographs was *The Break-Up* (2006), starring local-boy-made-good Vince Vaughn and Jennifer Aniston, and filmed on location throughout the city. Another hometown actor, John Cusack, starred in *High Fidelity* (2000), where hip Wicker Park makes an appropriate backdrop for the tale of a music-obsessed record store owner. Director Michael Mann, a Chicago native, filmed part of the gangster movie *Public Enemies* (2009) in town—appropriately enough, because this was the place where bank robber John Dillinger (played by Johnny Depp in the movie) was caught and killed by federal agents.

Though it technically takes place in Gotham City, the setting of the Batman blockbuster *The Dark Knight* is clearly recognizable as Chicago—although, rest assured, the real city isn't nearly as dark as the movie version! Swaths of downtown were also overrun by rampaging robots in *Transformers 3* (2011) and again in *Transformers 4* in 2013. Most recently, Chicago was transformed into a cinematic dystopia when *Divergent* was shot here.

Music

If Chicagoans were asked to pick one musical style to represent their city, most of us would start singing the blues. Thanks in part to the presence of the influential Chess Records, Chicago became a hub of blues activity after World War II, with musicians such as Muddy Waters, Howlin' Wolf, and Buddy Guy recording and performing here. (For a glimpse of what the music studio was like in its glory days, rent the 2008 movie

---

A CHICAGO playlist

The classic swingin' anthem of the city is Frank Sinatra's rendition of **"Chicago"** ("That toddlin' town . . . free and easy town, brassy, breezy town"), overblown versions of which show up regularly at local karaoke bars. Sinatra also sang his praises to the city in **"My Kind of Town (Chicago Is),"** which mentions the Wrigley Building and the Union Stockyards. But an even better pick for official city theme song is Robert Johnson's **"Sweet Home Chicago,"** with its appropriately bluesy riff ("Come on, baby don't you want to go, to the same old place, Sweet Home Chicago").

The 1970s pop-lite group Chicago didn't sing specifically about the city (probably because they moved to L.A. as soon as they hit it big), but their cheery **"Saturday in the Park"** captures the spirit of Grant Park and Lincoln Park in the summertime. Fast-forwarding a few decades, the blistering **"Cherub Rock"** by Smashing Pumpkins is a harsh take on the city's 1990s-era music scene (opening with the line: "Freak out, give in, doesn't matter what you believe in . . ."); more mellow is the elegiac **"Via Chicago"** by indie darlings Wilco. And no survey of Chicago music would be complete without mentioning the maestros of hip-hop, Common and Kanye West, who name-check their hometown in the songs **"Southside"** and **"Homecoming,"** respectively.

Cadillac Records, starring Jeffrey Wright as Muddy Waters and Beyoncé Knowles as Etta James.) Buddy Guy is still active on the local scene, making regular appearances at his eponymous downtown blues club (p. 206).

In the '60s and '70s, Chicago helped usher in the era of "electric blues"—low-tech, soulful singing melded with the rock sensibility of electric guitars. Blues-influenced rock musicians, including the Rolling Stones, Led Zeppelin, and Eric Clapton, made Chicago a regular pilgrimage spot.

Today the blues has become yet another tourist attraction, especially for international visitors, but the quality and variety of blues acts is still impressive. Hardcore blues fans shouldn't miss the annual (free) Blues Fest, held along the lakefront in Grant Park in early June. For a listing of the city's best blues clubs, see chapter 8.

EATING & DRINKING

Joke all you want about bratwurst and deep-dish pizza; Chicago is a genuine culinary hot spot. One of the city's most creative dining spots, **Alinea,** was even named the top restaurant in the United States by *Gourmet* magazine in 2007 (take that, New York and San Francisco!). What makes eating out in Chicago fun is the variety. We've got it all: stylish see-and-be-seen spots, an amazing array of steakhouses, chef-owned temples to fine dining, and every kind of ethnic cuisine you could possibly crave—and you've got to try the deep-dish, at least once.

Fueled in part by expense-account-wielding business travelers, high-end dining is a growth industry here. What makes Chicago's top restaurants unique, however, is their inclusive, low-key attitude. This isn't the kind of city where snooty waiters show off their foodie expertise or stare in horror if you have no idea what wine to order. By and large, hospitality is more than just a buzzword here, and as long as you can afford the eye-popping bill, the city's top chefs will welcome you. If you want to splurge on a one-of-a-kind meal—the kind you'll be describing to friends weeks later—Chicago is the place to do it. (See chapter 5, "Where to Eat.")

That said, ever-increasing restaurant prices are one of my pet peeves; eating out downtown has become more and more of a luxury. Although finding bargains in the Loop or around the Magnificent Mile isn't easy, you can still fill up without going broke by stopping at one of the food courts inside the malls along Michigan Avenue (as many locals on their lunch break do). Ethnic restaurants also tend to be less expensive, whether you're sampling *spanakopita* in Greektown (p. 79) or a picnic by the lake, which you can hand-pick from any number of our specialty grocers, including Mario Batali's Eataly (p. 95).

And about that pizza: Yes, Chicagoans hate to be stereotyped as cheese-and-sausage-devouring slobs, but it's a hard-earned reputation. In reality, we're more likely to eat thin crust than deep dish, but we'll join our visiting friends for the pizza casserole occasion at spots like **Lou Malnati's** (p. 88), just to ensure that you have a Sherpa on your decadent culinary adventure. We're pizza martyrs, here. You'll find a rundown of the best pizza spots on p. 88.

RESPONSIBLE TRAVEL

Chicago has become a breeding ground for urban environmental initiatives, starting with the green roof that was installed on the top of City Hall and the appointment of a chief environmental officer and chief sustainability officer on the mayor's staff.

Throughout the city, architects and contractors are building according to environmentally responsible principles, and an addition to the already massive McCormick Place Convention Center was the largest new construction building in the country to receive LEED (Leadership in Energy and Environmental Design) certification from the U.S. Green Building Council. An active pro-cycling community has pushed for more bike lanes in the city's streets, and Millennium Park provides secured bike parking and showers for two-wheeled commuters. (See p. 161 for bike rental information.)

A city-wide Green Hotels Initiative has encouraged hotels to become more energy-efficient and change back-room operations to minimize their impact on the environment. The nonprofit organization Green Seal and the U.S. Green Building Council have certified many local hotels for their role in minimizing waste, conserving water, and promoting energy savings; among those getting the highest marks are the **Hotel Allegro** (p. 51), **Hotel Burnham** (p. 52), **Hotel Felix** (p. 67), **InterContinental Chicago** (p. 61), **Hotel Monaco** (p. 52), **Radisson Blu Aqua** (p. 49) and **Talbott Hotel** (p. 62).

A focus on locally produced, organic ingredients has become a hallmark of the city's top chefs. Following the lead of well-known chefs such as Michael Kornick of **mk** (p. 90), Tony Mantuano of **Spiaggia** (p. 84) and **Bar Toma** (p. 87), and Rick Bayless of **Topolobampo** and **Frontera Grill** (p. 88), more and more local restaurateurs are highlighting seasonal ingredients on their menus, and the **Green City Market** (p. 87) has become a popular shopping destination for both culinary professionals and local foodies.

In addition to the resources for Chicago listed above, see www.frommers.com/planning for more tips on responsible travel.

SUGGESTED CHICAGO ITINERARIES

3

Remember last chapter, how I compared Chicago to an onion? Don't expect to discover all of the layers on your first visit. I've been here for years and am still discovering new-to-me museums, restaurants, theaters, and even whole neighborhoods. With that said, there's a certain expectation that you'll hit at least a few of the biggies on your visit here, from our towering skyscrapers to our belly-bombing deep-dish pizza. When you've made it through the "bucket list" items, you'll notice that a number of these itineraries— namely, "El Strolls"—take you on the El into our neighborhoods. These are my favorite jaunts, because that's where you'll discover the true Chicago.

You'll see from the map later in this chapter that Chicago is relatively compact, so it's possible to get a general sense of the city in 1 day (although, of course, I hope you're able to spend more than 24 hours here). How you spend your time depends in part on your interests and the weather. You could easily spend 3 days exploring Chicago's museums, and if you're here in the winter, that's going to be a lot more appealing than a day-long walking tour. On a sunny summer day, I encourage you to join us locals, and walk along the lakefront or in a neighborhood, without any particular destination in mind.

THE BEST OF CHICAGO IN 1 DAY

Just have 1 day in the Windy City? Better start walking! We've got a lot of ground to cover. *Start: Green, Orange, Brown, Pink, or Purple Line to State and Lake. Walk north on State one block to Wacker Drive. Turn right. Pass Wabash Avenue and arrive at Wacker Drive and Michigan Avenue. Take steps in the southeast corner down to River Walk.*

---

1 Chicago Architecture Foundation River Cruise ★★★

Where better to learn about architecture than the birthplace of the skyscraper? Even locals will tell you that the perfect morning begins with a Chicago Architecture Foundation (CAF) River Cruise. As this 90-minute boat ride moseys down the river and into Lake Michigan, docents explain the history of the city, which wouldn't exist as the booming metropolis and cultural hub it is today were it not for this very river. If you're here in the winter, check out the year-round CAF offerings, such as the "Skyscraper Walk Through Time," or, if it's too cold to walk, consider a bus or trolley tour. See p. 155.

Walk south on Michigan Avenue, past Wacker Drive, Lake Street. and Randolph Street and you'll arrive at:

2 Millennium Park ★★★

Known as "Chicago's front yard," Millennium Park is like Sara Lee: nobody doesn't like it. All summer long, Chicago residents and tourists flock here for free picnics, free concerts, movies, summer workouts, food and music festivals, and anything else Chicago decides to host there. After you've snapped a photo of a funhouse-like reflection of yourself (and 100 other spectators) in Anish Kapoor's sculpture, *Cloud Gate* (aka The Bean), splash around *Crown Fountain* (watch out, the sculpture will actually spit on you!) and take a walk through the 5-acre Lurie Garden. Then, relax on the Great Lawn in front of the Frank Gehry-designed Jay Pritzker Pavilion, a steel ribbon sculpture that doubles as a stage and sound system during the warmer months, and gaze at the beautiful Chicago skyline you just learned about on your tour. See p. 116.

Walk south from *Crown Fountain* to Monroe Street and cross Michigan Avenue. Head north to:

3 Lunch at The Gage 💭 ★★ (or Park Grill 💭 ★)

The closest and best lunch spot is The Gage ★★ (see p. 75), a lively gastropub with great service. Stop in for a sandwich, salad, or something a little more interesting, like a Scotch egg or brisket pot pie. If you're up for it, sample a local microbrew, like Half Acre's Daisy Cutter or a Gumballhead from Three Floyd's of Munster, Indiana. For families, Park Grill ★ in Millennium Park is a better pick. They have a kid-friendly menu with sandwiches and flatbreads, and on a nice day, you can dine alfresco. See p. 76.

If you went to the Gage, cross back over Michigan Avenue at Monroe and walk south for about a tenth of a mile to:

4 The Art Institute ★★★

Turn left at the regal lion statues to get to the main entrance of the art museum. At the country's second largest art museum (behind the Met in New York) you can, and will, easily lose the rest of the afternoon wandering through the 1 million square foot institution. Be sure to visit the extensive Impressionist collection, which the museum is known for, and don't miss Edward Hopper's iconic *Nighthawks* in the 20th-century American modern art gallery, the Rice Building. See p. 112.

Head west on Adams to Wabash and climb the stairs to hop on the Pink or Purple Line to Quincy/Wells.

5 The El ★

Welcome to the El, Chicago's above-ground (well, mostly, some is subterranean) elevated train, which has been rumbling over and under the Chicago streets since 1892.

Walk south one block on Wells and then head west on Jackson to the Skydeck entrance at Willis Tower.

6 The Skydeck at Willis Tower ★★★

End your day with a view of the city you've been exploring. From 103 floors up, the cars look like they were made by Matchbox and the city looks make-believe. Step out on to the glass-enclosed Ledge for sweaty-palm views looking up, around, and straight down.

Walk west on Jackson, past Franklin, to Giordano's, 233 W. Jackson.

7 Deep dish at Giordano's 🍺 ★

If you've never tried Chicago-style pie (they call it "stuffed pizza" here at Giordano's, p. 88), this is your chance. It's thick (so thick), loaded with cheese and a massacre on a plate. Consider walking back to your room after dinner to let things settle in. You won't want this for every meal, but it's a must-try if you're a deep-dish virgin.

THE BEST OF CHICAGO IN 2 DAYS

On your second day, take in the glitz, glamor, and hustle of the Magnificent Mile. Start at Michigan Avenue and the Chicago River. *Start: You can get there by walking or bus 3 or 26, which run along Michigan Avenue.*

1 The Magnificent Mile ★★

The 13-block stretch of Michigan Avenue from the river to Oak Street, known as the "Magnificent Mile," is the Rodeo Drive of Chicago. Here, locals rub elbows with tourists rubbing elbows with mimes and other street buskers. It's worth a look, whether you're interested in toting shopping bags or just watching the well-heeled tote theirs. See p. 167.

Walk north and make a stop at 625 N. Michigan, between Ohio and Ontario streets at:

2 Garrett Popcorn Shops 🍺 ★★★

You'll smell Garrett Popcorn before you see it, and the scent is what fills an Oompa Loompa's dream, I just know it. If there's a line out the door, get in it, and if not, consider yourself lucky. Head to the counter and order a small Chicago Mix. Trust me on this one. The caramel-meets-cheese mix may sound repulsive, but one bite and you'll see that this might be the ultimate sweet-meets-savory combination. *Note:* Eat it quickly, before the oil has a chance to darken the bag and taint the experience. See p. 172.

Continue heading north, shopping or window shopping on Michigan Avenue until you reach Michigan Avenue and Chestnut Street.

3 Oak Street Beach ★★★

This curved stretch of sand is a summertime hot spot and a great background for photos. Bikers, skaters, and joggers fill the paths while kids play in the sand. It's like Chicago's own mini-resort getaway—just don't plan on swimming in the frigid water unless you packed your wetsuit. If you're hungry, stop at the small cafe here for a casual lunch. For more on Chicago beaches, see p. 160.

4 Bike the lake path

There's a Divvy station (that's the name of the city-led bike share program) at Oak Street Beach. Swipe your credit card, and for $7 you can pedal a powder blue cruiser along the lake path. Keep in mind that every 30 minutes, you'll need to find a bike station and switch out your bike, but you can use the pass for up to 24 hours (p. 161).

If you head south on the path for about 6.5 miles, you'll arrive at:

5 Field Museum of Natural History ★★★

This is one of those classic something-for-everyone spots, and you can wander for hours here, staring at Sue, the largest and most complete Tyrannosaurus rex fossil ever discovered, admiring the old fashioned animal dioramas, and watching the kids play with the interactive displays. (If the Shedd Aquarium or Adler Planetarium are more to your liking, substitute one of those, they're all located in the same area; see p. 125).

Walk (or bike) north on the sidewalk that runs along the Museum Campus and pass under Lake Shore Drive. Continue north on Columbus and you'll walk along Grant Park until you arrive at:

6 Buckingham Fountain ★★

You may remember this tiered water feature from the intro to *Married with Children*. April through October, every hour on the hour from 9am–11pm, the fountain puts on a water show, shooting up to 150 feet in the air. It's particularly romantic at night, when canoodling couples gather to watch the light show and make kissy face (p. 118).

A TOUR OF CHICAGO IN 3 DAYS

For this itinerary, it's time to escape downtown completely and explore the city. *Start: Take the Pink or Green Line to Morgan/Lake. Walk one block south to Randolph Street and three blocks east to:*

1 Brunch at Little Goat 🍴 ★★★

Chicago is a huge brunch town, like no other I've ever seen. And the West Loop, being our dining hot spot, packs them in. Put your name on the list at Little Goat and then wander the neighborhood as you wait for them to text you that your table is ready. The old warehouse district is now filled with trendy restaurants, bars, and a winery. If your timing is right, check out the monthly Randolph Street Market, where you can find every kind of vintage hat (along with antiques and clothing) you ever imagined. See box p. 107.

Return to the Pink or Green Line and take it east to State/Lake. Transfer to the Red Line. Get off at Addison and walk west on Addison to:

2 Catch a Game at Wrigley Field ★★

If you're a baseball fan, Wrigley is hallowed ground: the second-oldest stadium in the major leagues, home to the perennially jinxed Chicago Cubs (see p. 164). The surrounding blocks are a good place to stock up on Cubs souvenirs, and, unless the game is a popular one, you should be able to buy a ticket in advance or at the box office.

Following the game, the streets around Wrigley fill with, what's the word, energized? No, drunken Cubs fans, looking to further dull their pain. Join them, if you're in the mood (the Cubby Bear, p. 217, is a magnet for intoxicated shenanigans). Prefer more Chicago culture and less inebriated tomfoolery? Keep reading.

Take the Red Line to Lawrence. Walk west one block to:

3 The Green Mill Jazz Club ★★★

Far removed from the tourist scene, The Green Mill fills with serious jazz fans and locals looking to check it off the list. Expect it to be packed here, especially on weekend nights. Music ranges from contemporary to traditional, and goes strong well into the morning hours (see p. 205).

5 DAYS IN THE WINDY CITY

Food, history, laughs, Old Town has it all. *Start: Take the Brown Line to Sedgwick. Walk north to North Avenue and head east, past Orleans Street, North Park Avenue, and Wieland Street until you reach Wells Street. Turn right.*

1 Foodie shopping for oil and spices

Wells Street is home to some fabulous specialty stores. Stop in at Old Town Oil (see p. 178) and learn to taste the difference between a grassy olive oil and a peppery one. Cleanse the palate in the vinegar section, where the staff will walk you through tangy fruit vinegars. Then, continue south on Wells to The Spice House, which specializes in spices and spice blends, including its own Chicago-centric creations (see p. 178).

From The Spice House, turn north and head back one storefront to:

2 Topo Gigio ☕ ★★

Tasting oils and smelling spices has a way of setting the stomach on rumble. Topo Gigio, situated conveniently between the two shops you just visited, serves up classic Italian, including some of the best fried calamari you may ever eat. Although this isn't a foodie destination, it's a great neighborhood spot, perpetually filled with regulars (see p. 102).

Walk north to North Avenue and turn right. Walk east, past Wells Street and LaSalle Street, and turn left on Clark Street. You'll arrive at the southwest corner of Lincoln Park and the:

3 Chicago History Museum ★★

This place is quirky and fun—much like Chicago's history, come to think of it. Step into an old El car, read about Chicago's past with the mob and racial tension, and wander through the halls of the town's colorful heritage (see p. 133).

Head back the way you came, going west on North Avenue Turn right on Wells Street to:

4 Second City ★★★

Chicago and comedy go together like mustard and hot dogs (never ketchup!), and if there's one comedy show you see while you're here, it ought to be Second City, an institution that's been busting bellies for more than 50 years with an alum list that includes John Belushi, Dan Aykroyd and Gilda Radner to name a few (see p. 204).

Ready for a nightcap? Continue west on North Avenue to Wieland Street and:

5 Old Town Ale House 🍺 ★★

It's a dive bar of the best variety. Don't expect a fancy wine list or craft cocktails. Order a local beer and take in the totally bizarre art, like former governor Rod Blagojevich in his orange prison wear getting strip-searched (see p. 216).

FAMILY FUN

Put on your walking shoes and sunscreen and prepare to spend the day outdoors. Although the following activities can all be done conveniently, back-to-back, I encourage you to pick and choose according to your little ones' interests, attention span, and energy level. *Start: Take a cab or bus 22, 36, 72, 73, 151 or 156 to North Avenue Beach.*

1 North Avenue Beach ★★★

Come summer, this is Lincoln Park's prime playground—a place to jog, play volleyball, build sandcastles, or simply pose. Even in August, the water is quite chilly, but if you want to at least dip your toe in Lake Michigan, this wide stretch of sand is the place to do it. Just south of the beach, a grassy stretch of park offers picture-perfect views of downtown, and the North Avenue Beach House, a giant, blue-and-white, ship-shaped structure, has snacks and refreshments (p. 160).

From the North Avenue Beach House, take the walkway that passes over Lake Shore Drive into Lincoln Park. Mosey north along Cannon Drive, through the park, and you'll arrive at:

2 Lincoln Park Zoo ★★★

A beloved local institution, this zoo won't dazzle you a la San Diego, but it does a good job of covering all the bases, with a mix of indoor habitats and naturalistic outdoor environments (plus, did I mention it's free?). Don't miss the Regenstein African Journey exhibit, which re-creates both a tropical jungle and a dusty African savanna, and the internationally renowned Great Ape House. Stop at the Children's Zoo, where a unique climbing structure gives little ones 2 and older a chance to release some energy (p. 134).

Exit at the north end of the zoo and walk up Stockton Drive to:

3 Lincoln Park Conservatory ★

Built in the late 1800s, the conservatory is home to four different greenhouses, filled with and surrounded by flora. It's a peaceful (and sun-protected) place to peruse while you get your energy back up (p. 133).

Continue north on Stockton Drive. Head east on Fullerton Avenue for one block and left on Cannon Drive. Arrive at:

4 Peggy Notebaert Nature Museum ★★

Kids will be aflutter at the Butterfly Haven, along with the rest of this bug-filled, nature-exploring museum. If the kids are too tired to take in another attraction, the grounds around it are quite beautiful and include a nature trail and bird walk (p. 135).

Head back the way you came, to the corner of Fullerton Parkway and Stockton Drive. Take a 20-minute ride on the 156 bus to LaSalle and Ontario streets. Walk a block west on Ontario and turn right on Wells.

5 Ed Debevic's 🍽 ★

Don't expect service with a smile at Ed Debevic's. Here, if you sass the servers, they'll sass you right back. Burgers, fries, hot dogs, chili, shakes, and malts are all the rage at this retro diner with an attitude (p. 83).

EL STOP STROLLS

The train makes it incredibly easy to get around Chicago, and in just 20 or 30 minutes, you can be in a neighborhood that feels like an entirely different city. Here are some strolls that take you from the train line into a handful of colorful neighborhoods for some urban exploring.

A Funky Stroll Through Wicker Park

Wicker Park is a melting pot of hipsters. Hipsters of all shapes, sizes, and accoutrement—some have piercings, others mustaches—and skinny jeans are the dress code. Whether or not that's your style, don't worry, there are plenty of non-disaffected folks, too, and it's a welcoming part of town. *Start: Blue Line to Damen Avenue.*

Take the Blue Line to Damen Avenue and walk north a few steps until you get to Milwaukee Avenue Turn right on Milwaukee, and take it all in. The sidewalks are filled with people, the bicycles are zipping by in their bike lanes, and even with all those tattoos, people are friendly and happy. Look around and shop to your heart's content up and down Milwaukee. I recommend stopping in at **Myopic Books** (p. 171), 1564 N. Milwaukee Ave., where you'll stumble into a rabbit hole of used books that you may never want to leave, while record lovers will encounter a similar time vacuum at **Reckless Records** (p. 180), 1532 N. Milwaukee Ave. After you pass Wolcott Avenue, before you get to Wood Street, you'll arrive at **Emporium Arcade Bar** (p. 218), 1366 N. Milwaukee Ave., one of a handful of Chicago's "barcades," combining vintage games and cocktails. Stop in for a couple of games of Asteroids or Donkey Kong and try whatever locally brewed Half Acre beer is on tap. But don't drink too much, there's more to be done! Head back the way you came on Milwaukee Avenue, shopping or just people watching. When you get to Damen Avenue, turn left and head to **Big Star** (p. 106), 1531 N. Damen Ave., for deliciously creative tacos and a margarita or whiskey (hey, it's what they're known for). Then, head directly across Damen Avenue for one last beverage at **Violet Hour** (p. 220), 1520 N. Damen Ave. You may not see the ever-so-subtle door, but you'll see the line of people leading up to it, awaiting their Prohibition-style speakeasy experience and superstrong drink.

An Eclectic Adventure in Logan Square

Logan Square today is similar to what Wicker Park was about a decade ago. It's a happening neighborhood, filled with incredible restaurants, cool shops, and an apartment scape that's being snatched up by cool 20- and 30-somethings. But it lacks the density of some of the more developed parts of the city, and there are large swaths of vacant property. With that said, it's worth an afternoon trip to shop, taste, and tipple the offerings. *Start: Blue Line to Logan.*

Take the Blue Line to Logan. Walking southeast on Milwaukee Avenue, you'll pass right by the square of Logan Square. It's surrounded by some cool spots, which you'll have to check out. First, pop into **Wolfbait & B-Girls** (p. 179), 3131 W. Logan Blvd., a small gift/accessory/clothing shop where most of the items are made by local artists, seamstresses, and artisans. Then, head west two storefronts and you'll come to **Billy Sunday** (p. 219), 3143 W. Logan Blvd., my new favorite Chicago bar. Don't expect to understand everything you read on the cocktail menu—I wasn't familiar with many of the drink ingredients. Fortunately, the bartenders are usually kind enough to let you try before you buy. Next, head back the way you came to the intersection of Milwaukee Avenue and Logan Boulevard. Turn right on Logan, a historic boulevard lined with beautiful old mansions. Pass Albany Avenue and Whipple Street, turn left on Sacramento Avenue, and walk north, past Schubert Avenue to Diversey and **Fat Rice** (p. 108), 2957 W. Diversey. Prepare for the best (or, possibly, first) Macanese meal of your life, with hints of Asia, Africa, India, and South America in the spices.

A Romantic Day on the Near North Side

Time to explore some lesser-known favorites in the Near North part of town, just off the beaten path of the tourist-filled Magnificent Mile. *Start: Red Line to Chicago.*

From Chicago Avenue, walk east to the **Museum of Contemporary Art** (p. 130), 220 E. Chicago Avenue, and spend an hour or two exploring what's happening right now in the art world. Then, head west on Chicago Avenue and south on Michigan Avenue Shop along the way, if you wish, and turn right on Ohio Street. Walk one block. There, looming before you, is the mother of all gourmet markets: **Eataly** (p. 95), 43 E. Ohio St. Mario Batali's Italian market is to a grocery store what a basilica is to a plain old church: holier than thou. Wander through the endless array of groceries, many of which come straight from Italy, or eat your way through the dozens of food stalls, restaurants, and bars inside (I highly recommend a glass of rosé and an assortment of salumi and cheese from La Piazza, followed by a crepe with Nutella from the cafe named Nutella). Stock up for a picnic for later in your trip, if you wish. Now it's time to switch gears from the Mediterranean to the Polynesian. Head west on Ohio, past Wabash Avenue, State Street, and Dearborn Street, and turn left on Clark Street. Walk two blocks south and turn left on Hubbard Street. Walk half a block and turn left into the alley. When you see a blue light, you've arrived at **Three Dots and a Dash** (p. 214), 435 N. Clark St., a dark, quirky little Tiki bar that doles out drinks that may look fruit-filled and girly, but they're seriously strong.

A Family-Friendly Trip to Lincoln Square

This friendly, family-dominated neighborhood was once home to a high concentration of Chicago's German immigrants, and you can still see traces of that heritage in the bars and shops throughout the mini downtown area of Lincoln Square (there's even a shop dedicated to selling dirndls.) *Start: Brown Line to Western.*

Take the Brown Line to Western Avenue. Walk east on Leland Avenue for about a minute, and you'll arrive at an aqua-colored "Lincoln Square" awning. Turn left and you've stepped into a Chicago's own little Bavaria. Stop in at **Merz Apothecary** (p. 170), 4716 N. Lincoln Ave., a throwback to pharmacies of old, filled with every natural salve, ointment, and beauty product you could want. Then, shop your way north to **The Book Cellar** (p. 171), 4736 N. Lincoln Ave., one of the city's great independently owned bookshops. Grab a cup of coffee (or wine) from the cafe and peruse the stacks—a high concentration of the books were penned by Chicago authors. Head north to **Gene's Sausage** (p. 177), 4750 N. Lincoln Ave., a sun-filled, bi-level market with Old World influences, including Europe-trained sausage makers who make 40+ different types of encased meats. Climb the stairs to the roof and enjoy a German beer in the prized beer garden, surrounded by herbs that the shop grows for its own use. Then, head south on Lincoln Ave. for about five minutes to the **Old Town School of Folk Music** (p. 210), 4544 N. Lincoln Ave. The school teaches all kinds of classes, from musical instruments to folk dancing, and brings in incredible talent to for concerts. Check the website to see what kind of performance, festival, or dance party is happening when you're in town.

Neighborhoods in Brief

Chicago proper has about 2.7 million inhabitants living in an area about two-thirds the size of New York City; another 7 million make up the Chicago metropolitan area, and the 'burbs sprawl into Wisconsin and Indiana. The **Chicago River** forms a Y that divides the city into its three geographic zones: North Side, South Side, and West Side. (Lake Michigan is where the East Side would be.) The downtown financial district is called **the Loop.** The city's key shopping street is **North Michigan Avenue,** also known as the **Magnificent Mile.** In addition to department stores and vertical malls, this stretch of property north of the river houses many of the city's most elegant hotels. North and south of this downtown zone, Chicago stretches along 26 miles of Lake Michigan shoreline that is, by and large, free of commercial development, reserved for public use as green space and parkland from one end of town to the other.

DOWNTOWN

THE LOOP

Best for: Architecture; museums (Art Institute); sights (Willis Tower); offices; dining; hotels; theater; Millennium Park; Macy's; public art; walking quickly and with a purpose (or risk getting mowed down by Loop workers).

What you won't find: Nightlife; neighborhoods; crowds that stick around past happy hour or on weekends.

Parameters: The Loop refers literally to a core of high-rises surrounded by a rectangular "loop" of elevated train tracks. But when Chicagoans use the term, they're referring to the city's downtown, bounded by the Chicago River to the north and west, Lake Michigan to the east, and Roosevelt Road to the south.

For the most part, the Loop is strictly business, filled with office buildings rather than residential developments. You will find a rich swath of hotels here, along with some shopping (Macy's on State Street, in particular), museums, and restaurants, most of which survive according to the appetites of hungry

Chicago Neighborhoods

Free Chicago Tours

Local Chicagoans give free tours through the **Chicago Greeter** program, ranging from neighborhood explorations to quick downtown detours. Here's how you can get in on the action: About two weeks before your trip, register on www.chicagogreeter.com. Take your pick of language, neighborhood, and interest, and you'll be matched with a volunteer for a 2- to 4-hour tour. For get to plan ahead? An hour-long tour is available through the **InstaGreeter** program. Tours of the Loop are available Fridays, Saturdays, and Sundays, year round, and when the weather is nice, tours also hit Millennium Park and the Magnificent Mile. Guides leave on the half hour, 10am–3pm, from the Chicago Cultural Center's Visitor Center (see p. 120).

office workers. Beautiful buildings and public art make for an enjoyable walk when the weather is nice. For a suggested walking tour of the Loop, see p. 183.

THE NORTH SIDE

MAGNIFICENT MILE

Best for: Shopping; major department stores; dining; hotels; architecture; 360 Chicago (formerly the Hancock Observatory).

What you won't find: Museums; independently owned stores; quiet.

Parameters: North Michigan Avenue from the bridge spanning the Chicago River to its northern tip at Oak Street is known as the Magnificent Mile (or, simply, "Michigan Avenue," although the street itself stretches much farther).

Many of the city's best hotels and most concentrated shopping can be found here. The area stretching east of Michigan Avenue to the lake is sometimes referred to as "Streeterville"—the legacy of George Wellington "Cap" Streeter. Streeter was an eccentric, bankrupt showman who lived in Chicago in the mid-1880s. Looking for a new way to make money, Streeter bought a steamship with a plan to become a gun runner in Honduras. The steamship ran aground during a test cruise in Lake Michigan, and Streeter left the ship where it was, staking out 200 acres of self-created landfill. He then declared himself "governor" of the "District of Lake Michigan." True story.

RIVER NORTH

Best for: Nightlife; clubs; views of the Loop; galleries; dining; steakhouses; hotels; high heels and short dresses; bathroom attendants.

What you won't find: Dive bars; cheap eats; serenity.

Parameters: Just west of the Magnificent Mile, bordered on the south and west by the Chicago River, and going as far north as Division Street.

The formerly industrial buildings of this old warehouse district have been transformed into one of the city's most vital commercial districts, with many of the city's hottest restaurants and nightspots. Large-scale residential loft developments have sprouted on its western and southwestern fringes.

THE GOLD COAST

Best for: Old money; historic sites; million-dollar mansions; boutique hotels; shops; dining; museums, Museum of Contemporary Art; beaches.

What you won't find: Cool dive bars; discount or thrift stores; grit.

Parameters: Along Lake Shore Drive, between Oak Street and North Avenue, west to LaSalle Street.

Some of Chicago's most desirable real estate and historic architecture are found in the Gold Coast. Despite trendy pockets of real estate that have popped up elsewhere, the moneyed class still prefers to live by the lake. On the neighborhood's southwestern edge, around Division and Rush streets, a string of raucous bars and late-night eateries contrasts sharply with the rest of the area's sedate mood. For a suggested walking tour of the neighborhood, see p. 187.

OLD TOWN

Best for: Dining; nightlife; bars; beautiful homes; Chicago History Museum; Second City; the lake and beaches; green space.

What you won't find: Chain stores; chain restaurants; dress codes.

Parameters: West of LaSalle Street, principally on North Wells Street between Division Street and North Avenue.

The residential district of Old Town boasts some of the city's best-preserved historic homes (a few even survived the Great Chicago Fire of 1871). This area was a hippie haven in the 1960s and '70s; now the neighborhood is one of the most expensive residential areas in the city. Old Town's biggest claim to fame, the legendary Second City comedy club, has served up the lighter side of life to Chicagoans for more than 30 years.

LINCOLN PARK

Best for: Family activities; theater; Lincoln Park (and zoo and conservatory); funky hotels; nature; nightlife; yuppies; music; dining; shopping; farmer's market; beaches; tasting menus.

What you won't find: Hippies; inexpensive shopping; genetically modified food.

Parameters: Stretching from North Avenue to Diversey Parkway, it's bordered on the east by the huge park of the same name, and west just past about Clybourn Avenue.

Chicago's most popular residential neighborhood for young singles and urban-minded families is Lincoln Park, home to one of the nation's oldest zoos (established in 1868). The trapezoid formed by Clark Street, Armitage Avenue, Halsted Street, and Diversey Parkway also contains many of Chicago's liveliest bars, restaurants, retail stores, music clubs, and off-Loop theaters—

including the nationally acclaimed Steppenwolf Theatre Company.

LAKEVIEW & WRIGLEYVILLE

Best for: Cubs fans; bros; drunken nightlife; music; casual dining; dive bars; wine bars; gay bars; Boystown; theaters; smaller hotels.

What you won't find here: Museums; fine dining; dress codes; attitude.

Parameters: The main thoroughfare is Belmont Avenue, between Broadway and Sheffield Avenue. Wrigleyville is the name given to the neighborhood in the vicinity of Wrigley Field—home of the Chicago Cubs—at Sheffield Avenue and Addison Street. Lakeview encompasses Wrigleyville and a much larger area, starting at Lake Michigan on the east to Ravenswood Avenue on the west, and from Addison Street on the north side to Belmont Avenue on the south.

Midway up the city's North Side is a one-time blue-collar, now mainstream middle-class quarter called Lakeview. It has become the neighborhood of choice for many gays and lesbians, recent college graduates, and residents priced out of Lincoln Park. Not surprisingly, the ball field is surrounded by sports bars and memorabilia shops.

UPTOWN & ANDERSONVILLE

Best for: Independent shops and restaurants; bakeries and cafes; friendly neighborhood feel; diversity; families and singles who have matured from Boystown.

What you won't find here: Fine dining; heavy tourist crowds; chain stores; pretension.

Parameters: Uptown runs along the lakefront as far north as Foster Avenue and west to Broadway. Andersonville is slightly to the north and west, and the main drag is Clark Street, between Foster and Bryn Mawr avenues.

Uptown has traditionally attracted waves of immigrants. Although crime was a major problem for decades, the area has mostly stabilized, with formerly decrepit buildings being converted into—you guessed it—condominiums. Vietnamese and Chinese immigrants have transformed Argyle Street between Broadway and Sheridan Road into a teeming market for fresh meat, fish, and all kinds of exotic vegetables. In the old Scandinavian neighborhood of Andersonville, the main drag is Clark Street, between Foster and Bryn Mawr avenues. The area has an eclectic mix of Middle Eastern restaurants, a distinct cluster of women-owned businesses, and a burgeoning colony of gays and lesbians.

LINCOLN SQUARE

Best for: German influenced dining and bars; stroller-filled, family-friendly neighborhoods; parks; independently owned shops; theater; Old Town School of Folk Music.

What you won't find here: Attitude; mansions; high-end boutiques; museums; chain stores and restaurants; hotels.

Parameters: West of Andersonville and slightly to the south, there's a charming downtown area where Lincoln, Western, and Lawrence avenues intersect, which runs south to Montrose Avenue. The eastern edge of Lincoln Square is Damen Avenue and the western edge is the Chicago River.

Lincoln Square still retains traces of Chicago's once-vast German-American community. The surrounding leafy residential streets have attracted many families, who flock to the Old Town School of Folk Music's theater and education center, a beautiful restoration of a former library building.

ROGERS PARK

Best for: Affordability; beaches; diversity; great Indian and Middle Eastern food; a touch of grit.

What you won't find here: Museums; heavy tourist traffic; shopping; ladies who lunch; hotels.

Parameters: Starts at Devon Avenue, on the northern fringes of the city bordering suburban Evanston. It's bordered to the east by Lake Michigan and to the west by Ridge Avenue.

The western half of Rogers Park has been a Jewish neighborhood for decades. The eastern half, dominated by Loyola University's lakefront campus, has become the most cosmopolitan enclave in the entire city: African Americans, Asians, East Indians, and Russian Jews live side by side with the ethnically mixed student population drawn to the Catholic university. The western stretch of Devon Avenue is a Midwestern slice of Calcutta, colonized by Indians who've transformed the street into a veritable restaurant row serving tandoori chicken and curry-flavored dishes.

THE WEST SIDE

WEST LOOP

Best for: The latest in dining; large, cavernous, warehouse-like restaurants; nightlife; music.

What you won't find here: A neighborhood feel; plain-Jane food; cheap eats; quiet romantic restaurants; shopping; museums; hotels.

Parameters: Also known as the "near west" side, it's just across the Chicago River from the Loop. It's bordered on the west by Ashland Avenue; Grand Avenue is to the north, and I-290 is to the south.

Welcome to the city's newest gentrification target, where old warehouses and once-vacant lots have been transformed into trendy condos and stylish restaurants. Chicago's old Greektown, still the Greek culinary center of the city, runs along Halsted Street between Adams and Monroe streets. Much of the old Italian neighborhood in this vicinity was the victim of urban renewal, but remnants still survive on Taylor Street. The same is true for a few old delis and shops on Maxwell Street, dating from the turn of the 20th century when a large Jewish community lived in the area. On Randolph Street, expect to wait at least an hour to get into the city's trendiest restaurants, like Girl and the Goat and Publican.

BUCKTOWN/WICKER PARK

Best for: Hipsters; nightlife; casual dining; boutiques; craft cocktails; Pabst Blue Ribbon; tattoos; piercings; irony.

What you won't find here: Museums; fine dining; Budweiser (unless it's being drunk ironically); chain stores and restaurants; bathroom attendants; dress codes; hotels.

Parameters: Disclaimer: The parameters of these two 'hoods are some of the most hotly contested in town, so we'll speak in approximations. Bucktown extends, approximately, from Ashland Ave. on the east to Western Ave. on the west and from Fullerton Ave. on the north to North Ave. on the south. Wicker Park is contained by, approximately, North Avenue on the north, Division Street on the south, Western on the West and Ashland on the east. But what you really need to know is this: The real action is centered near the intersections of North, Damen, and Milwaukee avenues.

This resurgent area has hosted waves of German-, Polish-, and, most recently, Spanish-speaking immigrants (not to mention writer Nelson Algren). In recent years, it has morphed into a bastion of hot new restaurants, alternative culture, and loft-dwelling yuppies. The terms Bucktown and Wicker Park are often used interchangeably, but Bucktown is technically the neighborhood north of North Avenue, and skews older, while Wicker Park is to the south, and skews younger. For a walking tour of the area, see p. 192.

LOGAN SQUARE

Best for: Innovative casual dining; dive bars; craft cocktails; farm-to-table sensibility; beer; hipsters; artists; beautiful homes, many of which have seen better days.

What you won't find: Museums; uppity airs; density; heavy traffic; major hotels or stores.

Parameters: Located west of Western and Bucktown, bounded by the Chicago River to the east. Diversey Avenue is to the north and Bloomingdale Avenue to the south.

Logan Square is a slowly-but-surely gentrifying area (the recession hasn't helped speed it along), interspersed with worth-the-wait restaurants, a brewery, and pockets of blight. The beautiful, mansion-lined boulevards of Logan Square speak to its heyday as a magnet for immigrants with new money. At the heart of Logan Square is its namesake square, a traffic circle/park honoring Civil War General John Logan. A number of trendy restaurants and bars are within walking distance of the square.

THE SOUTH SIDE

SOUTH LOOP

Best for: Dining; hotels; nightlife; music; architecture; diversity; history; Grant Park; proximity to Museum Campus and Financial District; new condo and loft developments.

What you won't find: Organic neighborhoods; single family homes; independent boutiques; artists; bohemian sensibility; fine dining.

Parameters: Stretching from Harrison Street's historic Printers Row south to Cermak Road (where Chinatown begins), and from Lake Shore Drive west to the south branch of the Chicago River.

The generically rechristened South Loop area was Chicago's original "Gold Coast" in the late 19th century, with Prairie Avenue (now a historic district) as its most exclusive address. But in the wake of the 1893 World's Columbian Exposition in Hyde Park, and continuing through the Prohibition era of the 1920s, the area was infamous for its Levee vice district, home to gambling and prostitution, some of the most corrupt politicians in Chicago history, and Al Capone's headquarters at the old Lexington Hotel. However, in recent years, its prospects have turned around.

PILSEN

Best for: Art galleries; artists; diversity; taquerias and Mexican bakeries; laid-back nightlife and restaurants, National Museum of Mexican Art.

What you won't find: Expensive meals; attitude; boutiques; chain stores or restaurants; North Side frat boys; expensive housing.

Parameters: Pilsen is centered at Halsted and 18th streets just southwest of the Loop. It runs from about 16th Street on the north to the Chicago River on the south and east, running west of Western.

Originally home to the nation's largest settlement of Bohemian-Americans, Pilsen (named for a city in what's now the Czech Republic) was for decades the principal entry point in Chicago for immigrants of every ethnic background. Pilsen now contains one of the largest Mexican-American communities in the U.S. This vibrant and colorful neighborhood, which was happily invaded by the outdoor mural movement launched years earlier in Mexico, boasts a profusion of authentic taquerías and bakeries. The artistic spirit that permeates the community isn't confined to Latin American art. In recent years, artists of every stripe, drawn partly by the availability of loft space in Pilsen, have nurtured a small but thriving artists' colony here.

HYDE PARK

Best for: Intellectuals (students, professors and neighbors); University of Chicago; diversity; lake and beaches; Museum of Science and Industry; Obamas.

What you won't find: Close-mindedness; boutiques; shopping; fine dining; upscale bars and nightlife; comedy; fearlessness—

most residents know the risk of crossing the boundaries into surrounding neighborhoods, where the crime rate is high and integration is less idyllic.

Parameters: Right off Lake Michigan and roughly a seven-mile, 30-minute train ride from the Loop. Stretching east to the lake, west to Cottage Grove Avenue and Washington Park, north to 51st Street/Hyde Park Boulevard, and south to Midway Plaisance. Fifty-Seventh Street is the main drag.

Hyde Park is like an independent village within the confines of Chicago, and is also the most successful racially integrated community in the city. The area is an oasis of furious intellectual activity and liberalism that, ironically, is hemmed in on all sides by neighborhoods suffering some of the highest crime rates in Chicago. Its main attraction is the world-famous Museum of Science and Industry, and the University of Chicago—with all its attendant shops and restaurants—is the neighborhood's principal tenant.

WHERE TO STAY

Ready to spin through that revolving door, directly onto State Street—that great street—and the heart of downtown Chicago? The hotels here make that quite easy to do. Of course, you'll pay for that convenient location. Chicago hotel rates rank among the most expensive in the country, at an average of just under $200 a night for leisure travelers. And with an occupancy rate surpassing 75%, don't expect that number to go down any time soon.

Unlike other major cities, though (we're looking at you, New York), most Chicago rooms don't totally skimp on real estate. It's entirely possible to find a spacious room in a central location at or even under that average rate. The thing you'll really pay for here is the view. If you want to look out at Lake Michigan, expect to pony up. When deciding where to stay, keep in mind that your odds of landing good rates increase exponentially if you know where to look—especially if you're open to staying in an area that's a few miles from downtown, or in less traditional (non-hotel) accommodations, like a room in someone's home or even a flat rented by a monastery. While some hotels are geared towards families and others have a distinct hipster vibe, the bulk of the properties here draw in a mixed crowd, packing in suits during the week and families and leisure travelers on the weekends.

4

I do want to point out that the majority of the hotels in and around Chicago are owned or managed by a familiar brand, and a property is often quite subtle about it. Take the Tremont House, for example. Sounds like a solid, independent, historic name, no? I thought so, too, until I emailed the property and the address had "@starwoodhotels" in it. Turns out, it's a "non-branded" Starwood property. The Wit isn't just a brand, it's a brand within a brand: DoubleTree by Hilton. With that said, completely avoiding chains in this section was simply unreasonable, but I made a point of finding the properties that had some kind of unique Chicago element, be it architecture, location, or just plain quirkiness, to highlight the most authentic representations of the Windy City. And, of course, there are a few independently owned spots in town that pay impeccable attention to design and service (see the listings for Dana Hotel & Spa, the Talbott, and the Whitehall Hotel below), while the many B&Bs and inns around the city are also a breath of fresh—and independent—air.

A note about smoking: Most Chicago hotels have adopted a no-smoking policy in recent years. If you want to make sure you can light up in your room, check the hotel's policy when making your reservation.

Practical Matters: Getting the Best Deal

In the listings below, I've highlighted the best finds in Chicago. While I selected some according to price, others are Chicago institutions, rich in history and, frankly, rate. Because hotel rates are so fluid, we can't speculate too much about how rates will fluctuate after this book has been published, or what deals might be offered at the time of your visit. But I can offer some general tips for finding the best value.

TIMING IS EVERYTHING   If you're willing to endure the cold, you can save well over 50% at many of the hotels by visiting during the off-season winter months. Rates skyrocket in the summer from Memorial Day to Labor Day, and hotels charge premium prices during major conventions, most notably the International Home + Housewares Show in early March and the National Restaurant Show in late May. Other conventions gobble up desirable rooms periodically throughout the year, so if you're surprised by a rate surge, that could be the culprit.

LOOK OUTSIDE OF THE LOOP   Sure, proximity makes things easier, but there are plenty of hotel options outside of the Loop that can save you big bucks, while putting you just a hop, skip, and jump away from the city center by train. Plus, I can't emphasize this point enough: Staying in a neighborhood is the best way to really get to know the city.

SEARCH FOR PACKAGE BUNDLES   If you're looking to book air, hotel, and even a car, search travel websites for package deals. Often, you can save hundreds of dollars by booking them all at the same time through major sites like Travelocity, Priceline, and Expedia. What you may sacrifice in choice (no, you likely won't be staying at The Langham and getting flight and car for less than $500), you'll make up for in value.

SET A PRICE ALERT   Travel sites such as Kayak.com invite you to set a "price alert" for a hotel (or airfare). You can select your dates of travel, a price limit and the number of stars you'd like. You'll receive an email letting you know if there's a hotel that fits the bill. Another site, Yapta.com, allows you to select particular hotels to track and the site will email you when the rates drop.

SEEK SITES WITH PRICE MATCHES   Orbitz.com offers a best price guarantee. That means that if you book a room (or flight or car) through that site and then find a lower rate elsewhere, Orbitz will send you 100% of that amount in "orbucks" (rewards you can redeem through the site) plus an additional $50 in "orbucks."

CHOOSE A CHAIN   My goal in this chapter has been to provide you with hotels with local character, so I've opted to not include many of the large chain properties in town. But if you're looking for a deal, chains are often the way to go. The sidebar, "Big Boxes," highlights some of the larger Chicago hotels. You can frequently find deals at these spots and other chains, because they have so much more real estate available.

AVOID EXCESS CHARGES AND HIDDEN COSTS   Use your own cellphone or prepaid calling card rather than using the hotel phone, which can rack up charges. Don't be tempted by expensive mini-bar items. All of the hotels listed are within a few steps or a few blocks of a drug store or grocery store. And ask about local taxes and service charges, which increase the cost of a room significantly. If a hotel insists on asking you to pay for an "energy surcharge" that wasn't mentioned at check-in, you can often contest it and have it removed.

ALTERNATIVE ACCOMMODATIONS

Across the globe, and certainly in Chicago, travelers have more options than ever when it comes to accommodations. Although downtown hotels are ready and waiting to dazzle visitors, an array of other options exists. I'm talking accommodations that will put you in the heart of some of Chicago's most wealthy/cultural/diverse neighborhoods, whether it's a mom-and-pop place, where welcoming B&B owners can dispense tourist advice, or a unique vacation rental (perhaps a penthouse, brownstone, or yacht?), where you can explore the city like a true Chicagoan. Here are some of my top picks on how to really best commune with the Windy City.

RENT A HOME, AN APARTMENT, OR A COUCH Unlike New York and other cities, it *is* still acceptable to lease your apartment, short term, as a vacation rental in Chicago. Legally speaking, the person listing the property is supposed to have a vacation rental license. With that said, to stay above the law when you're looking at listings, know that the ones that list their license numbers are generally the ones that are operating legally.

I rely on two sites, primarily, when searching for vacation rentals in Chicago and while traveling. **AirBnB** (www.airbnb.com) members tend to be a bit younger and the site has more of a college-ish, casual feel, likely because many of the places for rent here are just a room or a bed within a home or apartment. On this site, you can see photos of properties (and hosts), along with a brief description of the property. You'll find everything from a $22 bedroom in an artsy house in Pilsen, to a LEED-certified studio in Bucktown for $122 a night, to a mansion in the Gold Coast for about $2,400. One word of advice: Stick to the neighborhoods highlighted in this book, just to be on the safe side and to avoid getting stuck way out in the suburbs. On the sites **VRBO** (www.vrbo.com), which stands for Vacation Rental By Owner, and its affiliate, **Home Away** (www.homeaway.com), you won't find a couch or bedroom for rent, but there are more than 150 homes, apartments, and condos all across town that are up for grabs. With all rental sites, pay attention to the reviews that the previous renters left. They can be quite telling, pointing out issues and inconveniences about the location, cleanliness, and observations or insights about the owners.

For the best of both worlds—an apartment building that's run like a hotel in a great neighborhood—check out the **Guest House Hotel ★★** (4866 N. Clark St., btw. Lawrence Ave. and Ainslie St.; www.theguesthousehotel.com; ✆ **773/564-9568;** Subway/El: Red Line to Lawrence) in Andersonville. Owned by a condo developer and his wife, these one- to three-bedroom condos were built in 2005, right before the housing market collapsed. Unable to sell them, the couple initially listed the fully furnished apartments on vacation rental sites, and they were so impressed by the results that they decided offer even more properties. As I write this, they're on the verge of completing work on 15 more apartments, with access to a small gym and an organic grocery store with a local focus. All of the apartments are quite large, ranging in size from about 750 square feet to 1,800 square feet, and each has a balcony, fireplace, and washer/dryer. Having rented apartments in various countries, I can tell you from firsthand experience, the fact that this place is staffed 24 hours a day is a good thing. You won't have to play phone tag with your host trying to get into your room after flying all night. Plus, the Andersonville neighborhood is super walkable and filled with bars, restaurants and independent sho,ps. One word of warning to the superstitious: The apartments are across the street from a cemetery. Rates range from $160–$360 per night, depending on size and season.

COZY UP TO A B&B Although they're frequently overshadowed by the hotels in town, Chicago does have a B&B scene. A group of local B&B owners has formed the Chicago Bed and Breakfast Association, with a website that links to various properties throughout the city at www.chicago-bed-breakfast.com, so you can see for yourself.

I've indicated in the listings in this chapter those hotels that allow pets. However, understand that these policies might have limitations, such as weight and breed restrictions; may require an extra fee, deposit, and/or signed waiver against damages; and may be revoked at any time. Always inquire when booking if you're bringing Bowzer. Never just show up with a pet in tow.

For a truly unique experience, I recommend **The Monastery of the Holy Cross Bed and Breakfast ★★** (3111 South Aberdeen Street, $180 a night for one or two adults, $40 for additional adults, $25 for teens 16 and older, kids under 16 are free; www.chicagomonk.org/bed-and-breakfast; ℂ **773/927-7424** extension 202), located in the Bridgeport neighborhood, south of the Loop. Tucked in behind the monastery, the cozy, two-level house, which is owned by the monastery, is divided into two apartments. The loft apartment, upstairs, has three bedrooms, and the garden apartment, downstairs, has two bedrooms. Staying here felt, to me, like staying at grandma's house, with eclectic wood furnishings, an abundance of gold lamps, and the occasional crucifix. The bedrooms are small, but with a whole floor to yourself, that's a non-issue. The coolest part of staying here is, if you stay in the loft apartment, the monks deliver an enormous breakfast in the morning: French toast, eggs, hash browns, muffins, and fresh fruit, which when I stayed there was, oddly enough, smothered in maple syrup, leading me to believe that the monks moonlight as sugar elves. If you stay in the garden apartment, where there is a full kitchen, the fridge is stocked with breakfast items you can prepare for yourself. Those who aren't Catholic can rest assured that there is no religious expectation here, nor are there rules against unmarried couples renting a room. They do invite you to services, but I felt no pressure to participate. Also, the monks are quite quiet, which is a bonus for those who are leery of chatty B&B owners.

For a frock-free stay, **Ray's Bucktown B&B ★** (2144 N. Leavitt, at Webster Ave.; www.raysbucktownbnb.com; ℂ **773/384-3245;** rates $119–$219) is an affordable option in a quiet part of Bucktown. You won't find doilies and antiques, hee, but you will find a lot of folksy collections (owl art, Pez dispensers, pots on display, and so forth), communal areas and, a super chatty owner (Ray). Occupying two lots, Ray's has 11 rooms, the majority of which have more than one bed, and all have private baths (one is located across the hall, but is only for use of that occupant) with heated floors. Each room has different pros and cons, so if you're a light sleeper, ask for a quieter room in back, and if you prefer more sunlight, request an upstairs spot. In addition to fresh fruit, pastries, and yogurt, Ray and staff make a huge breakfast of omelets, stuffed French toast, and pancakes to order every morning at whatever time you request. The best part of Ray's is its location. It's six blocks from the Western stop on the Blue Line (he'll even pick you up from the train station, if he's around) and you're in the heart of a vibrant neighborhood, surrounded by dozens of shops, restaurants and bars, and, bonus, plenty of free parking.

Book a room at the **Flemish House of Chicago ★** (68 E. Cedar St. at Lake Shore Dr., www.innchicago.com; ℂ **312/664-9981;** rate $150–$379; Subway/El: Red Line to Clark/Division, cab or walk about a half mile east) and you'll be surrounded by million-dollar Gold Coast mansions. Each unit in the historic (and historically decorated)

We list double rooms only. Please assume that suites will be more pricey and those few hotels that offer single rooms will do so for less than the rate listed in this guide.

Inexpensive: $175 and under
Moderate: $175–$300
Expensive: $300 and up

Victorian/Arts and Crafts home, built in 1892, is actually its own apartment (studio, one or two-bedroom) and comes with a full fridge equipped with breakfast, a nice convenience before you head out to the nearby shops, parks, and beaches.

Landlubbers need not apply to stay at the **Windy City Sailing Bed and Breakfast** ★★ (Belmont Harbor, 3600 N. Recreation Drive; www.windycitysailing.com; ℰ **773/868-0096**), which is a B&B yacht. Because of the city lights, you won't see many stars above, but you will get to admire Chicago's glowing skyline from your own floating roost on Lake Michigan. The sleeping quarters are tight (it's a boat, after all) but the 40-foot yacht comfortably sleeps two, and has a kitchenette and dining area. Opt for a 2-hour sightseeing cruise in the morning or book the boat on a Wednesday or Saturday, when the Navy Pier fireworks color the sky. Rate is $500 for an overnight on the boat, plus $200 to $250 for sightseeing or fireworks.

INN THE KNOW For something less cookie cutter than a hotel but more private than a B&B, Chicago has some wonderful inn options. I'm in love with the **Ruby Room** ★★★ (1743-1745 W. Division St., between Wood Street and Hermitage Avenue; www.rubyroom.com; ℰ **773/235-2323;** rate $85–$385; Subway/El: Blue Line to Division). Thanks to spa-minded owners, each TV-free and phone-free room is as Zen as the lounge area of a spa, bathed in warm beige colors and equipped with ridiculously comfy beds. Attached to a salon, spa, boutique, and yoga studio, the eight rooms here are on the third and fourth floor (*warning:* no elevator). There's a small patio on the south side of the building from which you can see the Chicago skyline, and a tranquil healing garden with a waterfall to enjoy in warm months. It's located right smack in the heart of Division Street, a busy spot in Ukrainian Village (just south of Wicker Park), where you can walk to dozens of trendy cafes and bars and mix and mingle with cool area residents.

The quintessential hipster hotel is **Longman & Eagle Inn** ★ (2657 N. Kedzie at Schubert Ave.; www.longmanandeagle.com/sleep; ℰ **773/276-7110;** rates from $85–$250; Subway/El: Blue Line to Logan), which sits one floor above the equally hipster Longman & Eagle restaurant. This is a pretty great find if you're planning on making a night of rambling around Logan Square or visiting friends there. Located just a 2-minute walk from the Logan Square Blue Line stop, each of the six units here have hardwood floors, local art on the walls, free Wi-Fi, and charming retro touches, like a tape player with a stack of mix tapes. Plus, each room guarantees you a reservation to dinner or brunch at the restaurant (that could save you from a 30-minute to 2-hour wait, depending on the night) and two shots of $3 whiskey.

RESERVE A BED IN A HOSTEL Chicago has a number of dorm-style hostel options, with shared or private rooms, and they're available 24 hours a day for singles as well as families to rent. Rates start at $20 per night. Here are two of the city's well-maintained hostel options:

Chicago hotel rates vary widely throughout the year, making it difficult to pin down the average price for any given property. As you can see from the rates below, the high number might be more than twice as much as the low end of the range (such as $169–$429) for the exact same room. That's not a typo. Scoring a bed in this city does feel a bit like "dealer's choice." You never quite know which number will come up, because it all depends on occupancy rates. These numbers are simply meant to be used as a guide, because they can change at any time. **Note:** Quoted rates do not include Chicago's hefty hotel tax, a whopping 16.4%, which can add significantly to the cost of your stay.

Hostelling International Chicago. 24 E. Congress Parkway (at Wabash Ave.); www. hichicago.org; ✆ **312/360-0300;** Subway/El: Brown, Orange, Pink, or Purple Line to Harold Washington Library, Red Line to Harrison.

Chicago Getaway Hostel. 616 W. Arlington Place (at North Geneva Terrace); www. getawayhostel.com; ✆ **773/929-5380;** Subway/El: Brown, Purple or Red Line to Fullerton.

THE LOOP

Strictly speaking, "downtown" in Chicago means the area around Loop—the central business district, a six- to eight-block rectangle enveloped by elevated tracks on all four sides. Chicagoans aren't so strict with definitions, and we consider some areas outside of the tracks (but not too far outside) also a part of the Loop (Millennium Park, for example). Here's where you'll find the city's major financial institutions, trading markets, office buildings, and government buildings, making for a lot of weekday hustle and bustle during the day, and an eerie nighttime/weekend calm.

BEST FOR Business travelers and visitors who want a real "city" experience, with dramatic skyscraper vistas. Loop hotels are also within walking distance of Chicago's major museums, as well as Millennium Park and the lake. They're all convenient to public transportation, which can whisk you away to other parts of town.

DRAWBACKS Except for a few theaters and restaurants, the Loop shuts down at night. If nightlife is a priority, you won't find many options here. You also won't find many character-filled restaurants, bars, or small businesses.

Expensive

JW Marriott Chicago ★★ One of great things about Chicago is all of the architectural surprises, like the JW Marriott. I've passed the J-dub a dozen times, but I never expected the grandeur that I found in the hotel, which was originally built as the Continental and Commercial National Bank in 1914 by Daniel Burnham. With grand staircases on each side of the block-long lobby, thick, rectangular columns, and marble galore, I almost felt underdressed in my jeans when I visited. Located, appropriately enough, in the Financial District, you'll spot a lot of suits here during the week and a more leisurely crowd on weekends. Rooms are well-appointed, with natural light and marble baths. With 600-plus units, you can sometimes find some great deals here.

Where to Stay in the Loop

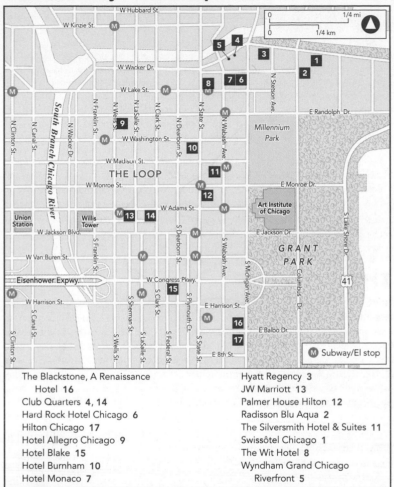

The Blackstone, A Renaissance Hotel **16**
Club Quarters **4, 14**
Hard Rock Hotel Chicago **6**
Hilton Chicago **17**
Hotel Allegro Chicago **9**
Hotel Blake **15**
Hotel Burnham **10**
Hotel Monaco **7**

Hyatt Regency **3**
JW Marriott **13**
Palmer House Hilton **12**
Radisson Blu Aqua **2**
The Silversmith Hotel & Suites **11**
Swissôtel Chicago **1**
The Wit Hotel **8**
Wyndham Grand Chicago Riverfront **5**

151 W. Adams St. (at LaSalle St.). www.jwmarriottchicago.com. (☎) **800/228-9290** or 312/660-8200. 610 units. $169–$429 double. Valet parking $60. Subway/El: Red or Blue Line to Jackson. **Amenities:** Restaurant; lounge; concierge; fitness center w/spa and indoor pool; room service; Wi-Fi at a surcharge.

Radisson Blu Aqua ★★ This LEED-Silver certified building is, hands-down, the most beautiful high rise to be built in Chicago in the last decade. It's also the tallest building in the world designed by a woman. True to its name, the outside is lined with irregularly shaped concrete slabs that, together, create an arresting nautical, wave-like image. The interior is just as dramatic. Throughout the property, you'll see an homage to Chicago, from the brick, light-studded lobby walls that call to mind the skyline, to

If you're staying anywhere near a train line in Chicago, I strongly encourage you to forgo the car rental. If you're flying in, you can hop on the Blue Line at O'Hare or the Orange Line at Midway and be downtown in less than an hour (see "Getting There," p 223). You won't just save money on the rental side, but also on the parking side. Hotels charge exorbitant rates for parking downtown. I've listed those rates within each entry, but they go up frequently. As of this writing, valet costs range from about $45 up to $72 (and those rates go up frequently) per night, adding up to half of what the hotel charges at some spots.

If you drive anywhere, you'll be paying to park in a parking lot or searching for street parking (and paying at a machine), which is at a premium. And that's not taking into account the general stresses of city driving—harried navigation, constant traffic, confusing parking restriction signs, and parallel parking.

If you do decide to drive, make note of this site: Park Whiz (www.parkwhiz.com). There, you can find a lot close to your destination and peruse the prices offered. It's not uncommon to see a $10 lot—for the entire day—just a block from one that charges $40. You can reserve a spot online and then show the attendant (often a valet at a hotel) the Park Whiz confirmation on your phone, and you're good to go.

the sketches of Chicago neighborhoods lining the hallways. Because of the unique shape of the building, rooms range in size; some are a bit small, others quite roomy. Some rooms look out on Millennium Park, while others have city views. If you get the latter, expect to be right in the thick of it, surrounded by high rise office buildings, with windows you can peer into and vice versa. About half of the rooms have balconies (a Chicago rarity) so request one; there's no extra charge.

The hotel is home to an Italian restaurant, Filini, as well as a small but impressive art gallery, fitness center, running track, spa, and indoor and outdoor pool—another downtown rarity. The location is ideal: it's about five minute's walk south to Millennium Park and north to the Magnificent Mile. *Warning:* if there's a fire nearby, you'll know it. The fire station is the hotel's neighbor.

221 N. Columbus Dr. (at Water St.). www.radissonblu.com. ℂ **800/333-3333** or 312/565-5258. 334 units. $197–$314 double. Valet parking $61. Pet friendly. Subway/El: Brown, Green, Pink, Purple, Orange Line to Randolph/Wabash or Red Line to Lake. **Amenities:** Restaurant; bar; concierge; spa; fitness center; indoor and outdoor pools; game room with pool and poker table; sauna; steam room; outdoor running track; room service; free Wi-Fi.

Moderate

The Blackstone, A Renaissance Hotel ★★★ Since it opened in 1910, the aristocratic Beaux Arts–style hotel has welcomed movie stars, royalty, sports celebrities, and nearly a dozen presidents into its marble-lined halls. Painstakingly restored, much of what you see in the lobby is original, from the crystal flower chandelier to the bronze elevator floor indicators, while the modern music and bright carpeting remind you that this isn't just a historic hotel, it's also quite hip. Up the swirling staircases is an art hall, which switches its for-sale works out quarterly. The large rooms all have marble-lined entryways and light earth tones, and once inside, it's easy to forget you're in a historic property. If you're looking for a splurge, reserve one of the two presidential suites. The palatial two-room, two-bath spaces have round, portal-style windows that look out at the lake, and the high ceilings give way to an enormous skylight directly over the bed. The downstairs Spanish tapas restaurant, Mercat a la Planxa, is frequented as much by locals as visitors (see p. 75).

636 S. Michigan Ave. (at Balbo St.). www.blackstonerenaissance.com. © **800/468-3571** or 312/447-0955. 332 units. $161–$242 double. Valet parking $62. Pet friendly. Subway/El: Red Line to Harrison. **Amenities:** Restaurant; concierge; art hall; executive rooms; exercise room; room service; pool table in lobby; Wi-Fi for a surcharge.

Hard Rock Hotel Chicago ★★

As a cool-kid chain, the Hard Rock Hotel has to work extra hard to make me pay attention to a property, and the one in Chicago truly does that. Towering over Michigan Avenue in the landmark Carbon & Carbide building, the gold-leaf-topped Art Deco skyscraper has a number of notable interior features, aside from its faux snakeskin reception area, ping pong table, and floors dedicated to famous rockers. Because it's a landmark, there are certain things about the hotel that the Hard Rock couldn't change, like the monstrous motherboard near the elevators, and the etched bronze elevator doors. Wood accents, lots of natural light, and the trendy decor you would expect from the hotel fill the good-sized rooms, and suites measure up to 1,300 square feet, with two bedrooms and two baths. Hard Rock touches greet you throughout, from the lyrics etched in mirrors of each room to the musical program that allows guests to borrow a guitar or DJ equipment. And exhibitionists take note: Bathroom windows are in front of the shower, so the offices across the way can and do see you if you don't pull the blinds down. The first-floor restaurant, Chuck's: A Kerry Simon Kitchen, serves a pan-ethnic menu, with everything from Thai curry to steaks. By night, the club scene from Angels & Kings spills into the lobby, filling it with loud music and beautiful people until the wee hours.

230 N. Michigan Ave. (at Wacker Pl.). www.hardrockhotelchicago.com. © **866/966-5166** or 312/345-1000. 387 units. $169–$266 double. Valet parking $60. Subway/El: Brown, Green, Pink, Purple or Orange to State/Lake; Red Line to Lake. Pet friendly. **Amenities:** Restaurant; bar; concierge; exercise room; spa; guitar and DJ equipment; room service; free Wi-Fi.

Hotel Allegro Chicago ★★

Families love this boutique hotel, not just because of the playful decor (giant curvy couches, humongous ottomans, a baby grand piano) or the fact that kids can choose a leopard or zebra print robe, but for the nightly "Kids Rule" hour between 4 and 5 pm, when the lobby serves popcorn, breaks out the Wii, and passes out coloring books. (As convenience would have it, a hosted wine hour follows from 5 to 6 nightly—cheers Mom and Dad!). But even with its focus on kids, the property is fresh and appeals to trendy travelers, not just the kid set. Although views aren't particularly special, rooms are spacious and stylish, with soft, blue velvet headboards and a dreamy aqua guitar painting on the walls. As a Kimpton property, expect to find a friendly staff with no airs and fun programming, such as "Guppy Love," which places a goldfish in your room upon request, and a bike borrowing option. The restaurant, 312 Chicago, which is adjacent to the hotel, fills up with power lunchers during the week.

171 W. Randolph St. (at LaSalle St.). www.allegrochicago.com. © **800/643-1500** or 312/236 0123. Fax 312/236-0917. 483 units. $159–$309 double. Valet parking $57. Subway/El: Brown, Orange, Pink, Purple, Blue Lines to Washington. Pets allowed. **Amenities:** Restaurant; lounge; concierge; exercise room; yoga mat in every room; complimentary bikes; room service; Wi-Fi free for hotel loyalty program members.

4

WHERE TO STAY | The Loop

Hotel Burnham ★ To stay here is to experience Chicago architectural history first-hand: the rehabbed Reliance Building is one of the world's first skyscrapers, built in 1895. The 14-story landmark hotel was named for architect Daniel Burnham, and the first floor remains a throwback to the Gilded Age, with its bronze chandeliers, marble columns, fireplace, mosaic tiles, and restored elevator, complete with dramatic grill. The vintage thread continues to the gold and blue guest rooms, which are quite small, with just enough real estate to fit a bed, desk, and chaise (in fact, suites here are the size of many standard rooms at other properties). History buffs who don't mind the squeeze will enjoy wandering the halls, where it's still easy to visualize when this was a functioning office building and the place where Al Capone's dentist worked. Visit the Atwood Cafe on the first floor for upscale comfort food, and stop by the lobby for hosted coffee in the morning and wine in the evening. The hotel also offers complimentary bike for guests to borrow.

1 W. Washington St. (at State St.). www.burnhamhotel.com. ℂ **866/690-1986** or 312/782-1111. 122 units. $142–$299 double. Valet parking $54 with in-out privileges. Subway/El: Blue Line to Washington, Red Line to Lake, Brown, Orange, Pink, Purple Line to Washington/Wells. Pet friendly. **Amenities:** Restaurant; concierge; exercise room; yoga mat in every room; complimentary bikes; hosted wine happy hour at 5pm nightly; room service; Wi-Fi free for hotel loyalty program members.

Hotel Monaco ★★★ Talk about prime location. With rooms overlooking the Chicago River, Hotel Monaco is convenient to the Loop, the Museum Campus, and nightlife and restaurants of River North and the Magnificent Mile. Just walking in the doors you'll get the sense of old-fashioned chivalry, as a doorman greets you and leads you inside. The lobby stretches into two rooms with cushy sitting nooks, a fireplace, and communal tables with lots of outlets. Behind the reception desk, backlit bright art of women in hats is a reminder of the building's history as a hat factory dating back to 1912. High ceilings make standard rooms feel even more spacious, and each of the units has a cushion-lined window seat, peering down on the city. Bathrooms are small, with a single sink and modest tub, while suites have tubs so big they just might qualify as wave pools. Room service is provided by the adjacent American restaurant, South Water Kitchen, and nightly wine receptions are a lovely way to unwind. Plus, the hotel offers guests bikes to borrow.

225 N. Wabash Ave. at Wacker Dr. www.monaco-chicago.com. ℂ **866/610-0081** or 312/960-8500. 192 units. $186–$280 double. Valet parking $56. Subway/El: Brown, Green, Orange, Pink or Purple Line to Randolph/Wabash, or Red Line to Lake. Pet-friendly. **Amenities:** Restaurant; concierge; fitness room; room service; hosted wine reception 5–6pm; Wi-Fi free for hotel loyalty program members.

The Wit Hotel ★ Entering The Wit isn't so dissimilar from entering a dance club. Everything is ultramodern and sparkly. Staff and guests alike are bubbly. Pants are tight. Whether that's your thing or not, it's fascinating to see what Hilton—which The Wit is—can do with a boutique property. Playful and bright with splashy colors, natural light streams in from the floor-to-ceiling windows, art fill each room, and touch-screen phones allow you to choose which Chicago voice you want to awaken you: Barack Obama or Al Capone, maybe? In the hallways, you can hear the sounds of birds chirping by day and crickets and owls at night. Wit stands for "Whatever it Takes," and clearly the staff does their best to have fun with that. Hotel guests also get first-in-line privileges to the ROOF, a Chicago hot spot with a retractable roof that's open year round. Room service comes from the onsite, locally focused restaurant, State and Lake.

201 N. State St. (at Lake St.). www.thewithotel.com. ℂ **312/467-0200.** 310 units. $165–$359 double. Valet parking $56 with in-out privileges. Subway/El: Red, Green, Orange, Brown, Purple, Pink

A No-Tell Motel for the Upper Crust

If you say the name, "Sybaris," to someone in Chicago, you'll get a knowing look and maybe a blushing giggle. That's because it's the name of an adult, or, "romance"-centric series of hotels located in the 'burbs, that's taken the concept of a cheap, no-tell motel and turned it into a high-end enterprise. Well, high-end may be generous, but it's a titillating—and fun—concept. Each room at Sybaris has all the typecast trappings of romance: soft lights, a fireplace, mirrors everywhere, including the ceiling, and at minimum, a Jacuzzi-style bathtub. But it gets better. The more you're willing to shell out for a suite, the more ridiculous the layout is, the highest end being the Chalet Swimming Pool Suite, which is a bi-level suite, complete with a full-on swimming pool, waterfall water slide(!), hot tub, steam room, and massage chair. Plus, the gift shop sells bottles of wine, champagne, chocolate-covered strawberries, and a variety of erotic products and games.

The hotel was actually started by a couple in the 1970s, dedicated to "the enhancement of romantic marriage." Today, the rooms are in private cottages with private garages, and you can book one for overnight (6pm to 11am, prices range from $248–$559) or just a little afternoon delight (12:30pm-4:30pm, $99–$199). From personal experience, I can tell you, blush firmly in place, an afternoon getaway to the room with the waterslide is money well spent. Sybaris has locations in Northbrook, Frankfort, and Downer's Grove, as well as Mequon, Wisconsin and Indianapolis, Indiana (you'll want to have a car to get to any of them). Check www.sybaris. com for locations, photos, videos, and rates.

Line to State/Lake Blue Line to Clark/Lake. **Amenities:** Restaurant; lounge; concierge; exercise room and spa; room service.

Wyndham Grand Chicago Riverfront ★   The Wyndham took over this lapis-blue, 39-floor riverfront property in 2013, transforming it into a space with a down-to-earth feel and luxury aspirations. When it was built in the 1950s, the building was originally a residence, and each apartment had terraces. Now, you can see where the terraces were enclosed, adding a little extra space to each fully window-lined, light-filled room. Of the hotels 334 rooms, 140 of them are double queens—a high number for downtown—and all of those are extra roomy, with a little nook for a seating area and couch. You won't find the same attention to style here that you will in independent boutique hotels—it's largely beige with splashes of color to and fro—but you also won't want for comfort. The art throughout the hotel portrays steely urban girders and train tracks, always reminding you that you're in the thick of a city on the move. And you are. The location on Wacker Drive puts you near Millennium Park, the museums and businesses of the Loop, as well as the shopping, dining, and nightlife of River North. There's a 24-hour fitness center on site and a restaurant.

71 E. Wacker Dr. (btw. Wabash and Michigan aves.) www.wyndham.com. *©* **877/999-3223** or 312/346-7100. 334 units. $236–$267 double. Valet parking $60. Subway/El: Brown, Orange, Pink, Purple, Green to State/Lake. **Amenities:** Restaurant; exercise room; room service; Wi-Fi free for hotel loyalty program members.

Inexpensive/Moderate

Club Quarters Central Loop ★   The no-nonsense Club Quarters has historically catered to the business traveler. Because of that, the hotel staff is unashamed of

THE big BOXES

Although I've focused primarily on highlighting the hotels that, in some way, really have a sense of Chicago to them, the hotel brands that really dominate Chicago are the ones that dominate nearly every city. We have no shortage of Best Westerns, Hiltons, Holiday Inns, Hyatts, Westins, and other large, reliable hotels, centrally located and with all the perks and amenities you've come to know those brands for. There are a few large properties that do warrant a brief mention. These are the big guns in town, with more than 1,000 rooms each. When their rates go down, other properties around town follow, and vice versa. Because of their sheer size, you won't find the personable service you'll find in the boutique hotels and smaller properties, but you will find a family-friendly attitude, along with multiple restaurants, large pools, and often, bargain-driving rates. Without going into too much detail, I've listed those properties below:

Chicago Marriott Downtown Magnificent Mile, 540 N. Michigan Ave. (at E. Ohio St.); www.marriott.com; ℭ **866/576-5456** or 312/836-0100; $189–$429 double. A shoppers dream, right in the thick of the Magnificent Mile action, the Chicago Marriott Downtown Magnificent Mile is filled with a crowd seeking a place a tad more refined than the Hilton and Hyatt. Expect to see the business crowd and conventioneers during the week, and the indoor pool draws large number of families on weekends. Standard rooms actually range in size and can be quite small, but with nearly 1,200 rooms to choose from, getting a reassignment shouldn't be a problem.

the small sizes of the rooms, and rightfully so. Standard rooms are big enough to fit a bed, a desk, and two nightstands, and bathrooms are small and most have just showers. But those interested in a serve-yourself mentality will appreciate the downstairs lounge area, where there's chocolate, cereal, fresh fruit, coffee, tea, bottled water, and sodas for the taking, along with four computers and meeting space for use by guests. The dated blue and aqua hallways could use some updating, but the rooms have recently been renovated, and while they won't be wowing any interior designers with their sparkly striped comforters and plush green chairs, you really can't beat the price or location. If you're looking for a beer and a burger, Elephant & Castle is right next door. A second Club Quarters, which looks out on the Chicago River, is located at 75 E. Wacker Dr. (just west of Michigan Ave.), ℭ 312/357-6400. Both properties are similar enough that I'd advise you to book purely based on rate.

111 W. Adams (at Clark St.). www.clubquarters.com. ℭ **312/214-6400.** 240 units. $94–$219 double. Valet parking $41. Subway/El: Brown, Orange, Pink, Purple Line to Quincy, Blue Line to Jackson. **Amenities:** Fitness center; complimentary fruit, snacks, and bottled water throughout the day; free Wi-Fi.

Hotel Blake ★ Aside from the "historic" designation plaque outside of Hotel Blake, you won't find many other historic references around the property. Rather, the hotel seems to be confident in its main attributes: It's an affordable, stylish property in a central location in the South Loop's Printer's Row. The marble-lined lobby is small and the kind staff is happy to tell you about the property's history as a former print shop, built in the early 1900s, if you ask. Rooms are beige and comfortable, and adornments are minimal. For more room, upgrade to a premium or corner king and you'll

Two restaurants and a Starbucks are on site.

Hilton Chicago, 720 S. Michigan Ave. (at Balbo Ave.); www.hilton.com; ℭ **855/760-0869** or 312/922-4400; $149–$299 double. It's not unusual to find rock-bottom rates at this 1,554-unit hotel, and because it's within walking distance of Grant Park, Millennium Park, the Museum Campus, and all of downtown, you'll also save on cab fare. With an indoor pool, it's a popular choice for families, and fitness buffs love the gym and indoor jogging track. On site, you'll find two restaurants and a snack bar.

Hyatt Regency, 151 E. Upper Wacker Dr. (at Stetson Ave.); www.chicagoregency.hyatt.com; ℭ **312/565-1234;** $139–$299 double. With more than 2,000 guest rooms, the Hyatt Regency is the largest hotel in Chicago, and it's convenient to Navy Pier, the Magnificent Mile, and other popular downtown attractions. Rooms have recently been updated, and there are four restaurants, a bar, and a fitness center.

Sheraton Chicago, 301 E. North Water St. (at Columbus Dr.); www.sheraton chicago.com; ℭ **877/242-2558** or 312/464-1000; $135–$329 double. Standing tall on the north side of the Chicago River, the Sheraton is in the thick of it all, so you can easily walk to Navy Pier, Millennium Park, the Magnificent Mile, and beyond. Upgrade to "club" level to get a room on the top four floors, which give way to stunning views of the city, river, and Lake Michigan. The hotel has 1,200 rooms, three restaurants, and two bars, along with a large indoor pool on the seventh floor.

still be paying less here than at many standard rooms downtown, at a property where I'd have no complaints. A word of advice: in addition to the discount sites, check the property's own website, which tends to publish even lower rates. The adjoining restaurant, Meli Cafe, has fresh and delicious salads, soups, and sandwiches.

500 S. Dearborn (at Congress Pkwy.) www.hotelblake.com. ℭ **312/986-1234.** 162 units. $127–$249 double. Valet parking $47. Subway/El: Brown, Orange, Pink, Purple to LaSalle/Van Buren, Red Line to Harrison. **Amenities:** Restaurant; lounge; exercise room; room service; free Wi-Fi.

Palmer House Hilton ★   History is the driving force at the Palmer House, which has continually operated longer than any other hotel in America. The current version is actually the third iteration of the hotel, the first of which burned 13 days after it opened in the Great Chicago Fire of 1871. To share the tales of the hotel's opulent past and guide guests through its elegant ball rooms, painted ceiling, and endless gold statuary and adornments, the Palmer House actually offers insightful daily tours by its own historian (actually, he's the director of public relations). This is, after all, the place where the brownie was created and it's the first hotel in Chicago to have a phone, an elevator, and electric lights. But once you move beyond the history of the property, I have to say that it's actually a good thing that the gathering spaces of this hotel are so grand, because the standard double rooms can run quite small here (those smaller ones are also less expensive). The hotel takes up a full block, which has its pros and cons. Pro: Rates can be low. Con: You risk getting lost in the winding hallways on the way to the elevator (I speak from experience).

17 E. Monroe St. (at State St.). www.palmerhousehiltonhotel.com. ℭ **800/HILTONS** (445-8667) or 312/726-7500. Valet $72, self parking in nearby hotel lot $41. 1,639 units. $115–$269 double.

Subway/El: Red Line to Monroe, Brown, Green, Orange, Pink, Purple to Adams/Wabash. Pet friendly. **Amenities:** Restaurant; lounge; concierge; executive-level rooms include access to lounge with complimentary breakfast, snacks, and hors d'oeuvres; health club and spa w/indoor pool and Jacuzzi; room service; Wi-Fi with surcharge.

The Silversmith Hotel & Suites ★★

If you can find a good rate at this place—and when the rates are good, they're good—grab it. Many locals haven't even heard of this lovely boutique hotel, which is in a central location in the thick of all of the Loop's action. The property underwent its first real, complete renovation in 2014, and it's now one of the more modern historic properties in town. Enter the black and white marble lobby, where large, shiny silver chandeliers splash bright light throughout. Upstairs, hallways are covered in shiny silvers and greys (that's as silver-smithy as it gets—the name is a nod to the property's early silversmith digs when it opened in 1897). Because it wasn't originally built as a hotel, the rooms are uniquely shaped, some narrow, some with more than one actual room, and all are of a good size. Furnishings have a fun, artsy flair and feel like they belong in a cool loft space. The El rumbles fairly close to the hotel, so expect to feel like a real Chicagoan and exist alongside the noise of city living.

10 S. Wabash Ave. (btw. Madison and Monroe streets). www.silversmithchicagohotel.com. ⓒ **855/695-6668** or 312/372-7696. 143 units. $115–$290 double. Valet parking $55. Subway/El: Brown, Green, Pink, Purple or Orange Line to Madison, or Red Line to Monroe. **Amenities:** Restaurant; lounge; small exercise room; room service; free Wi-Fi.

Swissôtel Chicago ★

There's no missing the Swiss sensibility of this hotel. It's efficient but keeps its eye on design, with artistic touches throughout. Designed by Evanston-born architect Harry Weese, the triangular shape of the building allows for extra space between neighboring buildings, and the result is gorgeous views on all sides, including the lake to the east. The rooms are more practical than plush, with large work desks and lots of natural light coming in from the windows, and bathrooms with separate tubs and showers. The generous health club and pool roost on the 42nd floor (cost is $15 to guests), with its view of Navy Pier and Lake Michigan, actually made me want to lift weights, just to stand in there longer. The hotel ownership is green-minded, and offers guests a dining credit in exchange for opting out of daily housekeeping. The hotel also relies on cold water for laundry, has energy-efficient lighting, and uses a composting system. Although many of the guests are here on business, families also frequently book here for the pool and the "kid-friendly" suites, which have kid-sized furniture, video games, stuffed animals, coloring books, and DVDs. The attached restaurant, The Palm, serves steaks and seafood.

323 E. Wacker Dr. (east of Columbus). www.swissotelchicago.com. ⓒ **888/737-9477** or 312/565-0565. 661 units. $183–$261 double. Valet parking $65. Subway/El: Red, Brown, Orange, Pink, or Green Line to Randolph or Red Line to Lake. **Amenities:** Two restaurants; lounge; coffee bar; concierge; executive-level rooms; health club and indoor pool for a surcharge; convenience store; FedEx; room service; sauna; Wi-Fi with surcharge.

THE MAGNIFICENT MILE

The stretch of North Michigan Avenue is home to some of Chicago's most luxurious hotels, not to mention megamall-style shopping galore. The Mag Mile attracts visitors year-round, but it's especially packed during the summer and Christmas vacation season. The area is safe, but keep your eye out for panhandlers and street performers on the take.

Where to Stay in the Magnificent Mile, Gold Coast, & River North

Acme Hotel Company **21**	The James Chicago **20**
The Allerton Hotel **15**	Kinzie Hotel **27**
Chicago Marriott Downtown Magnificent Mile **22**	The Langham **29**
Conrad Chicago **24**	Millennium Knickerbocker Hotel **11**
Dana Hotel and Spa **18**	Park Hyatt Chicago **12**
The Drake Hotel **10**	Peninsula Chicago **14**
Flemish House of Chicago **2**	Public Hotel **1**
Four Seasons Hotel **9**	The Ritz-Carlton Chicago **13**
The Godfrey Hotel **16**	Sheraton Chicago **31**
Hotel Cass Holiday Inn Express **19**	Sofitel Chicago Water Tower **6**
Hotel Chicago Downtown **28**	Talbott Hotel **4**
Hotel Felix **17**	The Thompson **3**
Hotel Palomar **23**	Tremont Hotel **8**
InterContinental Chicago **25**	Trump International Hotel & Tower **30**
Ivy Boutique Hotel **26**	Waldorf Astoria **5**
	Whitehall Hotel **7**

BEST FOR Serious shoppers, who can take advantage of everything from designer boutiques to large department stores. Travelers who like to be in the center of the action will enjoy the busy pace, as well as the easy access to bustling Oak Street Beach.

DRAWBACKS The crowds and the absence of a "neighborhood" feel. If you're looking for a peaceful getaway, head further north to the Gold Coast (see p. 69).

Expensive

Four Seasons Hotel ★★ The two real standout elements here are the pool and the views. For a second when I saw the indoor pool, I felt like I was in Vegas. This was actually the pool into which Macaulay Culkin jumped in *Home Alone 2,* although in the movie they said it was The Plaza in New York. The area is filled with natural light from a sky-lit dome, and Roman-style columns remind you that you're not in Kansas anymore. Head up to the rooms, which start on floor 30—a height where many hotels end or never quite reach—and tower up to floor 46, giving you views of the lake and city that rival some of the best vantage points in town. The rooms are spacious, but nothing really distinguishes them from others in the brand, aside from the stunning sites outside. *Bonus:* The hotel connects to the 900 North Michigan Avenue Shops, so on the coldest winter and hottest summer days, you can avoid the elements entirely.

120 E. Delaware Place (at Michigan Ave.). www.fourseasons.com/chicagofs. ℂ **800/332-3442** or 312/280-8800. 345 units. $276–$495 double. Valet parking $65. Subway/El: Red Line to Chicago. Pet friendly. **Amenities:** Restaurant; lounge; concierge; health club and spa w/indoor pool; room service; free Wi-Fi.

Park Hyatt Chicago ★★ As you hustle off busy Michigan Avenue into the Park Hyatt, you're met immediately with a hush—the type reserved for museums, galleries, and very nice hotels. Here, in fact, all of the above actually come together. In the lobby area is a museum-style collection of fossils, and a sculpture by Robert Rauschenberg sits by the check-in desk. "Before that we had a Gerhard Richter," the concierge tells me. "That just sold for $37 million." Well then. An Asian sensibility permeates the place, and each of the spacious rooms has a sumptuous cushioned window seat looking out on the city. You can also see that view from the soaking tub, which is separated from the room only by a sliding door. The onsite restaurant, NoMI, is a wonderful sushi restaurant, and it even offers a rather adventurous kids menu. Want a fun fact? The Hyatt has a local tie: It's owned by Chicago's Pritzker family. You'll likely see and hear their name a number of times during your visit, particularly if you see a performance at the Jay Pritzker Pavilion in Millennium Park.

800 N. Michigan Ave. (at Chicago Ave.). www.parkchicago.hyatt.com. ℂ **800/233-1234** or 312/335-1234. 198 units. $252–$400 double. Valet parking $62. Pet friendly. Subway/El: Red Line to Chicago. **Amenities:** Restaurant; lounge; concierge; health club and spa w/Jacuzzi and indoor pool; room service; free Wi-Fi.

Peninsula Chicago ★★ When I visited the Peninsula, I was actually surprised to recall that it's only been here since 2001. It seems like such an institution, I'd somehow assumed it was a historic property. No doubt that's because of the old-school grandeur, starting with the ballroom-sized, light-filled lobby, where there's live music 7 days a week. The hotel takes up a full city block, and you could spend days sampling all of the offerings: tea service by day, a chocolate buffet Friday and Saturday night, three onsite restaurants, a large gym, an indoor pool, 30 different fitness classes, the spa, and, in the winter, a skating rink, which donates all proceeds to charity. Rooms here are among the largest in town, measuring in at 530 square feet. They're also quite traditional and very beige (at the time of this writing the property was starting to schedule a renovation that would add more color and, we hope, update the Starship Enterprise–like electronics panels that tell you the weather and control lights). One notable standout in all rooms that I could get used to: The bathtubs each have a television at the end and a waterproof remote control sits at your fingertips.

108 E. Superior St. (at Michigan Ave.). http://chicago.peninsula.com. ℭ **866/382-8388** or 312/337-2888. 339 units. $444–$525 double. Valet parking $65. Subway/El: Red Line to Chicago. Pets accepted. **Amenities:** 3 restaurants; bar; tea; concierge; health club and spa w/indoor pool; ice skating rink in winter; room service; free Wi-Fi.

The Ritz-Carlton Chicago ★★ Bright, natural light spills into the 12th floor lobby and atrium of The Ritz-Carlton, which is one of the brightest and most welcoming lobbies I've seen. This luxury property has perks for all seasons. It's attached to Water Tower Place, so you can shop, dine, and sleep without ever setting foot outside, and it's just about a 10-minute walk to Oak Street Beach, which you can see from your room, if you luck into (read: pay for) a lake view. Rooms are on floors 13 through 31, which means the floors here (and at sister property The Four Seasons) begin where many hotels stop, and views are what you're really paying for. Even standard rooms are a generous size, although bathrooms are smaller than I'd expect, and the decor is stately but not terribly interesting. More interesting is the heated pool, which has LED lights that change its color and is a draw for many families, especially during "dive in" movie nights. The restaurant, Deca, serves primarily steak and seafood, and the lounge, which sits beneath the lobby's glass skylights, is a wonderful place to work or relax.

160 E. Pearson St. (at Mies van der Rohe Way). www.fourseasons.com/chicagorc. ℭ **800/621-6906** or 312/266-1000. 435 units. $292–$495 double. Valet parking $65 with in-out privileges; self-parking $35 with no in-out privileges. Subway/El: Red Line to Chicago. Pets accepted. **Amenities:** Restaurant; lounge; concierge; health club w/spa and indoor pool; room service; free Wi-Fi.

Moderate

The Drake Hotel ★★ The Drake Hotel was once the grand dame of Chicago luxury, and walking into its elegant, formal lobby is like entering Gatsby's West Egg. While modern hotels have really shrunken their lobbies, the entry here is multiple levels, and the harp music emanating from the Palm Court tearoom is the perfect soundtrack with which to explore. The comfortable rooms have been updated in a way that's actually taken away some of the character of years gone by, but considering the price and ideal location, I won't complain. Rooms facing north offer only-in-Chicago views of Lake Michigan and Lake Shore Drive (those rooms come at a premium). To experience even more grandeur, make a reservation for dinner at the Cape Cod Room (see p. 94) and enjoy classics such as clams casino and Lobster Thermidor before having a Manhattan at Coq d'Or, a boozy throwback of a lounge that opened at the end of Prohibition.

140 E. Walton Place (at Michigan Ave.). www.thedrakehotel.com. ℭ **800/555-7253** or 312/787-2200. 535 units. $129–$279 double. Valet parking $65. Subway/El: Red or Brown Line to Chicago. **Amenities:** 2 restaurants; 2 lounges; tea service; concierge; executive-level rooms; large exercise room; access to nearby health club with pool; room service; Wi-Fi with surcharge.

Hotel Chicago Downtown ★ In February 2014, this hotel seemingly changed overnight from Hotel Sax to The Hotel Chicago, a part of Marriott's Autograph Collection (to put it in PR speak, that means local flair, Marriott standards). As of this

Turning to the Internet or Apps for a Hotel Discount

Before going online, it's important you know why type of discount you're seeking. Currently, there are four types of online reductions:

1. **"Blind" bidding sites.** These offer extreme discounts on sites where you bid for lodgings without knowing which hotel you'll get. You'll find these on sites such as Priceline.com and Hotwire.com, and they can be real money-savers, particularly if you're booking within a week of travel (that's when hotels get nervous and resort to deep discounts to get beds filled). As these companies use only major chains, you can rest assured that you won't be put in a dump. For more reassurance, visit the website BetterBidding.com, where actual travelers spill the beans about what they bid on Priceline.com and which hotels they got.

2. **Hotel website discounts.** Sometimes these can be great values, because they'll often include nice perks, such as breakfast or parking privileges. Before biting, be sure to look at the discount sites below:

   Online travel agencies. These include Hotels.com, Quikbook.com, Expedia.com, and others. Some of these sites reserve rooms in bulk and at a discount, passing along the savings to their customers. But

instead of going to them directly, I'd recommend looking at dedicated travel search engines such as Hipmunk.com, HotelsCombined.com, Momondo.com, and Trivago.com. These sites list prices from all the discount sites, as well as the hotels directly, meaning you have a better chance of finding a deal. *Note:* Sometimes the discounts these sites find require advanced payment for a room (and draconian cancellation policies), so double check your travel dates before booking. Another good source for discounts, especially for luxury hotels, is Tingo.com, a site founded by TripAdvisor. Its model is a bit different than the others, in that users make a prepaid reservation through the site, and if the price of the room drops between the time you reserve and the time you arrive, the site refunds the difference in price.

HotelsTonight.com. This app works for the day on which you use it, but wow! Does it snare great prices for procrastinators—up to 70% off in many cases. A possible strategy: Make a reservation at a hotel. Then, on the day you're arriving, try your luck with HotelsTonight. Most hotels will allow you to cancel without penalty, even on the day of arrival.

writing, the lobby and lounge were in the renovation process, so I can't comment on those. The location, I can say, is pretty ideal. The hotel is in a complex with a bowling alley, wine bar, and House of Blues. To find entertainment, you barely need to leave your room. Speaking of which, they're quite lovely, with high ceilings, floor to ceiling windows, studded leather headboards, fluffy white comforters, and impressively large bathrooms. One word of warning: I'm not the only one who had a hard time finding the entrance, which is a revolving door in a parking lot facing Marina Towers, between Dearborn and State. If you're driving, the parking is on State, despite the fact that the hotel's address is on Dearborn.

333 N. Dearborn (at Carroll Ave.). www.thehotelchicago.com. © **888/236-2427** or 312/245-0333. 354 units. $144–$319 double. Valet parking $65 with in-out privileges. Subway/El: Brown, Green,

Purple, Pink, Orange to State/Lake or Red to Lake. **Amenities:** Wine bar/restaurant attached; lounge; exercise room; Wi-Fi with surcharge.

InterContinental Chicago ★★ This magnificent hotel is a nod to the Chicago of the roaring 20s, when it was built as Medinah Athletic Club, a luxury workout facility for men. You can still see where women were allowed to go: the ceilings in those rooms are painted blue. Hit hard by the Depression, the doors closed in 1934. Today, it's been restored to its full stately glory as the InterContinental. The marble-covered circular lobby is elegant and welcoming, but it has nothing on the "Historic Wing," located to the right. Request a room here (they're significantly larger than in the "Grand" wing, which was built in the '60s). Although they cost a bit more, the location within a maze of history is worth it. Wander around the hallways in front of the elaborate ballrooms, one of which is filled with images and stained glass relating to King Arthur. Visit the three-level fitness center, where that 1920s pool still remains in use, on the 12th floor of the hotel. If you want to learn more about the history, stop by the front desk and ask about the free iPod tour. The property's large size comes with perks: two restaurants, one of which is Michael Jordan's steakhouse (you can get steaks from here via room service); a wine bar; and a huge Starbucks, all of which look out on Michigan Avenue. One thing I appreciate about the InterContinental is that it doesn't just embrace its history; it looks to the future with its eco-friendly approach to hospitality. For example, Hungry Henry is the name of the contraption that turns all food waste to liquid.

505 N. Michigan Ave. (at Grand Ave.). www.icchicagohotel.com. (*) **800/628-2112** or 312/944-4100. 792 units. $148–$253 double. Valet parking $65. Subway/El: Red Line to Grand. **Amenities:** 2 restaurants; wine bar; lounge; Starbucks; FedEx office; concierge; executive-level rooms; health club w/sauna and indoor pool; room service; Wi-Fi free for loyalty card members.

Ivy Boutique Hotel ★★ As I made my way up the narrow, feminine, art-lined hallway of the Ivy, I wondered, briefly, if I'd just entered a spa. The narrowness continues to the top of this tiny, boutique hotel, which has 14 floors and only 63 rooms, 52 of which are suites. The 11 king rooms are quite large and have a lovely design, with hardwood floors, artsy purple striped rugs, and a sizable washroom. Suites measure in at two rooms and 675 square feet, and the bathrooms have deep soaking tubs. Located on a quiet, tree-lined street, just a block and a half off Michigan Avenue and a couple of blocks from the lake, this might be the best-kept secret in town. Strike that, the hotel staff says that it's actually quite popular with the business set, but I'd highly recommend it for a girls' getaway.

233 E. Ontario (btw. Fairbanks Ct. and St. Clair St.). www.thehotelchicago.com. (*) **312/335-5444.** 63 units. $199–$299 double. Valet parking: $48. Subway/El: Red Line to Grand. **Amenities:** Restaurant/bar, rooftop lounge (open seasonally), room service; free Wi-Fi.

Sofitel Chicago Water Tower ★ If you didn't realize the French origins of this hotel before you walked in, you will when you're greeted by the desk staff with "bonjour!" The glass, 32-floor, prism-like structure is by all definitions a large property, with 415 rooms. But each floor is limited to 16 rooms, which makes it feel boutique-like. Guest rooms are filled with natural light and are more daring than most with color choices, including bright red carpeting and chairs. The crowd here is primarily made up of business and international travelers, although families will stay here too. As a French property, there's a heavy emphasis on the food program, and the award-winning Café des Architectes is the onsite restaurant. If you stay here, order an extra croissant for me, please.

20 E. Chestnut St. (at Wabash St.). www.sofitel.com. © **800/SOFITEL** [763-4835] or 312/324-4000. 415 units. $167–$305 double. Valet parking $63. Subway/El: Red Line to Chicago. Pet friendly. **Amenities:** Restaurant; bar; concierge; exercise room; room service; free Wi-Fi.

Talbott Hotel ★★   Tucked away on a quiet street just a block and a half from the Mag Mile, the Talbott was constructed in the 1920s as a residential building. Today, the independently owned boutique hotel embraces its history, and welcomes guests with its English country home decor (complete with quite a few framed, serious dog portraits) and leathery fireside lounges. What comes as a pleasant surprise, in contrast to the old-world sensibilities and antique-styled rooms, is its embrace of technology and its certification as a Green Seal hotel. Each sizable room is equipped with an Apple Mac mini, which allows you to connect to your computer, check your bill, or watch your stories on TV. Guests can flip the thermostat into "eco mode," which alerts housekeeping, via iPad, to change linens and towels every other day. The onsite restaurant, Little Market Brasserie, serves up contemporary comfort food, including a killer grilled cheese with bacon, egg, avocado, and sriracha sauce.

20 E. Delaware Place (btw. Rush and State sts.). www.talbotthotel.com. © **800/TALBOTT** [825-2688] or 312/944-4970. 149 units. $165–$285 double; suites from $349. Valet parking $55, self-parking $44. Subway/El: Red Line to Chicago. Pet friendly. **Amenities:** Restaurant; lounge; concierge; complimentary access to nearby health club; room service; Apple computer in room; free Wi-Fi.

Inexpensive/Moderate

The Allerton Hotel ★   History and location are the motivators to book a room at this storied hotel, which dates back to the '20s. When it opened, the property served as a 1,000-room boarding house for men who moved to Chicago for work. Today, the 25-floor hotel has a stately presence, looming above the shops of Michigan Avenue, and the eyes of passersby are drawn to its Italian Renaissance style. Inside, jazzy hints of yesterday remain in the Art Deco lobby, but grow more tired as you get closer to the rooms, which, as with the other historic properties in town, are rather small, and elevators are tiny. King rooms and suites provide more room, but the guests here, mostly families and international travelers, are less interested in the decor and more tuned into what's going on outside of the hotel.

701 N. Michigan Ave. (at Huron St.). www.theallertonhotel.com. ℂ **877/701-8111** or 312/440-1500. 443 units. $137–$314 double. Valet parking $60. Subway/El: Red Line to Chicago. **Amenities:** Restaurant; lounge; concierge; exercise room; in-room massage treatments; room service; Wi-Fi with surcharge.

Hotel Cass Holiday Inn Express ★

Everything about this hotel is tiny. The lobby is tiny, the rooms are tiny, the bathrooms are tiny. But if you're looking to spend most of your time outside of your room, this spot, which maintains the bright and funky feel of a boutique hotel with the service and cleanliness of a Holiday Inn Express, is a reliable choice. The location is ideal, right in the heart of River North, a few blocks off the Magnificent Mile. And the relatively inexpensive rates even include a complimentary hot breakfast, with eggs, sausage, cinnamon rolls, and cereal. In fact, the lounge where breakfast is served is the only place I saw in the hotel that's not tiny.

640 N. Wabash Ave. (btw. Erie and Ontario sts.). www.casshotel.com. ℂ **800/799-4030** or 312/787-4030. 175 units. $129–$289 double. Valet parking $49. Subway/El: Red Line to Grand. **Amenities:** Fitness center; complimentary breakfast; free Wi-Fi.

Millennium Knickerbocker Hotel ★

This beautiful gothic building dates back to the 1920s, and legend has it that Al Capone's brother, Ralph, ran a speakeasy and casino from the penthouse during Prohibition. In 1970, Hugh Hefner and Playboy Enterprises purchased the property and it operated as Playboy Towers until 1979. The hotel revels in that history and invites guests to do so, too, during a free Friday tour at 3pm. Personally, I found the history of the hotel more interesting than its present, which feels a bit dated. Still, rooms and bathrooms are small but comfortable (upgrade to a Superior Room for more space), and the location is ideal: close to the lake, shopping, nightlife, restaurants, and more.

163 E. Walton Place (east of Michigan Ave.). www.millenniumhotels.com/millenniumchicago/index.html. ℂ **800/621-8140** or 312/751-8100. 305 units. $119–$243 double. Valet parking $65. Subway/El: Red Line to Chicago. **Amenities:** Restaurant; bar; concierge; exercise room; room service; Wi-Fi with surcharge.

Tremont Hotel ★

In a central location, filled with stylish, boutique properties with ever competitive amenities, the Tremont is quite staid and could use some fresh paint—but check out those rates! The European-style hotel is actually managed by Starwood, but because it's considered an "unbranded" property, you'll have to look pretty hard to see any sign of that. Here, what you see is what you get: a nice, clean room and straightforward, friendly service, gimmick free. Rooms vary in shape and size and some do veer on the small side. If you're staying longer, consider booking one of the Tremont "residences," which are larger and more apartment-like. The onsite restaurant is Ditka's, a steakhouse co-owned by former Bears coach Mike Ditka, which serves American fare with a side of sports memorabilia.

100 E. Chestnut St. (1 block west of Michigan Ave.). www.tremontchicago.com. ℂ **888/627-8281** or 312/751-1900. 135 units. $100–$211 double. Valet parking $61. Subway/El: Red Line to Chicago. **Amenities:** Restaurant; concierge; access to nearby fitness room; free Wi-Fi.

Whitehall Hotel ★★★

It feels like you're visiting a sophisticated urban friend's condo when the doorman welcomes you into the tiny lobby here, which is little more than a reception desk and small seating area. Little touches, like the Swarovski crystal chandelier and museum-grade screens from the Ming Dynasty, are a message of old-money confidence, as if the Whitehall Hotel is saying we don't have to hit you over

In Chicago, we're used to rushing around downtown, to and from architectural icons that double as our office spaces. Tourists can get that same experience when they book a room in a high-rise hotel. The **Hard Rock Hotel** (p. 51), located in the towering, green, gold-leaf-topped Carbon & Carbide building, has landmark status, so while the majority of the hotel is filled with musical paraphernalia, you can still see the bronze-gated elevators and the ancient-looking motherboard that controls them. The onion-like dome atop the **InterContinental** (p. 61) was once a dirigible landing for parking blimps. Formerly the Medinah Athletic Club, the elaborately elegant hotel is a throwback to the 1920s, when it was built, to a time when gyms were mighty different than they are today. **The Langham** (p. 65) is the only hotel to be built inside a Mies van der Rohe building. Located in floors 1 through 13 of the former IBM building, this is the last project the famous, steel-loving architect worked on before he died. The hotel even brought in his grandson, Dirk Lohan, to design the lobby. The initial plan when building the **Trump International Hotel & Tower** (p. 65) was to create the tallest building in the world. Those plans were altered following 9/11, but the building is still a dramatic addition to the skyline. Measuring in at 92 floors, the concrete, glass, and steel building is the second tallest in the city and the third tallest in the U.S. (if you count the height of the antenna on One World Trade Center, that is, which makes it the tallest building). Book a room in the gorgeous **Radisson Blu Aqua** (p. 49), which gracefully flows into the sky with its wave-like balconies, and you'll be spending the night in the tallest building ever to be designed by a woman.

the head with opulence to win you over. That sensibility continues in the small aristocratic lounge, lined with mahogany paneling, which is rumored to be the first place to serve a drink after Prohibition. Rooms are colored in earth tones, and even the standard variety is large enough for two beds, a couch, desk, and plenty of space to move around. Suites have the kind of furniture you'd find in a home, like a four-poster bed. Plus, you really can't beat the price. Two restaurants on site serve Italian and Chinese food.

105 E. Delaware Place (west of Michigan Ave.). www.thewhitehallhotel.com. ⓒ **866/753-4081** or 312/944-6300. 222 units. $90–$128 double. Valet parking $57 with in-out privileges. Subway/El: Red Line to Chicago. Pet friendly. **Amenities:** Two restaurants; lounge; concierge; exercise room; room service; free Wi-Fi.

RIVER NORTH/NEAR NORTH

North of the Loop and west of the Magnificent Mile, River North is a former industrial neighborhood that's been transformed into a thriving dining, shopping, and nightlife district, home to some of the city's trendiest restaurants and clubs. High heels and short skirts are the dress code here, and bathroom attendants aren't uncommon. I've seen them even in the most generic of lounges.

BEST FOR   Night owls, with lots of 20- and 30-somethings walking around in groups, often on the prowl. Restaurants in River North stay open late, and there are plenty of clubs and bars within walking distance.

DRAWBACKS Because of its large concentration of hotels, River North can feel overrun with tourists, especially in the summer. It's also lacking a neighborhood feel, and it's challenging to find any kind of low-key, super-casual gathering spot.

Expensive

The Langham ★★★ If Downton Abbey was transported in time and place to Chicago, it would be The Langham, where a team of butlers awaits you if you're a Langham Club member (that is, staying in a suite or paying a surcharge). This London-based outfit is the new belle to the Chicago luxury ball for its service and design. The property opened in 2013 in the first 13 floors of the 52-story former IBM building, which is a Chicago landmark designed by famous architect—and Chicago resident—Ludwig Mies van der Rohe. It's also the first hotel to live in one of his steel-and-glass, sharp-edged buildings. The first thing you'll see as you enter the hotel is art, art, art, and more art—140 piece of fine art, to be exact. "Mr." or "Ms." is the common greeting here, and "It's my pleasure," is a popular response. Still, even with the slightly stiff service, the property is refined and elegant, with soft beiges and chocolates throughout. Rooms go from big (starting at more than 500 sq. ft.) to absolutely huge (the Infinity and Regent suites are a whopping 2,700 sq. ft.) and have floor-to-ceiling windows that peer out on downtown, the Chicago River, and Lake Michigan. Bathrooms all have deep soaking tubs and rain showers. Be sure to visit the mid-century modern bar, Travelle Bar and Lounge (p. 215) on the second floor, a romantic spot with incredible views.

330 N. Wabash (at Illinois St.). www.chicago.langhamhotels.com. ℂ **312/923-9988.** 316 units. $256–$461 double. $71 valet parking. Subway/El: Brown, Orange, Purple, Pink, Green Lines to State/Lake. **Amenities:** Restaurant; bar; afternoon tea; butler services at club level; spa; health club; indoor pool; fitness classes; room service; concierge; free Wi-Fi.

Trump International Hotel & Tower Chicago ★★★ Regardless of how you feel about The Donald, I think we can all agree on one thing: Dude knows how to do hospitality. The towering, light blue concrete and glass structure, all 92 floors of it, sits on prime Chicago real estate, overlooking the river, lake, and downtown. And although the second tallest building in Chicago earned its stars for luxury, there's a comfort here that draws in many families, and kids are greeted with a backpack filled with a plush toy, coloring book, and cotton candy. Standard rooms are huge, with floor-to-ceiling windows, a bed, sofa-sleeper, chair, desk and bureau, and they are equipped with a full kitchen, complete with microwave, fridge, stove, Nespresso machine, ice maker, and dishwasher (reserved for housekeeping, but proof positive that glasses are actually washed and not just sprayed with disinfectant). One-to-three bedroom suites are enormous at 2,500 feet. The 14th floor fitness center and pool rivals many free-standing gyms, and guests can participate in 40-plus complimentary classes and even borrow UnderArmour workout clothes and shoes. Guests get first-come privileges at The Terrace, located on the 16th floor, which has views that even locals cherish (p. 214). Just try to keep your sense of humor when it comes to the over-the-top touches, like TVs in the bathroom mirrors and a "water library" that includes four bottled water options, one of which is a $25 bottle covered in Swarovski crystals. And, of course, expect to see the Trump name on anything that can be embroidered.

401 N. Wabash Ave. (at the Chicago River). www.trumpchicagohotel.com. ℂ **855/878-6700** or 312/588-8000. 339 units. $395–$446 double. Valet parking $71. Subway/El: Red Line to Grand. Pet friendly. **Amenities:** Restaurant; two lounges; concierge; fitness center w/spa and indoor pool; salon; room service; complimentary car service within 1 mile; room service; full kitchens in each room; free Wi-Fi.

family-friendly HOTELS

Kids and families can have a blast in Chicago with a little bit of planning. Here are some great places to stay when you have little ones in tow:

Chicago's four Kimpton properties (**Hotel Palomar, Hotel Allegro, Hotel Monaco,** and **Hotel Burnham**) all cater to the small ones, offering them mini animal-print robes, welcome gifts, and even kids' comment cards upon checkout. The **Allegro** (p. 51) even hosts a nightly "Kids Rule" hour, 4pm–5pm, when kids can nosh on popcorn, color in coloring books, and play Wii games in the lobby, and families love **Hotel Palomar** (p. 68) for its rooftop pool. At the south end of the Loop, the **Hilton Chicago** (p. 55) has lots of public space for wandering, and many of the rooms come with two bathrooms. Another bonus: Both the Field Museum and the Shedd Aquarium are within walking distance. At the north end of the Loop near the intersection of Lake Michigan and the Chicago River, the **Swissôtel Chicago** offers kids suites filled with kid-sized furniture, DVDs, stuffed animals, and coloring books (p. 56).

And, of course, luxury hotels can afford to be friendly to all of their guests. At **Trump International Hotel & Tower** (p. 65), kids get a backpack of activities on arrival, and milk and cookies are a part of the nightly turndown service. The **Four Seasons Hotel** (p. 58) indulges kids with little robes, balloon animals, Nintendo, and milk and cookies; the hotel also has a wonderful pool. The concierge at **The Ritz-Carlton Chicago** (p. 59) keeps a stash of toys and games for younger guests to borrow, and kids' menu items are available 24 hours; the hotel even provides a special gift pack just for teenage guests.

Moderate/Expensive

Dana Hotel and Spa ★★   The Dana is a rare bird in Chicago: a locally owned boutique hotel. The owners clearly have an eye for design, with hardwood floors throughout the property, exposed concrete ceilings, and smooth, flowing wood designs in the lobby. The wood floors continue into the rooms, with the exception of the area of the bed, where the carpet reveals an empathetic attention to detail—who wants to step on a cold, wood floor when they awaken? Rooms are spacious, with floor-to-ceiling windows and a glass wall that separates the shower from the room, allowing natural light in (and perhaps a shower show) as you rub-a-dub-dub. I'm particularly fond of the "cozy king" rooms, which are corner rooms that measure a bit smaller, but have panoramic views and small balconies—practically unheard of in Chicago—*and* they run about $30 less than standard rooms. Because of its contemporary appeal, expect to see the young, smart set as staff and guests, with the occasional tattoo and piercing. Vertigo, the lounge on the 27th floor, is a beautiful rooftop lounge.

660 N. State St. (at Erie St.). www.danahotelandspa.com. © **888/301-3262** or 312/202-6000. 216 units. $209–$334 double. Valet parking $49. Subway/El: Red Line to Chicago. **Amenities:** Restaurant; lounge; concierge; exercise room and spa; room service; free Wi-Fi.

The Godfrey Hotel ★★   A confident coolness emanates from The Godfrey, rather than the trying-too-hard-to-be-hip style of some boutique properties. Outside, the cubist-like metal and glass structure of the hotel looks a bit like a Transformer, or an abstract stack of LEGOs in the Chicago skyline. Inside, the front desk staff is so friendly, you might just feel like you know them from another life. The metallic design aesthetic continues into the spacious guest rooms, which are filled with varying tones of slates and grays, along with clean lines. The attention to design and the location just off the beaten tourist path draws in a savvy, 30- and 40-something clientele, adventurous enough to veer off the Mag Mile. Views from the building's south side are unhindered by nearby buildings, so you can see downtown from a vantage point that's just far enough away to appreciate the thickness of this city. Floor four is home to a restaurant and lounge called I|O (indoor|outdoor), which is the city's biggest "roofscape,"— PR speak for an enormous, retractable window-covered lounge with a mix of indoor and outdoor space that is well worth a visit. Also on site is a spa and fitness center, and bathroom products are L'Occitane (love it).

127 W. Huron (btw. Clark and LaSalle streets). www.godfreyhotelchicago.com. © **855/649-2200** or 312/649-2000. 221 units. $189–$369 double. $55 valet. Subway/El: Red Line to Chicago. **Amenities:** Restaurant; lounge with outdoor space; concierge; fitness center; spa; room service; free Wi-Fi.

Hotel Felix ★   It seems there's an eco-friendly story behind everything you touch at the Hotel Felix, from the lobby carpeting and wallpaper made from recycled materials, to the guest room and gym floors made from plastic bottles, to the cleaning products used, which don't include any bleach. At the same time, the hotel pays close attention to making those sustainable design principles visually appealing, and the lobby is a great example, with a fireplace, fountain, and fun blown glass globes that artfully dangle from the ceiling. Yes, the rooms are quite small at this Silver LEED-certified hotel, as are the bathrooms, but perhaps guests here are more interested in protecting the environment, not taking up more of it. A small spa and fitness center are on site if you want to get even more Zen.

111 W. Huron St. (at Clark St.). www.hotelfelixchicago.com. © **877/848-4040** or 312/447-3440. 225 units. $159–$364 double. Valet parking $49 (free for hybrid BMWs). Subway/El: Red Line to Chicago. **Amenities:** Restaurant; bar; concierge; exercise room; room service; free Wi-Fi.

Inexpensive/Moderate

Acme Hotel Company ★★★   If Acme were a beer, it would be a Pabst Blue Ribbon. While other hotels in this section could be compared to clubs or lounges, Acme is a cool hipster bar, and I mean that in the best possible way. Some hotels have fine art behind the front desk, Acme has graffiti art. Throughout the hotel, which is locally owned, a funky but accessible vibe emanates, from its nightlights—glowing lip prints on the bathroom mirrors—to its chalkboard door fixture, which you can make into your own note, be it "do not disturb" or something less practical. Rooms are all art splashed, with hardwood floors, a giant handprint on the headboard, and mid-century modern furniture and lamps. Foot for foot, standard rooms are tiny (about 200 sq. ft.), but the hotel has made smart moves, like taking out the closet for extra space and leaving racks exposed, so it somehow doesn't feel that small at all. For something bigger, about $40 extra will get you a larger room with two queens, and for about $80 more you can get a king suite, double the size, with a living room area. The Acme always seems to have something cool up its sleeve, whether it's sponsoring a Baconfest or introducing innovative amenities, like Google Glass, free for guest use. Plus, the bar and restaurant, the Berkshire Room, mixes up a good cocktail and feels like a neighborhood watering hole.

15 E. Ohio St. (btw. State St. and Wabash Ave). www.acmehotelcompany.com. © **312/894-0800**. 130 units. $174–$254 double. Self parking only, $35 with in-out privileges. Subway/El: Red Line to Grand. **Amenities:** Restaurant; lounge; fitness room; hot tub; sauna; laundry room; foosball table; room service; Google Glass free for guests to use for 3 hours; free Wi-Fi.

Many of Chicago's downtown hotels are in historical buildings. And although the rooms have all been renovated, that history still remains a deep part of the experience. A number of hotel offer tours to guests (and the general public) to share more about the hotel's heritage. The **Palmer House Hilton** (p. 55) has its own on-site museum (a room, really), filled with old relics, photos, and newspaper clippings that fill visitors in on the hotel's colorful Chicago history, dating back to 1871. This is also where the hotel's **"History is Hott"** tour begins. (www.palmerhousehiltonhotel.com/events/history-is-hott; $\textcircled{C}$ **312/917-1738**; Tues–Sat, noon; $65; includes lunch; reservations required). Led by Director of PR/Palmer House historian extraordinaire Ken Price, the tour explores the history of Chicago and Palmer House's place in it, and takes visitors through some of the most elaborate rooms of the hotel to view grand ballrooms, ceiling murals, and more. The **InterContinental Chicago** (p. 61) doesn't advertise it, but a free iPod tour is available. Inquire at the concierge desk, and the self-guided audio tour will lead your through the hotel, filling you in on the hotel's heyday back in the 20s, when it was built as a luxury athletic club for use by the Shriners. It fell into disrepair during the Depression, but today has been restored to its original state. The **Millennium Knickerbocker Hotel** (p. 63) supposedly has secret passageways that were once used by Al Capone's brother, who, they say, operated a casino in the penthouse. You won't get to tour any secret tunnels, but you'll learn a heck of a lot about the hotel's seedy underbelly on a free, weekly tour, Friday at 3pm (no reservation required).

4

River North/Near North

WHERE TO STAY

Hotel Palomar ★★ This River North spot manages to draw in all walks of life. Its art collection and playful sophistication appeal to young couples. Its indoor pool and kid-friendly perks (animal print robes, access to cribs and high chairs and babysitter service) appeal to families. And the eclectic American fare at its restaurant, Sable Kitchen & Bar (p. 93), appeals to foodies, many of whom are local, stopping in for a meal or a drink after work. The large rooms are designed with warm earth tones and punctuated with bright reds and blues. As a Kimpton property, Hotel Palomar offers fun fitness programs, such as barre workouts on the rooftop and morning runs with the manager, and every room has a yoga mat. Each night, guests are invited to the lobby to mix and mingle over a hosted wine happy hour (5–6pm) and pet "friendly" is an understatement here and at all Kimpton properties. There are no restrictions on pet size, and pet rooms are outfitted with a pet bed and bowl, along with other pet amenities. And for those sad about traveling Fluffy-free, the hotel also has a "Guppy Love" program, which puts a goldfish in your room for the night to keep you company.

505 N. State St. (at Illinois St.). www.hotelpalomar-chicago.com. $\textcircled{C}$ **877/731-0505** or 312/755-9703. 261 units. $195–$260 double. Valet parking $58. Subway/El: Red Line to Grand. Pet friendly.
Amenities: Restaurant; lounge; hosted wine hour 5pm nightly; concierge; exercise room; fitness programs (yoga and running); indoor pool; complimentary bike use; Wi-Fi free for hotel loyalty program members.

The James Chicago ★★ Walking past The James, you don't think much of the milquetoast brick building. Inside, it's a different story. The lobby could easily be a design store, with its warm, light colors, cushy mid-century modern orange couches, brown leather ottomans, and bookshelves. There's a surefire masculine feel to it, but it's more metrosexual than anything, like hanging out with your fun guy friend. Standard rooms are spacious, with a work nook that allows you to separate slightly from the bed area. Suites feel straight out of a design magazine photo shoot, and one of them even has a projector so that kids (or adults) can broadcast films on the wall. Although all of the surroundings are gorgeous and make this a hotel worth staying in on their own, the true standout here is David Burke's Primehouse, which is on the first floor. "You can get a dry-aged steak brought to your room," said my hotel tour guide. "Can't say that about a lot of places." In fact, a number of the guests return for that very reason. When you're ready to work off your steak, ask the hotel to make an appointment with their personal trainer, who will meet you in the fitness room.

55 E. Ontario St. (at Rush St.). www.jameshotels.com. © **877/526-3755** or 312/337-1000. 297 units. $188–$269 double. Valet parking $60. Subway/El: Red Line to Grand. Pets welcome. **Amenities:** Restaurant; two bars; concierge; large exercise room; room service; spa; free Wi-Fi.

Kinzie Hotel ★   Chicago is the theme at the Kinzie, which until 2014 was called the Amalfi. First, the name: John Kinzie was one of Chicago's early settlers. Next, the art: The small, brightly lit lobby doubles as a gallery, displaying Chicago-centric art, like the work by a popular street artist and a portrait of the Brown Line made of duct tape. Each room has a map of Chicago streets covering the wall behind the ridiculously comfortable bed. Continuing the Chicago theme, room service is available from Harry Caray's Italian Steakhouse, which is located across the street. Since the hotel doesn't have an onsite restaurant (as of this writing), it hosts happy hour every night with a complimentary drink, cold cuts, and cheese. A continental breakfast, with coffee, juice, pastries, fruit, and yogurt, is offered on each floor every morning. Assessment: A good boutique option in a great River North location.

20 W. Kinzie (btw. Dearborn Pkwy. and State St.). www.kinziehotel.com. © **312/395-9000.** 215 units. $171–$259 double. Valet parking $56. Subway/El: Brown Line to Merchandise Mart. Pet friendly. **Amenities:** Lounge with hosted nightly cocktail/hors d'oeuvres 5pm-8pm; free continental breakfast; fitness center; concierge; in-room spa services; free Wi-Fi.

THE GOLD COAST

Although it feels peaceful and secluded, the Gold Coast is still within easy walking distance to Michigan Avenue, the lakefront, Lincoln Park, and Old Town. Filled with mansions from the 19th and early 20th centuries, visitors here can see how some of Chicago's wealthiest live.

BEST FOR   Visitors who want to escape the noise and traffic of downtown and admire the residential architecture of one of Chicago's most exclusive neighborhoods. Shoppers, beachgoers, history buffs, and foodies will also find something worth exploring here.

DRAWBACKS   There are only a few hotel options in this largely residential district, but they're good ones.

Expensive

Waldorf Astoria ★★★   At first pass, I missed the turn into the walled, roundabout parking area of the Waldorf Astoria. Know why? Because I didn't know there was such a thing as a roundabout driveway in the Gold Coast, where every piece of real estate is treated like gold and used to its greatest potential. How wrong I was. The lavishness continues inside the hotel, which you could call "French manor-style," but "palatial" is more accurate. Built in 2008 as the Elysian, the Waldorf Astoria brand took over the space in 2012, and has done a superb job of maintaining its elegant, over-the-top image. Turn your eyes up in the bright white lobby and you'll see a starburst chandelier, which was based on a brooch that Coco Chanel used to wear, and the swirly designs in the marble are inspired by her apartment. The rooms here are among the largest in town, decorated with furnishings that are artfully residential, and many are equipped with balconies and fireplaces. Of the 188 units, only 38 are standards and the rest are suites, drawing in, surprisingly enough, a good number of families. One warning, though: Although there's a pool on site, it's more of a lap pool and less of a kid-friendly play area. Look close and you'll see hundreds of thousands of small, pink, Italian tiles on the bottom. The goal: so guests can feel as though they're swimming through a bed of roses. Seriously.

11 E. Walton St. (at Rush St.). www.waldorfastoriachicagohotel.com. © **800/500-8511** or 312/646-1300. 188 units. $405–$505 double. Valet parking $64. Subway/El: Red Line to Chicago. **Amenities:** Restaurant; lounge; concierge; health club w/spa and indoor lap pool; room service; free Wi-Fi.

Moderate

Public Hotel ★★   Color is one word that doesn't come to mind at Public Hotel, where the light marble matches the walls, which match the couches. This Gold Coast hotel is the brainchild of Ian Schrager, the co-founder of Studio 54, who is credited with coining the whole concept of boutique hotel. It opened in 2011, taking over the old Ambassador East and returning a sense of splendor to a property that was previously quite flea-baggy. The rooms are about as bright as the lobby (beige blanket, beige carpet, beige curtains, beige walls, beige chair, luxe white linens), yet the elevator and halls seem alarmingly dark. I wondered if my eyes were having issues and asked about it. "It's all about the contrast," I was told—a Schrager touch. The brights seem brighter when coming from the dark. Which is true, they do, but I'm still not sure I quite get it. Located in the Gold Coast, surrounded by million-dollar mansions, the property has managed to woo its neighbors, with whom you'll rub elbows at the popular Pump Room restaurant (p. 84). This is a great neighborhood to stay in and feel like a wealthy Chicagoan. You're within walking distance of Old Town, Lincoln Park, the Gold Coast, and the lake, and pleasantly removed from the tourist zone.

1301 N. State Pkwy. (at Goethe St.). www.publichotels.com. © **888/506-3471** or 312/787-3700. 285 units. $140–$257 double. Valet parking $65. Subway/El: Red Line to Clark/Division. Pet friendly. **Amenities:** Restaurant; lounge; concierge; fitness room; room service; free Wi-Fi.

The Thompson ★★   As I write this, The Thompson is the "it" place in Chicago, thanks to its quirky cool design, plus the popular onsite restaurant, Nico Osteria. The Thompson has made it a point to be comfortably un-hotel-like, and different from cookie-cutter-style, points-earning hotels (its sister property, Hotel Lincoln, see p. 72, takes the same approach). The lobby welcomes guests with a homey feel—a warm fireplace, living-room-style seating, and bookshelves to peruse. Upstairs, the rooms are a nice break from the beige hotel trend, with bright blue sectionals, window-facing glass desks, soft white linens, and modern art on the walls. USB chargers at the bed-side are like traveler's gold, and bathrooms have raised sinks and rain showerheads. The hotel makes a number of earth-friendly choices, which include a wall of plants—a "green wall"—in the lounge, and lights and thermostats that limit output when the room is unoccupied. And then there's the dining. Nico Osteria (p. 86) serves fresh and simple Italian food, with an emphasis on seafood, and diners are generally willing to wait quite a while to nab a seat here. Others simply book a room at The Thompson, where they can have it delivered straight to their room. On my visit, the GM told me that, to the hotel's surprise, the most popular time for room service isn't breakfast, as in most hotels. It's dinner, all because of Nico Osteria.

21 E. Bellevue Pl. (at Rush St.). www.thompsonhotels.com. $\copyright$ **866/378-8866** or 312/266-2100. 247 units. $195–$287 double. Valet parking $62. Subway/El: Red Line to Clark/Division. Pet friendly. **Amenities:** Restaurant; lounge; concierge; fitness room; room service; free Wi-Fi.

LINCOLN PARK

The North Side is a general term that encompasses the residential neighborhoods north of the Gold Coast; Lincoln Park is a particularly tony area area that sprawls westward from the lakefront park of the same name. Hotels in this area are actually quite affordable, and it's easy to feel like a local.

BEST FOR Living among Chicagoans; few tourists hang out this far from downtown. There are a number of smaller hotel options, and it's a great place to explore by bike or by foot, and there are a number of independent shops, neighborhood bars, and incredible restaurants, from molecular gastronomy to a great burger. Parking and hotel rates are much less expensive than downtown.

DRAWBACKS The distance from cultural institutions such as the Art Institute or Field Museum, both of which are a half-hour away by public transportation.

Inexpensive/Moderate

Best Western Hawthorne Terrace ★★ My own family has stayed here, repeatedly, when they come to visit, and they give this Lakeview hotel glowing reviews. I concur. First, the location is great if you want to feel like a local: it's within walking distance of Wrigley Field, Boystown, the lake, and dozens of restaurants and bars. Rates tend to be decent, and you can choose between the main building, which has 60 rooms—there's nothing special about them, but they're clean and comfortable and fairly big—or the new "annex," which has 24 apartment-style suites. Each has hardwood floors and sectioned off rooms, and some even have kitchens. Plus, the hotel provides an impressive continental breakfast with muffins and cinnamon rolls from the famous Chicago restaurant, Ann Sather (p. 92). There's also a fitness room and hot tub, and front desk staff couldn't be nicer.

3434 N. Broadway Ave. (at Hawthorne Place). www.hawthorneterrace.com. $\copyright$ **888/860-3400** or 773/244-3434. 84 units. $141–$216 double and $276–$419 suite. Rates include continental breakfast. Self-parking $30 with in-out privileges. Pet friendly. Subway/El: Red Line to Addison. **Amenities:** Complimentary breakfast, outdoor terrace, exercise room w/hot tub and sauna; free Wi-Fi.

City Suites Hotel ★ If you're in town for a Cubs game or taking in a show, and you'll take value over glamour and service, City Suites Hotel fits the bill. It's right by the Red Line, which can zip you to the Loop in less than a half hour (but also rumbles by 24 hours a day, so light sleepers might want to bring ear plugs), and the lake is less than a mile east. Plus, you're surrounded by residential areas, including Boystown, comedy clubs, bars, and restaurants. Standard rooms are quite small, so opt for a suite if you expect to spend much time in the room. Breakfast is included (pastries, cereal, breakfast sandwiches) and parking is only $22, so the hotel is a definite bargain. The neighborhood here is safe, but it does feels more urban and unpredictable than downtown and River North, so use common sense. (The fact that there's a "no public restrooms" sign at the hotel entrance says something). This property has two sister properties, The Willows and The Majestic (below), which are both a step up in appearance and an improvement in noise level.

933 W. Belmont Ave. (at Sheffield Ave.). www.chicagocitysuites.com. ℂ **800/248-9108** or 773/404-3400. 45 units. $127–$271 double. Parking $22 in nearby lot with in-out privileges. Subway/El: Red Line to Belmont. **Amenities:** Continental breakfast, free access to nearby health club; limited room service; free Wi-Fi.

Hotel Lincoln ★★★   Not only is Hotel Lincoln plopped in one of the best neighborhood locations in town (right in Lincoln Park, across from Lincoln Park Zoo and Lake Michigan), it's also among the most fun, lighthearted, and quirky hotels in Chicago. When you enter, expect an exuberant staff dressed in preppy uniforms (guys are in bowties, girls are in polka dots) to greet you and, quite possibly, compliment you on something (they did so to both of us; I think they were genuine, my boyfriend thinks it's part of their training). Although it has 184 rooms, the hotel manages to feel intimate, with its warm attention to homespun decor—the front desk is an assemblage of drawer fronts, for example. Standard rooms all have local art on the walls and vintage furniture that feels real rather than antiseptic, like many hotels. Request a room on floors nine and up for the best lake views (you'll pay about $40 more for it), and be sure to pop up to the J. Parker (p. 216), the rooftop lounge. Service there is so-so at best, but you can gaze at this beautiful city from up high. With complimentary bike rentals and even the hotel's pedicab, you can explore the neighborhoods without having to worry about a car.

1816 North Clark St. (at Lincoln Ave. and Wells St.). www.jdvhotels.com/hotels/illinois/chicago-hotels/hotel-lincoln. ℂ **855/514-8112** or 312/254-4700. 184 units. $179–$309 double. Valet parking $49. Bus: 22 or 36 Broadway. Pet friendly. **Amenities:** Restaurant; rooftop lounge; complimentary wine hour; coffee bar; rooftop yoga; complimentary bike rentals and pedicab rides; room service; free Wi-Fi.

The Majestic Hotel ★★   This is about as close as it gets to living local while also having access to the perks of a hotel. The Majestic is on a residential street, less than a block from Belmont Harbor and the lake, and less than a mile from Wrigley Field. The building looks like a typical Chicago apartment for a reason: It once served as a house for women and children who'd lost their husbands and fathers in World War I. Because of its residential location, the hotel is popular with relatives visiting family nearby. Rooms and suites were recently renovated, and some suites even have a small sunroom to sit in and watch the neighborhood outside. Continental breakfast is included. Parking is inexpensive compared to downtown hotels: It's $22 to park in a nearby lot. The Majestic shares the same owners as City Suites (above) and The Willows (below).

528 W. Brompton St. (at Lake Shore Dr.). www.majestic-chicago.com. ℂ **800/727-5108** or 773/404-3499. 52 units. $143–$369 double. Self-parking $22 in nearby lot with in-out privileges. Subway/El: Red Line to Addison; walk several blocks east to Lake Shore Dr. and then one block south. **Amenities:** Continental breakfast; free access to nearby health club; free Wi-Fi.

The Willows Hotel ★   Location, location, location. The Willows has a great one. If you haven't yet noticed, my goal in writing this book is to urge visitors into the neighborhoods, where Chicago's true energy is, and The Willows does just that. Plopped down in the tony Lincoln Park neighborhood, in an entirely residential area, it's within walking distance of the lake and a number of great nightlife and dining options, including my favorite restaurant, Senza (see p. 103). You won't find the refined service and amenities here that you will further south, but you'll get a comfortable room at a reasonable price, and, best of all, a taste of the true Chicago. **Bonus:** Continental breakfast is included and self-parking in a nearby lot is $22 (yes, that's a bonus).

555 W. Surf St. (east of Halsted Ave.). www.willowshotelchicago.com. ✆ **800/787-3108** or 773/528-8400. 55 units. $127–$344 double. Self-parking $22 in nearby lot with in-out privileges. Subway/El: Brown Line to Diversey; take a cab or walk several blocks east on Diversey, then left on Broadway and right on Surf. **Amenities:** Continental breakfast; free access to nearby health club; free Wi-Fi.

NEAR MCCORMICK PLACE

Although the sprawling McCormick Place Convention Center isn't far from downtown, it feels cut off from the rest of the city. The main reason to stay here is the easy access to conferences and conventions.

BEST FOR   Business travelers conducting work at McCormick Place.

DRAWBACKS   No great restaurants or stores within walking distance; you'll have to take a taxi or bus to explore the city.

Expensive

Wheeler Mansion ★★   You almost expect to find staff in period dress within Wheeler Mansion, a gorgeous home that was built 1 year before the Great Chicago Fire and managed to survive the disaster. Located just a 5-minute walk from McCormick Place, the historic property is actually a huge draw for those among the convention crowd who are looking for a place with more character than the nearby Hyatt. The 11 rooms, which range in size and layout, are all decorated a bit differently, although the antiques, luxurious linens, and elegance are consistent with the era in which the home was built. Out back is lovely outdoor space, with a peaceful porch and garden. Every morning, guests are offered an elaborate complimentary buffet breakfast, and even parking is free.

2020 S. Calumet Ave. (btw. 21st and Cullerton Sts.). www.wheelermansion.com. ✆ **312/945-2020.** 11 units. $295–$345 double. Free parking. Subway/El: Metra Electric to McCormick Place. **Amenities:** Complimentary breakfast; free shoe shine; free Wi-Fi.

Moderate

Hyatt Regency McCormick Place ★   You'll get great views of downtown and Lake Michigan if you're on one of the higher floors of this 33 level hotel, but it's an odd location on the city's South Side—there's not much to recommend within walking distance, and the area can get shady at night. The Hyatt Regency is really for convention goers. It's connected by a sky bridge to McCormick Place, so the hotel is perennially filled with suits. If you're in town for meetings and conferences and you stay here, you can literally avoid going outside for most of your journey. But if you're here to explore the city, resist the deals you'll see in the convention off-season and book someplace that has a little more soul than the fifth-largest Hyatt in the world. If you do stay here, you'll find clean rooms that are roomy and light filled. But get your elbows ready if you plan on leaving the hotel and exploring. You'll need to be assertive in your cab hailing, because you'll have some stiff competition.

2233 S. Martin Luther King, Jr. Dr. (at 22nd St.). www.mccormickplace.hyatt.com. ✆ **800/233-1234** or 312/567-1234. 1,258 units. $199–$299 double. Valet parking $49; self-parking $34. Bus: 3 or 4. **Amenities:** two restaurants; lounge; concierge; exercise room; indoor lap pool; room service; Wi-Fi with surcharge.

WHERE TO EAT

Whatever your budget is for food, plan on eating extremely well in Chicago. Here, people get just as excited about the perfect Chicago-style hot dog or slice of pizza as they do about eating at one of the top restaurants in the world (hello, Alinea, p. 96). Whether you're dropping a mortgage payment on a trendy tasting menu or spending just over $3 on an incredible banh mi sandwich at Nhu Lan (p. 105), you'll discover that one of the great things about the dining scene in Chicago is a lack of pretension, even at those places covered in diamonds and stars.

Classic steakhouses still have the same leathery allure today as they did when Old Blue Eyes crooned about this toddling town, and comfort food has made a comeback across town (might have something to do with those harsh winters). While many of the restaurants downtown and in River North fall comfortably in to the "American" category, if you get out into the neighborhoods, you'll find just about any kind of cuisine you could dream up, including entire neighborhoods dedicated to different regions and nationalities: the Asian population in Chinatown, the Indian and Middle Eastern influx on Devon Avenue, the German ties to Lincoln Square, the Latino concentration in Pilsen, and the list goes on.

In Chicago, eating is what we do, and we do it well. Although there's a chapter in this book dedicated to "Chicago after dark," many of us consider the perfect night one that involves a restaurant we've been dying to try, and lingering there over dinner and drinks until we're ready to go home.

Practical Information

Chicago has an enormous concentration of mind-blowingly delicious restaurants. Because of that, there's steep competition, and a restaurant that's in vogue one month could be out of business the next month. In this chapter, I've done my best to recommend those with staying power, but my soothsaying abilities are human, and therefore, unreliable. Be sure to call ahead to find out if these listings are still in business, just to be safe.

RESERVATIONS Reservations are always a good idea in Chicago, especially if you have your heart set on dining at a particular place. A number of restaurants' reservations lists fill up weeks if not months in advance, and I've made it a point to indicate that in the listing, when possible. I recommend that you either call the restaurant well in advance or see if it's on OpenTable.com, a reservation site, and secure a table at your earliest convenience.

TIPPING Don't forget to tip in Chicago. Many servers make less than minimum wage and are taxed on what the government expects them to make on tips. If you had decent service, leave at least 15%.

5

THE LOOP

Expensive

Atwood Café ★★ AMERICAN Power lunchers know it's best to make a reservation, even for lunch, when coming to the Atwood Café. Situated in the small lobby of the historic Hotel Burnham (p. 52), this is a comfort food favorite, with a gourmet twist: lobster pot pie, duck Reuben salads, and what could be the best veggie burger ever made. Dinner, which used to center around entrees, recently shifted to shared plates, and the pork cheek, lamb bacon, and duck hash are all artfully prepared and presented. At the same time, Executive Chef Derek Simcik manages to not take himself too seriously, and has fun playing with his food (foie gras quiche, anyone?). Sit back in a red velvet chair or on one of the soft blue couches and contemplate the notion that in Chicago, hotel lobby restaurants have become a destination in and of themselves. The restaurant also serves breakfast.

1 W. Washington St. (at State St.). www.atwoodcafe.com. (© **312/368-1900.** Main courses $15–$20 lunch; shared plates $8–$32 dinner. Breakfast Mon–Fri 7–10:30am; brunch Sat, Sun 8am–3pm; lunch Mon–Fri 11:30am–3pm; dinner Tues–Sat 4:45–9:30pm; Sun–Mon 4:45–9pm. Subway/El: Red Line to Washington.

The Gage ★★ IRISH/AMERICAN When I have friends in town who are unable—or unwilling—to leave the Loop, my go-to is The Gage. This gastropub, with a rollicking bar and quieter dining area, is just refined enough, without feeling buttoned down. With its prime location across from Millennium Park, you'll find suits stopping in for an after-work drink and visitors exhausted from a day at the Art Institute. The Gage makes one of the best burgers in town, along with a good mix of creative comfort food (brisket pot pie, house-crafted sausages) and more daring offerings (Scotch egg, poutine with smoked wild boar, grilled rack of elk), and the requisite but still delicious soups and salads. It's popular for pre- or post-dinner drinks, with a long beer list that pays special attention to local brews. As you tipple, admire the elegant tin ceiling, dark woods, and debonair decor.

24 S. Michigan Ave. (btw. Madison and Monroe sts.) www.thegagechicago.com (© **312/372-4243.** Main courses $11–$21 lunch, $11–$45 dinner. Mon 11am–10pm (bar open until midnight), Tues–Fri 11am–2am, Sat 10am–midnight (bar until 3am); Sun 10am–10pm (bar until midnight). Subway/El: Red or Blue Line to Monroe; Brown, Green, Pink, Orange, Purple Line to Madison/Wabash.

Mercat a la Planxa ★★ SPANISH & TAPAS Here, in the opulent Renaissance Blackstone Hotel, you'll find what I consider the best Spanish food in the city. Whereas many tapas can be bland and forgettable, Mercat creates dishes that burst with flavor, like the ham and chorizo croquetas, bacon-wrapped dates, and paellas. You'll also find a variety of meats and cured meats, cheeses, veggies, seafood and more. Even the flatbreads, usually an afterthought at a restaurant—particularly one with an ethnic

HOLD THE gluten, PLEASE

Where has all the flour gone? In Chicago, more and more restaurants and even bakeries are catering to those who are gluten intolerant or gluten avoidant. **Senza** ★★★ (2873 N. Broadway Ave., at Surf St.; www.senzachicago.com; ✆ **773/770-3527;** p. 103), a restaurant in Lakeview that offers seasonally inspired, gluten-free four or nine-course dinners by night, bakes the most amazing gluten-free bread this wheat-wary gal has ever tasted. By day, the restaurant operates as Wheat's End Café, serving bread, pastries and local coffee. **Sweet Cakes Bakery** ★ (1223 N. Milwaukee Ave., at Ashland Ave.; www.sweetcakeschicago.com; ✆ **773/772-5771**), a vibrant, cuter-than-cute bakery in Wicker Park, caters to folks with food allergies. Culinary Institute of America–trained

"chief baking officer" Emily Smith has a family filled with food allergies, so she churns out addictive cookies, cupcakes, and pastries for those who can't enjoy wheat, corn, eggs, or dairy. The bakery also makes treats for those who can have it all. **River Valley Farmer's Table** ★ (1816 W. Wilson Ave., btw. Wolcott and Ravenswood aves.; www.rivervalleyfarmerstable.com; ✆ **827/208-3267**), located in Ravenswood north of Lakeview, is a darling specialty store that sells a tempting selection of gluten-free baked goods, including delicious cookies and hand pies from local bakeries. The small cafe within the store also cooks up a variety of farm-fresh gluten-free dishes, including soups made with ingredients from the owner's Wisconsin farm.

theme—are worth coming back for. Although it's casual, the two-level restaurant has a flirty feel, with its bright and playful decor. It's a fun spot to grab a sangria and a snack to start the evening if you want to go light on the wallet, or a full meal if you're all in.

638 S. Michigan Ave. (at Balbo Dr.), in the Blackstone Hotel. www.mercatchicago.com. ✆ **312/765-0524.** Tapas $6–$14; entrees $13–$48. Mon–Thurs 11am–11pm; Fri–Sat 11am–midnight; Sun 11am–10pm. Subway/El: Red Line to Harrison.

Expensive/Moderate

Chuck's: A Kerry Simon Kitchen ★★ AMERICAN   Don't judge this restaurant, which is attached to the Hard Rock Hotel, by the sports bar in front, which you'll see from the windows on Michigan Ave. Behind the bar is a rather refined but still casual restaurant serving burgers, sandwiches, and salads by day, and more of a steakhouse-style menu by night (the tempura Brussels spouts and salmon were perfect when I was there). Chuck's is a Kerry Simon restaurant (which you'll know, immediately, by his wall-sized mug near the kitchen), a chef who was putting a twist on comfort food in Las Vegas, of all places, long before everyone else was doing it. I lived there at the time and have enjoyed watching his career really take off and infiltrate other cities. The restaurant also serves breakfast.

224 N. Michigan Ave. (in the Hard Rock Hotel). http://chuckschicago.com. ✆ **312/334-6700.** Lunch $10–$22, dinner $22–$34. Sun–Sat 6am–11pm. Subway/El: Red Line to State/Lake.

Park Grill ★ AMERICAN   Sitting in the heart of Millennium Park, you'd think Park Grill would be a tourist trap that serves overpriced, mediocre food. Surprise! At this kid-friendly spot, the food is fresh, honest, and varied. Sandwich highlights include falafel, turkey pastrami, and a lobster roll, while entrees rival nearby upscale eateries, with choices that include Skuna Bay salmon, steak and pommes frites, and

Where to Dine in the Loop & West Loop

Al's Bee² 14
Artopolis 11
Athena 10
Atwood Café 24
Au Cheval 5
The Berghoff 31
Chuck's: A Kerry
   Simon Kitchen 19
Everest 32
The Gage 28
The Girl and the Goat 6
Gold Coast Dogs 21
Greek Islands 9
Heaven on Seven 22
Hot Woks Cool Sushi 29
Little Goat 4
Lou Mitchell's 15
Macy's food courts 23
Mercat a la Planxa 33
Next 2
Park Grill 27
Parthenon 12
Pastoral 20
Pegasus 7
Petterino's 16
Pizano's 26
The Publican 3
Russian Tea Time 30
Santorini 8
Sepia 13
South Water
   Kitchen 18
Urban Market 25
Wishbone 1
Wow Bao 17
Yolk 34

ethnic DINING NEAR THE LOOP

CHINATOWN

You'll know you've arrived in Chinatown by the pagoda-style architecture and the large red and green gate with Chinese characters across it. Chinatown is about 20 blocks south of the Loop, and strung along two thoroughfares, Cermak Road and Wentworth Avenue, as far south as 24th Place. It's easy to get there by cab or take the Red Line to Cermak, but the most scenic route is by **Chicago Water Taxi** ★★★ (www.chicagowatertaxi.com; ⌀ **312/337-1446**), which runs a regular route along the river during warm months. You won't get the same narration as you'll hear on an architecture riverboat tour (p. 156), but the skyline view is the same. Buy a ticket ($4 on weekdays, $5 on weekends and holidays) on the river walk at the Michigan Avenue/Mag Mile stop, located at the northwest corner of the Michigan Avenue Bridge (DuSable Bridge) at Trump Plaza, and then get off at the Chinatown stop. You probably won't need a whole day here, but budget a few hours to browse for Chinese lanterns and trinkets and enjoy at least one good meal. One part of Chinatown is essentially a large, two-level outdoor strip mall across the street from the Chinatown Gate, a gigantic green and red gate spanning Wentworth Avenue (at Cermak Avenue) that leads to the other, more organic section of Chinatown. While you're there, check out these spots:

o The spacious, fairly elegant **Phoenix** ★, 2131 S. Archer Ave. (btw.

Wentworth Ave. and Cermak Rd.; www.chinatownphoenix.com; ⌀ **312/328-0848**), has plenty of room for big tables of family or friends to enjoy the Cantonese (and some Szechuan) cuisine. A good sign: The place attracts lots of Chinatown locals. It's especially popular for dim sum brunch, so come early to avoid the wait. Late night, stop by the more casual **Saint's Alp Teahouse** ★ downstairs (⌀ **312/842-1886**), an outpost of the Hong Kong chain, which serves refreshing bubble tea and other varieties until at least midnight daily.

o Open since 1927, **Won Kow** ★, 2237 S. Wentworth Ave. (btw. 22nd Place and Alexander St.; ⌀ **312/842-7500**) is the oldest continuously operating restaurant in Chinatown. You can enjoy dim sum in the mezzanine-level dining room from 9am to 3pm daily. Most of the items cost around $3. Other house specialties include Mongolian chicken and duck with seafood.

Two other great spots for lunch or dinner are located in Chinatown Square Mall, an open-air walking pavilion of restaurants, shops, and other businesses along Archer Avenue. The menu at **Lao Sze Chuan** ★★, 2172 S. Archer Ave. (www.tonygourmetgroup.com; ⌀ **312/326-5040**) reads like a book, but

lobster fra diavola, along with the requisite salads, burgers, and flatbreads. In the summer, head to the outdoor plaza, where you can bask in the sun, listen to live music, and ogle the hordes of visitors who flock to Millennium Park, aka Chicago's front yard.

11 N. Michigan Ave. (at Madison St.). www.parkgrillchicago.com. ⌀ **312/521-PARK** [7275]. Main courses $8–$28 lunch and dinner. Sun–Thurs 11am–9:30pm; Fri 11am–10:30pm; Sat 11am–10:30pm. Subway/El: Red Line to Washington, or Brown, Orange, Purple, or Green Line to Madison.

Petterino's ★ AMERICAN/ITALIAN   Located on the main floor of the Goodman Theatre, Petterino's is an obvious go-to for the theater crowd, and offers a $35 stick with the revered—and spicy—Tony's Chicken with Three Chili and you'll be happy. Head over to **Hing Kee ★★,** 2140 S. Archer Ave. (www.hingkeeonline.com; *☎* **312/808-9538**), where you can watch a noodle maker in action, pulling his own pasta, before it makes it to your bowl for slurping.

GREEKTOWN

A short cab ride across the south branch of the Chicago River will take you to the city's Greektown, a row of moderately- and inexpensively-priced Greek restaurants clustered on Halsted Street between Van Buren and Washington streets.

To be honest, there's not much here to distinguish one restaurant from the other: They're all standard Greek restaurants with similar looks and similar menus, but some have better patios than others (read on). That said, **Greek Islands ★,** 200 S. Halsted St. (at Adams St.; www.greekislands.net; *☎* **312/782-9855**); **Santorini ★,** 800 W. Adams St. (at Halsted St.; www.santorinichicago.com; *☎* **312/829-8820**); and **Parthenon ★,** 314 S. Halsted St. (btw. Jackson and Van Buren sts.; www.theparthenon.com; *☎* **312/726-2407**) are all good bets for gyros, Greek salads, shish kabobs, and the classic moussaka. On warm summer nights, opt for either **Athena ★★,** 212 S. Halsted St. (btw. Adams and Jackson streets; www.athenarestaurantchicago.com; *☎* **312/655-0000**), which has a huge outdoor seating area, or **Pegasus ★★,** 130 S. Halsted St. (btw. Monroe

and Adams streets; www.pegasus chicago.com; *☎* **312/226-3377**), with its rooftop patio serving drinks, appetizers, and desserts. **Artopolis ★,** 306 S. Halsted St. (at Jackson St.; www.artopolis chicago.com; *☎* **312/559-9000**), is a more casual option offering up Greek and Mediterranean specialties, wood-oven pizzas, breads, and French pastries, all of them tasty.

PILSEN

Just south of the Loop and convenient to McCormick Place and Chinatown, Pilsen is a colorful blend of Mexican culture, artists, and bohemians. The area's restaurant scene is drawing more and more Northsiders to step away from their usual hotspots and make a trip south, where there's nary a dress code.

On weekends, prepare to wait in line at **Nuevo Leon ★★,** 1515 W. 18th St. (at Laflin St.; *☎* **312/421-1517**), a popular Mexican restaurant serving down-home enchiladas, tacos, and menudo like mami used to make. Adventurous spirits will find something to push even the most generous of comfort zones at **Birrería Reyes de Ocotlan ★,** 1322 W 18th St. (btw. Blue Island Ave. and Throop Street; *☎* **312/733-2613**), where you can feast like a king on $2 *cabeza* (cow head), *lengua* (cow tongue), and goat tacos, along with the popular goat meat stew (*birria*). Don't scrutinize the cheap eats too much, or you might miss a sighting of celeb chef Rick Bayless (Frontera Grill, p. 88), who's a regular here.

three-course theater menu. With its dark woods, leather booths, and dim lighting, it's a throwback to the days of old Chicago, and the walls are covered in the caricatures of celebs to prove it. The menu is traditional Italian, with classic pastas, such as potato gnocchi, baked ravioli, and spaghetti and meatballs, along with a number of steak and seafood options and more casual burgers and sandwiches. Overall, the food is reliably good but uninspired. Pre-theater convenience and its Loop location are key here.

150 N. Dearborn St. (at Randolph St.). www.petterinos.com. *☎* **312/422-0150.** Main courses $9–$29 lunch, $14–$40 dinner. Mon 11am–10pm; Tues–Thurs 11am–10:30pm; Fri–Sat 11am–11pm; Sun 11am–7:30pm. Subway/El: Red Line to Washington; or Brown Line to State/Lake.

Russian Tea Time ★ RUSSIAN/TEA   Culture-seekers need sustenance, and at Russia Tea Time, you can mix your uppers (tea, lots of it) with your downers (vodka, lots of it). Located steps from the Art Institute and Chicago Symphony Center, this restaurant, open since 1993, is bustling before and after performances and shows, but during off hours on weekdays, it takes on the feel of a once elegant hotel, straight out of *The Shining*, with its dated '90s decor, rich in red fabrics and dark woods. Crowds are a mix of young business types, older arts patrons, and hard scrabble vodka guzzlers from the old country. Stop in to snack on finger sandwiches and sip from a floral pot during the afternoon tea service, or savor caviar and beef stew with a shot from the extensive vodka list. I guarantee that a vodka flight with horseradish vodka, served with brown bread, pickles, and instructions on how to shoot it the Russian way, will jumpstart just about any evening.

77 E. Adams St. (btw. Michigan and Wabash aves.). www.russianteatime.com. © **312/360-0000.** Main courses $14–$30 lunch, $20–$34 dinner. Sun–Thurs 11am–9pm; Fri–Sat 11am–11pm (the restaurant sometimes closes earlier during the summer months). Tea service daily 2:30–4:30pm. Subway/El: Brown, Purple, Green, or Orange Line to Adams; or Red Line to Monroe or Jackson.

South Water Kitchen ★ AMERICAN   Considering the sea of business suits that fill the Loop, it's not easy finding a spot that both caters to kids and tastes good to adults. That explains why South Water Kitchen has such a, shall we say, young clientele. (Considering they're located adjacent to the Hotel Monaco, it makes sense that they cater to families.) In addition to a seasonally rotating kids' menu, South Water doles out coloring books and crayons to keep kids happy. That gives parents more time to explore the extensive craft beer list, which was assembled by the restaurant's own *cicerone* (that's basically a sommelier of beer) and the American comfort food menu— deviled eggs, short ribs, rabbit sausage, salmon, flatbread, and some veg options—with an emphasis on Midwestern flavors and products. Childless diners shouldn't be put off by the inviting attitude the restaurant has towards kids. There's a large bar area, in case you're looking for a more adult ambience. It's also open for breakfast and brunch, but the menu gets more interesting later in the day.

Adjacent to the Hotel Monaco, 225 N. Wabash Ave. (at Wacker Dr.). www.southwaterkitchen.com. © **312/236-9300.** Main courses $11–$27 lunch, $19–$32 dinner. Mon–Fri 6:30–10:30am breakfast, 11am–3pm lunch; Sat–Sun 7am–3pm brunch; Mon–Sun 4:30–10pm dinner. Subway/El: Red Line to State/Lake.

Inexpensive

Heaven on Seven ★ CAJUN & CREOLE/DINER   The "seven" in Heaven on Seven is a clue to its location, tucked away on the seventh floor of an office building/ movie theater. The walls at this loud breakfast/lunch spot are covered in Mardi Gras/ Big Easy decor and an impressive collection of hot sauces, and that theme carries over to the giant servings of packed-with-flavor New Orleans food, like the red beans and rice, Hoppin' John, po' boys, and jambalaya. Breakfast items run the gamut from standard diner fare (pancakes, eggs, omelets) to born-on-the-bayou specialties, like shrimp and grits and bananas Foster French toast. Their chocolate peanut butter pie is so good, if you try it, you risk ruining all other peanut butter pies.

Looking for a Cajun dinner? On the third Friday of every month, the original location serves it up. Or there's a second downtown location just off the Mag Mile at **600 N. Michigan Ave.** (© 312/280-7774; they accept reservations and take credit cards). Both spots are good choices for families, and you'll see a number of kids there.

111 N. Wabash Ave. (at Washington St.), 7th floor. www.heavenonseven.com. ✆ **312/263-6443.**
Breakfast $7–$14, sandwiches $11–$13, main courses $10–$30. No credit cards. Mon–Fri 9am–4pm;
Sat 10am–3pm; 3rd Fri of each month 5:30–9pm. Subway/El: Red Line to Washington.

Hot Woks Cool Sushi ★ SUSHI/JAPANESE   It's not easy to find good, afford-able sushi near the Loop, which is why the fish-loving masses embrace Hot Wok Cool Sushi, located close to Millennium Park and the Art Institute. Yeah, the name is kind of cheesy, and sure, it looks like a chain (there are four Chicago locations) but don't hold that against it. Choose from sushi, sashimi, or a wide range of maki (I prefer the simple ones here, like spicy tuna and salmon avocado, over the more elaborate and more expensive options). Mixed parties, meaning those with non-sushi lovers, will be relieved to find a number of traditional Chinese options, like beef and broccoli or General Tso chicken, and noodle dishes. *Bonus:* you can order online and pick up a Bento box for an easy Millennium Park picnic.

30 S. Michigan Ave (at Monroe St.). www.hotwokscoolsushi.com. ✆ **312/345-1234.** Entrees $8–$14, maki $6–$14. Mon–Thurs 11:30am–9:30pm; Fri–Sat 11:30am–10pm. Subway/El: Brown, Pink, Purple, Green, Orange Line to Madison/Wabash; Red or Blue Line to Monroe.

Pastoral ★★ AMERICAN/SANDWICHES   It's tempting to curse the overload of mediocre sandwiches near the Loop. But when you discover Pastoral, you forget about all the others. This neighborhood specialty shop, which peddles wine, cheese, bread, and yes, sandwiches, is a secret among in-the-know Chicagoans who have eschewed chain vehicles of lunchmeat and embraced this European-style, fresh-baked, made-to-order handheld meal, made with cured meats and artisanal cheeses. One glimpse at the menu, which reveals traditional-with-a-twist options—the Mediterranean turkey is roasted local turkey with house-made basil pesto, white bean puree, red onion, and oven-roasted tomatoes; and the Atun a Tuna is Spanish tuna with house-made black olive tapenade, piquillo peppers, red onions, shaved celery, tomatoes, and field greens—and you may never order your sandwich by its lengths (6-inch or 12) again. Quick and affordable, Pastoral is an easy stop for a quick bite to eat between meetings or for packing into a picnic and heading to the beach or Millennium Park.

53 E. Lake St. (east of Wabash Ave). www.pastoralartisan.com. ✆ **312/658-1250.** Sandwiches $5–$13. Mon–Fri 10:30am–8pm; Sat–Sun 11am–6pm. Subway/El: Red Line to Lake; Brown, Pink, Purple, Orange, Green Line to Randolph/Wabash.

Wow Bao ★ ASIAN/FAST FOOD   This fast-casual Asian spot is a bit confusing. First, it's not immediately clear which line to choose or where or how to place your order. Then, I had trouble finding the forks. But once you get past that anxiety, it's a nice change from the boring subs and fast food that dominates the Loop. Wow Bao serves bao (a Chinese steamed bun with your choice of filling), potstickers, soup, Asian salads, and bowls with teriyaki chicken, Thai curry chicken, Kung Pao chicken, Mongolian beef, and vegetarian dishes. Although I wouldn't make this a dining des-tination, if you're in the area it's a relatively healthy lunch and affordable spot, and there are multiple locations around downtown, including one inside of Water Tower Place, 835 N. Michigan Ave., ✆ **312/642-5888.** If you're extra calorie conscious, you can even forgo the rice and replace it with Napa cabbage, lettuce cups, multi-grain rice, or quinoa.

1 W. Wacker Blvd. (entrance is at corner of State and Lake sts.). www.wowbao.com. ✆ **312/658-0305.** Lunch/dinner $5–$10. Mon–Fri 8am–9pm; Sat 11am–9pm; Sun noon–6pm. Subway/El: Brown, Pink, Orange, Green, or Purple Line to State/Lake.

THE WEST LOOP & NEAR WEST

Expensive

Girl and the Goat ★★★ AMERICAN   First things first: Yes, it's worth the wait, even if that wait is 2 hours on a Friday or Saturday night, which is not unexpected at this West Loop hot spot. Girl and the Goat is a name that even the most seasoned Chicago foodies utter with reverence. The restaurant is the brainchild of celebrity Chef Stephanie Izard (you may remember her as the winner of *Top Chef* in 2008), who's as talented with creating the exotic (say, wood-oven roasted pig face or duck tongues) as the more staid, such as Hamachi crudo, sautéed green beans, and a delectable bread selection. And, of course, there are a number of goat options: goat liver moose, goat carpaccio, goat neck, and even goat legs. Despite the sophisticated food, the restaurant has a sultry-but-casual style with top-notch servers in black t-shirts and jeans hustling to and fro from the open kitchen. Don't be afraid to start a conversation with your neighbors here—if you're not at a communal table, odds are you'll be rubbing elbows with the party next to you in this tight, but somehow never too crowded, space. Reservations are available and recommended, but they're hard to get, unless you're willing to eat early (like, 4:30 or 5pm on a week night). Otherwise, grab a spot at the bar and join the bubbly crowd. Waiting is practically a rite of passage here.

809 W. Randolph St. (at Halsted St.). www.girlandthegoat.com. ✆ **312/492-6262.** Small plates $7–$25. Sun–Thurs 4:30–11pm; Fri–Sat 4:30–midnight. Subway/El: Green or Pink Line to Morgan.

The Publican ★ AMERICAN   Carnivores, pescetarians, and beer lovers will feel right at home here. Modeled after a European beer hall, Publican is a big, open room, with a series of long, wooden, communal tables interspersed with individual tables. Decor is sparse, which makes the so-serious-they're-funny pig portraits on the walls stand out even more, especially considering the pig-heavy menu offerings, such as aged ham, spicy pork rinds, pork belly, and porchetta. Non-swine options include an impressive selection of oysters and fish, and the veggies, particularly the Brussels sprouts with burrata, Parmesan, lemon, and sesame seeds, are so good they almost outshine the proteins. With a farm-to-table focus, many of the shared plates come from the Midwest, like the La Quercia Rossa aged ham from Norfolk, Iowa and shrimp farmed in Hope, Indiana. But Publican also brings in specialties from afar, like salt-crusted loup de mer from the Aegean Sea. Although there is a solid wine list, beer is clearly the beverage of choice here, with an emphasis on German,

family-friendly RESTAURANTS

One of the city's first "theme" restaurants, **Ed Debevic's** ★ (640 N. Wells St., at Ontario Street; www.eddebevics.com; ⓒ **312/664-1707**), is a temple to America's hometown lunch-counter culture. The burgers-and-milkshakes menu is kid-friendly, but it's the staff shtick that makes this place memorable. The waitresses play the parts of gum-chewing toughies who make wisecracks, toss out good-natured insults, and even sit right down at your table. If you're in the mood for something a little more funky, **Wishbone** ★★ (p. 83) is a popular option for families. The food is diverse enough that both adults and kids can find something to their liking (you can mix and match side dishes, a big plus), and there's also a menu geared just toward children. Another all-American choice in the Loop is **South Water Kitchen** ★ (p. 80), which offers a kids' menu and coloring books. At **Gino's East** ★ (p. 94), the famous Chicago pizzeria, long waits can be an issue during the prime summer tourist season. But once you get your table, the kids can let loose: Patrons are invited to scrawl all over the graffiti-strewn walls and furniture with chalk.

Want more? Restaurants across Chicago offer "kids eat free" nights throughout the week. Many of those are located in neighborhoods, and a great website that rounds up kid-friendly/wallet-friendly restaurants is www.mykidseatfree.com.

Belgian, and Austrian brews. Service is good if a bit pretentious. Say a French word wrong and prepare to be corrected. Reservations strongly recommended.

837 W. Fulton Market St. (btw. Morgan and Halsted streets). www.thepublicanrestaurant.com. ⓒ **312/733-9555.** Shared plates $4–$42. Mon–Thurs 3:30am–10:30pm; Fri–Sat 3:30–11:30pm; Sun 10am–2pm (brunch) and 5–9pm. Subway/El: Pink or Green Line to Morgan.

Sepia ★★ AMERICAN I visited here with colleagues, but look forward to returning with my date. Although regulars sing its praises, the classically elegant restaurant is just off the beaten path enough to make it accessible, which, in Chicago, means there are nights you can pop in without a reservation and score a seat. Sophisticated but without airs, the restaurant sits in a former 1890s print shop, and its vintage photos and glamorous chandeliers perfectly mix old with new. Chef Andrew Zimmerman's (not to be confused with Andrew Zimmern, of *Bizarre Foods* fame) ever-evolving seasonal menu brings together Mediterranean, French, and American influences, but regardless of what you choose, expect simple, fresh flavors. For starters, order the seasonal soup, whatever it is. Zimmerman truly shines here. The tea-smoked duck breast and skate wing (deboned tableside, something I'd never seen before with skate) are also standouts, and don't leave until you've sampled the sweet potato pecan pie. *Tip:* To save money, visit Sepia at lunchtime. The lunch menu has quite a bit of overlap with the dinner menu, but for far less.

123 N. Jefferson St. (at Randolph St.). www.sepiachicago.com. ⓒ **312/441-1920.** Main courses $28–$36 dinner, $13–$20 lunch. Mon–Fri 11:30am–2pm; Mon–Thurs 5:15–9:30pm; Fri–Sat 5:15–10:30pm; Sun 5–9pm. Subway/El: Pink, Brown, Orange, or Purple Line to Washington/Wells.

Inexpensive

Wishbone ★★ BREAKFAST & BRUNCH/SOUTHERN This folksy breakfast/lunch/brunch diner is known for its Southern specialties, such as shrimp and grits, corn cakes, and Andouille hash. But the health conscious should take note: Despite the

Southern-fried delights (and there are many) it's actually easy to eat somewhat healthily here, with a number of fish and vegetarian choices, and gluten-free options are even highlighted on the menu. When this place is hopping, and it usually is for weekend brunch, in particular, expect it to be loud and filled with families taking advantage of the extensive kids' menu. Looking around at the expressive cartoon animal and flying food paintings that fill the walls, the kid-friendly attitude makes perfect sense. There's also a second location on the North Side, at 3300 N. Lincoln Ave. (at W. School St.; ℂ 773/549-2663).

1001 Washington St. (at Morgan St.). www.wishbonechicago.com. ℂ **312/850-2663.** Main courses $6–$14 breakfast and lunch, $4–$12 dinner. Mon 7am–3pm; Tues–Thurs 7am–9 pm; Fri 7am–10pm; Sat 8am–3pm and 5–10pm; Sun 8am–3pm. Subway/El: Green or Pink to Morgan.

THE MAGNIFICENT MILE & THE GOLD COAST

Expensive

Spiaggia ★★★ ITALIAN   Executive Chef Tony Mantuano has elevated Italian food in Chicago, literally and figuratively, with Spiaggia. For the literal part, Spiaggia looks down from the second floor on one of the city's toniest shopping corners, Michigan Avenue and Oak Street, and its floor-to-ceiling windows give way to a gorgeous view of Lake Michigan. (*Spiaggia*, by the way, is Italian for "beach.") On the figurative note, Spiaggia was the first (and remains the only) four-star Italian restaurant in Chicago. As of deadline, the dining room was undergoing a redesign, so we can't speak to the decor, other than to say Spiaggia has a deserved reputation for lavishness (as evidenced by its dress code requiring jackets and banning jeans). At $85, a mere shaving of white Italian truffles on your meal costs as much as a meal for two at a more modest restaurant. But if you've come to Spiaggia, you're clearly not counting your pennies, so splurge on the $115 four-course menu (which includes antipasto, pasta, protein, and dessert) and taste all of the vibrant straight-from-Italy flavors, such as risotto with Parmigiano Reggiano and balsamic, and Wagyu beef with mushroom and potato, all paired perfectly (upon request) with a red or white from the exhaustive wine list.

If you're not prepared to shell out the big bucks, visit the adjacent **Café Spiaggia** (ℂ 312/280-2755) for a less formal meal for lunch or dinner.

980 N. Michigan Ave. (at Oak St.). www.spiaggiarestaurant.com. ℂ **312/280-2750.** Main courses $34–$41; tasting menu $115–$125. Sun–Thurs 6–9:30pm; Fri–Sat 5:30–10:30pm. Subway/El: Red Line to Chicago.

Pump Room ★★ AMERICAN   To give you a hint of just how historic the Pump Room is, it's referenced in the song "Chicago (That Toddlin' Town)," which was published in 1922. "Chicago, we'll meet at the Pump Room, Ambassador East." This used to be the gathering place for celebs and politicians back in the day, and you can still see their photos plastered throughout. Today, the crowd is quite a mix: tourists who are staying at Public Hotel (formerly the Ambassador East, where Pump Room roosts), hip 20- and 30-somethings, wealthy Gold Coast neighbors, and cougars on the prowl. The restaurant has been reimagined by hotelier Ian Schrager (of Studio 54 fame), who brought in vaunted Chef Jean-Georges Vongerichten to devise the farm-to-table menu. Although the selections have quite a bit of overlap with ABC Kitchen, Vongerichten's New York restaurant, there are also a number of dishes inspired by the original Pump Room menu, and choices range from decadent short ribs and an incredible burger to

Where to Dine in the Magnificent Mile, Gold Coast & River North

| 0 | 1/4 mi |
| 0 | 1/4 km |

Ⓜ Subway/El stop

Al's Beef **15**
Billy Goat Tavern **32**
Bar Toma **9**
Cape Cod Room **7**
Chicago Cut Steakhouse **20**
Chicago q **2**
David Burke's Primehouse and
 Burke's Bacon Bar **30**
Ditka's **8**
Eataly **29**
Ed Debevic's **14**
Foodlife **10**
Frontera Grill & Topolobampo & Xoco **24**
Gene & Georgetti **17**
Gibsons Bar & Steakhouse **4**
Gino's East **18**
GT Fish & Oyster **16**

Harry Caray's Italian Steakhouse **25**
House of Blues **26**
India House **23**
La Madia **22**
Lou Malnati's Pizzeria **19**
mk **11**
Mr. Beef **12**
Morton's **3**
Nico Osteria **5**
Pizzeria Uno **28**
Portillo's **21**
Pump Room **1**
The Purple Pig **31**
Sable Kitchen & Bar **27**
Spiaggia **6**
Sumi Robata **13**

lighter fish dishes, pasta, and flatbread. Desserts are incredible (I wish the butterscotch pudding had been bottomless) as are the classic cocktails—in particular the sour cherry old fashioned. As for decor, this place is swank incarnate—a large, dimly lit, open room with planetary-like lighted orbs hanging throughout, with diners dressed to the nines. The hotel is also open for lunch and dinner, but scenesters come here for dinner. *Bonus:* If you're staying at Public Hotel, your room service comes from the Pump Room.

1301 N. State Pkwy. (at Goethe St.). www.pumproom.com. ℂ **312/787-3700.** Main courses $22–$47. Breakfast Mon–Fri 7–11am; lunch Mon–Fri 11:30am–2:30pm; dinner Sun–Thurs 5–11pm and Fri–Sat 5pm–midnight; brunch Sat–Sun 9am–3pm. Subway/El: Red Line to Clark/Division.

Moderate/Expensive

Nico Osteria ★★ ITALIAN   This Italian seafood restaurant hit the ground running in late 2013, quickly becoming one of the hottest reservations in town. Located in the Thompson Hotel, the hotel staff actually report that dinner has been the most popular room service meal for them, because room service comes from, you guessed it, Nico. If you do get into the restaurant, you'll notice the array of fresh fish on ice. They're line caught and flown in from across the world, giving the restaurant a rather unique selection (branzino, turbot, and Dover sole were all on the menu on my visit), which changes seasonally. Also delicious: the house-made pasta and house-made bread, along with the sandwiches served on that bread during lunch, like the artichoke, burrata, and pesto sandwich. Food is prepared in traditional Italian style: fresh and simple, using the best ingredients available. It's one of my top picks for dining in the Gold Coast.

1015 N. Rush St. (at E. Lake Shore Dr.). www.nicoosteria.com. ℂ **312/994-7100.** Lunch $13–$32; dinner $17–$48. Mon–Thurs 7:30am–11pm; Fri 7:30am–midnight; Sat 9am–midnight; Sun 9am–11pm. Subway/El: Red Line to Clark/Division.

The Purple Pig ★★★ MEDITERRANEAN   There's a reason The Purple Pig has a line out the door nearly every single night: It is porcine perfection, and the bubbly after-work crowd can't leave work fast enough to get here (lines usually start forming by 5pm). This casual, meat-heavy Mag Mile bistro, with a broad and affordable wine list, serves up shared plates from all parts of the animal, including pig tails and tripe, while also excelling at veggies such as shaved Brussels sprouts and braised baby artichokes. The "JLT," an open-faced sandwich with pork jowl, tomato, frisee, and fried duck egg, is also a stand-out. But don't steer away from the more familiar choices, like

farmers' MARKETS

If you're lucky enough to be here during good weather, celebrate by enjoying at least one picnic. Peruse the city's farmers' markets and then carry your lunch off to Grant Park or a spot along the lakefront.

The city-sponsored farmers' markets operate from late May through October. Two locations in the Loop are easy for visitors to get to: **Daley Plaza** ★ (at Washington and Dearborn sts.; open on Thurs) and **Federal Plaza** ★ (at Adams and Dearborn sts.; open on Tues), both open from 7am to 3pm and are good places to pick up fresh fruit or bakery treats. For more information, call the Mayor's Office of Special Events at *ℂ* **312/744-3315.** At the south end of Lincoln Park (btw. Clark St. and Stockton Dr.), local chefs and civilian foodies head to the **Green City Market** ★★★ (greencitymarket.org; *ℂ* **773/880-1266**) for seasonal produce. Pick up some fresh bread, locally produced cheese, and in-season fruit, and enjoy an alfresco meal; Lincoln Park Zoo is just steps away. The market is open Wednesdays and Saturdays from 7am to 1pm, from mid-May through October, and often features cooking demonstrations by chefs from Chicago restaurants.

the chicken thigh kebab or milk-braised pork shoulder, which are just as delicious as the glandular offerings. No reservations are accepted, so aim at getting there early or plan on a wait.

500 N. Michigan Ave. (btw. the Chicago River and Ohio St.). www.thepurplepigchicago.com. *ℂ* **312/464-1PIG** [464-1744]. Most dishes $8–$17. Sun–Thurs 11:30am–midnight; Fri–Sat 11:30am–1am (bar open until 2am). Subway/El: Red to Grand Ave.

Moderate

Bar Toma ★★ ITALIAN/PIZZA   This wood-fired pizza spot is a welcome addition to the glitzy, pricey, and often touristy Gold Coast offerings. The pizzas by Chef Tony Mantuano, the same chef behind Spiaggia (see above), are the perfect melding of chewy and crisp at this casual neighborhood trattoria. Sit at the bar for quick, amicable service or sink into one of their comfortable booths for a more leisurely meal. Pizza toppings range from traditional (margherita and quattro formaggi) to creative, with duck or lamb sausage, pistachios, and Manchego cheese as toppings. There are also plenty of non-pizza items, from sandwiches to proteins. And with 14 flavors of gelato daily, Bar Toma is also a great stop for espresso and dessert.

110 E. Pearson St. (btw. the Rush St and Michigan Ave.). www.bartomachicago.com. *ℂ* **312/266-3110.** Pizza $14–$22, lunch entrees $9–$18, dinner entrees $15–$37. Sun 11am–9pm; Mon–Thurs 11:30am–10pm; Fri–Sat 11:30am–11pm. Subway/El: Red or Brown Line to Chicago.

Inexpensive

Billy Goat Tavern ★ FAST FOOD   First, let me be clear: People do not come to Billy Goat Tavern for a delicious meal. The hamburgers are mediocre at best and, if you've seen the *Saturday Night Live* skit that made this place famous, then you already know what they'll say when you try to order fries or a soda. "No fries, cheeps!" "No Pepsi, Coke!" What you will find at the original subterranean Michigan Avenue joint is more than 80 years of history, a steady stream of newspaper reporters (Tribune Tower, where the *Chicago Tribune* is located, is within stumbling distance) and a disinterested staff made famous by *SNL* (actually, they're pretty nice if you shake them

pizza pie (CHICAGO-STYLE & OTHERWISE)

Although **Pizzeria Uno** ★ (29 E. Ohio St., at Wabash Ave.; www.unos.com; (☎ **312/321-1000**) claims creation credit for Chicago deep dish (like all food origin stories, it's murkier than that), I'm more partial to **Lou Malnati's Pizzeria** ★★, which has multiple locations, including 439 N. Wells St., at Hubbard St. (www.loumalnatis.com; (☎ **312/828-9800**), where you generally won't have to wait in a winding line of tourists, and the pizza, with its golden crust brushed with corn meal, just tastes better. The same goes for the Malnati-owned **Pizano's Pizza & Pasta** ★★, also with multiple locations, including one in the Loop at 61 E. Madison St., at Wabash Ave (www.pizanoschicago.com;

(☎ **312/236-1777**). Another popular chain—known for its stuffed pizza—is **Giordano's** ★ (www.giordanos.com), with downtown locations off the Magnificent Mile at 730 N. Rush St., at Superior St. (☎ **312/951-0747**), and at the Prudential Plaza, 135 E. Lake St., just east of Michigan Ave. (☎ **312/616-1200**). **Gino's East** ★★, which has four locations in Chicago, including the original at 162 E. Superior St., btw. Michigan Ave. and Fairbanks Court (www. ginoseast.com; (☎ **312/266-3337**; p. 94), has been slinging the Windy City favorite since 1966. Or if you want to go where the locals go for deep dish, head to Lincoln Park's **Pequod's Pizza** ★★ (2207 N. Clybourn Ave., just north of Webster

out of their act). My recommendation: Come for the dive bar atmosphere and know that the *cheezborgers* are there, should you really need one after a few brews.

A number of Billy Goat outposts have opened across town (including one on Navy Pier, which is much more kid-friendly; (☎**312/670-8789**), but you don't get the same grit and reputation as with the original.

430 N. Michigan Ave. www.billygoattavern.com. (☎ **312/222-1525.** Menu items $3–$6. No credit cards. Mon–Fri 6am–2am; Sat 10am–2am; Sun 10am–1:30am. Subway/El: Red Line to Chicago.

RIVER NORTH

For restaurants listed in this section, see the map "Where to Dine in the Magnificent Mile, Gold Coast & River North" on p. 85.

Expensive

Frontera Grill ★★★, **Topolobampo** ★★, **Xoco** ★ MEXICAN   Since winning Bravo's *Top Chef Masters,* Rick Bayless has become a household name, synonymous with fresh, organic Mexican food that uses ingredients from local farms. Dining at any Rick Bayless spot is popular on Chicago bucket lists, and you have a number to choose from. **Topolobampo** is the top-tier restaurant, and it's quite a change from the "expected" Mexican restaurant atmosphere, with its linen tablecloths and museum-grade art on the walls. The menu changes monthly, but expect to find bold, soulful flavors—different chilies, fruits, and nuts—complementing game, seafood, and meat dishes. If you plan to visit Topolobampo, it's best to make a reservation in advance.

The casual and energetic **Frontera Grill** is the most fun of the bunch, and serves up top-notch versions of Mexican classics—quesadillas, grilled meats, rich moles, and tender braised items, along with Mexican street snacks. You may need to wait during

Ave.; www.pequodspizza.com; (℃ 773/327-1512), where even the gut-busting 10-inch small pie will deliver more than a day's supply of delicious calories.

Lest you think that Chicago only excels at crust as thick as a bicycle tire, we also love our thin crust. If you're in Wrigleyville or Wicker Park, stop by **Dimo's**, which slings slices until the wee hours, with out-there toppings like chicken and waffles with syrup or mac and cheese pizza (www.dimospizza.com; (℃ 773/525-4580; in Wrigleyville: 3463 N. Clark, btw. Cornelia and Newport aves.; in Wicker Park/Bucktown at 1615 N. Damen Ave., btw. Wabansia and North aves.). **La Madia ★★★** (59 W.

Grand Ave., btw. Clark and Dearborn sts.; www.dinelamadia.com; (℃ 773/755-1777; p. 95), a pizzeria with a sense of River North sophistication paired with great pizza deals, serves red or white thin crust with toppings that border on fancy, like cracked egg, wild mushrooms, and shaved artichokes (although the above aren't served together) and salads that are mind-blowingly good. And the top Neapolitan style in town, hands down, comes from **Spacca Nappoli** (1769 W. Sunnyside Ave., at Ravenswood Ave.; www.spaccanapolipizzeria.com; (℃ 773/878-2420), located just east of Lincoln Square, where the slightly charred pizzas are served uncut, with a knife and fork, just like in Italy.

Chicago Treats

Deep-dish pizza may be Chicago's culinary claim to fame, but the city has added to the national waistline in other ways. Twinkies and Wonder Bread were invented here, as was the brownie.

Chicago businessman James L. Kraft created the first processed cheese, and Oscar Mayer got his start as a butcher in the Old Town neighborhood.

prime dining hours at Frontera, but it's a good excuse to put your name on the list and hit the bar for a margarita. To taste Bayless for less, stop by the fast-casual **Xoco** (pronounced SHO-ko), which offers straightforward counter service (soups, salads, sandwiches, and churros) and churns people in and out at lightning speed (after sitting at the cramped shared tables, you'll understand why). Bayless really excels at *caldos* (soups), so take advantage of those whenever and wherever you can.

Bayless's reach has spread beyond his River North haunts, and you can find his fast-food spots, called Frontera Fresco, around the city and even at O'Hare. If you're in The Loop, visit the **Frontera Fresco** on the seventh floor of Macy's (111 N. State St.; (℃ 312/781-4884), for tortas, salads, soup, and other Mexican items, all for less than $9.

445 N. Clark St. (btw. Illinois and Hubbard sts.). www.fronterakitchens.com. (℃ **312/661-1434.** **Topolobampo** main courses $18–$39; chef's 7-course tasting menu $120 (add $80 with wine pairings). **Frontera Grill** main courses $13–$29. **Xoco** sandwiches and soups $9–$13. **Frontera Grill** Tues–Fri 11:30am–2:30pm; Sat 10:30am–2pm; Tues 5:20–10pm; Wed–Thurs 5–10pm; Fri–Sat 5–11pm. **Topolobampo** Tues 11:45am–2pm; Wed–Fri 11:30am–2pm; Tues–Thurs 5:30–9:30pm; Fri–Sat 5:30–10:30pm. **Xoco** Tues–Thurs 8am–9pm; Fri–Sat 8am–10pm; Sun–Mon closed. Subway/El: Red Line to Grand Ave.

LET THEM EAT steak

Chicago and steakhouses go hand-in-hand. Sure, there's the meat-and-potatoes reputation of the Midwest, but there's also that classic, leather-booth, no-nonsense sensibility that comes to mind when thinking the quintessential steakhouse—and the old days of Chicago. With a steakhouse, you know what you're going to get: a hearty, working-man's meal (at expense account prices)—meat, potatoes, creamed spinach, and some kind of chocolate dessert to email home about. **Tip:** to save money, visit a steakhouse for lunch, when the menu is almost the same but prices are much lower. Here are some of our favorite Chicago steakhouse picks:

First, the classics. Legendary Chicago restaurateur Arnie Morton no longer prowls the dining room, but **Morton's** ★★ (1050 N. State St., at Rush St.; www.mortons.com; ℂ **312/266-4820;** or 65 E. Wacker Place, between Michigan and Wabash avenues; tel] **312/201-0410)** remains the king of the city's old-guard steakhouses, serving up gargantuan wet-aged steaks and baked potatoes. **Gene**

& Georgetti ★ (500 N. Franklin St., at Illinois St.; www.geneandgeorgetti.com; ℂ **312/527-3718),** is another blast from the past, a long-time hangout for the city's movers and shakers that's barely changed since it opened in 1941—and that's exactly why the regulars like it. *Bonus:* Vegetarian companions will appreciate the Italian focus and array of meat-free pasta dishes available here. Open for more than two decades, **Gibsons Bar & Steakhouse** ★★ (1028 N. Rush St., at Bellevue Place; www.gibsonssteakhouse.com; ℂ **312/266-8999),** is still a see-and-be-seen scene in River North, delighting its trendy crowd with huge portions of melt-in-your-mouth steaks, chops, and seafood (the smallest steak portion at dinner is 10 ounces—you might want to plan to share) and dangerously large martinis in 10-ounce glasses.

The belle-of-the-bovine ball right now is **Chicago Cut** ★★ (300 N. LaSalle St., at the Chicago River; www.chicagocutsteakhouse.com; ℂ **312/329-1800),**

GT Fish & Oyster ★★ SEAFOOD   It's pretty easy to find heavy, meat-filled foods in River North. More of a challenge is discovering delicate, fresh seafood, like the kind at GT Fish & Oyster. Ask a local to suggest a great upscale spot for seafood that's not sushi in Chicago, and this usually tops the list. Overall, the food is seasonal, simple, and meant to be shared, with decadent choices like fish and chips, a lobster roll, and mac and cheese with lobster, along with healthier options such as whole roasted fish, a crudo platter, tuna poke, oysters, and caviar service. At lunch, you can get a number of dinner menu items as well as sandwiches and shared plates, and GT serves a decadent brunch on weekends.

531 N. Wells St. (at Grand Ave.). www.gtoyster.com. ℂ **312/92-3501.** Shared plates $9–$28. Lunch Mon–Fri 11:30am–4:30pm; dinner Sun–Thurs 4:30pm–11pm; brunch Sat, Sun 10:30am–2:30pm; dinner Fri, Sat 4:30pm–midnight. Subway/El: Brown Line to Merchandise Mart, Red Line to Grand Ave.

mk ★★★ AMERICAN   You won't find test tubes, edible menus, or other telltale signs of molecular gastronomy at mk. Instead, expect a confident spot that excels at serving fresh, simple dishes that are exceedingly well prepared. Located in a refurbished paint factory from the 1920s, the three-level, loft-style restaurant is warm and where, looking out on the Chicago River, gussied up diners enjoy a creative take on the classic steakhouse menu (clever meat glazes, innovative sauces, an impressive seafood list, truffle scalloped potatoes, and decadent lobster mac and cheese) and spend a hearty portion of their paychecks while doing it. And hotel guests actually regularly choose to stay at The James because of the steakhouse attached: **David Burke's Primehouse** ★★ (616 N. Rush St., at Ontario St.; www.davidburkesprimehouse.com; ⓒ **312/660-6000**), where guests can enjoy dry-aged steaks in the leather-filled restaurant or have them delivered via room service. The adjoining **Burke's Bacon Bar** ★ relies on the same kitchen to offer on-the-go bites in the form of "handwiches," filled with braised beef and all sorts of bacon.

Sports fans can take their pick between two famous Italian steakhouses, which are workingman's restaurants compared to the dining rooms above, which expect more refined attire. **Ditka's** ★ (100 E. Chestnut St., in the Tremont Hotel, btw. Michigan Ave. and Rush St.; www.ditkasrestaurants.com; ⓒ **312/587-8989**) is da restaurant of Da Coach, Mike Ditka. Here, you won't find the same hushed tones that accompany many white-linen steakhouses. The light-hearted crowd comes for the meat-heavy man-food and abundance of sports memorabilia. **Harry Caray's Italian Steakhouse** ★ (33 W. Kinzie St., at Dearborn St.; www.harrycarays.com; ⓒ **312/828-0966** and at Navy Pier, 700 E. Grand Ave.; ⓒ **312/527-9700**) is a walk through the baseball diamond of yesteryear, brimming with relics from the collection of the famous Cub's announcer. You'll find wet- and dry-aged steaks here, along with Italian classics like rigatoni and chicken Vesuvio, as well as a popular burger. The dining room is casual and kid friendly, and service is swift, if not entirely friendly (*warning:* it gets packed when a game is on). In late spring of 2014, Harry Caray's also opened up a new restaurant and sports museum in Water Tower Place, 835 N. Michigan Ave., ⓒ **312/202-0500.**

welcoming with its soft lighting, exposed bricks, and wooden beams. mk, which dates back to 1998, when it was *the* place to see and be seen, was a farm-to-table restaurant before anyone was using that catchphrase. Today, its chef Michael Kornick, who co-owns the restaurant with his wife, Lisa, is known as a champion of sustainable practices in fishing and farming, and his seasonal menu reflects that. With a heavy seafood focus, you can't go wrong with any of the restaurant's gracefully carried out fish dishes (oysters and Hamachi were recent winners). Landlubbers will appreciate the naturally raised and roasted chicken, grilled bison, or steak, and all of the above can be expertly paired with a selection from the 750-bottle-deep wine list. *Tip:* Make the most of mk by going on a Sunday, when you can get three courses for $44. Reservations are highly recommended here.

868 N. Franklin St. (1 block north of Chicago Ave.). www.mkchicago.com. ⓒ **312/482-9179.** Main courses $33–$52. Sun–Thurs 5:30–9:30pm; Fri–Sat 5:30–10pm. Subway/El: Brown Line to Chicago.

Sumi Robata ★★ JAPANESE The decor is simple at this tiny Japanese restaurant, with wood-paneled walls and minimalist clean lines throughout. Your attention will be focused on the open kitchen, which you can see from most seats. There, the

BREAKFAST & brunch

Chicago is a breakfast and brunching town, and here are some of my favorite spots for a great morning meal, or one that can stretch well into the afternoon.

A local breakfast favorite since 1923 is **Lou Mitchell's** ★ (565 W. Jackson Blvd., btw. Jefferson and Clinton streets; loumitchellsrestaurant.com; ℂ **312/939-3111**), across the south branch of the Chicago River from the Loop, a block farther west than Union Station. You'll be greeted at the door with a basket of doughnut holes and Milk Duds so that you can nibble while waiting for a table. Those who prefer a long and creative menu to peruse will love **Yolk** ★ (1120 S. Michigan, btw. Roosevelt Rd. and 11th St.; www.eatyolk.com; ℂ **312/789-9655**), which does a little of everything and does it well, from the traditional (smoked salmon platter) to the frou-frou (bananas Foster crepes). For a Southern-style breakfast of spicy red eggs, cheese grits, or biscuits and gravy, head over to **Wishbone** ★★ (p. 83), a family-friendly, laid-back spot in a converted warehouse building in the West Loop. For brunch with some soul, head to **House of Blues** ★ (329 N. Dearborn St., at Kinzie St.; ℂ **312/527-2583**; p. 209), for its popular Sunday gospel brunch. To guarantee seating, it's a good idea to book a spot 2 weeks in advance.

If you're on the city's North Side, **Ann Sather** ★ (909 W. Belmont Ave.,

chefs are using a charcoal (*sumi*) robata grill to perfectly cook everything from vegetables (asparagus, romaine lettuce, onion, shishito peppers) to seafood (salmon, shrimp, king crab, octopus) and meat (skirt steak, beef tongue, chicken thigh, lamb). The grill makes everything incredibly tender and slightly smoky, and each bite seems to elicit an "Mmmm." Most items are served on skewers, but a few, like the oh-my-God-good beef sliders, are a little more elaborate, served in a bun. Service is excellent, with fine-tuned attention to detail.

702 N. Wells (at Huron Street). www.sumirobatabar.com. ℂ **312/988-7864.** Small plates $4–$16. Mon–Fri 11:30am–2:30pm; Mon–Wed 5–11pm; Thurs–Sat 5–midnight. Subway/El: Brown Line to Chicago Ave.

Moderate

India House ★★★ INDIAN   India House ranks up there with the best Indian food I've ever had, and certainly the best Indian buffet (context: I'm an Indian food junkie). If you can, visit during lunch—it'll be packed, but manageable, during the week—when you can sample a bit of everything on the buffet. The menu offers a tasty tour of India, with flavors from Bombay and Delhi, as well as tandoor cooking and street-food influences. Dinner prices can run steep, but prices are on par with other area rates. Whatever you do, order the Kashmiri naan, which is stuffed with pineapple, cherries, and walnuts. It's so good, it's ridiculous, and makes the perfect dessert (even if it's not intended to be dessert). The interior here was recently redone, and it's quite a fashionable place, with hints of sparkly gold and hot pink. Its River North hipness is above and beyond the neighborhood Indian joint that I, for one, am accustomed to.

59 W. Grand Ave. (btw. Clark St. and Dearborn Pkwy.). ℂ **312/645-9500.** Buffet $18, Main dishes $13–$33. Mon–Fri 11am–2:30pm; Sat–Sun 11:30am–3pm; Mon–Thurs 5:30–10pm; Fri–Sat 5:30–11pm; Sun 5–10pm. Subway/El: Brown to Merchandise Mart or Red to Grand Ave.

btw. Clark St. and Sheffield Ave.; www.annsather.com; © **773/348-2378**), famous for its homemade cinnamon rolls, is a perfect breakfast or brunch spot if you're heading up to Wrigleyville for a Cubs game or a walk through Lincoln Park. The **Nookies** ★ restaurants are Chicago favorites for all the standard morning fare. Locations include 2114 N. Halsted Street, in Lincoln Park (www.nookiesrestaurants.net; © **773/327-1400**); 1748 N. Wells Street, in Old Town (© **312/337-2454**); and 3334 N. Halsted Street, in Lakeview (© **773/248-9888**). Especially in Old Town, be prepared to stand outside on the weekends until a table opens for you. It's quite a scene on the sidewalk, which is packed with baby strollers, dogs on leashes, large groups chatting, and singles reading the newspaper. **Elly's Pancake House** ★★ (p. 101), located across from the Chicago History Museum and Lincoln Park (101 North Ave. at Clark St.; © **312/643-2300**), serves up helium-light omelets and greats from the griddle. Or head to **Orange** ★★, 3231 N. Clark St., at Belmont Ave. (orangerestaurantchicago.com; © **773/549-4400**), for a fun twist on breakfast foods. Try the Green Eggs and Ham—eggs scrambled with pesto, tomatoes, mozzarella, and pancetta—and the fruishi, which is fruit sushi.

Inexpensive

Burke's Bacon Bar ★ SANDWICHES   Ready to get your bacon on? This tiny, counter-service spot serves not sandwiches, but "handwiches," filled with some of the best, bacony fillings around. That's because the kitchen is shared with David Burke's Primehouse ★★ (p. 91), and it's famous for its protein prowess. Duck in for a bacon burger, bacon dog, beef and cheddar, or all of the above (three make up an order) and then head to the lake for a carnivorous picnic. It's a super cute concept, but take my word for it and don't eat these while walking; they can make quite a mess.

610 N. Rush St. (at Ontario St.). www.burkesbaconbar.com. © **312/660-7200.** Sandwiches are $4 each or three for $11. Mon–Sun 11am–10pm. Subway/El: Red Line to Grand Ave.

Sable Kitchen & Bar ★★ AMERICAN   Despite its location in Hotel Palomar, Sable draws in as many (if not more) locals as it does visitors, thanks to its inviting bar with an impressive whiskey selection and always cheerful bartenders (although table service isn't always as pleasant or reliable). The menu, created by former *Top Chef: Texas* contestant Heather Terhune, takes the concept of bar food to new heights, with around the-world influences in its tuna tartare tostadas, South Indian vegetable curry, and chicken confit poutine, along with new takes on American favorites, like the crispy pork belly BLT, baked mac and cheese, and deviled eggs with truffle oil. The plates are meant to be shared, and you can choose half or full portions. Although Sable is open for breakfast and brunch, and it does an okay job, I really recommend visiting during lunch or dinner.

505 N. State St. (at Illinois St.), in the Hotel Palomar. www.sablechicago.com. © **312/755-9704.** Main courses $12–$35. Mon–Fri 6:30–10:30am; Sat–Sun 10–2; Sun–Wed 5–10pm; Thurs 5–11pm; Fri–Sat 5pm–midnight. Closed Thanksgiving and Christmas. Subway/El: Red Line to Grand Ave.

THE old guard

Although many of the most popular spots in Chicago today tend toward jeans-casual and serve shared plates, no guidebook would be complete without paying homage to the gourmet spots of old—the places my parents and, in some cases, their parents, equate with fine dining. These are places that were, in their day (and some remain) status dining spots, bringing in cuisine and old-world charm from Europe. Back then, it wasn't quite as easy to find a spot at these places as it is today. I searched for same day reservations on a Saturday and had no problems.

Open since 1898, **The Berghoff ★** (17 W. Adams St. btw. State and Dearborn sts.; www.theberghoff.com; Ⓒ **312/427-3170**), is legendary for its hearty German fare, like Wiener Schnitzel, sauerbraten, and encased meats galore, along with their house-made beers. For those less inclined toward the heavy, Teutonic food, there are also salads, soups, and sandwiches in the downstairs cafe. Bedecked in intricate woodwork and stained glass, the turn-of-the-century decor (and, it often seems, servers) are a throwback to the Chicago of yesterday. It gets particularly rowdy here in September, during Oktoberfest.

Fast forward 30 years after the opening of the Berghoff, and the **Cape Cod Room ★** in The Drake Hotel (140 E. Walton Place, at Michigan Ave.; www.thedrakehotel.com/dine/cape-cod-room; Ⓒ **312/932-4615**), is a glimpse of Chicago's fine dining scene in the 1930s. In its glory days, Marilyn Monroe and Joe DiMaggio carved their initials on the bar here. Today, diners include older devotees and younger curiosity seekers who are willing to shell out big bucks for Old World classic cuisine (oysters Rockefeller, lobster Thermidor, and Dover sole) and, most importantly, peer back in time.

When **Everest ★★** (440 S. LaSalle St., 40th floor, at Congress Pkwy.; www.everestrestaurant.com; Ⓒ **312/663-8920**) opened in the '80s, the notion of paying $80 per person for a fine-dining experience that included some of the best views of the city from the 40th floor of the Chicago Stock Exchange was a steep concept in Chicago. Today, those amazing views remain and the price has risen to $130 per person, not including beverages (although you can get a three-course pre-theater menu for $54). The restaurant is still revered by Chicago chefs and old-school gourmands for the seven-course degustation menu of traditional Alsatian cuisine (cold-pressed lobster and potato terrine, sautéed foie gras, loin of venison), prepared by beloved French chef Jean Joho.

Inexpensive

Gino's East ★ PIZZA Splurging on calories is an understatement when eating a deep-dish slice at Gino's East, but you've got to do it. Thick, golden-crusted, drowning in cheese, and smothered in tomatoes (which are on top of the cheese), this casserole-style dish, served in a hefty, cast-iron pan, is as Chicago as it gets. Gino's East has been engorging bellies since 1966, and while there are four locations around Chicago (and more in the suburbs), I recommend going to the original, where chalk graffiti covers the exposed brick walls, and generations of families have waddled out those very front doors. But if you're not in that area, the food is just as good at the enormous new three-story River North location, 500 N. La Salle (at Illinois St.) Ⓒ **312/988-4200.** Keep in mind that because the pizzas are so thick, they take about 45 minutes to cook, so don't

FOOD COURTS FOR foodies

We're a city of Midwest sensibilities. And, while some of us may be willing to splurge for an Alinea-sized bill on special occasions, lunch is a different story. People who work in the Loop are constantly looking for the quickest, cheapest, and best tasting lunch, and because of that, downtown is buzzing with inventive food courts and on-the-go meal options. My personal favorite is River North's **Eataly** ★★★ (43 E. Ohio St., btw. Wabash Ave. and Rush St.; www.eataly.com/chicago; ℭ **312/521-8700**). I bring visitors here to explore the elaborate selection of Italian imports (tomatoes, truffles, and artichokes galore, as well as a fresh pasta counter, where they make it before your eyes and sell it by the pound), before grabbing a glass of wine or beer at one of the two bars, and then lunch at one of its 23 dining options, serving pizza, pasta, rotisserie meats, sandwiches, and just about anything else with an Italian stamp.

The lower level of the **Chase Building** gets packed during the week (it's closed after hours and on weekends) with Loop workers looking for variety at **Urban Market** ★★ (10 S. Dearborn St., at

Madison St.; www.urbanmarketchicago.com). Here, 12 different food stations include Indian, a salad bar, potato bar, sushi, soup, and more. It gets loud inside, and there's not much to see, but if the weather is nice, take your food outside to the courtyard, where you can sit by a fountain and gaze at a mosaic by Marc Chagall.

Located in the mezzanine of Water Tower Place, **foodlife** ★ (835 N. Michigan Ave.; www.foodlifechicago.com; ℭ **312/335-3663**) offers more healthy options than you'd expect from a food court, with juices, rotisserie chicken, sushi, salads, and taco and Chinese bowls. There are also plenty of old food court standbys, too, in case you're craving pizza, pasta, and hot dogs. The lower level of **Macy's** ★★ (111 N. State St., at Washington; www.visitmacys chicago.com, ℭ **312/781-4483**) fills with Loop workers seeking a quick bite—sushi, salads, pizza—while the seventh floor buzzes with lunch goers choosing between tacos at Frontera Fresco, noodles at Noodles by Takashi Yagihashi, or a farm-fresh burger at Marc Burger.

arrive here with a family that's hungry and ready to eat. Not ready to say goodbye? Gino's is so popular that you can actually order a frozen pizza via the restaurant's website and have it shipped home, ready to heat.

162 E. Superior St. (btw. Michigan Ave. and Fairbanks Ct.). www.ginoseast.com. ℭ **312/266-3337**. Reservations not accepted. Pizza $14–$33. Mon–Thurs 11am–10pm; Fri–Sat 11am–11pm; Sun noon–9pm. Subway/El: Red, Brown Line to Chicago Ave.

La Madia ★★★ PIZZA   Not all pizza in Chicago is Chicago pizza, which helps explain why not all Chicagoans are morbidly obese. I'd be willing to bet that most Chicagoans actually prefer their thin crust to thick. That explains, in part, why La Madia packs them in at every meal, lunch or dinner. With an airy, thin crust and eclectic toppings, such as clam and Fresno chiles, shaved artichoke, and roasted grapes, these wood-fired pizzas are the best in the vicinity of the Loop (as are the salads). This spot bucks the cavernous feel of traditional Chicago pizzerias, and its attention to interior design makes it feel comfortably upscale, well suited for date night, a business dinner, girls' night out, or a family meal. La Madia also offers one of the best restaurant lunch deals in the area: Two can share a pizza, salad, and cookies for $19. Add two glasses of the $6 wine of the week for $31 (Did you hear that? Six dollar glasses of wine!).

59 W. Grand Ave. (btw. Clark St. and Dearborn Pkwy.). www.dinelamadia.com. ✆ **312/329-0400.** Pizzas $12–$18. Mon–Thurs 11am–11pm; Fri–Sat 11am–midnight; Sun 11am–10pm. Subway/El: Brown to Merchandise Mart or Red to Grand Ave.

Portillo's ★ AMERICAN/FAST FOOD   Kids love Portillo's for its hot dogs and burgers. Parents love the chain, which originated locally, for the broad and inexpensive menu that goes above and beyond meat-on-a-bun options, including salads and relatively healthy sandwiches. Then again, when in Chicago, consider throwing caution to the wind and double down with a combo beef and chargrilled sausage, which is, as it sounds, an Italian sausage buried in Italian beef on a bun. Before you leave, order a slice of the famous chocolate cake, and as you lick your lips and savor its rich, moist goodness, consider its not-so-secret ingredient: mayonnaise. Reliably loud and frenetic, you won't feel out of place here if you bring along your noisy brood.

100 W. Ontario St. (at Clark St.). www.portillos.com. ✆ **312/587-8910.** Reservations not accepted. Main courses $3–$8. Sun–Thurs 10am–11pm; Fri–Sat 10am–midnight. Subway/El: Red Line to Grand Ave., Brown Line to Chicago.

LINCOLN PARK & OLD TOWN

Alinea ★★★ AMERICAN   Sure, there's a fair amount of cockiness to a restaurant that doesn't even bother to put its name out front. But Alinea, which has been named among the top restaurants in the world, clearly isn't having many issues drawing diners to its unmarked Lincoln Park digs. Once you step inside, you'll know where you are by the flames, ice, and foam that make Alinea unlike any place you've ever been. Here, Chef Grant Achatz has perfected the art of molecular gastronomy, and the only way to sample it is through the tasting menus, which are priced just as extravagantly, starting at $210. The menu changes in number of courses and offerings (the current one is 18 courses), but is consistent in its blow-your-mind factor. Take one of the dessert courses that was served at the time this was written: a translucent, floating, apple-flavored balloon that you suck in, only to then talk like Mickey Mouse from the helium. Other highlights have included a dessert that's literally painted on the table as you watch, taking the form of modern art; leafy branches used as skewers for a goose course; and aromatic pillows that release scents, such as nutmeg, as you dine. I should note that if you do go to Alinea, you may want to make arrangements for someone to watch your kids. You'd think that would be a given, but there was an uproar recently when a couple brought their 8-month-old baby to the restaurant. The child was actually allowed to stay, mind you, but the couple, who were never named, were completely castigated by media (and, of course, online commenters) for taking their child to dine in a library-quiet restaurant for a meal that, with wine pairings, will run two people more than $700. If you can afford that, you can afford a sitter. You must purchase a ticket in advance to dine at Alinea (see box on facing page), and prices change according to the date and time that you plan on dining. It's best to nab tickets months in advance, to be safe.

1723 N. Halsted St. (btw. North Ave. and Willow St.). www.alinea-restaurant.com. ✆ **312/867-0110.** Tickets required; purchase online well in advance. $210–$265. Wed–Sun 5–9:30pm. Subway/El: Red Line to North/Clybourn, Brown Line to Armitage.

Boka ★★★ AMERICAN   Take fine-dining-style attention to food, mix it with sophisticated playfulness—like a moss- and greenery-filled wall punctuated with portraits of regally dressed cats—and you've got Boka. This Lincoln Park restaurant,

A HOT ticket

Two of the hottest meal tickets in town are, literally, tickets, and you have to buy one in order to secure a spot at Alinea and Next, where Chicago's most renowned chef and molecular gastronomist, Grant Achatz, is at the helm.

The ticketing all started with **Next** ★★ (953 W. Fulton Market Ave., btw. Morgan and Sangamon sts.; www.nextrestaurant.com; ✆ **312/226-0858**). When the West Loop restaurant opened in 2011, it did so using a prepaid system, where diners had to log on and nab a date and time in order to secure a spot. Sold in 3-month increments, the tickets sold out in seconds. The restaurant operates on a theme concept that changes quarterly, which, to this day, keeps the ideas fresh and the tickets selling. "Paris, 1906," "Kyoto," "Childhood," and "Chicago Steakhouse" have been on the list in the past, and each tasting menu ties into the motif and has a varying number of courses, the highest of which, so far, has been 29 (prices are generally $130 and up, not including beverage pairings). Service here is borderline perfect, and can feel as though you're on the stage of a ballet with multiple waiters descending on you to explain the latest course. It can also be a bit odd. I visited Next during the Tour of Thailand menu. Our server presented a panang beef cheek course, and then proceeded to gross out the table by announcing, "We have a person on staff who runs through fields cutting the faces off of cows." None of us were quite sure what to do with that. But every course was incredible (including that ol' beef cheek) and the dinner, which lasted 3 hours, was no doubt a meal and a show—a thought that helps me justify the expense.

After the success of the ticket sales at Next, **Alinea** ★★★ (p. 96; 1723 N. Halsted St., btw. North Ave. and Willow St.; www.alinea-restaurant.com; ✆ **312/867-0110**) followed suit. This hallowed Lincoln Park restaurant elevates food to the level of fine art, and that creativity and precision have earned it the title of best restaurant in the country by no less than *Gourmet* magazine. Alinea regularly sells out of tickets to its 12- to 24-course tasting menus, which are currently priced at just over $200 as of this writing, not including beverages. At Alinea, you can expect the same level of seemingly choreographed service as you get at Next, and the menu is punctuated with even more notes of molecular gastronomy. One course may be served on, say, driftwood; another may be trapped in an ice block or balloon; the next may be presented on a lavender-scented pillow. Falling somewhere between ridiculously over-the-top and absolutely divine, each course comes with an explanation and often instructions on how to consume what's in front of you. Tickets to Alinea are the most sought-after and expensive in town, and people do, in fact, travel to Chicago solely to enjoy a 3-hour-plus meal here.

With both ticketing systems, a limited number of tickets are available (buy them online) and prices change according to when you go. A Wednesday evening, for example, might cost $40 or so less, per person, than a peak weekend time, and tickets sell out regularly. A limited number of tickets are also available through the restaurants' respective Facebook and Twitter pages, but because there are a lot of people vying for those day-of tickets, I'd strongly advise booking well, well in advance, if you want to guarantee a spot during your visit.

Where to Dine in Lincoln Park, Old Town & Wrigleyville

Alinea **15**
Ann Sather **4**
Bistrot Margot **20**
Boka **14**
Café Ba-Ba-Reeba! **13**
The Chicago Diner **7**
Elly's Pancake House **18**
L2O **11**
Murphy's Red Hots **3**
New England Seafood
  Company **1**
Nhu Lan's Bakery **8**
Nookies **6, 12, 17**
Old Jerusalem **21**
Orange **5**
Senza **9**
Tac Quick **2**
Topo Gigio **19**
Twin Anchors **16**
The Wieners Circle **10**

Lake Michigan

1/4 mi

1/4 km

LINCOLN PARK

41

Yacht Club

Belmont Harbor

Bird Sanctuary

Harbor Dr.

N Sheridan Rd.

N Lake Shore Dr.

41

N Pine Grove Ave.

W Melrose St.

W Briar Pl.

W Barry Ave.

W Oakdale Ave.

N Surf St.

N Broadway St.

8

W Buckingham Pl.

W Aldine Ave.

N Belmont Ave.

N Clark St.

W Diversey Pkwy.

9

7

W Roscoe St.

6

N Halsted St.

5

N Mildred Ave.

4

W George St.

W Wellington Ave.

W Oakdale Ave.

N Sheridan Rd.

N Fremont St.

N Wilton Ave.

N Sheffield Ave.

N Kenmore Ave.

N Seminary Ave.

N Clifton Ave.

N Racine Ave.

19

2

N Kenmore Ave.

N Seminary Ave.

Wrigley Field

W Waveland Ave.

WRIGLEYVILLE

Graceland Cemetery

Wunders Cemetery

Jewish Graceland Cemetery

N Clark St.

W Grace St.

W Addison St.

W Eddy St.

W Cornelia St.

W Newport Ave.

W School St.

N Southport Ave.

N Greenview Ave.

1

N Lakewood Ave.

N Lincoln Ave.

W Fletcher St.

W Barry Ave.

3

W Melrose St.

W Wolfram St.

W Irving Park Rd.

W Byron St.

located two doors down from the much more serious Alinea, recently got a new chef and a new look. "Same Boka, just a little facelift," the host smiled, during our visit. And that nip and tuck has served it well. Rather than presenting diners with a tasting menu, Boka breaks their menu into four sections: salads, starters, entrees, dessert. The idea is that you can create your own array of courses, picking and choosing according to appetite and taste, rather than sitting through an elaborate tasting menu. I have to say that everything Chef Lee Woolen touches turns to culinary gold. Light, fresh flavors dominate (the fluke with ginger, grapefruit, and cilantro goes on my list of top bites, ever, and the loup de mer with blood orange, olives, artichokes, and calamari wasn't far behind), and while you won't find molecular gastronomy or organ meats that push you too far out of your comfort zone, you will find a meal that borders on perfection, with simple, honest flavors from start to finish. It all swirls together in an atmosphere that feels celebratory and energetic, rather than the museum-like feel of many fine-dining establishments in Chicago. Reservations strongly recommended.

1729 N. Halsted St. (btw. North Ave. and Willow St.). www.bokachicago.com. ℂ **312/337-6070.** Main courses $20–$32. Sun–Thurs 5–10pm; Fri–Sat 5–11pm. Subway/El: Red Line to North/Clybourn, Brown Line to Armitage.

L2O ★★★ SEAFOOD Speaking of museum-like, L2O is the refined, hushed counterpart to the fine-dining experience, where the diners are reserved, serious, and dressed for the occasion. Each course is presented with reverence, and you can opt for the four-course prix fixe menu or the more elaborate tasting menu (when I was there it had 11 courses). Each course has a story behind it and was inspired by Francophile Chef Matthew Kirkley's travels across France. Expect masterfully assembled creations, some of which were so beautiful—and so un-food-like, in appearance—I was hesitant to eat them (I was that annoying girl photographing each and every course). Although the menu changes seasonally, there are some mainstays, like the stunning, bright green avocado-wrapped sphere of ahi tuna tartare, topped with black beads of caviar. You can play it safe here and stick with seafood you've heard of (Dover sole, lobster, mussels), or go out on a limb and try something more daring, like geoduck or bone marrow with abalone and black truffles. On our visit, my boyfriend had the pigeon, which still looked like a pigeon, although its leg was smoked and turned to sausage, claw still intact. He resisted pocketing the claw, although I know he secretly really wanted to freak me out later and scratch me with it. Despite the hallowed hall feel, the servers are down-to-earth and fun, if you engage them. You'll need to make a reservation here to guarantee seating. (There's no formal dress code, but jackets are recommended for men.)

2300 N. Lincoln Park West (at Belden Ave., inside the Belden-Stratford). www.l2orestaurant.com. ℂ **773/868-0002.** Prix fixe and tasting menus $140–$210. Mon, Thurs 6–10pm (closed Tues, Wed); Fri 5:30–11pm; Sat 5–11pm; Sun 5:30–9:30. Bus: 151.

Moderate

Bistrot Margot ★★ BISTRO/FRENCH This cozy spot is forever bustling, and regulars love it for its true Parisian bistro feel. The French staples are all here—steak frites, brined and roasted chicken, roasted duck over saffron and asparagus risotto. And they're just as delicious as you'll find anywhere in the Loop, but far more affordable. Bistrot Margot also serves a number of sandwiches, including croque monsieur, for lunch, and weekend brunch offerings include a number of inventive benedicts, like *confit de canard,* with two poached eggs, duck leg confit, spinach, portabella, and orange hollandaise.

smoke it IF YOU'VE GOT IT

No, we're not Kansas City, Memphis, the Carolinas or St. Louis, but we Chicagoans still love our barbecue, and a wealth of new spots have opened in the last few years. Looking for something smoky? Hit these spots:

County Barbeque ★★ (1352 W. Taylor St., at Loomis St.; www.dmkcounty barbeque.com; 𝐂 **312/929-2528**) is the newcomer to the barbecue scene, and it's a welcome addition. Perfuming the Little Italy neighborhood with hunger-pang-inducing smell of smoked meats, this is where roadhouse meets trendy: American flags and animal heads cover walls and the bourbon menu goes on forever (try one of the carbonated bourbon cocktails). The barbecue is inspired by all the American greats— St. Louis ribs, Texas brisket, Chicago rib tips, KC burnt ends, and more—and the sides, like the cheddar grits and mac and cheese with burnt ends, could be a meal in and of themselves.

The Kobe beef ribs and brisket at **Chicago q** ★ (1160 N. Dearborn St., at Division St.; www.chicagoqrestaurant. com; 𝐂 **312/642-1160**) are a bit gimmicky (why go with a pricey cut for such a slow, tenderizing process?) but one bite of the "Competition" baby back ribs and you won't give it a second thought. The crowd tends toward the buttoned-up Gold Coast variety, but that's what you get when you put "artisanal rubs" on your meats, right?

At **Twin Anchors** ★★ (1655 N. Sedgwick St., 1 block north of North Ave.; www.twinanchorsribs.com; 𝐂 **312/266-1616**), a hidden dive in Old Town, Sinatra is the soundtrack and 'cue is the main attraction, specifically ribs so tender you could gum them. Unfortunately, the cat is long out of the bag on this family-friendly joint, and you may have to wait a good hour or more on weekends.

1437 N. Wells St. (at W. Schiller St.). www.bistrotmargot.com. 𝐂 **312/587-3660.** Main courses $9–$19 lunch, $16–$26 dinner. Mon 11:30am–9pm; Tues–Thurs 11:30am–10pm; Fri 11:30am–11pm; Sat 10am–11pm; Sun 10am–9pm. Subway/El: Red Line to Clark/Division, or Brown Line to Sedgwick St.

Café Ba-Ba-Reeba! ★ SPANISH & TAPAS   Got a group? Head to Café Ba-Ba-Reeba!, which has been serving tapas and *pinxtos* (bite-sized tapas popular in Northern Spain) since before many Americans had uttered the words "small plate." Here, you'll share Spanish small plates galore in a loud and festive setting. Favorites include chorizo-wrapped Medjool dates and cheese, spicy potatoes, braised short ribs, paella, and too many others to list. Get tipsy with the rest of the crowd on pitchers of sangria while you debate whether or not you should order just one more plate. Ba-Ba-Reeba is also a great date spot, but try to come with other couples so that you can sample more items.

2024 N. Halsted St. (at Armitage Ave.). www.cafebabareeba.com. 𝐂 **312/266-9355.** Tapas $5–$20. Mon–Thurs 4–10pm; Fri 4pm–midnight; Sat 10am–midnight; Sun 10am–10pm. Subway/El: Red or Brown Line to Fullerton, or Brown Line to Armitage Ave.

Elly's Pancake House ★★ BREAKFAST   This darling breakfast spot, with its bright green walls decorated with an eclectic plate collection, is, in a word, awesome. First, you've got the location across from Chicago History Museum and the south end of Lincoln Park. Then you've got the huge menu with all the breakfast classics, like steak and eggs, corned beef hash, and biscuits and gravy, along with every griddle

TASTES LIKE chicken

Fried chicken is having something of a, yes, golden moment in Chicago. In addition to showing up on menus everywhere, dedicated fried chicken spots are also delivering it by the bucketful. The calorie conscious should stay away from **Honey Butter Fried Chicken ★** (3361 N. Elston Ave., at Roscoe; www.honeybutter.com; ℃ **773/474-4000**), where each order of fried chicken is served with a dollop of honey-kissed butter that you spread on the bird. Although the fried chicken is just fine without it—hot, tender and juicy, as it should be—the sweetness does add a nice contrast, if you can accept the absurdity of buttering something fried. Logan Square's **Parson's Chicken & Fish ★★** (2952 W. Armitage Ave., at Humboldt Blvd.; www.parsonschickenandfish.com;

℃ **773/384-3333**) is at its peak in the summer, when patrons sip Negroni slushies and margaritas with a Sour-Patch-covered rim on the sunny outdoor area. But don't count it out during the cooler months, when the fried-chicken-and-fried-fish fiends fill the 40-seat restaurant, savoring hush puppies, mashed potatoes, butterbeans, and crispy chicken brined for max juiciness. And then there's **Harold's Chicken Shack ★** (multiple locations, including No. 36 in Wicker Park at 1631 N. Milwaukee, at Wood Street; ℃ **773/252-2424**), a local franchise with 65 chicken joints across the state. Don't expect to find anything fancy here; Harold's is just good, down-home, no glitz or shtick fried bird, served on a piece of grease-sopping white bread.

creation you can imagine, like waffles, French toast, pancakes, crepes, and blintzes, and add in helium-light omelets, skillets, and even a number of tasty healthy options, along with sandwiches and salads. And last, it's open 24 hours, so it's booming in the early morning with families, fills up mid-morning with kid-free couples, and late at night it draws in the post-bar-crawl patrons in need of beer-absorbing pancakes.

101 W. North Road (at Clark St.). www.ellyspancakehouse.com. ℃ **312/643-2300.** Breakfast $6–$15, lunch $7–$14. Open 24 hours a day. Subway/El: Brown Line to Sedgwick St.

Old Jerusalem ★ MIDDLE EASTERN   Not to be eclipsed by the trendy spots of Old Town, the understated Old Jerusalem holds its own and has done so since 1976. The falafel sandwich here has been heralded as one of the best in Chicago, but don't limit yourself to that. The Middle Eastern fare keeps it traditional, with shawarma, hummus, grape leaves, salads, and kebabs, all of which actually taste quite healthy if you've been indulging in hot dogs and pizza for days. Feel like a glass of wine? Old Jerusalem doesn't have a liquor license, but encourages diners to bring their own bottle, at no added fee (see BYO box p. 82). And there's a great little wine shop called Galleria Liquors about a block north on Wells Street.

1411 N. Wells St. (btw. Schiller Street Ave. and Burton Place). www.oldjerusalemrestaurant.net. ℃ **312/944-0459.** Main courses $13-15. Mon–Sun 11am–10:30pm. Subway/El: Brown Line to Sedgwick St.

Topo Gigio ★★ ITALIAN   Full disclosure: I dream of Topo Gigio's fried calamari, so much so that after gorging on fried squid and Topo Gigio's soft, warm bread, served with cheese and olive oil, I usually take most of my entree—which is a huge portion—home. This old-world Italian joint is reliably filled with a well-heeled and energized Old Town crowd, who come here for the pastas, like the popular *rigatoni al filo di fumo* (rigatoni in tomato sauce with pancetta, fresh mozzarella, and fresh basil, topped with pecorino cheese) and traditional proteins, like veal saltimbocca and fish al limone, plus reasonable wine prices. Despite the perennially busy speed, servers are attentive and down to earth.

1516 N. Wells St. (btw. North Ave. and Schiller St.). www.topogigiochicago.com. ℂ **312/266-9355.** Main courses $14–$26. Mon–Sat 11:30–10:30pm; Sun 4–10pm. Subway/El: Brown Line to Sedgwick St.

WRIGLEYVILLE & THE NORTH SIDE

Expensive

Senza ★★★ AMERICAN Senza has become my go-to restaurant for special occasions. It's a rare combination: neighborhood restaurant (a non-touristy spot with friendly, down-to-earth service) with food fit for a gastronomer. The intimate Lakeview restaurant offers two different menus, a four-course prix fixe and a nine-course tasting menu. Personally, I prefer the prix fixe, because I like to make the choice of what I'm going to eat and be done with dinner in 2 hours or less. The menus are seasonal and change frequently, but expect an array of proteins served with fruit- or herb-inspired sauces, prepared simply but beautifully. Another unique thing about Senza: It's gluten free. Now, I get nervous saying that because I know, for many people (including my boyfriend), the GF label is an immediate turn off, or often an apology for not being as good as a place with gluten. Here, that couldn't be further from the truth. Our first visit, we both unhinged our jaws in order to stuff more of the gluten-free bread, served hot and fresh with whipped butter, into our maws. We saved just enough room for the meal, and left comfortably satisfied but not stuffed. In the mornings, Senza operates as Wheat's End Café and serves gluten-free baked goods and local coffee.

2873 North Broadway St. (at Surf St.). www.senzachicago.com. ℂ **773/770-3527.** Tues–Sat 5:30–10:30pm. Dinner: $75 for the prix fixe menu, $125 for tasting menu. Wheat's End Café hours: Sun 10am–2pm; Mon–Fri 9am–noon. Subway/El: Brown Line to Wellington.

Moderate

Kuma's Corner ★★★ AMERICAN/BURGERS The Kuma's demographic wears black, bangs his or her head, and appreciates a huge hunk of beef. But the normal among us are welcome here, too. Kuma's names its burgers after metal bands, and the toppings are a reminder that in the Midwest, a burger is never just a burger; it's an artist's palette upon which to build. The Pantera, a personal favorite, has homemade ranchero salsa, tortilla chips, bacon, and cheese, while the Slayer is a mess of a meal, with a pile of fries topped with a burger, sausage, chilis, "and anger." There are non-burger sandwiches too (the "pig destroyer" is pulled pork and "hate beak" is chicken), and the salads here are surprisingly decent for a rage-filled burger joint. Kuma's has fewer than a dozen tables, so waits can border on obscene (2 to 3 hours on weekends). If you do come, put your name on the list and head across the street to a bar named Square, where you can enjoy drinks away from the crowds (and loud music) until it's time for dinner. Kuma's recently opened a second location, Kuma's Too (666 West Diversey Pkwy, btw. Orchard and Clark Streets; ℂ **773/472-2666**), in Lakeview, which has a larger kitchen and shorter wait times, but a little less rage than the original.

2900 W. Belmont Ave. (at Francisco Ave.). www.kumascorner.com. ℂ **773/604-8769.** No reservations. Main courses $12–$15. Mon–Wed 11:15am–11:45pm; Thurs–Sat 11:15am–12:45am; Sun

Aside from pizza, the dishes that the city truly calls its own are bovine-centric: hot dogs and Italian beef. It may not be haute cuisine, but I promise you've never had anything quite like the city's spin on these indulgences. The classic Chicago hot dog includes a frankfurter by Vienna Beef (a local food processor and hallowed institution), heaps of chopped onions and green relish, a slather of yellow mustard, pickle spears, fresh tomato wedges, a dash of celery salt, and, for good measure, two or three "sport" peppers, those thumb-shaped holy terrors that turn your mouth into its own bonfire.

Chicago is home to many standout hot-dog spots. **Gold Coast Dogs ★** (159 N. Wabash Ave., at Randolph St.; www.goldcoastdogs.net; ⓒ **312/917-1677**), in the Loop just a block from Michigan Avenue, serves a great classic Chicago dog. **Portillo's ★** (p. 96) is another local chain that specializes in hot dogs, as well as burgers and sandwiches for the non-tubular inclined. **Murphy's Red Hots ★** (1211 W. Belmont Ave., at Racine Ave.; www.murphyshotdogs.com; ⓒ **773/935-2882**) is a neighborhood spot not too far from Wrigley Field; while **The Wieners Circle ★** in Lincoln Park at 2622 N. Clark St. (btw. Wrightwood Ave. and Drummond Place; ⓒ **773/477-7444**), is a late-night favorite where the counter server's rudeness is part of the,

er, charm. If you order a $20 chocolate shake, don't expect ice cream. Prepare to lose part of your innocence, as the large-and-in-charge cashier's shirt goes up and the shaking begins.

Encased meats aren't the only thing we Chicagoans love on a bun. There's also the Italian beef, a sandwich that seems to thrive primarily within Chicago's borders (maybe because our winter coats can hide the fat-flinging side effects). **Al's Beef ★**, www.alsbeef.com, with a downtown location at 601 West Adams (at Jefferson St., ⓒ **312/559-2333**) and a River North joint at 169 W. Ontario (at Wells, ⓒ **312/943-3222**), is one of the spots that lays claim to the Italian beef, a messy, heart attack of a sandwich, filled with shaved beef, slathered with enough meat juice to make the bun soggy, and topped with *giardiniera* (a marinated pepper relish). Artery clogs aside, the sandwich is delicious. You can find also find Italian beef at a number of generic burger joints, but I'd stick to the big names, like **Mr. Beef ★** (666 N. Orleans St. at Erie St., ⓒ **312/337-8500**), an Italian beef dive that is nevertheless hopping with construction boots, suits, and everything in between at lunchtime. Or head to **Portillo's ★,** where you can get an Italian beef and an Italian sausage, all on the same bun (see p. 96).

11:45am–11:45pm. Closed Thanksgiving, Christmas Eve, Christmas Day, New Year's Eve, New Year's Day. Subway/El: Blue Line to Belmont Ave.

Inexpensive

New England Seafood Company ★★ SEAFOOD   Aside from the seafood counter/fish market/lobster tank, there's not much to look at in this small, fish-centric joint. But one bite of a lobster roll, one slurp of the clam chowder, and attention to little details like aesthetics and distance from the ocean vanish. It's that good. The owners of this Lakeview hole-in-the-wall are from Boston and speak the language of the lobster shack, and a visit here totally justifies the 30-minute Brown Line commute from

DETOUR TO devon avenue

Bollywood, here we come! If you're looking for an inexpensive lunch and, perhaps, a sari, head to Devon Avenue and consider this itinerary. This single street, which runs for about 10 blocks starting in West Rogers Park, is a glimpse into just how diverse Chicago is. Devon is considered the "Little India" of Chicago, with the occasional punctuation of Jewish, Middle Eastern, Pakistani, and Asian stores and restaurants (see, we really can all get along!). Not quite gritty, but not entirely clean, it's a bit of a hike from the Loop via public transportation (just under an hour) or 10 miles by car, but fun if you're up for the adventure. Take the Red Line to Loyola and then walk one block south on Sheridan. Hop on the 155 bus heading west, to **ISP (India Sari Palace)** ★ (2534 W. Devon Ave., btw. Rockwell St. and Maplewood Ave.; no website; ✆ **773-338-2127**), and peek in at the bright silk and pashmina saris. Then head across the street and peruse the Bollywood video selection at **India Book House/Atlantic Video** ★ (2551 W. Devon Ave., btw. Rockwell St. and Maplewood Ave; no website; ✆ **773/338-3600**), and wander through aisles of spices, chutneys, and pickles at

Patel Brothers ★★ (2610 W. Devon Ave., at Rockwell St.; www.patelbros. com; ✆ **773/262-7777**) before heading to lunch. The following rank as my favorites in the area, so take your pick. Savor a southern Indian crepe, called a *dosa*, at **Uru Swati** ★★ (2629 W Devon Ave., at Talman Ave; www.uru-swati.net; ✆ **773/381-1010**). The savory pancake, filled with potatoes, rice, lentils, and other spicy delectables, is about two feet in length, and for about $6 it's a meal in itself. Load your plate at the buffet with chicken tikka masala, dal makhani, and saag paneer at **Viceroy of India** ★★ (2520 W Devon Ave., at Maplewood Ave.; www.viceroyofindia. com; ✆ **773/743-4100**), where they deliver hot, buttery naan to your table. Or to try a bit of everything, get a table at **Mysore Woodlands** ★ (2548 W Devon Ave., btw. Maplewood Ave. and Rockwell St.; www.mysorewoodlands. com, ✆ **773/338-8160,** and order one of their *thalis* (choose one with meat or veggies) and watch as your table is filled with tiny dishes, with curries, lentils, pickles, soup, and more, served with rice and bread. It's enough for two to share and costs just $14 to $17.

the Loop. Just ask my mom, who has declared visiting here a "tradition" every time she flies into town.

3341 N. Lincoln Ave. (btw. Roscoe and School sts). www.neseafoodcompany.com. ✆ **773/871-3474.** Sun, Tues–Thurs 11am–8pm; Fri–Sat 11am–10pm. Closed Mondays. Subway/El: Brown Line to Paulina.

Nhu Lan's Bakery ★★★ VIETNAMESE   This counter-service spot specializes in banh mi sandwiches, aka "Saigon subs," which range in price from $2.95 to $4.25 (buy five get one free). Whether you're a vegetarian or not, I beg you—beg you!—to try the veggie lemongrass tofu (No. 10) or the veggie ginger tofu (No. 11). The tofu isn't the mushy stuff that many people hate. It's more of a textured, meat-like substance that absorbs all of the delicious spices of the sandwich, and the flavor is phenomenal. I've delivered these to vegetarians, only to see panic cross their face after they take a bite. "I think this is meat," one said. It's not though. It's just that good. Nhu Lan has a second location in Lakeview (602 W. Belmont Ave., at Broadway, www.nhulansaigonsubs.com; ℂ **773/857-6868**). The sandwiches are about $1 more expensive there, but it's closer to the lake and picnic territory.

2612 W. Lawrence (btw. Rockwell St. and Talman Ave). www.nhulansbakery.com. ℂ **773/878-9898.** Sandwiches $2.95–$4.25. Mon- Fri 8am–7pm Sat-Sun 7am–7pm. Closed Tuesday. Subway/El: Brown Line to Rockwell St.

Tac Quick ★★★ THAI   My all-time favorite go-to for Thai is conveniently close to Wrigley Field (9 minutes north on foot or 6 minutes on the Red Line). This spot gets packed at night, so it's not a bad idea to make a reservation. What I love most is the "secret menu," a slightly more daring menu (raw shrimp, pork hock, Thai omelets, fermented pork and rice sausage), which they serve right along with the regular menu (not so secretive!). Full disclosure: The curry here is so good I've never ventured to try anything else. Prices are incredibly reasonable and it's BYO.

3930 N. Sheridan Rd. (at Dakin St.). www.tacquick.net. ℂ **773/327-5253**. Entrees $7.95–$12. Sun 11am–9:30pm; Mon, Wed–Sat 11am–10pm; closed Tues. Subway/El: Red Line to Sheridan.

WICKER PARK/BUCKTOWN
Moderate

Hot Chocolate ★ AMERICAN   If it sounds like the perfect spot for dessert, that's because the owner, Mindy Segal, cut her culinary teeth as a pastry chef. Her sweets, particularly the hot chocolates—of which there are seven flavors, each served with house-made marshmallows—are the stand out here, but comfort classics like the meat-loaf sandwich, mac and cheese, and hamburger all hold their own. Although the name Hot Chocolate sounds like a cafe, there's an undeniable lounge feel to the restaurant, which has a long list of beer, wine, and cocktails.

1747 N. Damen Ave. (at Willow St.). www.hotchocolatechicago.com. ℂ **773/489-1747.** Main courses $10–$15 lunch, $13–$28 dinner. Sat, Sun brunch 10am–2pm; Wed–Fri 11:30am–2pm; Sun, Tues–Thurs 5:30–10pm; Fri–Sat 5:30pm–12am; closed Monday. Subway/El: Blue Line to Damen Ave.

Inexpensive

Big Star ★★★ MEXICAN   There's no question what you'll get if you score a seat at Big Star: tacos. And we're not talking about boring old Americanized tacos (so don't expect flour tortillas, cheddar, or sour cream). At this former gas station turned hipster hangout, you're in for fancy meets traditional: steamed corn tortillas overflowing with fresh flavors, like crispy braised pork belly, queso fresco, onion, and cilantro. Add on a Big Star margarita or bourbon and take in the Wicker Park skinny jean scene. The menu is small (there are more bourbons than there are tacos), but each stuffed tortilla is pretty darn close to perfection. When the weather is nice, the large patio is perpetually packed.

1531 N. Damen Ave. (btw. Milwaukee and Wicker Park aves.). www.bigstarchicago.com. ℂ **773/235-4039.** No reservations. Sun–Fri 11:30am–2am; Sat 11:30am–3am. Subway/El: Blue Line to Damen Ave.

Piece ★★ AMERICAN/PIZZA   Piece serves up New-Haven style pizza (read: thin crust, a little bit crispy, a little bit chewy, and round-ish) and an impressive beer list, including Piece's own brews, in a lofty, loud, communal table setting. Pick your base: plain (no cheese), red (traditional) or white (olive oil, garlic, and mozzarella) and your toppings (mashed potatoes, anyone?), and get your nosh on. If you're here on a

A new TAKE ON THE OLD DINER

It's okay to break the rules and eat eggs after dark in Chicago. Two diners in the West Loop are revving up the often-tired diner concept and injecting it with new life—and craft cocktails. **Little Goat** ★★★ (820 W. Randolph St., at Green St.; www.littlegoatchicago.com; *©* 312/888-3455) is goat-themed restaurant No. 2 of Stephanie Izard (Girl and the Goat is No. 1, p. 82, and it's right across the street). Here, people happily wait in line to try the ever-inventive flavors and textural twists on traditional fare, and pay a fraction of what they would across the street. Breakfast is served from 7am daily until late at night, and meals range from cross-cultural (the parathas burrito is Indian flatbread, egg, avocado, bean salad, and sheep's milk cheddar) to weird-but-kind-of-amazing American (the bulls eye French toast with eggs, fried chicken, sweet onion brioche, and BBQ maple syrup). Everything's a la carte, so don't forget to add on an order of tempura mashed potatoes and a Sloe Punch cocktail to the mix for the breakfast of champions.

Grab a counter spot at **Au Cheval** ★★ (800 W. Randolph, at Halsted St.;

www.auchevalchicago.com; *©* 312/929-4580) if you can, and prepare to get your meat on. It may feel like a dimly lit, nothing-to-see-here bar, until you get the menu, which takes diner food and injects it with carnivore crack. While the foie gras with eggs is a little rich for my blood, I will personally swear by the crispy potato hash with duck's heart gravy. And one bite of the fried, house-made bologna sandwich, served on an airy roll and paired, perhaps, with a Horse's Neck cocktail, and you'll curse your elementary school sandwiches for failing to live up to their potential.

Farther north in Wrigleyville, **The Chicago Diner** ★ (3411 N. Halsted St.; www.veggiediner.com; (*©* 773/935-6696) might sound like the kind of place you load up on greasy burgers, but it's actually one of the city's best and longest-lasting vegetarian restaurants. (Most dishes are vegan, too.) The wide-ranging menu includes salads, sandwiches (including a "California Reuben" with seitan instead of corned beef), tacos, and pastas. And for dessert, save room for a chocolate peanut butter or vanilla chai vegan milkshake.

Saturday, stick around for the live band karaoke. Who knows? You may see co-owner Rick Nielsen of Cheap Trick take the stage.

1927 W. North Ave. (at Milwaukee Ave.). www.piecechicago.com. *©* **773/772-4422.** Pizza $11–$17. Mon–Wed 11am–10:30pm; Thurs 11am–11pm; Fri–Sat 11am–12:30am; Sun 11am–10pm. Subway/El: Blue Line to Damen Ave.

LOGAN SQUARE & THE NORTHWEST

Moderate

Kai Zan ★★★ ASIAN/SUSHI   I didn't realize the sushi I'd eaten for years was mediocre until I ate at Kai Zan, and all else paled in comparison. This small spot south of Logan Square is just far enough off the beaten path that you can get a same-day reservation to savor the melt-in-your-mouth sushi bites, most of which cost less than $9. Each is created and plated with precision akin to one of the city's much finer dining

To find out more about restaurants that have opened since this book went to press, check out the *Chicago Tribune*'s entertainment website (**www.chicago. metromix.com**), the websites for the monthly magazine *Chicago* (**www.**

chicagomag.com) and the weekly *Time Out Chicago* (**www.timeoutchicago. com**), and the local foodie website LTH Forum (**www.lthforum.com/bb/index. php**).

establishments, and served in an array of tiny dishes. In favorites like the Angry Crab—spicy crab wrapped with tuna—flavor and texture come together so intricately you don't want the chewing to end. The makimono rolls start out with the basics— spicy tuna and cucumber, salmon and avocado, and so forth—and a fun build-your-own option allows you to add those decadent extras, like tempura flakes or cream cheese, for $1 each. Make a reservation and nab a tiny booth made for two, or grab a seat at the sushi bar and watch the chefs work their magic. Service is good, but expect a disaffected air of cooler-than-thou to fall upon your table. Oh, and it's BYO, so what you save on booze you can spend on more plates.

2557 W. Chicago Ave. (at Rockwell St.). www.eatatkaizan.com. © **773/278-5776.** Small plates $4–$16. Mon–Tues, Thurs, Sun 5pm–10pm; Fri–Sat 5pm–11pm. Bus: 49, 50, 52, 66 or cab.

Fat Rice ★★★ MACANESE   You don't have to know anything about the cuisine of Macau to appreciate Fat Rice. The Macanese food at this tiny, exceedingly popular Logan Square restaurant has influences of India, Europe, and Asia, which make it exotic yet still familiar. The dishes here are meant to share, and they're large enough that if you come solo or with one other person, you won't be able to sample a lot. I suggest coming with at least two other people (but fewer than six—they restrict party size here), to sample the black-ink-colored squid fried rice (one of my all-time favorite dishes anywhere), the spice-filled vegetable curry, and, if you have at least four people, the namesake Fat Rice, a dish similar to paella and comedic in size, overflowing with rice, sausage, duck, prawns, clams, pickles, and sauces. The Logan Square location guarantees a hipster crowd with piercings and skinny jeans, who clearly have good enough taste to be here.

2957 W. Diversey Ave. (at Logan Blvd.) www.eatfatrice.com. © **773/661-9170.** Main courses $14–$42. Tues–Sat 5:30–10pm. Subway/El: Blue Line to Logan.

RESTAURANTS BY CUISINE

AMERICAN

Alinea ★★★ p. 96
Ann Sather ★ p. 92
Atwood Café ★★ p. 75
Au Cheval ★★ p. 107
Boka ★★★ p. 96
Chuck's: A Kerry Simon Kitchen ★★ p. 76
Ditka's ★ p. 91
Ed Debevic's ★ p. 83

The Gage ★★ p. 75
Girl and the Goat ★★★ p. 82
Harry Caray's Italian Steakhouse ★ p. 91
Honey Butter Fried Chicken ★ p. 102
Hot Chocolate ★ p. 106
Kuma's Corner ★★★ p. 103
Little Goat ★★★ p. 107
mk ★★★ p. 90
Next ★★ p. 97

Orange ★★ p. 93
Park Grill ★ p. 76
Parson's Chicken & Fish ★★ p. 102
Pastoral ★★ p. 81
Petterino's ★ p. 79
Piece ★★ p. 106
Portillo's ★ p. 96
The Publican ★ p. 82
Pump Room ★★ p. 84
Sable Kitchen & Bar ★★ p. 93
Sepia ★★ p. 83
Senza ★★★ p. 103
South Water Kitchen ★ p. 80

ASIAN/FUSION
Kai Zan ★★★ p. 107
Wow Bao ★ p. 81

BARBECUE
County Barbeque ★★ p. 101
Chicago q ★ p. 101
Twin Anchors ★★ p. 101

BREAKFAST/BRUNCH/BAKERY
Ann Sather ★ p. 92
Elly's Pancake House ★★ p. 93
House of Blues ★ p. 92
Lou Mitchell's ★ p. 92
Nookies ★ p. 93
Orange ★★ p. 93
River Valley Farmer's Table ★ p. 76
Sweet Cakes Bakery ★ p. 76
Wishbone ★★ p. 83
Yolk ★ p. 92

CAJUN & CREOLE
Heaven on Seven ★ p. 80

CHINESE
Hing Kee ★★ p. 79
Lao Sze Chuan ★★ p. 78
Phoenix ★ p. 78
Saint's Alp Teahouse ★ p. 78
Won Kow ★ p. 78

DINER
Au Cheval ★★ p. 107
The Chicago Diner ★ p. 107
Heaven on Seven ★ p. 80
Little Goat ★★★ p. 107

FAST FOOD/COUNTER SERVICE
Al's Beef ★ p. 104
Billy Goat Tavern ★ p. 87
Burke's Bacon Bar ★ p. 93
foodlife ★★ p. 95
Gold Coast Dogs ★ p. 104
Harold's Chicken Shack ★ p. 12
Macy's food courts ★★ p. 95
Mr. Beef ★ p. 104
Murphy's Red Hots ★ p. 104
Portillo's ★ p. 96
Urban Market ★ p. 95
The Wieners Circle ★ p. 104
Wow Bao ★ p. 81

FRENCH
Bistrot Margot ★★ p. 100
Everest ★★ p. 94

GERMAN
The Berghoff ★ p. 94

GREEK
Artopolis ★ p. 79
Athena ★★ p. 79
Greek Islands ★ p. 79
Parthenon ★ p. 79
Pegasus ★★ p. 79
Santorini ★ p. 79

INDIAN
India House ★★★ p. 92
Mysore Woodlands ★ p. 105
Uru Swati ★★ p. 105
Viceroy of India ★★ p. 105

IRISH
The Gage ★★ p. 75

ITALIAN
Bar Toma ★★ p. 87
Eataly ★★★ p. 95
Nico Osteria ★★ p. 86
Petterino's ★ p. 79
Spiaggia ★★★ p. 84
Topo Gigio ★★ p. 102

JAPANESE
Hot Woks Cool Sushi ★ p. 81
Sumi Robata ★★ p. 91

MACANESE
Fat Rice ★★★ p. 108

MEDITERRANEAN
The Purple Pig ★★★ p. 86

MEXICAN
Big Star ★★★ p. 106
Birrería Reyes de Ocotlan ★ p. 79
Frontera Grill ★★★ p. 88
Topolobampo ★★ p. 88
Xoco ★ p. 88
Nuevo Leon ★ p. 79

MIDDLE EASTERN
Old Jerusalem ★ p. 102

PIZZA
Bar Toma ★★ p. 87
Dimo's p. 89
Gino's East ★ p. 94
Giordano's ★ p. 88
La Madia ★★★ p. 95
Lou Malnati's Pizzeria ★★ p. 88
Pequod's Pizza ★★ p. 88
Piece ★★ p. 106
Pizano's ★ p. 88
Pizzeria Uno ★ p. 88
Spacca Nappoli p. 89

RUSSIAN
Russian Tea Time ★ p. 80

SANDWICHES
Burke's Bacon Bar ★ p. 91
Pastoral ★★ p. 81

SEAFOOD
Cape Cod Room ★ p. 94
GT Fish & Oyster ★★ p. 90
L20 ★★★ p. 100
New England Seafood Company ★★
   p. 104

SOUTHERN
Wishbone ★★ p. 83

SPANISH & TAPAS
Café Ba-Ba-Reeba! ★ p. 101
Mercat a la Planxa ★★ p. 75

STEAK
Chicago Cut ★★ p. 90
David Burke's Primehouse ★★ p. 91
Ditka's ★ p. 91
Gene & Georgetti ★ p. 90
Gibsons Bar & Steakhouse ★★ p. 90
Harry Caray's Italian Steakhouse ★
   p. 91
Morton's ★★ p. 90

SUSHI
Hot Wok Cool Sushi ★ p. 81
Kai Zan ★★★ p. 107

TEA
The Lobby ★, The Peninsula Hotel
   p. 86
Palm Court ★★, The Drake Hotel
   p. 86
Russian Tea Time ★ p. 80
Tiffin at The Langham ★★ p. 86

THAI
Tac Quick ★★★ p. 106

VEGETARIAN
The Chicago Diner ★ p. 107

VIETNAMESE
Nhu Lan Bakery ★★★ p. 105

EXPLORING CHICAGO

P undits and poets alike often refer to Chicago as the quintessential American city. Standing proud in America's heartland, the Windy City is packed with museums, art galleries, world-famous cultural institutions, historical homes, stunning architecture, parks, zoos, concerts, and theaters, but it's also brimming with beautiful, tree-lined streets, a stunning, beach-lined lake, and neighborhoods loaded with character. In a single day, you can view one of the largest collections of Impressionist works in the world at the Art Institute; pay a visit to the Field Museum to wave at Sue, the largest, most complete Tyrannosaurus Rex ever found; stand on the highest viewing deck in the U.S. at Willis Tower; and then sleep it all off in an iconic skyscraper hotel and wake up to choose another adventure. It's a city of contrasts, from the bustling Loop on a weekday morning to the serene Lake Michigan on summer afternoon.

One piece of advice: Take a deep breath and don't try and fit it all into one visit. First off, it's impossible. And besides that, to be a true Chicagoan is to appreciate the city's playfulness. If the weather's nice, that means packing a picnic and heading to the lake or Millennium Park. If it's dreary or cold, head to an art house movie theater or even a neighborhood tavern for a spell. Our cultural institutions have been here, in some cases, for more than 100 years. They'll still be here when you visit next.

In this chapter, I've done my best to highlight the standouts, from the major museums, like the Art Institute, to those lesser known oddball draws, like the International Museum of Surgical Science, along with historical homes, architectural icons, family-friendly destinations, and more.

For itineraries that hit on a number of these spots, see chapter 3, or assemble your own itinerary according to your interests and energy. The city's museums alone could keep you busy for at least a week. And come summertime, a stroll through picturesque Lincoln Park Zoo is the perfect way to spend an afternoon. The setting makes it worth visiting even if you don't have kids along. (Added bonus: It's free!)

From a traveler's perspective, visiting Chicago is especially hassle-free because the majority of the places you'll want to see are in or near downtown, making it easy to plan your day and get from place to place. Extensive public transportation makes it simple to reach almost every tourist destination, but some of your best memories of Chicago may come from simply strolling along the sidewalks. Chicago's neighborhoods, also easily reached by the El, each have their own distinct mood, and you'll have a more authentic experience if you don't limit yourself solely to the prime tourist spots.

IN & AROUND THE LOOP: THE ART INSTITUTE, THE WILLIS TOWER & GRANT PARK

The heart of the Loop is Chicago's business center, where you'll find some of the city's most famous early skyscrapers, the Chicago Board of Trade (the world's largest commodities, futures, and options exchange), and the Willis Tower (formerly the Sears Tower, which many Chicagoans still call it). If you're looking for an authentic big-city experience, wander the area on a weekday, when commuters are rushing to catch trains and businesspeople are hustling to get to work. The Loop is also home to one of the city's top museums, the Art Institute of Chicago, as well as a number of cultural institutions including the Symphony Center (home of the Chicago Symphony Orchestra), the Auditorium Theatre, the Civic Opera House, and the Goodman Theatre. On the eastern edge of the Loop in Grant Park, three popular museums are conveniently located within a quick stroll of each other on the landscaped Museum Campus. Busy Lake Shore Drive, which brings cars zipping past the Museum Campus, was actually rerouted years ago to make the area easier to navigate for pedestrians.

The Top Attractions in the Loop

Art Institute of Chicago ★★★ ART MUSEUM   If you're planning to visit the Art Institute of Chicago, I'll give you fair warning that you may want to schedule a nap in your afternoon. With more than 300,000 works in its permanent collection, spanning 5,000 years of creativity, the gargantuan and seemingly ever-expanding campus is the second-largest art museum in the country, at nearly 1 million square feet. You'll need to wind your way through the maze-like galleries and ancient displays of pottery and other items that people tiptoe past to get to the more popular halls.

The Art Institute is an encyclopedic art museum, which means there's a little bit of everything, from everywhere—Indian, Southeast Asian, and Himalayan art; Chinese, Japanese, and Korean art; African art; American art; American decorative art; pottery; bronzes; sculpture; installations; modern art; miniatures and more. That's a good thing if you're a true art lover interested in spending an entire day here. It's a challenge if you just want a quick walk through before packing other museums into a compact visit.

If you're short on time, the Art Institute's must-sees include its extensive collection of Impressionist and Post-Impressionist art, which is considered one of the finest in the world. Since 2009, the airy, light-filled Modern Wing has been showcasing the museum's extensive collection of 20th- and 21st-century art. And two of the museum's most beloved works are on display in the American art, pre-1950 gallery: *American Gothic* by Grant Wood and *Nighthawks* by Edward Hopper.

To help you navigate the endless halls, visit the Art Institute's website and download the new free app, which offers 50 different tours and makes the museum feel more manageable than getting lost on your own. A separate app guides you through Impressionist works, enriching your visit with detailed descriptions of the art and the artists who created it.

If you've visiting with kids, stop by the Ryan Education Center in the Modern Wing, where kids and teens can sit at a workstation and get hands-on lessons from artists. Children also love the Thorne Miniature Rooms, where dollhouse-like structures, all constructed to scale, showcase European and American homes, buildings, and

Although Chicago is a great city to explore on foot, Lake Shore Drive is no place for pedestrians or cyclists. People have been seriously injured and even killed attempting to dodge traffic on the busy road. Near Grant Park, cross only in crosswalks at Jackson Boulevard or Randolph, East Monroe, or East Balbo drives, or by using the underpass on the Museum Campus. North of the river, use underpasses or bridges at East Ohio Street, Chicago Avenue, Oak Street, and North Avenue.

interiors. The Art Institute offers a variety of lectures and workshops, so check their calendar to see what's happening during your visit.

A word of advice: The Art Institute can get incredibly crowded on weekends. If you can avoid visiting on a Saturday or Sunday, do so. Many people don't realize that the museum is, indeed, open on Monday, which makes it a great time to visit. Also, many visitors are unaware of the late Thursday hours, so consider visiting then, too, to avoid rush hour.

If you get hungry during your visit, stop by the museum's Caffe Moderno for soups, salads, and sandwiches, or visit Terzo Piano for a more elegant, sit-down meal. And save time for the enormous gift shop, which sells beautiful art, jewelry, accessories, books, and more. Allow at least 3 hours.

111 S. Michigan Ave. (at Adams St.). www.artic.edu. (✆ **312/443-3600.** Admission $23 adults, $17 seniors and students with ID, free for children 13 and under. Illinois residents can enter free Thurs evenings 5pm–8pm. Daily 10:30am–5pm (Thurs until 8pm). Closed Jan 1, Thanksgiving, and Christmas. Subway/El: Green, Brown, Purple, Pink, or Orange Line to Adams, or Red or Blue Line to Monroe.

Willis Tower Skydeck ★★★ Before the Ledge opened at the Skydeck at Willis Tower (formerly Sears Tower) a few years ago, people were faced with a difficult choice for the best views: Willis or Hancock? Now, there's really no competition. It takes a slightly wobbly 60-second elevator ride to get to the 103rd-floor Skydeck, which actually consists of a series of 4-foot-long, 1.5-inch-thick glass ledges that place you, hovering, 1,353 feet above the city. From your vantage point on the tallest observation deck in the U.S. and the second-tallest building in the Western Hemisphere, vehicles look like Matchbox cars and the skyline of Chicago looks miniature. That's the reason 1.5 million people visit this very spot every year, posing for a souvenir photo while floating above the Windy City. In addition to 50 miles of views on a clear day (you can see four states: Wisconsin, Michigan, Indiana, and Illinois), you'll also get to engage with fun, kid-friendly interactive displays that show you, comparatively, what other Chicago landmarks look like from 1,353 flights. Zoom above Wrigley Field and Millennium Park to see just how tall you really are, and measure yourself to determine how many of you, stacked, would reach the top of the tower. You'll also get a brief Chicago history lesson from a 9-minute movie, which talks about the building of the tower for Sears in 1970. When it opened in 1973, it was the tallest building in the world, although it's since been surpassed in height multiple times (the Burj Khalifa in Dubai holds the current record). Sears actually sold the building and moved out in the late '80s, but the name remained until 2009, when global insurance broker Willis Group Holdings, the building's largest tenant, acquired the naming rights and the

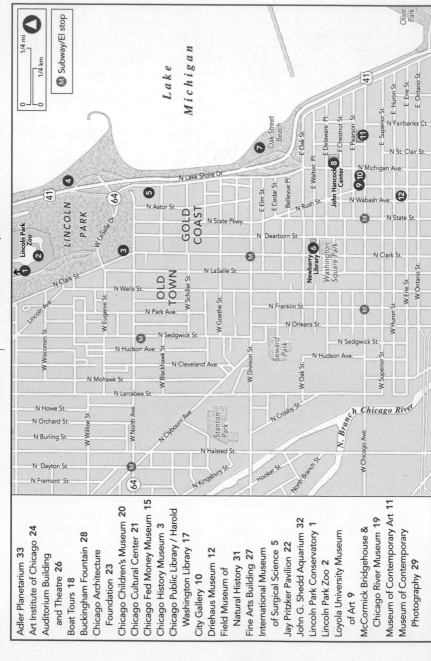

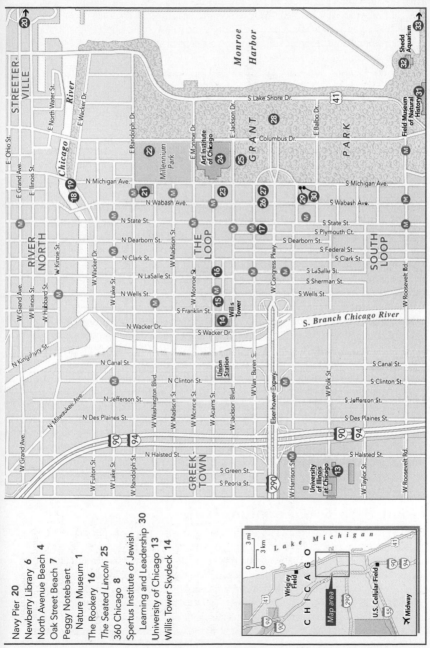

Navy Pier **20**
Newberry Library **6**
North Avenue Beach **4**
Oak Street Beach **7**
Peggy Notebaert
Nature Museum **1**
The Rookery **16**
The Seated Lincoln **25**
360 Chicago **8**
Spertus Institute of Jewish
Learning and Leadership **30**
University of Chicago **13**
Willis Tower Skydeck **14**

skyscraper became Willis Tower (many Chicagoans still insist on calling it Sears). In the winter, you can zip up to the top without much of a wait, but in the summer, budget a half hour to 45 minutes in line, or purchase the "Fast Pass" for $40 and skip the wait. The cafe on your way out sells Chicago-centric snacks—hot dogs and deep dish pizza—and if you want to take a piece of Willis home with you, pick up a Willis Tower Legos kit from the gift shop; it's the shop's most popular item. Allow 1½ to 2 hours, including wait time.

233 S. Wacker Dr. (enter on Jackson Blvd.). www.theskydeck.com. © **312/875-9696.** Admission $19 adults, $12 children 3–11, free for children 2 and under. Apr–Sept daily 9am–10pm; Oct–Mar daily 10am–8pm. Subway/El: Brown, Purple, Pink, or Orange Line to Quincy; Red or Blue Line to Jackson.

The Loop Sculpture Tour

Grand monuments, statues, and contemporary sculptures are scattered in parks throughout Chicago, but the concentration of public art within the Loop and nearby Grant Park is worth noting. The best known of these works are by 20th-century artists including Picasso, Chagall, Miró, Calder, Moore, and Oldenburg. (You can conduct a self-guided tour of the city's best public sculptures by following "The Loop Sculpture Tour" map, below.)

The most popular is the massive elliptical sculpture *Cloud Gate* (known as "The Bean" because it looks like a giant silver kidney bean) by British artist Anish Kapoor. The sculpture, in Millennium Park, was Kapoor's first public commission in the U.S., and you'll find crowds taking photos of it, along with their own reflection and that of the Chicago skyline, even in the middle of winter.

The single most famous sculpture in Chicago is **Pablo Picasso's** *Untitled,* located in Daley Plaza and constructed out of Cor-Ten steel, the same gracefully rusting material used on the exterior of the Daley Center behind it. Viewed from various perspectives, its enigmatic shape suggests a woman, bird, or dog; the artist himself never discussed its inspiration or meaning. Perhaps because it was the first monumental modern sculpture in Chicago's conservative business center, its installation in 1967 was met with hoots and heckles, but today "The Picasso" enjoys semiofficial status as the logo of modern Chicago. It is by far the city's most popular photo opportunity among visiting tourists. Year round at noon on weekdays, you'll likely find a dance troupe, musical group, or visual-arts exhibition here as part of the city's long-running "Under the Picasso" multicultural program (they perform indoors when it's cold or rainy). Call © **312/744-3116** or visit www.underthepicasso.us for event information. And if you have kids, they might enjoy joining the other little people who have transformed the slanted lower part of the sculpture into an urban slide.

Grant Park & Millennium Park

Thanks to architect Daniel Burnham and his coterie of visionary civic planners—who drafted the revolutionary 1909 Plan of Chicago—the city boasts a wide-open lakefront park system unrivaled by most major metropolises. Modeled after the gardens at Versailles, **Grant Park** ★★★ (www.chicagoparkdistrict.com; © **312/742-7529**) is Chicago's front yard, composed of giant lawns segmented by *allées* of trees, plantings, and paths, and pieced together by major roadways and a network of railroad tracks. Incredibly, the entire expanse was created from sandbars, landfill, and debris from the Great Chicago Fire; the original shoreline extended all the way to Michigan Avenue. A few museums are spread out inside the park, but most of the space is wide open (a legacy

The Loop Sculpture Tour

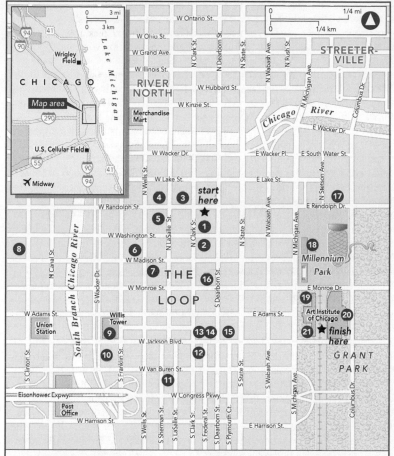

1 *Untitled ("The Picasso"),*
   Pablo Picasso (1967)
2 *Chicago,* Joan Miró (1981)
3 *Monument with Standing Beast,*
   Jean Dubuffet (1984)
4 *Freeform,* Richard Hunt (1993)
5 *Flight of Daedalus and Icarus,*
   Roger Brown (1990)
6 *Dawn Shadows,* Louise Nevelson (1983)
7 *Loomings* and *Knights and Squires,*
   Frank Stella
8 *Batcolumn,* Claes Oldenburg (1977)
9 *The Universe,* Alexander Calder (1974)
10 *Gem of the Lakes,* Raymond Kaskey (1990)
11 *San Marco II,* Ludovico de Luigi (1986)

12 *The Town-Ho's Story,* Frank Stella (1993)
13 *Ruins III,* Nita K. Sutherland (1978)
14 *Flamingo,* Alexander Calder (1974)
15 *Lines in Four Directions,* Sol Lewitt (1985)
16 *The Four Seasons,* Marc Chagall (1974)
17 *Untitled Sounding Sculpture,*
    Harry Bertoia (1975)
18 *Cloud Gate,* Anish Kapoor (2004)
19 *Large Interior Form,* Henry Moore (1983)
20 *Celebration of the 200th Anniversary
    of the Founding of the Republic,*
    Isamu Noguchi (1976)
21 *The Fountain of the Great Lakes,*
    Lorado Taft (1913)

of mail-order magnate Aaron Montgomery Ward's late-19th-century campaign to limit municipal buildings).

The northwest corner of Grant Park (bordered by Michigan Ave. and Randolph St.) is the site of **Millennium Park ★★★**, one of the city's grandest public works projects. Who cares that the park cost hundreds of millions more than it was supposed to, or the fact that it finally opened a full 4 years *after* the actual millennium? It's a winning combination of beautiful landscaping, elegant architecture (the classically inspired peristyle), and public entertainment spaces, including an ice rink and theater. The park's centerpiece is the dramatic Frank Gehry-designed **Jay Pritzker Pavilion,** featuring massive curved ribbons of steel, which sits over 4,000 fixed seats, with room for an additional 7,000 in the abutting Great Lawn. Throughout the summer, the park is a cultural oasis, and people from all over learn to shake their thang to live music on a 4,900 square foot outdoor dance floor during Chicago SummerDance dance lessons. Grant Park Symphony Orchestra and Chorus stages a popular series of free outdoor classical music concerts here most Wednesday through Sunday evenings in the summer, and the lawn fills with a younger crowd on Mondays for "Downtown Sound: New Music Mondays." For a schedule of concert and dance times and dates, visit www. millenniumpark.org or call © **312/742-1168.**

Two public artworks well worth checking out are the kidney bean–shaped sculpture *Cloud Gate* and the *Crown Fountain,* where children splash in the shallow water between giant faces projected on video screens. Free walking tours of the park are offered daily from May through October at 11:30am and 1pm, through the Chicago Cultural Center's Millennium Park **Greeter Tours ★★★** program. Meet at the Cultural Center's Visitor Center, 77 E. E. Randolph St. (© **312/945-4231;** www.chicago greeter.com). The first-come, first-served tours are limited to 10 people, and no reservations are required.

During the summer, a variety of music and food festivals take over central Grant Park. Annual events that draw big crowds include a blues music festival (in June) and a jazz festival (Labor Day). The **Taste of Chicago** (www.cityofchicago.org/special events; © **312/744-3315**) is purportedly the largest food festival in the world, with attendance estimated at more than 3 million people during the 5-day July hullabaloo. Local restaurants serve up more ribs, pizza, hot dogs, and beer than you'd ever want to see, let alone eat, and headliners take the stage nightly at the Petrillo Music Shell (although the music used to be free, today, tickets are $25). Admission to the festival itself is free (you buy tickets for food and drink) so if you go, get your elbows ready. The crowds are enormous and traffic is terrible throughout Taste. Many locals go once to this event and then make an effort to avoid it, preferring the many neighborhood street festivals that occur throughout the summer.

Head south to the lake via Congress Parkway, and you'll find **Buckingham Fountain ★★,** the baroque centerpiece of Grant Park, composed of pink Georgia marble and patterned after—but twice the size of—the *Latona Fountain* at Versailles, with adjoining esplanades beautified by rose gardens in season. From April through October, the fountain spurts columns of water up to 150 feet in the air every hour on the hour for 20 minutes, and starting at dusk, a whirl of colored lights and dramatic music amps up the drama. The last fountain show of the night starts at 10:35; concession areas and bathrooms are available on the plaza.

Sculptures and monuments stand throughout the park, including a sculpture of two Native Americans on horseback, *The Bowman and the Spearman* (at Congress Pkwy. and Michigan Ave.), which was installed in 1928 and has become the park's trademark.

Have You Seen the Puppet Bike?

If you come upon a small crowd of children and their parents gathering along Michigan Avenue or elsewhere downtown, you've likely found **The Puppet Bike** ★★ (www.puppetbike.com). Judging by their wide eyes and giggle output, to a kid, this stage-topped tricycle is one of the best forms of Chicago entertainment out there. The Puppet Bike is home to nine puppets, which peek out of the holes of the stage that's mounted on a bicycle and put on a show. It's all controlled by the cyclist, who's standing within the parked wooden box, working his (or her) magic. When the show's over, the performer hops back on the bike and commutes to the next happening corner. The show must go on! The Puppet Bike also travels throughout Chicago neighborhoods, but finding it is a stroke of luck: There's no published tracking system, although its Facebook page will sometimes share location clues.

Also here are likenesses of Copernicus, Columbus, and Lincoln, the latter by the great American sculptor Augustus Saint-Gaudens, located on Congress Parkway between Michigan Avenue and Columbus Drive. On the western edge of the park, at Adams Street, is the **Art Institute** (see above), and at the southern tip, in the area known as the Museum Campus, are the **Field Museum of Natural History** ★★★, the **Adler Planetarium** ★★, and the **Shedd Aquarium** ★★★ (see below for all three).

To get to Grant Park, take the subway/El, get off at any stop in the Loop along State or Wabash streets, and walk east.

Along South Michigan Avenue

The high-fashion boutiques may be clustered along the Magnificent Mile, but aesthetically, Chicago's grandest stretch of boulevard is still the stretch of Michigan Avenue that runs south of the river. Streaming from the Michigan Avenue Bridge all the way down to the Field Museum, it serves as the boundary between Grant Park on one side and the Loop on the other. A stroll along this boulevard in any season offers both visual and cultural treats. Particularly impressive is the great wall of buildings from Randolph Street south to Congress Parkway (beginning with the Chicago Cultural Center and terminating at the Auditorium Building) that architecture buffs refer to as the "Michigan Avenue Cliff."

The following attractions are listed from north to south.

McCormick Bridgehouse & Chicago River Museum ★ MUSEUM This small museum tells the water-rich history of Chicago, which today has more moveable bridges than any city. The rapid growth of Chicago wouldn't have been possible without its position on the river, where boats could haul goods in and out on a regular basis, solidifying the Midwestern city's instrumental role in farming, agriculture and other industries. In addition to a history lesson, museum visitors will get to explore five floors of a historic bridgehouse, and stand on an observation deck beneath the Michigan Avenue Bridge, where you can see the enormous gears that make it mobile. This bridge opens nearly 40 times a year, between April and November, to allow river traffic to pass through, and for $10 you can reserve a spot to see it happen. (Check the museum's website for upcoming dates). Today, as I write this, the Chicago River Walk, where the museum is located, isn't much to look at. There are few bars and restaurants, and many visitors have no idea it exists. The city is working on changing that, and is in the process of adding landscaping and businesses to the riverfront. It's still in the early phases, so all I can say now is I'll believe it when I see it.

376 N. Michigan Ave. (at the Chicago River). www.bridgehousemuseum.org. © **312/977-0227.** Admission $5, seniors and children 6–12 $4, free for children 5 and under. May–Oct Thurs–Mon 10am–5pm. Subway/El: Brown, Green, Orange, Pink, or Purple Line to Randolph, or Red Line to Lake.

Chicago Cultural Center ★ CULTURAL INSTITUTION

The Chicago Cultural Center was built in 1897 as the city's public library, and there's actually a funny story behind it. Following the Great Chicago Fire of 1871, a sympathetic Great Britain sent more than 8,000 books to the city to help rebuild its library. What our English compatriots didn't know was that Chicago never actually had a library to begin with. In 1872, Chicago's City Council passed an ordinance to build a library. Originally, that library was a water tank, used to store the books sent from England, and it moved from one location to another for the next 24 years, until the $2 million Central Library, now the Chicago Cultural Center, was complete, and crowned with an incredible centerpiece: the largest Tiffany dome in the world. Today, it's one of the most visited attractions in Chicago. People come to view its formal Beaux Arts exterior and a sumptuous interior of rare marble, fine hardwood, stained glass, and mosaics of Favrile glass, colored stone, and mother-of-pearl inlaid in white marble.

The Cultural Center also houses a Visitor Information Center, which makes it an ideal place to kick-start your visit. If you stop in to pick up tourist information and take a quick look around, your visit won't take longer than 15 minutes, but the Chicago Cultural Center also schedules an array of art exhibitions, concerts, theater and dance performances, films, lectures, and special events (most free), which might convince you to extend your time here. A long-standing tradition is the Dame Myra Hess classical concert series every Wednesday at 12:15pm in Preston Bradley Hall. On the first and third Friday of most months, toddler-friendly music and performance is offered at 11am, and a lunchtime dance party for Loop office workers begins at noon. Free guided architectural tours of the Chicago Cultural Center run at 1:15pm on Wednesday, Friday, and Saturday. A permanent exhibit in the Landmark Chicago Gallery on the first floor features images and artifacts gathered to tell the story of the city's architectural treasures and historic preservation in Chicago.

78 E. Washington St. www.chicagoculturalcenter.org. © **312/744-3316** for basic information. Free admission. Mon–Thurs 9am–7pm; Fri–Sat 9am–6pm; Sun 10am–6pm. Closed major holidays. Subway/El: Brown, Green, Orange, Pink, or Purple Line to Randolph; Blue or Red Line to Washington.

Chicago Architecture Foundation ★★ ARCHITECTURE

Architecture is one of Chicago's main claims to fame, and a quick swing through this non-profit foundation's visitor center, conveniently located across the street from the Art Institute, will help you understand why. Permanent exhibits include a scale model of downtown Chicago, profiles of the people and buildings that shaped the city's look, and a searchable database with information on many of Chicago's best-known skyscrapers. Two galleries also feature changing exhibits about ongoing Chicago design projects, so you can see firsthand how local architecture continues to evolve. "Architecture ambassadors" are on hand to provide information on the excellent tours run by the foundation, which are well worth experiencing, especially for visitors new to the city (see "Sightseeing Tours," p. 155), and free lunchtime lectures and evening programs delve into urban planning and design topics. If you're here with a LEGO-loving kid (ages 8 and up), or are a LEGO-lover yourself, stop by the new ArcelorMittal Design Studio (www.architecture.org/designstudio), a LEGO architecture studio, where you can spend the day designing your own project or people watching as others build their own mini skyscrapers. And don't forget to hit the gift shop, a Chicago shoppers' favorite that's filled with architecture-focused books, cool toys and arts and crafts, design-centric jewelry, and LEGO sets that create iconic Chicago buildings. Allow 30 minutes, more if you want to browse in the store or play with LEGOs.

224 S. Michigan Ave. www.architecture.org. © **312/922-3432.** Free admission. Exhibits daily 9:30am–5pm. Sun–Fri 9:30am–6pm, Sat 9am–6pm. Subway/El: Brown, Green, Purple, Pink, or Orange Line to Adams; Red or Blue Line to Jackson.

Fine Arts Building ★ ARCHITECTURE A worthwhile brief stop for architecture and history buffs, this 1885 building was originally a showroom for Studebaker carriages. In 1917 it became an arts center, with offices, shops, two theaters, and studios for musicians, artists, and writers. Its upper stories sheltered a number of well-known publications (the *Saturday Evening Post, Dial*) and provided offices for luminaries such as Frank Lloyd Wright, sculptor Lorado Taft, and L. Frank Baum, author of *The Wonderful Wizard of Oz*. Harriet Monroe published her magazine, *Poetry*, here, and introduced American readers to Carl Sandburg, T. S. Eliot, and Ezra Pound. Before the literary lions prowled its halls, the building served as a rallying base for suffragettes. Located throughout the building are a number of interesting studios and musical instrument shops. Take at least a quick walk through the marble-and-wood lobby (a half hour is enough), and ride the vintage elevator to the top floor to see the Art Nouveau–era murals and an impressive, ornate staircase. Although it's quiet during the week, stop in the second Friday of each month between 5pm and 9pm, when the building has more of a festive atmosphere, studios are open, and musicians are playing during "Second Fridays."

410 S. Michigan Ave. www.fineartsbuilding.com.© **312/566-9800.** Free admission. Mon–Fri 7am–10pm; Sat 7am–9pm; Sun 10am–5pm. Subway/El: Brown, Green, Purple, or Orange Line to Adams, or Red or Blue Line to Jackson.

Auditorium Theatre ★★ ARCHITECTURE/THEATER A truly grand theater with historic landmark status, the Auditorium gives visitors a taste of late-19th-century Chicago opulence. Designed and built in 1889 by Louis Sullivan and Dankmar Adler, the 4,000-seat Auditorium was a wonder of the world: The heaviest (110,000 tons) and most massive modern edifice on earth, the most fireproof building ever constructed, and the tallest building in Chicago. It was also the first large-scale building to be lit by electricity, and its theater was the first in the country to install air-conditioning. Originally the home of the Chicago Opera Company, Sullivan and Adler's masterpiece is defined by powerful arches lit by thousands of bulbs and features Sullivan's trademark ornamentation—in this case, elaborate golden stenciling and gold plaster medallions. It's equally renowned for otherworldly acoustics and unobstructed sightlines.

During World War II, the building sheltered GIs, and its theater stage was turned into a bowling alley. The theater reopened in 1967 following a $3-million renovation made possible through the fundraising efforts of the nonprofit Auditorium Theatre Council. Remnants of the building's halcyon days remain in the Michigan Avenue lobby, with its faux-marble ornamental columns, molded ceilings, mosaic floors, and Mexican onyx walls.

Because it's still a working theater and resident home to the Joffrey Ballet, it's not usually open to the public during the day; to make sure you'll get in, join a guided tour, offered on Monday at 10:30am and noon, and Thursday at 10:30am. Tours cost $10 per person, and you can purchase tickets 30 minutes prior at the Box Office, or via

ONLY IN CHICAGO: THE MASTER builders

Visitors from around the world flock to Chicago to see the groundbreaking work of three major architects: Louis Sullivan, Frank Lloyd Wright, and Ludwig Mies van der Rohe. They all lived and worked in the Windy City, leaving behind a legacy of innovative structures that still inspire architects today. Here's the rundown on each of them:

Louis Sullivan (1865–1924)

o **Quote:** "Form ever follows function."

o **Iconic Chicago building:** Auditorium Building, 430 S. Michigan Ave. (1887–1889).

o **Innovations:** Father of the Chicago school, Sullivan was perhaps at his most original in the creation of his intricate, nature-inspired ornamentation.

Frank Lloyd Wright (1867–1959)

o **Quote:** "Nature is my manifestation of God."

o **Iconic Chicago building:** Frederick C. Robie House, 5757 S. Woodlawn Ave., Hyde Park (1909).

o **Innovations:** While in Chicago, Wright developed the architecture of the Prairie School, a largely residential style combining natural materials, communication between interior and exterior spaces, and the sweeping horizontals of the Midwestern landscape. (For tours of Wright's home and studio, see "Exploring the 'Burbs," p. 146.)

Ludwig Mies van der Rohe (1886–1969)

o **Quote:** "Less is more."

o **Iconic Chicago building:** Chicago Federal Center, Dearborn Street between Adams Street and Jackson Boulevard (1959–74), former IBM Building/Langham Hotel, Wabash Avenue and Kinzie Street.

o **Innovations:** Mies van der Rohe brought the office tower of steel and glass to the United States. His stark facades don't immediately reveal his careful attention to details and materials.

Ticketmaster, www.ticketmaster.com/venue/57351. (To schedule a group tour for 20 or more, call ✆ **312/341-2357**.)

An insider tip: If you can't get in for a tour, you can still get a glimpse of the building's historic past. Around the corner on Michigan Avenue, walk in the entrance that now houses Roosevelt University, and you'll get a sense of the building's grand public spaces. Take the elevator to the school's 10th-floor library reading room to see the theater's original dining room, with a barrel-vaulted ceiling and marvelous views of Grant Park. Allow 1 hour for the guided tour.

50 E. Congress Pkwy. (at Wabash Ave.). www.auditoriumtheatre.org. ✆**312/341-2310.** For tickets to a performance at the Auditorium, call ✆ **800/982-2787.** Subway/El: Brown, Green, Orange, Pink, or Purple Line to Library/Van Buren; Red Line to Jackson, Blue Line to LaSalle St..

Museum of Contemporary Photography ★ ART MUSEUM This approachable, three-floor photography museum brings in cutting-edge exhibits from local, national, and international artists, thanks to its connection, literally and figuratively, to Chicago's Columbia College—not to be confused with New York's Columbia University—a small arts school with a stellar photography program. With intimate, navigable galleries on each of its floors, some showing videos, others digital photos and occasionally even Polaroids, the museum is an enjoyable and quick daytime jaunt

MUSEUM free DAYS

If you time your visit right, you can save yourself some admission fees—but not during prime tourist season. Although some major museums offer free admission at specific times year-round (check individual websites for details), others schedule free days only during the slowest times of the year, usually late fall and the dead of winter, and it's often only aimed at Illinois residents. Keep in mind that you will still have to pay for special exhibitions and films on free days. The good news? Some smaller museums never charge admission.

Illinois residents can take advantage of the following free days: Art Institute, Thursday evenings, 5–8pm; Museum of Contemporary Art, Tuesdays; Peggy Notebaert Nature Museum, Thursdays (suggested donation).

Free for All:
Sunday: Free entry to DuSable Museum of African American History; first Sunday of each month is free for kids 15 and under at Chicago Children's Museum at Navy Pier.

Tuesday: Free admission to the Loyola University Museum of Art and the International Museum of Surgical Science.

Wednesday: Tours are free at Glessner House Museum, Clarke House Museum and Charnley-Persky House.

Thursday: Free evening visits to Chicago Children's Museum at Navy Pier, 5–8pm.

Always Free: Chicago Botanic Garden, Chicago Cultural Center, Chicago Fed Money Museum, Garfield Park Conservatory, David and Alfred Smart Museum of Art, Jane Addams Hull-House Museum, Lincoln Park Conservatory, Lincoln Park Zoo, National Museum of Mexican Art, Museum of Contemporary Photography, Oriental Institute Museum (suggested donation) and Newberry Library, Spertus Institute for Jewish Learning and Leadership.

and a breath of playfully fresh air if you've spent the day at heavier museum brethren, like the Art Institute and Museum of Contemporary Art. Exhibits change about every three months here. Allow 30 minutes.

600 S. Michigan Ave. www.mocp.org. © **312/663-5554.** Free admission. Mon–Sat 10am–5pm (Thurs until 8pm); Sun noon–5pm. Subway/El: Red Line to Harrison.

Spertus Institute for Jewish Learning and Leadership ★ CULTURAL CENTER/ARCHITECTURE Although this educational center collects and preserves an array of historic Jewish ceremonial objects, textiles, and sculptures, I have to say I was most excited to come here for the architecture and the view. The stunning modern building, which resembles a chunky, enlarged prism, is among the most conversation-worthy in the city (that conversation often starts with, "What *is* that building?" and ends with "I don't know!"). The exterior glass, which reflects the sky and clouds, is made up of 726 pieces of glass in 556 different shapes and sizes. As you enter the light-filled atrium, you'll notice that the geometric wall in front of you mimics the same shapes of the exterior. Stop in the gift shop and the friendly staff will give you a self-guided tour pamphlet, which provides an overview of the Jewish-inspired art throughout the quiet, airy institute. Ultimately, it leads you up to the 8th floor Asher library, where the floor-to-ceiling glass windows look out on Grant Park and beautiful Lake Michigan. The building also includes a 400-seat theater for lectures, films, and performances. Allow 30 minutes.

610 S. Michigan Ave. www.spertus.edu. © **312/322-1700.** Free admission. Sun, Mon, Wed 10am–5pm, Thurs 10am–6pm, Fri 10am–3pm. Closed Saturday and for major national holidays and

Jewish religious holidays. Subway/El: Red Line to Harrison, Blue Line to Jackson, Brown Line to State/Van Buren, or Green Line to Adams.

Elsewhere in the Loop

Chicago Fed Money Museum ★ MUSEUM Walking into the Money Museum feels a little like walking onto a game show set (or so I imagine). Hidden within the stately Federal Reserve Bank of Chicago, here you'll see lots of flashy exhibits brimming with dollar signs, a new interactive display that lets you design your own money, a game that detects which bills are counterfeit, and three different displays showing off $1 million (one is a giant cube of $1 bills, the others are smaller and made of $20 and $100 bills). Policy wonks will likely get the most out of the money museum, but it's an informative (and free) stop if you're in the area. Plus, there's a brief movie about the Fed that doubles as a great resting spot on a hot or cold day. Expect to show your ID and plan on being scanned by security before entering. Allow a half hour.

230 S. LaSalle St. (at Quincy St.). www.chicagofed.org. ✆ **312/322-2400.** Free admission. Mon–Fri 8:30am–5pm. Closed federal holidays. Subway/El: Brown Line to Quincy/Wells or Red or Blue Line to Jackson.

Chicago Public Library/Harold Washington Library Center LIBRARY/ ARCHITECTURE A hulking building that looks like an Italian Renaissance fortress, Chicago's main public library is the largest in the world, and even has its own El stop. Named for the city's first and only African-American mayor, who died of a heart attack in 1987 at the beginning of his second term in office, the building fills an entire city block at State Street and Congress Parkway. The interior design has been criticized for feeling cold and impersonal (you have to go up a few floors before you even see any books), but the stunning, 52-foot glass-domed **Winter Garden** on the top floor, with its terrazzo and marble floors and giant glass dome, is worth a visit. On the second floor is another treasure: The vast Thomas Hughes Children's Library, which makes an excellent resting spot for families traveling with kids. The library also offers an interesting array of events and art exhibitions that are worth checking out. A 385-seat auditorium is the setting for a unique mix of dance and music performances, author talks, and children's programs, and visitors can stop by the third-floor Computer Commons, which has about 75 terminals available for public use, to check email. Allow a half hour.

400 S. State St. www.chipublib.org. ✆ **312/747-4300.** Free admission. Mon–Thurs 9am–9pm; Fri–Sat 9am–5pm; Sun 1–5pm. Closed major holidays. Subway/El: Red Line to Jackson; Brown, Pink, Orange, or Purple to Harold Washington Library.

The Rookery ★ ARCHITECTURE From the outside, this gloomy building gives no hint of the beauty within. Designed by master architect Daniel Burnham in the 1880s, it was one of Chicago's largest and most expensive office buildings when it was completed. (The name was a carryover from the old City Hall that previously occupied the site, a favorite of roosting birds.) In 1898, a young architect starting up an independent practice, Frank Lloyd Wright, rented an office here; a few years later, he was commissioned to update the building's interior. The resulting work is one of the loveliest commercial interiors in the city, including a two-story glass pavilion filled with natural light and gleaming white marble. Half-hour long tours cost $5 and are offered by the Frank Lloyd Wright Preservation Trust on Mondays, Tuesdays, Thursdays, and Fridays at noon; longer tours, including the on-site library, start at noon on Wednesdays and cost

If you're planning on visiting lots of Chicago museums, you should invest in a **CityPass,** a prepaid ticket that gets you into five of the biggest attractions in Chicago: the Art Institute or Adler Planetarium (you have to choose one or the other), Field Museum of Natural History, Shedd Aquarium, Museum of Science and Industry or 360 Chicago (choose one), and The Ledge at Willis Tower. The cost at press time was $94 for adults and $79 for children, which is about 50% cheaper than paying all the museums' individual admission fees. Plus, the City Pass lets you skip the line. You can buy a CityPass at any of the museums listed above or purchase one online before you get to town (www.citypass.com).

$10. The ShopWright store stocks a well-edited collection of books and decorative accessories. Allow 5 minutes for a quick look, up to 45 minutes if you stay for a tour. 209 S. LaSalle St. (at Adams St.). www.flwright.org/visit/rookery.html. © **312/994-4000.** Tours Mon–Friday at noon, $5-$10. Mon–Fri 9am–5pm. Closed federal holidays. Subway/El: Brown, Orange, Pink, or Purple Line to Quincy/Wells or Red or Blue Line to Jackson.

THE GRANT PARK MUSEUM CAMPUS'S BIG THREE

With terraced gardens and broad walkways, the Museum Campus at the southern end of Grant Park makes it easy for pedestrians to visit three of the city's most beloved institutions: the Field Museum of Natural History, Shedd Aquarium, and Adler Planetarium. To get to the Museum Campus from the Loop, walk south on Michigan Avenue to East Balbo Drive. Head east on Balbo, across Grant Park, then trek south along the lakeshore path to the museums (about a 15-min. walk). Or follow 11th Street east from South Michigan Avenue, which takes you across a walkway spanning the Metra train tracks. Cross Columbus Drive, and then pick up the path that will take you under Lake Shore Drive and into the Museum Campus. The CTA no. 146 bus will take you from downtown to all three of these attractions; it also stops at the Roosevelt El stop on the Red Line. Call © **312/836-7000** for the stop locations and schedule.

There are a few garages to choose from at the Museum Campus, accessible from Lake Shore Drive, and you can pre-pay online if you choose by going to soldierfield. clickandpark.com. Here's a breakdown of what you'll spend: The North Garage costs $19 for up to 4 hours, $22 for anything longer (capped at 12 hours); the Adler Lot costs $11 if you're there earlier than 9:30am, $19 between 9:30am and 4pm and $13 after 4pm; the East Museum garage is a flat $22 for up to 12 hours. Be aware that there is no public parking during Chicago Bears games in the fall; Soldier Field is next to the Museum Campus, and football fans get first dibs on all the surrounding parking spaces.

Adler Planetarium ★★ PLANETARIUM   The stately, 12-sided building may be historic (it was the first planetarium in the Western Hemisphere), but thanks to cutting-edge technology, the attractions here will hold the attention of even the most jaded video game addict.

Since 2011, the most technologically advanced digital projection center in the world has wowed visitors at the **Grainger Sky Theater,** taking them on an astral journey to see nebula, supernova, and sky views. This is the one spot you absolutely can't miss at Adler. The theater takes 3D films to new levels—there are times you'll actually feel

Dedicating just a few minutes to the websites of museums and other attractions before you visit can really enhance your trip. At the **Field Museum of Natural History** website (www.fieldmuseum.org), download the mobile app that helps you follow suggested routes or customize your own tour, complete with behind-the-scenes insights, videos, and trivia from museum scientists. **The Art Institute Tours App** (available through www. artic.edu/visit/maps-guides-and-apps) will guide you, step-by-step, on 50 different tours. Choose a guide by collections, amount of time you have, and what your goal is (whether to wow out-of-town guests or meander at your own pace). And download the **Museum of Contemporary Art's** app (www.mca. com.au/apps) to see interviews with artists and curators who explain the art you're looking at and why it matters.

like you're floating, it's so immersive. Two other 3D theaters on site, Delfiniti Space Theater and Samuel C. Johnson Family Star Theater, also play movies throughout the day.

The planetarium's exhibition galleries feature a variety of displays and interactive activities. If you're going to see only one exhibit, check out *Shoot for the Moon,* an interactive lunar exploration station. (It also showcases the personal collection of astronaut Jim Lovell, captain of the infamous Apollo 13 mission, who now lives in the Chicago suburbs.) If you've got little ones in tow, your first stop should be *Planet Explorers,* a series of immersive play stations where kids can experience a simulated rocket launch and crawl through the caves and tunnels of a mysterious "Planet X."

Café Galileo's serves soups and sandwiches and has gorgeous views of the lakefront and skyline. On the third Thursday evening of the month, the museum stays open until 10pm for **Adler After Dark**, and visitors 21 and older can listen to music, sip cocktails, and view dramatic close-ups of the moon, the planets, and distant galaxies through a closed-circuit monitor connected to the planetarium's Doane Observatory telescope.

Allow 2 hours, more if you want to see more than one show.

1300 S. Lake Shore Dr. www.adlerplanetarium.org. © **312/922-STAR** [7827]. Admission $22 adults (includes show), $12 adults general; $20 seniors/students (includes show), $10 seniors/student general; $18 children 3–11 (includes show) $8 children general; free for children 2 and under. Memorial Day to Labor Day daily 9:30am–6pm; early Sept to late May Mon–Fri 9:30am–4pm; Sat–Sun 9:30am–4:30pm; 3rd Thurs of every month until 10pm. Bus: 146 year round, 130 May through Labor Day.

Field Museum of Natural History ★★★ MUSEUM   The Art Institute gets a lot of love when it comes to Chicago Museums, but I've always had a soft spot for the Field Museum of Natural History. The museum, which was named for one of Chicago's most famous early residents and the museum's first major donor, Marshall Field, is one of the largest natural history museums in the world, filling 9 acres with 25 million artifacts and specimens, and there's a surprise around every corner—beginning with one of Chicago's most famous residents: Sue, the biggest and most complete Tyrannosaurus rex fossil in the world. Don't expect to see it all in one visit. Instead, hit the highlights, such as the dioramas of the man-eating **Lions of Tsavo,** two cats that killed an estimated 35 people in Kenya. In **Underground Adventure,** you'll see the world through the eyes of a bug, as your surroundings—worms, crayfish, spiders—

If you want to taste food at a festival in Chicago, skip the crazy-crowded Taste of Chicago and go to one of the city's more than 400 neighborhood festivals that happen throughout the year but especially during the summer. Every summer, the neighborhoods come alive, celebrating just about any event or food you can think of: Ribfest (one in Uptown, one on Lincoln Ave.), Oysterfest in Roscoe Village, German-American Fest in Lincoln Square, Midsommarfest in Andersonville, Cinco de Mayo in Little Village, and so many more. Locals love these celebrations, because it gives them a chance to sample their neighborhood restaurants, meet their neighbors, and listen to rollicking live entertainment. A visit to one of these celebrations is a visit to the real Chicago—you won't find many tourists here. Some festivals are free, while others ask for a nominal donation (they make it sound as though it's mandatory, but don't feel pressure to give unless you want to). Visit www.chicago.metro mix.com to see what's going on during your visit.

dwarf you, measuring in at 100 times their normal size. Peer into an ancient tomb, filled with more than 20 mummies, in **Inside Ancient Egypt,** and visit the many science labs throughout the museum, such as the **DNA Discovery Center,** where scientists are hard at work studying DNA, and the **Fossil Preparation Laboratory,** where preparators toil away, readying the latest fossil findings for further research. If you're here with kids 7 or younger, take a detour to the **Crown Family Playlab,** where they can dress up like animals, pound on drums, and uncover fossils (Thurs–Mon 10am–4pm). Every Friday from 10am to noon, scientists are on hand at the east entrance of Stanley Field Hall to chat with kids about their careers.

Too much to choose from? The museum offers a highlights tour daily at 11am and at 2pm Monday through Friday and 1pm Saturday. And before you visit, be sure and visit the Field Museum's website for behind-the-scenes info. The museum recently began producing apps that take you on a historical adventure, guiding you through the latest exhibits. For a snack break, head to The Field Bistro and Explorer Café, which offer globally influenced sandwiches, soups, salads, and burgers.

1400 S. Lake Shore Dr. (at Roosevelt Rd.). www.fieldmuseum.org. © **312/922-9410.** Admission $18 adults, $15 seniors and students with ID, $13 children 3–11, free for children 2 and under. Extra fees apply for special exhibits. Daily 9am–5pm. Closed Christmas. Bus: 146.

John G. Shedd Aquarium ★★★ AQUARIUM The Shedd is one of the world's largest indoor aquariums and houses thousands of river, lake, and sea denizens in standard aquarium tanks and elaborate new habitats within its octagon-shaped marble building. Truly, the only problem with the Shedd is its relatively steep admission price. You can keep your costs down by buying "Aquarium Only" tickets; the tradeoff is that you'll miss some of the most stunning exhibits. A CityPass (see "Museums for Less," box, p. 15) can save you money if you visit enough of the other included attractions.

The first thing you'll see as you enter is the **Caribbean Coral Reef.** This 90,000-gallon circular tank occupies the Beaux Arts–style central rotunda, entertaining spectators who press up against the glass to ogle divers feeding nurse sharks, barracudas, stingrays, and a hawksbill sea turtle. A roving camera connected to video monitors on the tank's periphery gives visitors close-ups of the animals inside, but I'd

HISTORIC HOMES OF prairie avenue

Prairie Avenue, south of the Loop, was the city's first "Millionaire's Row," and its most famous address is **Glessner House Museum** ★ (1800 S. Prairie Ave.; www. glessnerhouse.org; ✆ **312/326-1480**). A must-see for anyone interested in architectural history, and the only surviving Chicago building designed by Boston architect Henry Hobson Richardson, the 1886 structure represented a dramatic shift from traditional Victorian architecture and inspired a young Frank Lloyd Wright.

The imposing granite exterior gives the home a forbidding air. So much so that railway magnate George Pullman, who lived nearby, complained, "I do not know what I have ever done to have that thing staring me in the face every time I go out my door." But step inside, and the home turns out to be a welcoming, cozy retreat, filled with Arts and Crafts furnishings. Visits are by guided tour only; tours begin at 1 and 3pm Wednesday through Sunday (except major holidays) on a first-come, first-served basis (advance reservations are taken only for groups of 10 or more). Tours cost $10 for adults, $9 for students and seniors, and $6 for children 5 to 12.

While you're in the area, book a back-to-back tour at the neighboring home, **Clarke House Museum,** which is the oldest in the city, built in 1836. The owner, Henry Brown Clarke, moved to Chicago in 1835, when it was still a new settlement, and built the house in Greek Revival Style the next year. The Clarke family home survived the Great Chicago Fire and has moved twice to make it to its Prairie Avenue address. Tours are given at noon and 2pm. If you can, stop by on a Wednesday, when tours are free. Otherwise, combination tickets are $15 for adults, $12 for seniors and students, $8 for children 5 to 12, and free for kids under 5; stand-alone tickets are $10 for adults, $9 for seniors and students, $6 for children 5 to 12, and free for children under 5.

To get to Prairie Avenue, catch the no. 1, 3, or 4 bus from Michigan Avenue. Get off at 18th Street and walk two blocks east.

recommend sticking around to catch one of the daily feedings, when a diver swims around the tank and (thanks to a microphone) talks about the species and their eating habits.

The exhibits surrounding the Caribbean coral reef recreate marine habitats around the world. The best is **Amazon Rising: Seasons of the River,** a rendering of the Amazon basin that showcases frogs and other South American species, as well as fish (the sharp-toothed piranhas are pretty cool).

You'll pay extra to see the other Shedd highlights, but they're quite impressive, so I'd suggest shelling out for them if you plan to spend more than an hour here. The **Abbott Oceanarium,** with a wall of windows revealing the lake outside, replicates a Pacific Northwest coastal environment and creates the illusion of one uninterrupted expanse of sea. On a fixed performance schedule in a large pool flanked by an amphitheater, a crew of trainers puts dolphins through their paces of leaping dives, breaches, and tail walking (there's an extra charge of $2 per person to see the show). If you're visiting during a summer weekend, consider buying tickets in advance to make sure you can catch a show that day.

Wild Reef—Sharks at Shedd is a series of 26 connected habitats that house a Philippine coral reef patrolled by sharks and other predators. The floor-to-ceiling windows bring the toothy swimmers up close and personal (they even swim over your head at certain spots). And if you're here with kids, you'll want to stop by the **Polar Play Zone,** where little ones can pet a starfish, try on a penguin suit, or get a good look at the real thing—the Play Zone is home to a dozen rockhopper penguins (the newest member of the family was born in the spring of 2014).

If you want a quality sit-down meal in a restaurant with a spectacular view of Lake Michigan, check out the kid-friendly Soundings. There's also a food court.

Allow 2 to 3 hours.

1200 S. Lake Shore Dr. www.sheddaquarium.org. ℭ **312/939-2438.** Total Experience Pass (includes all shows/exhibits) $35 adults, $26 children 3–11; Shedd Pass Plus includes regular exhibits plus one show) $36 adults, $27 children 3–11; Shed Pass (includes regular exhibits) $29 adult, $20 children 3–11); Aquarium only, $8 adults, $6 children; free for children 2 and under. Memorial Day to Labor Day daily 9am–6pm; early Sept to late May Mon–Fri 9am–5pm, Sat–Sun 9am–6pm. Bus: 146.

NORTH OF THE LOOP: THE MAGNIFICENT MILE & BEYOND

360 Chicago (formerly The Hancock Observatory) ★★ ARCHITEC-TURE/VIEWS   The Hancock may not be quite as famous as the Willis (nee Sears) Tower, but it's more central to the Loop and River North than its taller brethren. A high-speed elevator carries passengers to the observatory in 39 seconds, and on a clear day, you can see portions of the three states surrounding this corner of Illinois (Michigan, Indiana, and Wisconsin), for a radius of 40 to 50 miles. The view up the North Side is particularly dramatic, stretching from nearby Oak Street and North Avenue beaches, along the green strip of Lincoln Park, to the suburbs that trace the shoreline beyond. During your visit, you're given a handheld PDA that delivers a **"Sky Tour,"** using audio and video to highlight features of interest across the skyline (kids get their own version). The Skywalk open-air viewing deck, surrounded on all sides by a safety screen, allows visitors to feel the rush of the wind at 1,000 feet. In spring of 2014, the Hancock launched its latest feature, **Tilt,** a glass and steel enclosed platform that actually tilts forward, while holding eight people, to give better views of the surrounding city. It's enough to get your heart rate going, that's for sure, and does so without feeling gimmicky or taking away from the experience (like, say, a roller coaster would). There's also a cafe with an adjoining kids' play area if you want to linger over a cappuccino and snack. Allow 1 hour.

Tip: "Big John," as some locals call the building, also has a restaurant, the **Signature Room at the 95th,** and a bar, the Signature Lounge, on the 95th floor, which is one floor above the observation deck. To get there, you don't have to pay for the elevator ride up. You simply pay for a soda or beverage to sip while taking in the view in a more relaxed fashion.

94th floor, John Hancock Center, 875 N. Michigan Ave. (enter on Delaware St.). www.360chicago.com. ℭ **888/875-8439** or 312/751-3681. Admission $18 adults (12 and up), $12 children 3–11, free for children 2 and under. Daily 9am–11pm. Subway/El: Red Line to Chicago.

Loyola University Museum of Art ★ MUSEUM   Tucked away in the downtown Loyola University campus, right next door to Bottega Veneta, oddly enough, is the Loyola University Museum of Art. Although the museum's website describes it as "dedicated to the exploration of the spiritual in art," its revolving exhibits aren't necessarily tied to such ethereal topics. When I visited, there was a delightful display exploring the rather morbid illustrations of artist Edward Gorey. Other past exhibits have

A river RUNS THROUGH IT

The **Chicago River** remains one of the most visible of the city's major physical features. More bridges span it within the city limits (52 at last count) than any other city in the world. An almost-mystical moment occurs downtown when all the bridges spanning the main and south branches—connecting the Loop to both the Near West Side and the Near North Side—are raised, allowing for the passage of some ship, barge, or contingent of high-masted sailboats. The Chicago River has long outlived the critical commercial function that it once performed. Most of the remaining millworks that occupy its banks no longer depend on the river alone for the transport of their materials, raw and finished.

The river's main function today is to serve as a fluvial conduit for sewage, which, owing to an engineering feat that reversed its flow inland in 1900, no longer pollutes the waters of Lake Michigan. Recently, Chicagoans have begun to discover other roles for the river, including water cruises, park areas, cafes, public art installations, and a riverside bike path that connects to the lakefront route near Wacker Drive. Actually, today's developers aren't the first to wonder why the river couldn't be Chicago's Seine. A look at the early-20th-century Beaux Arts balustrades lining the river along Wacker Drive, complete with comfortably spaced benches and Parisian-style bridge houses, shows that Chicago architect and urban planner Daniel Burnham knew full well what a treasure the city had.

been similarly unexpected, including photos that kids took illustrating life in a Nairobi slum, along with a number of themes connected to Christianity, Buddhism, and other belief systems. Because of the wide range of topics, what's showing on your visit could be hit or miss, so I suggest you check the site for upcoming exhibits to see if one piques your interest. The gallery's third floor houses one of the Midwest's largest collections of Renaissance, medieval, and baroque art, all of it with religious overtones.

820 N. Michigan Ave. (at Pearson St.). www.luc.edu/luma. ℂ **312/915-7600.** Admission $8 adults; $6 seniors; Tuesdays free. Subway/El: Red Line to Chicago.

Museum of Contemporary Art ★ MUSEUM   The MCA recently scored a major art coup by booking the David Bowie exhibition (Sept 2014–Jan 2015). It's the only museum in America to land the exhibit, which sold out handily when it was in London, and that speaks well to the art muscle of Chicago's contemporary museum—one of the nation's largest of its genre. Despite that ranking, MCA is a spot that's actually quite easy to breeze through, with three floors of exhibition space dedicated to sculpture, video, painting, and film created since 1945. Although the museum holds a permanent collection of more than 2,500 objects, it frequently rotates them, showcasing a small percentage at a time, while also bringing in traveling exhibits and, bonus, showcasing Chicago artists. If you're not a huge fan of modern art, I highly recommend taking a podcast audio tour for a primer on the latest works, or join in one of the free tours (Tues at 1, 2, and 6pm; Wed–Fri at 1pm; Sat–Sun at noon, 1, 2, and 3pm), which take less than 45 minutes. The tours are quite helpful to those of us, including myself, who leave some art museums feeling like the only kid in the room who didn't get the joke.

The MCA is also home to a 300-seat theater, and is a great spot to take in performances and art house films. Puck's at the MCA is a far better than average museum

The impressive Gothic **Tribune Tower,** just north of the Chicago River on the east side of Michigan Avenue, is home to the *Chicago Tribune* newspaper. It's also notable for an array of architectural fragments jutting out from the exterior of the first floor. The newspaper's notoriously despotic publisher, Robert R. McCormick, started the collection shortly after the building's completion in 1925, gathering pieces during his world travels. *Tribune* correspondents then began supplying building fragments that they acquired on assignment. Each one now bears the name of the structure and the country whence it came. There are nearly 150 pieces in all, including chunks and shards from the Great Wall of China; the Taj Mahal; the White House; the Arc de Triomphe; the Berlin Wall; the Roman Colosseum; London's Houses of Parliament; the Great Pyramid of Cheops in Giza, Egypt; and the original tomb of Abraham Lincoln in Springfield, Illinois.

restaurant, and it looks over a lovely sculpture garden. The museum springs to life the first Friday of every month, when music fills the halls and patrons sip cocktails while perusing the latest art. Allow 1 to 2 hours.

220 E. Chicago Ave. (1 block east of Michigan Ave.). www.mcachicago.org. ℂ **312/280-2660.** Admission $12 adults, $7 seniors and students with ID, free for children 12 and under. Closed Jan 1, Thanksgiving, and Christmas. Subway/El: Red Line to Chicago.

Navy Pier ★ ATTRACTION   Built during World War I, this 3,000-foot-long pier served as a Navy training center for pilots during World War II. The military aura is long gone, and Navy Pier now thrives as a major tourist attraction, drawing more than 8 million visitors a year to the carnival rides, large food court, T-shirt shops, and boat rides. Whether or not you enjoy Navy Pier depends on your tolerance for crowds—especially in the summer. If you shy away from chain restaurants, high prices, and thick throngs of tourists, I recommend you skip Navy Pier and head to any of Chicago's other beaches for beautiful lake and city views. Speaking from a local's point of view, unless we're heading to the Chicago Children's Museum or Chicago Shakespeare Theatre, most of us make a point of avoiding Navy Pier.

But if you do go to the pier, here's what you'll see: Midway down the pier are the **Crystal Gardens,** a lovely, glass-enclosed atrium with 70 full-size palm trees, dancing fountains, and various flora; a carousel and kiddie carnival rides; and a 15-story Ferris wheel, a replica of the original that made its debut at Chicago's 1893 World's Fair. The pier is also home to the **Chicago Children's Museum** ★★★ (p. 154), a **3D IMAX theater** (ℂ 312/595-5629), and the **Chicago Shakespeare Theatre** (p. 198). The shops tend to be bland and touristy, but you won't go hungry. **Harry Caray's Tavern, Billy Goat Tavern,** and **Landshark Beer Garden** are your best bets for casual local options (otherwise, you're looking at Jimmy Buffet's Margaritaville and Bubba Gump Shrimp Co.), or for something more upscale, make a reservation at the white-tablecloth seafood restaurant **Riva** (www.rivanavypier.com; ℂ 312/644-7482). There's also a food court with hot dogs, pretzels, pizza, and, most importantly, Garrett Popcorn (p. 172). Summer is one long party at the pier, with fireworks on Wednesday and Saturday evenings.

The quietest spot on Navy Pier is the **Smith Museum of Stained Glass Windows.** It's a bit dull for those of us who aren't into decorative arts, but colored-glass lovers

Free Fireworks!

Yes, Navy Pier can be chaotic, crowded, and loud, but come summer, it's also a prime gathering spot for visitors from around the world. Memorial Day through Labor Day, the pier sponsors twice-weekly **fireworks** shows, where you can watch spectacular light displays reflected in the water of Lake Michigan below. It's a great way to appreciate the city at night (along with a few thousand of your fellow travelers). If you hate crowds, head for any of the city's beaches, where you can still nab a front-row view without the human traffic. The shows start at 9:30pm on Wednesday and 10:15pm on Saturday.

will enjoy the 150 windows on display, which include works by Louis Comfort Tiffany and John LaFarge. Although well trafficked, the dark gallery is a nice, cool reprieve on a hot summer day—plus it's free.

When the noise and commercialism get overwhelming, take the half-mile stroll to the end of the pier, where you can enjoy the wind, the waves, and the city view, which is the real delight of a place like this. Or unwind in **Olive Park,** a small sylvan haven with a sliver of beach just north of Navy Pier.

You'll find more than half a dozen sailing vessels moored at the south dock, including a couple of dinner-cruise ships, the pristine white-masted tall ship *Windy,* and the 70-foot speedboats *Seadog I, II,* and *III.* In the summer months, water taxis speed between Navy Pier and other Chicago sights. For more specifics on sightseeing and dinner cruises, see "Setting Sail on a Lake or River Cruise," p. 156. Allow 1 hour.

600 E. Grand Ave. (at Lake Michigan). www.navypier.com. © **800/595-PIER** [7437], or 312/595-PIER [7437]. Free admission. Summer Sun–Thurs 10am–10pm, Fri–Sat 10am–midnight; fall–spring Sun–Thurs 10am–8pm, Fri–Sat 10am–10pm; winter Mon–Thurs 10am–8pm, Fri–Sat 10am–10pm, Sun 10am–7pm. Closed Thanksgiving and Christmas. Parking: $21/day Mon–Thurs; $25/day Fri–Sun (lots fill quickly). Bus: 29, 65, 66, 124.

Newberry Library ★ LIBRARY   The Newberry Library, housed in a stately five-story granite building, is a bibliophile's dream. Established in 1887, thanks to a bequest by Chicago merchant and financier Walter Loomis Newberry, the noncirculating research library contains many rare books and manuscripts (such as Shakespeare's first folio and Jefferson's copy of *The Federalist Papers*). The library is also a major destination for genealogists digging at their roots, with holdings that are free to the public (over the age of 16 with a photo ID). The collections include more than 1.5 million volumes and 75,000 maps, many of which are on display during an ongoing series of public exhibitions. For an overview, take a free 1-hour tour Thursday at 3pm or Saturday at 10:30am. The Newberry operates a fine bookstore and also sponsors a series of concerts (including those by its resident early music ensemble, the Newberry Consort), lectures, and children's story hours throughout the year. One popular annual event is the **Bughouse Square debates.** Held across the street in Washington Square Park in late July, the debates recreate the fiery soapbox orations of the left-wing agitators in the 1930s and 1940s. Allow a half hour.

60 W. Walton St. (at Dearborn Pkwy.). www.newberry.org. © **312/943-9090,** or 312/255-3700 for programs. Reading room Tues–Fri 9am–5pm; Sat 9am–1pm. Exhibit gallery Mon, Fri, and Sat 8:15am–5pm; Tues–Thurs 8:15am–7:30pm. Closed Sundays and major holidays. Subway/El: Red or Brown Line to Chicago.

WHAT TO SEE & DO IN LINCOLN PARK

Lincoln Park is the city's largest park, and certainly one of the longest. Straight and narrow, the park begins at North Avenue and follows the shoreline of Lake Michigan north for several miles. Within its 1,200 acres are a world-class zoo; half a dozen beaches; a botanical conservatory; two excellent museums; a golf course; and the meadows, formal gardens, sporting fields, and tennis courts typical of urban parks.

The park, named after Abraham Lincoln, is home to the **statue of the standing Abraham Lincoln** (just north of the North Ave. and State St. intersection), one of the city's two Lincoln statues by Augustus Saint-Gaudens (the seated Lincoln is in Grant Park). Saint-Gaudens also designed the *Bates Fountain* near the conservatory.

Chicago History Museum ★★ HISTORY MUSEUM What do the atomic bomb, birth control pill, and Lincoln Logs have in common? They were developed in Chicago, which you'll learn about when you visit here. The museum's name is far more straightforward and boring than what's within, so if you're not a history buff, don't let it scare you off. This place is pretty great. On any given day, a visit here could reveal dramatic photo exhibits, luxurious fashion explorations, stories from the lives and times of railroad workers, and more. Year-round, the museum, which sits on the southwest boundary of Lincoln Park, does a great job of capturing just how fascinating the history of Chicago is, rife with gangsters and race riots; riddled with tragedies and fire; rich with inventions and innovations. Although the bulk of the museum is best suited for older kids and adults, a number of interactive exhibits, including a hands-on El train from the late 1800s, will keep little ones entertained, at least for a little while. Programming in recent years has shown a particularly fun edge, drawing in younger patrons, including historic bar crawls, same-sex wedding events, energetic history tours, and family trolley tours. Check the website to see what the museum has in store during your visit. The museum is also home to a small gift shop and cafe. Allow 1 to 2 hours.

1601 N. Clark St. (at North Ave.). www.chicagohistory.org. ℭ **312/642-4600.** Admission $14 adults, $12 seniors and students, free for children 12 and under. Mon–Sat 9:30am–4:30pm; Sun noon–5pm. Subway/El: Brown Line to Sedgwick or Red Line to Clark/Division.

Lincoln Park Conservatory ★ CONSERVATORY Just beyond the Lincoln Park Zoo's northeast border is a lovely botanical garden housed in a soaring glass-domed structure. Inside are four great halls filled with thousands of plants. If you're visiting Chicago in the wintertime, this lush haven of greenery provides a welcome respite from the snow and ice outside. Built between 1890 and 1895, this historic house was created to nurture the plants and flowers used in Chicago parks. The Palm House features giant palms and rubber trees (including a 50-foot fiddle-leaf rubber tree dating back to 1891); the Fern House nurtures plants that grow close to the forest floor; and the Orchid House is home to hundreds of colorful orchids, as well as tropical carnivorous plants. The fourth environment is the Show House, where seasonal flower shows take place.

Even better than the plants inside, however, might be what lies outside the front doors. The expansive lawn, with its French garden and lovely fountain on the conservatory's south side, is one of the best places in town for an informal picnic (especially nice if you're visiting the zoo and want to avoid the congestion at its food concession venues).

The Lincoln Park Conservatory has a sister facility on the city's West Side, in Garfield Park, that is even more impressive. The two-acre **Garfield Park Conservatory** (300 N. Central Park Ave.; www.garfield-conservatory.org; ℂ **312/746-5100**), designed by the great landscape architect Jens Jensen in 1907, is one of the largest gardens under glass in the world. Unfortunately, it's surrounded by a pretty rough neighborhood with a high crime rate, so it's best to visit if you have a car, rather than using public transportation to get there. It's open 365 days a year from 9am to 5pm, and on Wednesday until 8pm.

Allow a half hour for the Lincoln Park Conservatory or 1 to 2 hours for Garfield Park.

2391 N. Stockton Dr. (at Fullerton Ave.). www.chicagoparkdistrict.com. ℂ **312/742-7736.** Free admission. Daily 9am–5pm. Bus: 22, 36, 151, or 156.

Lincoln Park Zoo ★★★ ZOO   One of the city's treasures, this family-friendly attraction is not only open every day of the year, but it's also free. Even if you don't have time for a complete tour of the various habitats—there are 49 acres, after all—it's worth at least a quick stop during a stroll through Lincoln Park. The term *zoological gardens* truly fits here: Landmark Georgian Revival brick buildings and modern structures sit among gently rolling pathways, verdant lawns, and a kaleidoscopic profusion of flower gardens. The late Marlon Perkins, legendary host of the *Mutual of Omaha's Wild Kingdom* TV series, got his start here as the zoo's director and filmed a pioneering TV show called *Zoo Parade* (*Wild Kingdom*'s predecessor) in the basement of the old Reptile House.

Don't miss the **Regenstein African Journey,** a series of linked indoor and outdoor habitats home to giraffes, rhinos, and other large mammals. Large glass-enclosed tanks allow visitors to go face-to-face with swimming pygmy hippos, meerkats, colobus monkeys, and other exotic species, including (not for the faint of heart) a rocky ledge filled with Madagascar hissing cockroaches.

Your second stop should be the **Regenstein Center for African Apes.** Lincoln Park Zoo has had remarkable success breeding gorillas and chimpanzees, and watching these ape families interact can be mesmerizing (and touching). One caveat: The building can get incredibly noisy when it's crowded, so be prepared.

Other exhibits worth a visit are the **Small Mammal–Reptile House,** which features a glass-enclosed walk-through ecosystem simulating river, savanna, and forest habitats; and the popular **Sea Lion Pool** in the center of the zoo, which is home to harbor seals, gray seals, and California sea lions (walk down the ramp and take a look at the underwater viewing area). The zoo's large carousel features beautifully rendered figures of endangered species. If you're here for a while and need nourishment, there's an indoor food court, as well as a cafe located on a terrace above the gift shop. And don't let the winter weather stop you from going to the zoo. The annual holiday lights display, "Zoo Lights," along with an ice skating rink and, of course, polar bears and other hearty animals, make the zoo a worthwhile stop year round. Allow 3 hours. For the adjoining children's zoo, see "Kid Stuff," p. 154.

2200 N. Cannon Dr. (at Fullerton Pkwy.). www.lpzoo.com. ℂ **312/742-2000.** Free admission. Buildings daily Nov–March 10am–4:30pm (grounds open 7am–5pm); Memorial Day to Labor Day Mon–Fri 10am–5pm (grounds open 7am–6pm), Sat–Sun 10am–6:30pm (grounds open 7am–7pm); Sept to Oct daily 10am–5pm (grounds open 7am–6pm). Parking $20 for up to 2 hr. in on-site lot. Bus: 22, 36, 151, or 156.

After a visit to Lincoln Park Zoo or the Peggy Notebaert Nature Museum, take a quick stroll along the south side of Fullerton Avenue toward the lakefront. Standing on the bridge that runs over the lagoon (just before you get to Lake Shore Dr.), you'll have a great view of the Chicago skyline and Lincoln Park behind you—an excellent backdrop for family souvenir photos. This path can get very crowded with bikers and runners on summer weekends, so pay attention to the painted lines on the path and treat the traffic like you would on the street. Keep to the right, and be aware of cyclists zipping by. If you hear someone call out "on your left" (a cyclist's warning cry) don't turn and look, just keep to the right.

Peggy Notebaert Nature Museum ★★ NATURE MUSEUM   I love that the third largest city in the U.S. is home to a nature museum. And it's not tucked away in the 'burbs, either: Peggy Notebaert is on prime Lincoln Park property, across from the zoo, Lincoln Park, Lake Michigan and surrounded by plenty of, well, nature. One of the museum's most popular spots, particularly among kids, is the Judy Istock Butterfly Haven, a greenhouse where visitors can walk in the home of more than 1,000 butterflies. There's even butterfly "security" at the door, to make sure you don't accidently walk out with a winged passenger (I've been stopped). Interactive exhibits are the rule and not the exception here, and kids can do science experiments, explore giant rope spider webs, get up close and personal with a turtle skeleton, peer in at the museum's living collection (tarantula warning!), learn about Chicago's history as a former marsh, and more. Temporary exhibits combine history, nature, and a touch of whimsy, whether they're exploring the history of the bicycle or paying tribute to the courier pigeon, as recent shows did. The nature museum is actually built into a sand dune and surrounded by a nature trail and bird walk—two pretty cool spots to discover in the shadow of the Chicago skyline. Allow 1 to 2 hours.

2430 N. Cannon Dr. (at Fullerton Ave.). www.naturemuseum.org. © **773/755-5100.** Admission $9 adults, $7 seniors and students, $6 children 3–12, free for children 2 and under. Mon–Fri 9am–5pm, Sat–Sun 10am–5pm. Closed Jan 1, Thanksgiving, and Christmas. Bus: 22, 36, 76, 151, or 156.

EXPLORING HYDE PARK

Hyde Park, south of the Loop, is the birthplace of atomic fission, home to the University of Chicago and the popular Museum of Science and Industry, and definitely worth a trip. It's gotten an added boost of publicity ever since a certain former resident, Barack Obama, came to national prominence. The Obamas are such fans of the area that they've kept their house here (see more on that below). Allow at least half a day to explore the University of Chicago campus and surrounding neighborhood (one of Chicago's most successfully integrated). If you want to explore a museum or two as well, plan on a full day.

SOME HYDE PARK HISTORY   When Hyde Park was settled in 1850, it became Chicago's first suburb. A hundred years later, in the 1950s, it added another first to its impressive résumé, one that the current neighborhood is not particularly proud of: an urban-renewal plan. At the time, a certain amount of old commercial and housing stock—just the kind of buildings that would be prized today—was demolished rather

Did You Know?

The world's first Ferris wheel was built on Hyde Park's midway during the World's Columbian Exposition in 1893. Not to be confused with the Navy Pier Ferris wheel, the original was blown up and sold for scrap metal.

than rehabilitated and replaced by projects and small shopping malls that actually make some corners of Hyde Park look more like a post–World War II suburb than an urban neighborhood.

What Hyde Park can be proud of is this: In racially divided Chicago, this neighborhood has found an alternative vision. As Southern blacks began to migrate to Chicago's South Side during World War I, many whites fled. But most whites here, especially those who wanted to stay near the university, chose integration as the only realistic strategy to preserve their neighborhood. The 2010 census and 2011 American Community Survey proved that integration still works: About 32% of the residents are white and 33% are black and there is also a significant Hispanic population (28%). Hyde Park is decidedly middle class, with pockets of affluence that reflect the early-20th-century period when the well-to-do moved here to escape the decline of Prairie Avenue. A well-known black resident from the area is the late Elijah Muhammad, and numerous Nation of Islam families continue to worship in a mosque, formerly a Greek Orthodox cathedral, that is one of the neighborhood's architectural landmarks. Surrounding this unusual enclave, however, are many marginal blocks where poverty and slum housing abound. For all its nobility, Hyde Park's achievement in integration merely emphasizes that socioeconomic differences are even more unwieldy than racial ones.

The University of Chicago is widely hailed as one of the more intellectually exciting institutions of higher learning in the country and has been home to some 89 Nobel laureates (including alumni and faculty), including physicist Enrico Fermi, novelist Saul Bellow, and economist Milton Friedman. Almost one-third of all the Nobel Prizes in Economics have gone to University of Chicago professors, twice as many as any other institution. Another long-time faculty member was English professor Norman Maclean, author of *A River Runs Through It*. Though they may joke about the school's staid social life, U of C undergrads take pride in their school's nerdy reputation.

The year the university opened its doors in 1892 was a big one for Hyde Park, but 1893 was even bigger. In that year, Chicago, chosen over other cities in a competitive international field, played host to the World's Columbian Exposition, commemorating the 400th anniversary of Columbus's arrival in America. To create a fairground, the landscape architect Frederick Law Olmsted was enlisted to fill in the marshlands along Hyde Park's lakefront and link what was to become Jackson Park to existing Washington Park on the neighborhood's western boundary with a narrow concourse called the Midway Plaisance. On the resulting 650 acres—at a cost of $30 million—12 exhibit palaces, 57 buildings devoted to U.S. states and foreign governments, and dozens of smaller structures were constructed under the supervision of architect Daniel Burnham. Most of the buildings followed Burnham's preference for the Classical Revival style and white stucco exteriors. With the innovation of outdoor electric lighting, the sparkling result was the "White City," which attracted 27 million visitors in a single season, from May 1 to October 31, 1893. The exposition sponsors, in that brief time, had remarkably recovered their investment, but within a few short years of the fair's closing, vandalism and fire destroyed most of its buildings. Only the Palace of Fine Arts, occupying the eastern tip of the midway, survives to this day, and it now houses the Museum of Science and Industry. For more on the behind-the-scenes drama at the

Hyde Park Attractions

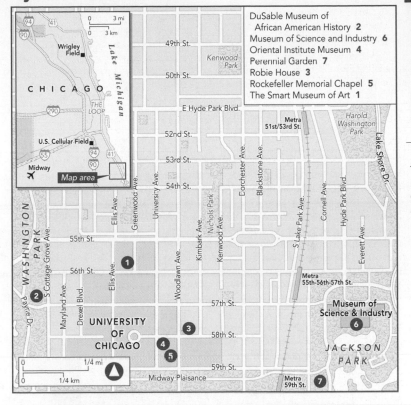

DuSable Museum of
  African American History **2**
Museum of Science and Industry **6**
Oriental Institute Museum **4**
Perennial Garden **7**
Robie House **3**
Rockefeller Memorial Chapel **5**
The Smart Museum of Art **1**

Exposition, read *The Devil in the White City* (2002), by Erik Larson, a nonfiction history book that reads like a thriller.

GETTING THERE From downtown, ride to Hyde Park on the **no. 6 Jackson Park express bus or the no. 2 Hyde Park express bus,** which both depart from State Street and take about 30 minutes. The fare is $2.25. For a faster trip, take the **Metra Commuter Train on the Metra Electric District (ME),** which goes from downtown to Hyde Park in about 15 minutes. Trains run every hour (more frequently during rush hour) Monday through Saturday from 5:15am to 12:50am, and every 30 to 90 minutes on Sunday and holidays from 5am to 12:55am. Downtown stations are at Randolph Street and Michigan Avenue, Van Buren Street and Michigan Avenue, and Roosevelt Road and Michigan Avenue (near the Museum Campus in Grant Park). Printed schedules are available at the stations. The fare is approximately $3 each way.

For CTA bus information, call ✆ **312/836-7000** or 888/968-7282 or visit **www.transitchicago.com**. For Metra train information call ✆ **312/322-6777** or visit **www.metrarail.com**.

For taxis, dial ✆ **312/829-4222** for **Yellow Cab** or ✆ **312/243-2537** for **Checker.** The one-way fare from downtown is around $25 to $30.

Though his primary residence is now a certain White House in Washington, D.C., the first couple still own a home here and maintain strong local ties. Tourists from around the world make pilgrimages to the Obamas' house at 5046 S. Greenwood Ave. on the city's South Side. You can get a glimpse of the home from a distance, but you won't see much; the whole block is closed to passersby for security reasons. However, the surrounding neighborhood of Kenwood—with its lovingly restored historic mansions—as well as adjacent Hyde Park, are well worth a stroll. After visiting the campus of the University of Chicago—where President Obama once taught constitutional law—you can browse the stacks at the **Seminary Co-op Bookstore** (p. 173), where he was a regular.

Chicago-based fashion maven Ikram Goldman helped cultivate Michelle Obama's sense of style. For a First-Lady-worthy makeover, head to her boutique, **Ikram** (p. 174), which stocks pieces by up-and-coming and off-the-radar designers.

For dinners out, the Obamas have often eaten at the upscale Mexican restaurant **Topolobampo** (p. 88). Another favorite for special occasions is **Spiaggia** (p. 84), one of the best Italian restaurants in the country—and among the most expensive. To celebrate their first

Valentine's Day as first couple, the Obamas chose **Table Fifty-Two** (52 W. Elm St., btw Clark and Dearborn sts.; www.tablefifty-two.com; (✆ **312/573-4000**), an unassuming spot that gives classic Southern dishes an upscale twist. Not only is the restaurant's owner, Art Smith, a friend and former South Side neighbor, but he also happens to be Oprah's former personal chef.

For more casual meals in Hyde Park, the Obamas were regulars at **Italian Fiesta Pizzeria** (1400 E. 47th St.; italianfiestapizzeria.com; ((✆ **773/684-2222**), a take-out pizza joint that was also a favorite of Michelle and her parents when she was growing up. In fact, when the Obamas moved to D.C., Italian Fiesta followed. President Obama has also mentioned the **Valois Cafeteria** (1518 E. 53rd St.; www.valoisrestaurant.com; (✆ **773/667-0647**), a no-frills, old-school neighborhood landmark, as his top breakfast spot in the city. For family outings on the North Side, the Obamas liked to stop in at **R. J. Grunts** (2056 N. Lincoln Park West; www.rjgruntschicago.com; (✆ **773/929-5363**), known for its all-American lineup of burgers and Tex-Mex specialties, as well as its enormous salad bar. An added bonus for kids: It's right across the street from Lincoln Park Zoo.

A SUGGESTED ITINERARY A long 1-day itinerary for Hyde Park should include the following: a walk through the University of Chicago campus (including a stroll along the Midway Plaisance); a visit to the Museum of Science and Industry (for families), Frank Lloyd Wright's Frederick C. Robie House, or one of the other local museums; and lunch or dinner in the neighborhood's commercial center.

The Top Attractions

DuSable Museum of African American History ★ HISTORY MUSEUM
One of the first thoughts I had while reading the displays in this museum, was, "Wow, it's nice to be reading the version of history that wasn't written by old white men." More specifically, I was reading a blurb on the Revolutionary War that focused on African Americans, rather than paying total attention to the colonies. You'll get a lot of

When you're ready to take a break, Hyde Park has an eclectic selection of restaurants. As in any university town, you'll find plenty of affordable, student-friendly hangouts. The most famous University of Chicago gathering spot is **Jimmy's Woodlawn Tap** (1172 E. 55th St.; ✆ **773/643-5516**). This dive of a bar and grill doesn't have much to offer much in the way of atmosphere, but the hamburgers and sandwiches are cheap, and the person sitting next to you might just be a Nobel Prize–winning professor. Another casual spot near campus is **Medici** (1327 E. 57th St.; www.medici57.com; ✆ **773/667-7394**), where a few generations' worth of students have carved their names into the tables while chowing down on pizza, the house specialty, or an apple pie so flaky and perfect you'll want to come back for more. About a block from the main Hyde Park Metra station you'll find **La Petite Folie** (1504 E. 55th St.; www.lapetitefolie.com; ✆ **773/493-1394**), a French bistro that offers a refined escape from student life.

that at the DuSable Museum of African American History, located in Washington Park a few minutes' walk from the University of Chicago campus. The museum was named for Jean Baptiste Point du Sable, a Haitian man who is considered Chicago's first permanent settler, or, as the museum somewhat awkwardly puts it, "the first non-Indian to establish a permanent settlement in the territory," and showcases art, artifacts, and history related to the African and African-American experience. You'll see exhibits about the march on Birmingham, Rosa Parks, segregation, white and black water fountains, and other more recent additions, such as a stirring quote from President Barack Obama: "I will never forget that the only reason I'm standing here today is because somebody, somewhere stood up for me when it was risky." While it does a good job of covering history, I think the museum misses a ripe opportunity to explore the strongly divided race relations that exist in Chicago. I look forward to checking out the museum's expansion, the Round House, which promises to be a more modern institution, when it opens across the street sometime in 2014 or 2015, depending on funding. Allow 1 hour.

740 E. 56th Place. www.dusablemuseum.org. ✆ **773/947-0600.** Admission $10 adults, $7 students and seniors, $3 children 6–11, free for children 5 and under. Free admission Sun. Tues–Sat 10am–5pm; Sun noon–5pm. Closed major holidays. Subway/El: Green Line to Garfield, Bus: 6 or Metra Electric train to 57th St. and Lake Park Ave., and then a short cab ride or 1-mile walk.

Museum of Science and Industry ★★★ MUSEUM If Disney were to make a purely educational theme park, it probably wouldn't be too far off from the this humongous museum—the largest science museum in the Western Hemisphere—where exploring, playing, squealing, and climbing isn't just encouraged, it's practically required. Here, you can stand in front of a real German submarine that the U.S. Navy captured during World War II; watch a chick hatch from its egg; control a 40-foot tornado; and travel through an enormous digestive system. The five-story, domed Omnimax is also a cool spot for relaxing after all that hard work.

Not surprisingly, the museum is super tech-savvy, and in recent years it opened up the Wanger Family Fab Lab, where guests can explore their creative side and make anything from a t-shirt to a robot, using the different CAD work stations, electronics workshop, 3D printer, and other hardware and software. Check the website for upcoming workshops on laser cutting, 3D printing, sticker design, and more. The museum also recently created a number of fun games and apps, available on www. msichicago.org. Allow 3 hours.

The museum is a hike from downtown, but it's easy to get to, with or without a car, or taking the bus or Metra (see below). If the weather's nice, it's just an 8- mile bike ride down the Lake Path to get to the museum.

5700 S. Lake Shore Dr. (at 57th St.). www.msichicago.org. © **800/468-6674** outside the Chicago area, or 773/684-1414. Admission to museum only: $18 adults, $17 seniors, $11 children 3–11, free for children 2 and under. Memorial Day to Labor Day daily 9:30am–5:30pm; early Sept to late May daily 9:30am–4pm. Closed Thanksgiving and Christmas. Bus: 2, 6, or 10 or Metra Electric train to 57th St. and Lake Park Ave.

Oriental Institute Museum ★ HISTORY/ARCHAEOLOGY MUSEUM They had me at the Egyptian mummy. Two of them, in fact, are on display here, one in a coffin, the other enshrouded in linen. The mummies, and all of the artifacts, statues, palace corridors, jewels, and other Near Eastern art items are here because they were unearthed in excavations by the Oriental Institute at the University of Chicago, which is dedicated to studying archaeology, languages, and culture as it moved west out of Africa. The museum's 170,000 items come from Egypt, Iran, Iraq, Israel, Nubia, Syria, and Turkey—once considered "the Orient"—and date back as far as 10,000 B.C. The Chicago connection of every item housed here gives it added appeal, in my mind. To enhance your visit, get the iPod self-guided tour from the Suq gift shop ($5). They may not tell you about it when you walk in, but it's available and really adds to the visit. Allow 1 hour.

1155 E. 58th St. (at University Ave.). www.oi.uchicago.edu. © **773/702-9520.** Free admission; suggested donation $7 adults, $4 children. Tues–Sat 10am–6pm (Wed until 8:30pm); Sun noon–6pm. Closed major holidays. Bus: 6 or Metra Electric train to 57th St. and Lake Park Ave.

Frederick C. Robie House ★★ ARCHITECTURE/HISTORIC HOME For architectural history hounds, Robie House is a must-see. Frank Lloyd Wright designed this 20th-century American architectural masterpiece for Frederick Robie, a bicycle and motorcycle manufacturer. The home, which was completed in 1909, is a classic example of Wright's Prairie School of design, with its open layout and linear geometry of form. Wright prided himself on creating all-encompassing, stylistically harmonious environments, and he oversaw everything from the furniture to the exquisite leaded- and stained-glass doors and windows. It was also among the last of Wright's Prairie School–style homes. During its construction, he abandoned both his family and his Oak Park practice to follow other pursuits, most prominently the realization of his Taliesin home and studio in Spring Green, Wisconsin. Docents from Oak Park's Frank Lloyd Wright Home and Studio Foundation lead tours of the interior, and after a massive, 10-year restoration in honor of the house's 100th anniversary, it looks better than ever. Right now, three different tours are available. The hour-long Guided Interior Tour gives the best overview of Wright and the home, taking visitors through all of the rooms. The 90-minute Private Spaces tour is a more in-depth tour, offered Saturdays and Sundays, delving into areas that are usually off limits, like the billiards room and servants' wing, and is best for those who are true Wright fans and not just curiosity seekers. The 35- to 40-minute kid-centric Wright Mystery Tour is based on Blue Balliett's novel *The Wright 3,* and students in grades 5 through 10 lead visitors through the house, exploring the ghosts and plot twists in the novel. (Kids on the tour must be accompanied by an adult.) *Note:* Advance reservations are a good idea in summer.

In addition to Robie House, several of Wright's earlier works, still privately owned, dot the streets of Hyde Park. They include the **Heller House,** 5132 S. Woodlawn Ave. (1897); the **Blossom House,** 1332 E. 49th St. (1882); and the **McArthur House,** 4852 S. Kenwood Ave. (1892). **Note:** These houses are not open to the public, so they can only be admired from the outside.

A **Wright specialty bookshop** is in the building's former three-car garage—which was highly unusual for the time in which it was built. Allow 1 hour for the tour, plus time to browse the gift shop.

5757 S. Woodlawn Ave. (at 58th St.). www.flwright.org/visit/robiehouse. ✆ **773/994-4000.** Admission for Guided Interior and Wright 3 Mystery: $15 adults, $12 seniors and children 4–17, free for children 3 and under. $55 for Private Spaces tour. Closed major holidays. Mon, Thurs–Sun 10:30am–3pm. Check website for exact schedules. Bookshop 10am–4pm on days tours are given. Bus: 6 or Metra Electric train to 57th St. and Lake Park Ave.

Rockefeller Memorial Chapel ★★ ARCHITECTURE/CHAPEL   To call the Rockefeller Memorial Chapel a chapel is false modesty, even for a Rockefeller. When the university first opened its doors, the students sang the following ditty:

> *John D. Rockefeller, wonderful man is he*
> *Gives all his spare change to the U of C.*

John D. was a generous patron, indeed. He founded the university (in cooperation with the American Baptist Society), built the magnificent mini-cathedral that now bears his name, and shelled out an additional $35 million in donations over the course of his lifetime. Memorial Chapel, designed by Bertram Goodhue, an architect known for his ecclesiastical buildings—including the Cadet Chapel at West Point and New York City's St. Thomas Church—was dedicated in 1928.

In keeping with the rest of the campus, which is patterned after Oxford, the chapel is reminiscent of English Gothic structures; however, it was built from limestone using modern construction techniques. Its most outstanding features are the circular stained-glass window high above the main altar (the windows, in general, are among the largest of any church or cathedral anywhere) and the world's second-largest carillon, which John D. Rockefeller, Jr., donated in 1932 in memory of his mother, Laura. The chapel's organ is nearly as impressive, with four manuals, 126 stops, and more than 10,000 pipes. Choir concerts, carillon performances, and other musical programs run throughout the year, usually for a small donation. Allow a half hour.

5850 S. Woodlawn Ave. http://rockefeller.uchicago.edu. ✆ **773/702-2100.** Free admission. Daily 8am–5:30pm (except during religious services). Bus: 6 or Metra Electric train to 57th St. and Lake Park Ave.

The Smart Museum of Art ★ ART MUSEUM   Small and plain on the outside, but incredibly scrappy within, this University of Chicago museum has an impressive array of items that span 5,000 years of humanity. That's the same as the Art Institute, if you're keeping score. The permanent collection draws from four categories: Asian art, contemporary art, European art, and modern art and design, and includes paintings, sculpture, furnishings, and even silver. It's worth dropping in if you're in the area, but I wouldn't recommend commuting to Hyde Park just for the museum, unless there is a special exhibit that catches your eye—and there well could be; in the recent past, exhibits have a ranged from political and sociological commentary to an exploration of opera in Chinese visual culture. Allow 1 hour.

5550 S. Greenwood Ave. (at E. 55th St.). www.smartmuseum.uchicago.edu. © **773/702-0200.** Free admission. Tues–Sun 10am–5pm (Thurs until 8pm); Sat–Sun 11am–5pm. Closed major holidays. Bus: 6 or Metra Electric train to 57th St. and Lake Park Ave.

Exploring the University of Chicago

Walking around the Gothic spires of the University of Chicago campus is bound to conjure up images of the cloistered academic life. Allow about an hour to stroll through the grassy quads and dramatic stone buildings. (If the weather's nice, do as the students do, and chill out for a while on the grass.) If you're visiting on a weekday, your first stop should be the university's **Information Center** (© 773/702-1234) on the first floor of Edward H. Levi Hall, 5801 S. Ellis Ave., where you can pick up campus maps, get information on university events, and learn about tours. The center is open Monday through Friday from 10am to 7pm. If you stop by on a weekend when the Visitors Information Desk is closed, you can get the scoop on campus events at the **Reynolds Clubhouse** student center (© 773/702-8787).

Start your tour at the **Henry Moore statue,** *Nuclear Energy,* on South Ellis Avenue between 56th and 57th streets. It's next to the Regenstein Library, which marks the site of the old **Stagg Field,** where, on December 2, 1942, the world's first sustained nuclear reaction was achieved in a basement laboratory below the field. Directly in front of the library is another eye-catching curiosity of a building: a gentle dome of glass also known as the **Joe and Rika Mansueto Library,** designed by Helmut Jahn. Then turn left and follow 57th Street until you reach the grand stone Hull Gate; walk straight to reach the main quad, or turn left through the column-lined arcade to reach **Hutchinson Court** (designed by John Olmsted, son of revered landscape designer Frederick Law Olmsted). The **Reynolds Clubhouse,** the university's main student center, is here; you can take a break at the C-Shop cafe or settle down at a table at Hutchinson Commons. The dining room and hangout right next to the cafe will bring to mind the grand dining halls of Oxford and Cambridge.

Other worthy spots on campus include the charming, intimate **Bond Chapel,** behind Swift Hall on the main quad, and the blocks-long **Midway Plaisance,** a wide stretch of green that was the site of carnival sideshow attractions during the World's Columbian Exposition in 1893. (Ever since, the term *midway* has referred to carnivals in general.)

The **Seminary Co-op Bookstore,** 5751 S. University Ave. (www.semcoop.com; © 773/752-4381), is a treasure trove of academic and scholarly books. Its selection of more than 100,000 titles has won it an international reputation as "the best bookstore west of Blackwell's in Oxford." It's open Monday through Friday from 8:30am–8pm, Saturday from 10am–6pm, and Sunday from noon–6pm.

Enjoying the Outdoors in Hyde Park

Hyde Park is not only a haven for book lovers and culture aficionados; the community also has open-air attractions. Worthy outdoor environments near Lake Michigan include **Lake Shore Drive,** where many stately apartment houses follow the contour of the shoreline. A suitable locale for a quiet stroll during the day is **Promontory Point,** at 55th Street and Lake Michigan, a bulb of land that juts into the lake and offers a good view of Chicago to the north and the seasonally active 57th Street beach to the south.

Farther south, just below the Museum of Science and Industry, is **Wooded Island** in Jackson Park, the site of the Japanese Pavilion during the Columbian Exposition and today a lovely garden of meandering paths. In the **Perennial Garden** at 59th Street and Stony Island Avenue in Jackson Park, more than 180 varieties of flowering plants display a palette of colors that changes with the seasons.

MORE MUSEUMS

City Gallery ★ ART GALLERY   Along with the pumping station across the street, the **Chicago Water Tower** is one of only a handful of buildings to survive the Great Chicago Fire of 1871. It has long been a revered symbol of the city's resilience and fortitude, although today the building is dwarfed by the high-rise shopping centers and hotels of North Michigan Avenue. The Gothic-style limestone building is now an art gallery. The spiffed-up interior is intimate and sunny, and it's a convenient, quick pit stop of culture on your way to the Water Tower shopping center or the tourist information center across the street in the pumping station. Exhibits focus mostly on photography, usually featuring Chicago-based artists. Allow 15 minutes.

806 N. Michigan Ave. (btw. Chicago Ave. and Pearson St.). ℭ **312/742-0808.** Free admission. Daily 10am–6:30pm; Holidays 10am–4pm. Subway/El: Red Line to Chicago.

Driehaus Museum ★★ HISTORIC HOME   It's like the Gilded Age never quite left the Driehaus Museum, and that's just how owner and investment manager Richard Driehaus likes it. Driehaus, an art collector and philanthropist, whose Driehaus Capital Management firm is cattycorner from the museum, "discovered" this home in 1994 and in 2003 founded the museum. The home was originally built in 1879 by Samuel Nickerson, who'd made his money by scoring a contract to sell alcohol to the Union army during the Civil War (he later became president of First National Bank of Chicago). Constructed by more than 600 artisans from Italy and Germany, it was, at the time, the largest and most opulent house in the city, and its 17 types of marble earned it the nickname The Marble Palace. Over the years, the home changed hands a number of times, but thanks to restoration by Driehaus, it remains in pristine condition.

Today, the art inside is a combination of art owned by the Nickerson family, along with the Driehaus collection, which includes an extensive array of glass from Louis Comfort Tiffany. Although self-guided audio tours are available, I highly recommend taking one of the staff-guided tours offered throughout the day (tours focus on the house, the revolving second-floor exhibits, or both and cost only $5 more than general admission). The guides are not only knowledgeable about Driehaus and Nickerson, but also adept at discussing the home's place in the larger context of Chicago history. The museum also offers themed tours seasonally, and my tour guide mentioned an upcoming tour led by characters dressed as servants, speaking about the house from their perspective, which has quite a bit of quirky potential. *Tip:* As you're wandering around the house, ask to see the servants' quarters, and one of the staff members will take you to where the current offices are, today. It's a narrow hallway with access to the back-of-the-house stairs and photos of the cots where the help slept. It's an eye-opening contrast to the elegance surrounding you. Allow 1 to 2 hours.

40 E. Erie St. (at Wabash Ave.). www.driehausmuseum.org. ℭ **312/482-8933.** Admission $20 adults, $13 seniors, $10 students and children 12–16. Children 5 and younger free. Museum is open Tues–Sun 10am–5pm. First and third Tuesdays open til 8pm. Closed Mondays and major holidays. Tours offered daily 10:30am, 11:30am, 1:30pm, 3:30pm. First and third Thurs at 6:30pm. Subway/El: Red Line to Grand Ave.

Historic Pullman ★★ HISTORIC NEIGHBORHOOD Railway magnate George Pullman may have been a fabulously wealthy industrialist, but he fancied himself more enlightened than his 19th-century peers. So when it came time to build a new headquarters for his Pullman Palace Car Company, he dreamed of something more than the standard factory surrounded by tenements. Instead, he built a model community for his workers, a place where they could live in houses with indoor plumbing and abundant natural light—amenities almost unheard of for industrial workers in the 1880s. Pullman didn't do all this solely from the goodness of his heart: He hoped that the town, named after him, would attract the most skilled workers (who would be so happy that they wouldn't go on strike). As one of the first "factory towns," Pullman caused an international sensation and was seen as a model for other companies to follow. The happy workers that Pullman envisioned did go on strike in 1894, however, frustrated by the company's control of every aspect of their lives.

Today the Pullman district makes a fascinating stop for anyone with a historical or architectural bent. Although most of the homes remain private residences, a number of public buildings (including the Hotel Florence, the imposing Clock Tower, and the two-story colonnaded Market Hall) still stand. You can walk through the area on your own (stop by the visitor center for a map), or take a guided tour at 1:30pm on the first Sunday of the month from May through November ($7 adults, $5 seniors, $4 students). Allow 1½ hours for the guided tour.

11141 S. Cottage Grove Ave. www.pullmanil.org. ✆ **773/785-8901.** Free admission. Visitor center Tues–Sun 11am–3pm. Train: Metra Electric Line to Pullman (111th St.), turn right on Cottage Grove Ave., and walk one block to the visitor's center.

Hull-House Museum ★ HISTORY MUSEUM Jane Addams was the daughter of a wealthy miller, who leased a mansion on Chicago's poor west side in 1889, welcoming the area's residents, many of whom were poor immigrants, into the home, called the Hull-House. Today, that mansion is a museum that highlights the accomplishments of the social reformer, who provided childcare services so parents could work, supported the labor movement, drew attention to issues of immigration, pushed for universal education, and more. She went on to become the first American woman to win the Nobel Peace Prize. The first floor gives an overview of the social services that Addams and her co-worker, Ellen Gates Starr (also most likely her lover at one time, although the museum doesn't come right out and say that), provided to the neighborhood, all in the backdrop of a comfortable, welcoming home—a far cry from the kind of stripped-down soup kitchen of many charities. Wander up to the second floor and you can see Addams's sparsely furnished room and the desk where she worked, which was the centerpiece. Around the halls are photos of former residents and reformists who joined in Addams's mission to understand poverty in order to move beyond it. The Hull-House does assume a basic knowledge of Jane Addams, a household name in Chicago, where a tollway, elementary school and high school bea,r her name. I've tried to supply you with that here, so you should be set to explore. The Hull-House also recently began a farm to educate visitors about gardening, and offers tours Monday, Wednesday, and Friday between 9am and 3pm. Call ✆ **312/413-5353** ahead to schedule a tour. Allow a half hour.

University of Illinois at Chicago, 800 S. Halsted St. (at Polk St.). www.uic.edu/jaddams/hull. ✆ **312/413-5353.** Free admission. Tues–Fri 10am–4pm; Sun noon–4pm. Closed university holidays. Subway/El: Blue Line to Halsted/University of Illinois.

International Museum of Surgical Science ★ MEDICAL SCIENCE MUSEUM Although it's not quite as macabre as Philadelphia's Mütter Museum, the International Museum of Surgical Science will be of interest to those with an appreciation for the weird, as well as surgeons and others in the medical field. Tucked into a 1917 Gold Coast mansion—the last lakefront one open to the public—and modeled after Le Petit Trianon at Versailles, it does feel rather odd to wander the quiet, elegant rooms with eight fireplaces while gazing at specimens in jars, old cringe-inducing surgery videos, prosthetics, bloodletting devices, X-ray machines, and plenty of scalpels. It's a great place to pick up facts that could win you the next round at Trivial Pursuit, such as my personal favorite: Before sutures were created, ants were used to close wounds. In the 10th century B.C., an ant was held over a wound until it bit the edges. "The ant was then decapitated and the death grip from the ant's jaws kept the wound closed." In addition to more than 7,000 medical artifacts, there are galleries that showcase art with ties to medicine, and a new exhibit called "RX for Success" highlights the many medical careers associated with modern and ancient surgery. Allow 1 hour.

1524 N. Lake Shore Dr. (btw. Burton Place and North Ave.). www.imss.org. ℂ **312/642-6502.** Admission $15 adults, $10 seniors, students, $7 children ages 4–13. Free admission Tues. Tues–Fri 10am–4pm, Sat–Sun open until 5. Closed major holidays. Bus: 151.

Intuit: The Center for Intuitive and Outsider Art ★ ART MUSEUM It sounds like an *X-Files* kind of name, and, true, the art can get a little weird here, but you have no alien abductions to fear in this warehouse district gallery. "Outsider art," is a term attached to a group of unknown, unconventional artists who do their work without any formal training or connection to the mainstream art world, and it ranges from fairly conventional paintings to enormous canvases, bottle cap art, and beyond. Visitor's reactions run the gamut from intrigued to "what the . . .?" as they explore the permanent collections of art, including the fascinating Henry Darger room, a replica of the one-bedroom apartment the Chicago recluse/custodian/artist/hoarder lived in prior to moving to a nursing home. One standout recent exhibit came from a photographer who purchased 30 boxes of slides at a secondhand store that captured a family he'd never met. He became obsessed with finding out who the people really were, as his exhibit showed. The gallery is also home to educational lectures, along with workshops, independent film screenings, and fun events, like drawing competitions. Allow 1 hour.

756 N. Milwaukee Ave. (at Chicago and Ogden aves.). www.art.org. ℂ **312/243-9088.** Admission $5 adults, free for children 11 and under. Tues–Sat 11am–6pm (Thurs until 7:30pm). Subway/El: Blue Line to Chicago.

National Museum of Mexican Art ★ ART MUSEUM Exploring the Latino-heavy Pilsen neighborhood is a bit like stepping into a different city, where the smell of spicy meats and soft corn tortillas fills the air, emanating from the many tempting taquerias. One of the cultural highlights here is the National Museum of Mexican Art, which, with more than 7,000 items, is one of the largest collections of Hispanic art in the country. With that said, it's a small, friendly, and easy to navigate museum, and it's free. What I love about this museum is the wide range of mood of its works, from serious to whimsical to laugh-out-loud funny. I've thought back many times to the lawn-mower sculpture I once saw there: It was a pimped-out lowrider on hydraulics, with spinners on the tires and a light-up steering wheel. The museum is family-friendly and offers art classes and family-centric tours. Allow 1 hour.

1852 W. 19th St. (a few blocks west of Ashland Ave.). www.nationalmuseumofmexicanart.org. ℂ **312/738-1503.** Free admission. Tues–Sun 10am–5pm. Closed major holidays. Subway/El: Pink Line to Damen/Cermac.

National Veterans Art Museum ★ A stroll through this intense museum is akin to peering into a soldier's soul. Although it's not exactly comfortable, it opens our eyes to the ways that war can affect soldiers, right down to their synapses. The works here, from sculpture to photography to portraits and more, were all created by veterans, many of whom fought in Vietnam. Located in the second floor of a loft in the Portage Park neighborhood, some of the themes touched on include suicide and alcohol, and renderings of camo gear, bullets, and weapons abound. I can tell you from a recent visit that some of the works are heart wrenching, while others are downright weird, like a sculptural tribute to Barbie on her 50th birthday, which included a number of Barbie heads in a box along with a museum-grade real shrunken head. The most visceral part of the museum is the text posted by a fair number of the works, describing, in the veteran's words, the exact memory or moment that inspired the piece. Talk about chills. Allow a half hour.

4041 N. Milwaukee (btw. Irving Park Rd. and Cuyler Ave.). www.nvam.org. ⓒ **312/326-0270.** Free admission. Tues–Sat 10am–5pm. Closed major holidays. Bus: 80.

EXPLORING THE 'BURBS
Oak Park

Architecture and literary buffs alike make pilgrimages to Oak Park, a nearby suburb on the western border of the city that is easily accessible by car or train. Bookworms flock here to see the town where Ernest Hemingway was born and grew up, while others come to catch a glimpse of the Frank Lloyd Wright–designed homes that line the well-maintained streets.

GETTING THERE
BY CAR Oak Park is 10 miles due west of downtown Chicago. By car, take the I-290 west to Harlem Avenue (Ill. 43) and exit north. Continue on Harlem north to Lake Street. Take a right on Lake Street and the **Oak Park Visitor Center** (see below) will be on your left.

BY PUBLIC TRANSPORTATION Take the Green Line west to the Harlem stop, roughly a 25-minute ride from downtown. Exit the station onto Harlem Avenue, and proceed north to Lake Street. Take a right on Lake Street, follow it to Forest Avenue, and then turn left to the **Oak Park Visitor Center** (see below). This part of the green line takes you through some shady parts of town, so I would suggest timing your visit well before dark.

VISITOR INFORMATION
The **Oak Park Visitor Center,** 1118 Westgate (www.visitoakpark.com; ⓒ **888/OAK-PARK** [625-7275]), is open daily from 10am to 5pm. Stop here for an orientation, maps, and guidebooks. The heart of the historic district and the Frank Lloyd Wright Home and Studio are only a few blocks away.

THE WRIGHT STUFF
Frank Lloyd Wright Home and Studio ★★★ ARCHITECTURE/HISTORIC HOME For the first 20 years of Wright's career, this remarkable complex served first and foremost as the sanctuary where he designed and executed more than 130 of 430 completed buildings. The home began as a simple shingled cottage that the 22-year-old Wright built for his bride in 1889, but it became a living laboratory for his revolutionary reinvention of interior spaces. Wright remodeled the house constantly until 1911,

wright's OAK PARK

Oak Park has the highest concentration of Frank Lloyd Wright-designed and -built houses or buildings anywhere. People come here to marvel at the work of a man who saw his life as a twofold mission: to wage a single-handed battle against excessively ornamental architecture (Victorian, in particular), and to create in its place a new form that would be, at the same time, functional, appropriate to its natural setting, and stimulating to the imagination.

Not everyone who comes to Oak Park shares Wright's architectural philosophy, but scholars and enthusiasts admire him for being consistently true to his vision, out of which emerged a unique and genuinely American architectural statement. The reason for Wright's success could stem from the fact that he was a living exemplar of a quintessential American type. In a deep sense, he embodied the ideal of the self-made and self-sufficient individual who had survived, even thrived, in the frontier society—qualities that he expressed in his almost-puritanical insistence that each spatial or structural form in his buildings serve some useful purpose. He was also an aesthete in Emersonian fashion, deriving his idea of beauty from natural environments, where apparent simplicity often belies a subtle complexity.

The three principal ingredients of a tour of Wright-designed structures in Oak Park are the **Frank Lloyd Wright Home and Studio Tour,** the **Unity Temple Tour,** and a **walking tour**—guided or self-guided—to view the exteriors of homes throughout the neighborhood that were built by the architect. Oak Park has 25 homes and buildings designed by Wright, constructed between 1892 and 1913, which constitute the core output of his Prairie School period.

when he moved out permanently. During Wright's fertile early period, the house was his showcase, but it also embraces many idiosyncratic features molded to his own needs, rather than those of a client. With many add-ons—including a barrel-vaulted children's playroom and a studio with an octagonal balcony suspended by chains—the place has a certain whimsy that others might have found less livable. This was not an architect's masterpiece, but rather the master's home, and visitors can savor every room for the view it offers into of the workings of a remarkable mind. The Home and Studio offers two tours: the Guided Interior Tour explores the inside of the house and the career or Frank Lloyd Wright, while the Historic District Walking Tour is a self-guided tour pointing out different Wright properties and Wright-inspired properties in the neighborhood.

Advance reservations are recommended, especially during the busy summer months; you can book online or by phone (📞 **312/994-4000**). Allow 1 hour for the tour, more time if you want to browse in the bookshop.

951 Chicago Ave. www.flwright.org. 📞 **312/994-4000.** Admission $15 adults, $12 seniors and children 4–17, free for children 3 and under; combined admission for the home and studio tour and guided or self-guided historic district tour $25 adults, $20 seniors and students 4–17. Admission to the home and studio is by guided tour only; tours depart from bookshop daily, 10am–3pm home tour, 9am–4pm walking tour. Closed Thanksgiving, Christmas Eve, Christmas, New Year's Day. Facilities for people with disabilities are limited; please call in advance.

Unity Temple ★ ARCHITECTURE After a fire destroyed its church around 1900, a Unitarian Universalist congregation asked one of its members, Frank Lloyd

Die-hard fans of the architect will want to be in town on the third Saturday in May for the annual **All Wright House Walk.** The public can tour several Frank Lloyd Wright–designed homes and other notable Oak Park buildings, in both the Prairie School and Victorian styles, in addition to Wright's home, his studio, and the Unity Temple. The tour includes 10 buildings in all. Tickets, which go for $125, go on sale March 1 and can sell out by mid-April. Call the Frank Lloyd Wright Home and Studio (© **708/848-3559**) or visit www.flwright. org for details and ticket information.

Wright, to design an affordable replacement. Using poured concrete with metal reinforcements—a necessity due to a small $40,000 budget—Wright created a building that, on the outside, seems as forbidding as a mausoleum, but inside contains all the elements of the Prairie School that has made Wright's name immortal. Wright believed conventional church architecture was overpowering—he complained that he didn't feel a part of the Gothic-style cathedral across the street, for example—and Unity Temple was intended to offer a new model for houses of worship. Today, it's the only remaining public building from his Prairie period. It's worth the extra $3 for the guided tour, where the docent explains why Unity Temple still feels groundbreaking 100 years later—and why Wright would consider that the ultimate compliment. Allow an hour.

875 Lake St. www.flwright.org. © **312/994-4000.** Admission for guided tours $15 adults, $12 seniors and children 4–17, free for children 3 and under. Self-guided tours $12 adults, $10 students & seniors (65+). Mon, Wed–Sat 9:30am–2pm; Closed Tues, Sun, Thanksgiving, Christmas Eve, Christmas Day, New Year's Day. Church events can alter schedule; call in advance.

ON THE TRAIL OF HEMINGWAY

Hemingway Museum ★ Ernest Hemingway was born in Oak Park, but judging from the museum dedicated to him, it seems that the city may have had a greater affinity with him than he with it. When you think of Hemingway, after all, Key West, Paris, and Cuba come to mind. But the Village of Oak Park, Illinois? It comes as a surprise even to some of us locals. That's because he left after graduating high school, embarking on the life we've come to know, as he traveled the world and wrote about it. You can follow his path through the exhibits here, even if you haven't read his books.

Housed in a former church that's now an arts center, the modest museum is filled with photographs, unpublished writing samples, book covers, movie posters, and other snippets that give hints into the life of the famous storyteller, as well as shedding light on the history of Oak Park. There are a couple of different videos, including a recently acquired 4-hour long Hemingway video produced by the BBC. The items that interested me most were those that gave insights into the slightly bizarre viewpoint of the Hemingway family. For example, his mother, Grace, buried a time capsule when the family moved to a new house, filling it with her baby shoes and a newspaper article about a recent San Francisco earthquake. Those little offbeat pieces of trivia give some fun insight into the forces that shaped the author.

The **Ernest Hemingway Birthplace Home ★★** is a block and a half north, at 339 N. Oak Park Ave. The lovely Queen Anne house—complete with wraparound porch and turret—was the home of Hemingway's maternal grandparents, and it's where the writer was born on July 21, 1899. Its connection to Hemingway is actually pretty tenuous—he spent most of his boyhood and high school years at 600 N. Kenilworth Ave., a few blocks away (that house is still privately owned). And according to the volunteer who led my tour, about 99% of the furnishings are not original (the exceptions include a couple of chairs, a sewing kit that Ernest used, and his sister's toy chest), but it has been fashioned to replicate what it looked like back in the early 1900s. Still, the tour is fascinating (and included in the museum price), thanks to dedicated volunteer guides who are Hemingway scholars. I walked out of it feeling like I'd learned some great family lore. Such as the fact that Ernest's mother raised him and his older sister, Marcelline, as though they were twins, styling their hair the same and putting them in matching outfits (some days they wore dresses, others pants) until the school demanded that she stop. Fans of historic house tours will also really enjoy this visit, whether they're Hemingway devotees or not. Tours are offered on the hour during the museum's hours. Last tour begins at 4pm.

200 N. Oak Park Ave. www.ehfop.org. © **708/848-2222.** Combined admission to Hemingway Museum and Ernest Hemingway Birthplace Home $10 adults, $8 seniors and children 6–12, free for children 5 and under. Sun–Fri 1–5pm; Sat 10am–5pm. Closed major holidays.

Skokie

Abutting Chicago to the north is the Village of Skokie, a working-class area filled with modest Chicago-style bungalows that has the benefits of proximity to the perks of the city without the terrible traffic. Skokie is most easily accessible by car. While the El's Yellow Line does come here, and runs about every 10 to 12 minutes from the Howard Stop, getting around the sprawling suburb without a car is much more challenging than in the city.

Skokie is known, historically, for its concentrated Jewish population. In 1976, nearly half of the population of 70,000 was Jewish, an estimated 7,000 of whom were Holocaust survivors. The city made headlines when a neo-Nazi group planned to march through the Village in 1977. Ultimately, the American Civil Liberties Union defended the group's right to march, only to have the American Nazis themselves decide to hold their demonstration in Chicago, rather than Skokie.

That history puts into context the sedate but impressive **Illinois Holocaust & Education Center ★★** (9603 Woods Dr., at Golf Rd.; www.ilholocaustmuseum. org; © **847/967-4800**). A large, concrete fortress, the museum has a commanding and graceful presence—think castle meets bunker. Upon entry, it's dark and tomb-quiet. You pass through a metal detector and put your bags on an X-ray conveyor belt—an immediate reminder that the threat of hate and destruction are neither gone, nor forgotten. Inside the museum, the rooms are arranged by year, giving a brief historical glimpse into anti-Jewish sentiments through the rise in power of Hitler and the German Nazi Party. The museum is peppered with personal artifacts—letters, clothing, photos, and other memorabilia that bring the events out of history and into real life. Mini-documentaries also tell the stories of survivors and their families, as men and women who now live in Illinois talk viscerally about their experiences. The names of those lost are written across the Room of Remembrance. In addition to revisiting the past, the message here is a call to action to never let something like this happen again. The museum also pays tribute to genocides in Bosnia and Rwanda. The museum is open Monday through Wednesday and Friday 10am to 5pm, Thursday 10am to 8pm, Sat and Sun 11am to 4pm; $12 adults, $8 seniors 65 and up and students 12–22; $6 children ages 5 to 11.

After the museum, you'll be ready for something a little lighter. If the weather is nice, take a walk along the **Skokie Northshore Sculpture Trail ★★,** www.sculpture park.org, a 2-mile path that runs from Touhy Avenue on the south to Dempster Street on the north, and parallels the Chicago River (and busy McCormick Blvd.). The trail, which is surprisingly serene considering the traffic, malls, and strip malls in its wake, has more than 60 sculptures by locally and nationally known artists, and is filled with cyclists, walkers, and joggers when the weather is nice.

The North Shore

Between Chicago and the state border of Wisconsin is one of the nation's most affluent residential areas, a swath of suburbia known as the North Shore. Although towns farther west like to co-opt the name for its prestige, the North Shore proper extends from Evanston, which is just north of Skokie, along the lakefront to tony Lake Forest, originally built as a resort for Chicago's aristocracy. Dotted with idyllic, picture-perfect towns such as Kenilworth, Glencoe, and Winnetka, this area has long attracted filmmakers such as Robert Redford, who filmed *Ordinary People* in Lake Forest, and the North Shore's own John Hughes, who shot most of his popular coming-of-age comedies (*Sixteen Candles, Ferris Bueller's Day Off, Home Alone,* and so on) here.

Although a Metra train line extends to Lake Forest and neighboring Lake Bluff, I highly recommend that you rent a car and drive north along **Sheridan Road,** which winds its leisurely way through many of these communities, past palatial homes and mansions designed in a startling array of architectural styles. Aside from Lake Shore Drive in Chicago, you won't find a more impressive stretch of roadway in the entire metropolitan area.

EXPLORING EVANSTON

Despite being frequented by Chicagoans, Evanston, the city's oldest suburb, retains an identity all its own. A unique hybrid of sensibilities, it manages to combine the tranquility of suburban life with a highly cultured, urban charm. It's great fun to wander amid the shops and cafes in its downtown area or along funky Dempster Street at its southern end. The beautiful lakefront campus of **Northwestern University** (633 Clark St., www.northwestern.edu; *©* **847/491-3741**) is here, and many of its buildings—such as Alice Millar Chapel, with its sublime stained-glass facade, and the Mary & Leigh Block Gallery, a fine-arts haven that offers a top-notch collection and intriguing temporary exhibitions—are well worth several hours of exploration.

For a bit of serenity, head to **Grosse Point Lighthouse** (2601 Sheridan Rd.; www. grossepointlighthouse.net; *©* **847/328-6961**), a historic lighthouse built in 1873, when Lake Michigan still teemed with cargo-laden ships. Tours of the lighthouse, situated in a nature center, take place on weekends from June to September at 2, 3, and 4pm ($6 adults, $3 children 8–12; children 7 and under not admitted, for safety reasons). The adjacent Lighthouse Beach is a favorite spot for local families during the summer. If you're here between Memorial Day and Labor Day, you'll have to pay to frolic on the sand ($8 adults, $6 children 1–11), but it's a great place for a (free) stroll on a sunny spring or fall day.

OTHER AREA ATTRACTIONS

Bahá'í House of Worship ★★ ARCHITECTURE   Up the road from Evanston in Wilmette is the most visited of all the sights in the northern suburbs, the Bahá'í House of Worship, an ethereal edifice that seems not of this earth. The gleaming white stone temple, designed by the French-Canadian Louis Bourgeois and completed in

If you've made it to the Bahá'í temple, take a stroll across Sheridan Road to the 60-acre **Gillson Park** for a taste of north suburban life. Check out the sailors prepping their boats for a day cruise, families picnicking and playing Frisbee, and kids frolicking on the sandy beach. (Boats are also available for rent at the harbor (© **847/256-9656**) if you'd like to explore Lake Michigan from the water.) Access to the beach is restricted to local residents in the summer, but in the fall and spring, you're welcome to wander. Just don't expect to take a dip in the frigid water, unless you're wearing a wet suit, like the locals do.

1953, is essentially a soaring, nine-sided, 135-foot dome, draped in a delicate lacelike facade, which reveals the Eastern influence of the Bahá'í faith's native Iran. Surrounded by formal gardens, it is one of seven Bahá'í temples in the world and the only one in the Western Hemisphere. The dome's latticework is even more beautiful as you gaze upward from the floor of the sanctuary, which, during the day, is flooded with light. Downstairs, displays in the visitor center explain the Bahá'í faith and give you a glimpse of the other temples around the world. Friendly temple members offer informal tours of the building and exhibits to anyone who inquires. Allow 45 minutes.

100 Linden Ave. (at Sheridan Rd.), Wilmette. www.bahai.us/bahai-temple. © **847/853-2300.** Free admission. Daily 7am–10pm; visitor center 10am–5pm (until 8pm May–Sept). From Chicago, take the El Red Line north to Howard St. Change for the Evanston train and go to the end of the line, Linden Ave. (Or take the Purple/Evanston Express and stay on the same train all the way.) Turn right on Linden and walk 2 blocks east. If you're driving, go north on the Outer Dr. (Lake Shore Dr.), which feeds into Sheridan Rd.

Chicago Botanic Garden ★★ BOTANIC GARDEN Despite its name, the world-class Chicago Botanic Garden is actually 25 miles north of the city, in the suburb of Glencoe. But if you're looking for an afternoon of serenity, it makes for a tranquil day trip. Made up of islands, lagoons, prairie, and forest, this 385-acre living preserve is really a city of gardens, complete with bridges, greenhouses, bonsai, vertical gardens, children's gardens, and more. Winding landscaped paths takes visitors around the world, through the English walled garden, the Japanese garden, the waterfall garden, and even a fruit and vegetable garden, where you'll get tips on how to grow your own. Tram tours are available for those who don't feel up to the hike. If you're here in the summer, don't miss the extensive rose gardens, with more than 7,750 plants. The Botanic Garden also has an exhibit hall, auditorium, museum, library, education greenhouses, outdoor pavilion, carillon, cafe, designated bike path, and garden shop. Carillon concerts take place at 7pm Monday evenings from June through August; tours of the carillon are offered beforehand. Allow 3 hours.

Starting in June, the gardens remain open until 9pm. The public is invited to remain for a beautiful nighttime stroll through Evening Island, where the paths glow upon the surrounding lagoon. The garden also recently began working with local farmers, chefs, brewers, and wine makers to host monthly summer farm dinners. Check the website or call for event schedules.

1000 Lake-Cook Rd. (just east of Edens Expwy./I-94), Glencoe. www.chicago-botanic.org. © **847/835-5440.** Free admission. Parking $25. Daily 8am–sunset fall, winter, spring. Summer hours June–September 7am–9pm. Tram tours start June 7, 10am–5pm. Closed Christmas. From

Chicago, take Sheridan Rd. north along Lake Michigan or I-94 to Lake-Cook Rd. Metra Union Pacific North Line to Braeside Station.

Ravinia Festival ★★★ CONCERT   Want to know where the natives get away from it all? Come summertime, you'll find them chilling on the lawn at Ravinia, the seasonal home of the highly regarded Chicago Symphony Orchestra in suburban Highland Park. In operation since 1904, Ravinia started off as an amusement park. The **Martin Theatre**—built in the Prairie style—still remains and is the only building still standing from the early days. Over the years, the festival has hosted an amazing array of performers, from Louis Armstrong, Duke Ellington, George Gershwin, and Ella Fitzgerald to Janis Joplin and Steven Sondheim. The season runs from mid-June to Labor Day and includes far more than classical concerts: You can also catch pop acts, dance performances, operatic arias, and blues concerts. Tickets are available for the covered pavilion, where you get a reserved seat and a view of the stage, but the real joy is sitting in the lawn, lazing under the stars and a canopy of leafy branches while listening to music and indulging in an elaborate picnic. (It's a local tradition to try to outdo everyone else by bringing candelabras and fine china.)

Don't let the distance from downtown discourage you from visiting, because Ravinia is served by an extremely convenient public-transportation system. On concert nights, you can take the Metra Union Pacific North Line (from Chicago to Kenosha), which stops right in front of the gate at the Ravinia Park stop (the Ravinia stop and the Braeside stop will also get you there). After the concert, trains wait right outside the gates to take commuters back to the city. The round-trip train fare is $7—a real bargain, considering that traffic around the park can be brutal.

Dining options at the park range from the fine-dining restaurant **Mirabelle** (𝄐 **847/432-7550** for reservations) to prepacked picnic spreads, burgers, pizza, and ice cream sold around the park, or you can bring your own food and drinks, including alcohol. You can also bring your own blanket and chairs, or for $14, rent a pair of lawn chairs and a table from booths set up near the park entrance. If you're wondering about the weather conditions at concert time, Ravinia's weather page, www.crh.noaa.gov, provides updates.

418 Sheridan Road, Highland Park. www.ravinia.org. 𝄐 **847/266-5000.** Pavilion tickets $25–$120; lawn $10–$45. Most concerts are in the evening. Take the Metra Union Pacific North Line to Ravinia or Braeside.

'Burb Highlights Worth the Trek

In Chicago, a trip to the 'burbs is a day trip. Traffic can be bumper-to-bumper at any given time, whether it's rush hour or mid-day on a weekend, so it can take a good hour or more to get to the surrounding communities. With that said, these spots are worth the traffic nightmare. (Although it's possible to get to the following places by public transportation, a car is really the most reliable and quickest option.)

Arlington International Racecourse ★ HORSE RACING   With its gleaming-white, palatial, six-story grandstand and lush gardens, this racecourse is one of the most beautiful showcases for thoroughbred horse racing in the world. Its storied history stretches back to 1927, and such equine stars as Citation, Secretariat, and Cigar have graced the track. The annual Arlington Million (the sport's first million-dollar race, held in mid-Aug) attracts top jockeys, trainers, and horses, and is part of the World Series Racing Championship, which includes the Breeders' Cup races.

Arlington's race days are thrilling to behold, with all of racing's time-honored pageantry on display—from the bugler in traditional dress to the parade of jockeys.

Arlington likes to say that it caters to families, and the ambience is more Disney than den of iniquity. "Family days" throughout the summer include live music and entertainment ranging from petting zoos to puppet shows.

2200 W. Euclid Ave., Arlington Heights. www.arlingtonpark.com. ℂ 847/385-7500. May–Sept Wed–Sun gates open 11:15am, 1st post 1pm. No racing Oct–Apr. General admission $8 adults, $3–$6 additional per person for reserved seating. Take the Kennedy (I-94) Expwy. to the I-90 tollway, and exit north on Rte. 53. Follow 53 north to the Euclid exit. Or take Metra train to Arlington Heights. Free parking.

Brookfield Zoo ★★ ZOO In contrast to the more modest Lincoln Park Zoo, Brookfield, located in the western suburbs, is enormous, spreading out over 216 acres and housing thousands of animals—camels, dolphins, giraffes, baboons, wolves, tigers, green sea turtles, Siberian tigers, snow leopards, and more—in naturalistic environments that put them side by side with other inhabitants of their regions. These creative indoor and outdoor settings, filled with activities to keep kids interested, are what set Brookfield apart.

Start out at **Habitat Africa!**, a multiple-ecosystem exhibit that encompasses 30 acres—about the size of the entire Lincoln Park Zoo. Then wander through some of the buildings that allow you to see animals close up; my personal favorites are **Tropic World,** where you hang out at treetop level with monkeys, and **Australia House,** where fruit bats flit around your head. **The Living Coast** explores the west coast of Chile and Peru, and includes everything from a tank of plate-size moon jellies to a rocky shore where Humboldt penguins swim and nest as Inca terns and gray gulls fly freely overhead. **The Swamp** re-creates the bioregions of a southern cypress swamp and an Illinois river scene, and discusses what people can do to protect wetlands. The dolphins at the **Seven Seas** put on an amazing show that has been a Brookfield Zoo fixture for years. If you go on a weekend, buy tickets to the dolphin show at least a couple of hours before the one you plan to attend, because they tend to sell out quickly. Stop by the **Hamill Family Play Zoo,** where kids can pet animals, build habitats, learn how to plant a garden, and even play animal dress-up. The only catch: the separate admission fee ($2.50 for ages 3 to adult). Allow 3 hours.

8400 31st St. (at 1st Ave), Brookfield. www.brookfieldzoo.org. ℂ 708/688-8000. Admission $16.95 adults, $11.95 seniors and children 3–11, free for children 2 and under; free for military personnel. Parking $10. Free admission Tues, Thurs, Sat, and Sun Jan–Feb. Memorial Day to Labor Day daily 9:30am–6pm (Sun until 7:30pm); fall–spring daily 10am–5pm. Bus: 304 or 311. Take I-55 and I-290 14 miles west of the Loop.

Morton Arboretum ★★ ARBORETUM This suburban oasis, located in Lisle, about 27 miles west of the Loop, covers almost 2,000 acres and is dedicated to preserving an amazing variety of trees and shrubs. You can follow walking trails through solemn forests, explore a re-creation of an original Illinois prairie, or wander the twisting pathways of the **Maze Garden.** (If you'd rather watch others wander, climb up to the viewing platform built around the trunk of a 60-ft.-tall sycamore tree.) Covering the arboretum's vast acreage requires some driving—and you'll need a car to get here, since it's not accessible by public transportation.

The arboretum's modestly named **Children's Garden** is more like a family wonderland, with dozens of nature-friendly attractions (and secret gnomes). Highlights include streams built for splashing, hidden grottoes, and a wooden walkway suspended between evergreen trees. The Visitor Center has an attractive gift shop and restaurant. *Hint:* Schedule your visit on a Wednesday, if you can, when admission is discounted $3 to $4 per person.

4100 Illinois Rte. 53, Lisle. www.mortonarb.org. ℰ **630/968-0074.** Admission $12 adults, $11 seniors, $9 children 2–17. Grounds open daily year-round 7am–7pm (or sunset, whichever comes soonest). Visitor Center 9am–4pm Jan–Feb, 9–5 March–April, 9–6pm May–Oct. Closed Thanksgiving, Christmas Eve at 3pm, Christmas Day. Take I-290 west from downtown Chicago to I-88. Exit north onto Rte. 53 and follow the signs for ½ mile to the entrance.

KID STUFF

Chicago Children's Museum ★★★ KIDS MUSEUM   I know I've already said this, but the Children's Museum is the main reason to visit Navy Pier (that is huge praise!). It also happens to be the second-most visited kids' museum in the country. The entire three-floor building is like a giant playground that also happens to be educational. With 15 permanent exhibits and a number of revolving activities, kids can dig for dinosaur bones, build their own skyscraper, construct a fort under a tree house, take a quick art lesson, climb three floors of ship rigging and get sweaty—and maybe even smarter—while doing so. The museum even has a fun-filled space designated for kids who aren't yet steady on their feet. And in 2013, CCM opened a new permanent exhibit called the Tinkering Lab, which, inspired by the maker movement, seeks to draw in older kids in the 9 to 13 range. Kids can design, hack, experiment, and try their hand at power tools in this supervised creative space. Allow 2 to 3 hours, plus an additional hour to explore the Ferris wheel and other rides and games on Navy Pier.

Navy Pier, 700 E. Grand Ave. www.chicagochildrensmuseum.org. ℰ **312/527-1000.** Admission $14 adults and children, $13 seniors, kids under 1 are free. Free admission Thurs 5–8pm; free for ages 15 and under the first Sun of every month. Daily 10am–5pm (Thurs until 8pm). Closed Thanksgiving and Christmas. Bus: 29, 65, 66, or 124. Subway/El: Red Line to Grand; transfer to city bus or Navy Pier's free trolley bus (Memorial Day through Labor Day).

Lincoln Park Pritzker Children's Zoo & Farm-in-the-Zoo ★ ZOO   After hours of looking at animals from afar in the rest of Lincoln Park Zoo, kids can come here to get up close and personal. Unlike many other children's zoos, there are no baby animals at the **Pritzker Family Children's Zoo;** instead, the outdoor habitats feature wildlife of the North American woods, including wolves, beavers, and otters. Although there are a few interactive displays outside, most kids head inside to the Treetop Canopy Climbing Adventure, a 20-foot-high wood-and-fabric tree (encased in soft safety netting) where they can scramble up and down. There are also a few small padded play areas for little ones.

The **Farm-in-the-Zoo** is a working reproduction of a Midwestern farm, complete with a white-picket-fenced barnyard, chicken coops, and demonstrations of butter churning and weaving. You'll also spot plenty of livestock, including cows, sheep, and pigs. Inside the Main Barn (filled with interactive exhibits), the main attraction is the huge John Deere tractor that kids can climb up into and pretend to drive (Can you say "photo opp"?). In the winter (late Nov–early Mar), Farm-in-the-Zoo is home to an ice skating rink, where you can rent skates or bring your own. Allow 1 hour.

2001 N. Clark St. www.lpzoo.com. ℰ **312/742-2000.** Free admission. Daily 9am–5pm. Bus: 151 or 156.

Six Flags Great America ★ AMUSEMENT PARK   One of the Midwest's biggest theme and amusement parks, Six Flags is midway between Chicago and

As anyone who's traveled with little kids well knows, children can take only so much museum-going. Sometimes they have to let loose and run around—luckily, there are playgrounds tucked away in unassuming spots, as long as you know where to look. The **Seneca Playlot** (220 E. Chicago Ave.) is directly east of the Chicago Water Works Visitor Center and across the street from Water Tower Place mall. The play structures are mostly low-to-the-ground, making it a good choice for toddlers. Walk a few blocks east and you'll come to **Lake Shore Park** (808 N. Lake Shore Dr.), which has a good assortment of slides and climbing equipment. As an added bonus, you'll enjoy views of the lake. An adjoining athletic field has a running track and plenty of space for impromptu soccer or football games. Occupying a large corner lot on the ritzy Gold Coast, **Goudy Square Park,** at the corner of Astor and Goethe streets, is a tranquil oasis surrounded by high-rises. There are three separate play areas, along with plenty of benches for parents to lounge. For more Chicago park options, visit the Chicago Park District's website, www.chicagoparkdistrict.com.

Milwaukee on I-94 in Gurnee, Illinois. The park has more than 100 rides and attractions and is a favorite of roller coaster devotees. Excitement is brewing over the new, wooden dare-devil coaster, Goliath, which opened in 2014 (think mind-blowing, record-breaking heights, speeds, and inversions). That's in addition to the nausea-inducing Déjà Vu, where riders fly forward and backward over a twisting, looping inverted steel track; and Superman, where you speed along hanging headfirst (with your legs dangling). Other don't-miss rides for the strong of stomach include the Iron Wolf, where you do corkscrew turns and 360-degree loops while standing up, and the American Eagle, a classic wooden coaster. Because this place caters to families, you'll also find plenty to appeal to smaller visitors, with three distinct kids areas. Hurricane Harbor, a massive water park with a giant wave pool, is fun on a hot day, but you risk heatstroke waiting in the long lines. Six Flags also has live shows, IMAX movies, and restaurants. If you take the trouble to get out here, allow a full day.

I-94 at Rte. 132 E., Gurnee. www.sixflags.com. ℰ **847/249-4636.** Admission (including unlimited rides, shows, and attractions) $65 adults, $45 children under 48 in. tall, free for children 2 and under. Daily hours change by day, check website for details; on average, expect May–Sept opening daily at 10:30am closing between 7 and 10pm; water park open 11am–5pm or noon–6 dep on day, check website. Parking $22 when purchased online, $25 at park. Take I-94 or I-294 W. to Rte. 132 (Grand Ave.). Approximate driving time from Chicago city limits: 45 min.

SIGHTSEEING TOURS

If you're in town for a limited time, an organized tour may be the best way to get a quick overview of the city's highlights. Some tours—such as the boat cruises on Lake Michigan and the Chicago River—can give a whole new perspective on the city's landscape, and most tours give fascinating insights into Chicago's colorful history as a city.

Chicago Architecture Foundation (CAF) ★★★ Chicago's architecture is world famous. Luckily, the Chicago Architecture Foundation offers first-rate guided tours to help visitors understand what makes this city's skyline so special.

setting sail ON A LAKE OR RIVER CRUISE

Although the Architecture Foundation is my personal favorite for architecture boat tours (see below), a number of other companies also lead informative explorations of the city's skylines. **Chicago Line Cruises** ★★ (465 N. McClurg Court, at the end of E. Illinois St.; www.chicagoline. com; ☏ **312/527-1977;** tickets $42 adults, $35 seniors, $23 children 7–18, free for children 6 and under; April–Nov daily) runs two types of 90-minute cruises: a tour of architecture along the Chicago River, and excursions that travel on the lake and river to explore the development of the city. The atmosphere is more upscale-educational than party-hearty, with knowledgeable guides who make no attempt to double as stand-up comedians. **Shoreline Sightseeing** ★ (departing from Navy Pier, Shedd Aquarium, and Sears Tower; www.shorelinesightseeing. com; ☏ **312/222-9328;** $17–$33 adults, $15-$30 seniors, $8–$21 children 11 and under; May–Sept) launches 40-minute lake cruises every hour, and has also gotten in on the popularity of architecture tours. But the real unique offering of this company is the **water taxi** service, which is a great way to tour the Chicago waterways without paying big bucks. It runs every half hour between Navy Pier and the Willis Tower, Michigan Avenue, and the Shedd Aquarium, and tickets for the water taxi cost $5 to $8, depending how far you travel. Operating since 1935, **Wendella Sightseeing Boats** ★ (400 N. Michigan, departing from Michigan Ave. and Wacker Dr., north side of the river, at

The foundation offers walking, bike, boat, Segway, El, and bus tours to more than 80 architectural sites and environments in and around Chicago, led by nearly 450 trained and enthusiastic docents (all volunteers). I highly recommend taking at least one CAF tour while you're in town—each one will help you look at (and appreciate) the city in a new way. Tours are available year-round but are scheduled less frequently in winter.

One of the CAF's most popular tours is the 1½-hour **Architecture River Cruise,** which glides along both the north and the south branches of the Chicago River. Although you can see the same 50 or so buildings by foot, traveling by water lets you sit back and enjoy the buildings from a unique perspective. The excellent docents provide interesting historical details, as well as some fun facts. (David Letterman once called the busts of the nation's retailing legends that face the Merchandise Mart the "Pez Hall of Fame.") The docents do an applause-worthy job of making the cruise enjoyable for visitors with all levels of architectural knowledge. In addition to pointing out buildings—Marina City, the Civic Opera House, the Willis Tower—they approach the sites thematically, explaining, for example, how Chicagoans' use of and attitudes toward the river have changed over time.

In the summer (late May–mid Oct), cruises run on the hour or half hour (10am–5:30pm Mon–Thurs [7:30pm Thurs], from 9:30am–7:30pm, 9am–5:30pm Sat and 9am–7:30pm Sun); the cost is $38 per person. The trips are popular in the summer, so I'd definitely purchase tickets in advance online if you're hoping for a particular date or time.

If you have a limited amount of time in Chicago and want to squeeze in a lot of sightseeing, try the **Highlights by Bus** tour, a 3½-hour overview that covers the Loop, Hyde Park—including a visit to the interior of Frank Lloyd Wright's Robie House—and the Gold Coast, plus several other historic districts. Tours start at 9:30am on Friday the Wrigley Building, and the Wendella dock at Trump Tower, west of the Wrigley Building at Kinzie and Rush; www.wendellaboats.com; ℭ **312/337-1446;** tickets $29 adults, $26 seniors, $14 children 3–11, free for children 2 and under; weather dependent, March–Nov daily) operates a 75-minute tour along the Chicago River and a 1½-hour tour along the river and out onto Lake Michigan. One of the most dramatic events during the boat tour is passing through the locks that separate the river from the lake. One of the more breathtaking scenes on the lake is **Tall Ship Windy ★★** (departing from Navy Pier; ℭ **312/451-2700;** www.tallshipwindy.com; tickets $30 adults, $25 seniors and students, $10 children 3–12; May–Oct) approaching the docks at Navy Pier. The 148-foot four-masted schooner sets sail for cruises that last about 75 minutes each, and because the course depends on the wind, no two cruises are alike. Cruise themes here are, far and away, the most creative in town and change frequently (as of this writing, the upcoming schedule was still a work in progress) so check the website for details. Past topics have explored pirates, the maritime history of the Great Lakes, haunted harbors, and more. Passengers are welcome to help raise and trim the sails and occasionally take turns at the ship's helm (with the captain standing close by). Definitely an only-in-Chicago experience! The boats are not accessible for people with disabilities.

and Saturday year-round, with additional tours on Wednesdays and Sundays from April through October; tickets are $45 per person.

A 4-hour bus tour of Frank Lloyd Wright sights in **Oak Park** ($45) is available on the first Saturday of the month from May to October. The tour includes walks through three neighborhoods and commentary on more than 25 houses—but does not take visitors inside Wright's home and studio.

The CAF offers a variety of guided walking tours. For first-time visitors, I highly recommend two tours for an excellent introduction to the dramatic architecture of the Loop. **Historic Downtown: Rise of the Skyscraper** (daily 10am) covers buildings built between 1880 and 1940, including the Rookery and the Chicago Board of Trade; **Modern Skyscrapers** (daily 1pm) includes modern masterpieces by Mies van der Rohe and postmodern works by contemporary architects. The 2-hour tours cost $17 each.

The CAF also offers more than 50 **neighborhood tours** (see website for full list), visiting the Gold Coast, River North, Grant Park, Old Town, the Jackson Boulevard Historic District, and even Lincoln Park Zoo. Most cost $10 and last a couple of hours.

Departing from the Chicago ArchiCenter, 224 S. Michigan Ave.; a few tours leave from the John Hancock Center, 875 N. Michigan Ave. www.architecture.org. ℭ **312/922-3432,** or 312/922-TOUR [8687] for recorded information. Tickets for most walking tours $10–$17. Subway/El: Brown, Green, Purple, Pink, or Orange Line to Adams, or Red Line to Jackson.

Chicago Trolley & Double Decker Company ★★ Chicago Trolley Company offers guided tours on a fleet of rubber-wheeled "San Francisco–style" trolleys that stop at a number of popular spots around the city, including Navy Pier, the Grant Park museums, the historic Water Tower, and the Willis Tower. You can stay on for the full 2-hour ride or get on and off at each stop. During the summer, the trolleys also offer trips to residential neighborhoods, and I highly recommend the West

Architecture junkies may want to visit the **Charnley-Persky House,** 1365 N. Astor St., in the Gold Coast (www. charnleyhouse.org; © **312/915-0105**), designed by Frank Lloyd Wright and Louis Sullivan in 1891. Sullivan was Frank Lloyd Wright's architectural mentor, and although Wright was a junior draftsman on this project, Sullivan allowed him to become involved in the design process. The result is an important landmark in modern architecture that rejected Victorian details and embraced symmetry and simplicity. Free 45-minute tours of the interior are given on Wednesday at noon. A 90-minute tour of the home and the surrounding neighborhood is offered Saturdays at 10am year-round ($10). Reservations are not accepted.

Neighborhood Tour. The witty guide sums up the history of Chicago, points out iconic buildings, and fills you in on the diverse neighborhoods, while also driving through Chinatown, Pilsen, and Little Italy; you can hop off for dim sum and then hop on the next trolley and continue on to tacos followed by pasta, and you never have to worry about navigating public transportation or search for parking. The trolleys operate year-round and are enclosed and heated during the chilliest months. The same company also operates the **Chicago Double Decker Company,** which has a fleet of London-style red buses. The two-level buses follow the same route as the trolleys; if you buy an all-day pass, you can hop from bus to trolley at any point.

615 W. 41st St. www.coachusa.com/chicagotrolley. © **773/648-5000.** Three-day hop-on, hop-off pass $45 adults, $40 seniors, $17 children 3–11. Daily 9am–6pm. No tours New Year's Day, Thanksgiving, or Christmas.

Chicago Detours ★★★ ARCHITECTURE/HISTORY TOURS This small, independently owned company knows what it's doing and the result is creative, informative, and fun tours. That's because the owner of the company worked for nearly a decade as a tour guide and guidebook researcher herself. I recently went on a tour called "Interior Architecture of the Loop," which has the bonus of being indoors for the majority of the time (I took the tour mid-winter), and was pleasantly surprised to find that my group was made up of 95% locals—a rave review if there ever was one. The tour took us through Chicago's pedway, an underground system that lets downtown workers get from building to building without facing the elements in the winter, and also highlighted different pieces of public art and architecture, while sharing stories of developmental failures and weaving tales about famous Chicago names, like Marshall Field. The guide was well versed in history, art, architecture, and Chicago, and was also an excellent storyteller. Detours also offers tours that include a historic bar crawl and a visit to the Chicago Temple (aka "The Skyscraper Church").

Loop Interior Architecture Tour, $26/person, departs from the southeast corner of Chase Tower, 10 S. Dearborn St. Times are Mon 11am; Wed/Thurs 10am; Fri 3pm; Sat/Sun 11am, 1:30pm. Historic bar tours, $34/person, leaves from Argo Tea in Tribune Tower, 435 N. Michigan Ave. Times are Thurs/Fri 5:30pm; Sat 5pm and 5:45pm. www.chicagodetours.com. © **312/350-1131.**

Untouchable Tours ★ The days of Al Capone are long gone, but Chicago's notorious past is still good for business, it seems, given the popularity of these "Gangster Tours." The 2-hour bus trip takes you to all of the city's old hoodlum hangouts from the Prohibition era, including O'Bannion's flower shop and the site of the St.

Valentine's Day massacre. The focus is definitely more on entertainment than history (guides with names such as "Al Dente" and "Ice Pick" appear in costume and role-play their way through the tour). It has its cheesy moments, for sure, but the trip does give you a pretty thorough overview of the city and its mobster ties.

Departs from the southeast corner of Clark and Ohio sts. www.gangstertour.com. © **773/881-1195.** Tickets $30. Tours depart Mon–Thurs 11am; Fri 11am, 1pm, 7pm; Sat 11am, 1pm, 3pm, 5pm, 7pm; Sun 11am, 1pm.

NEIGHBORHOOD TOURS

I highly encourage picking a neighborhood, hopping on a train, and exploring on your own. But if you're limited on time and sense of direction, the city puts on some enlightening tours. Sponsored by the Department of Cultural Affairs, **Chicago Neighborhood Tours** ★ (www.chgocitytours.com; © 312/742-1190) are 4- to 5-hour narrated bus excursions to about a dozen diverse communities throughout the city. Departing at 10am from the **Chicago Cultural Center** (p. 120), 77 E. Randolph St., every Saturday, the tours visit different neighborhoods, from Chinatown and historic Bronzeville on the South Side to the ethnic enclaves of Devon Avenue and Uptown on the North Side. Neighborhood representatives serve as guides and greeters along the way as tour participants visit area landmarks, murals, museums, and shopping districts. Tickets (including a light snack) are $25 for adults and $20 for seniors, students, and children 8 to 18. Tours do not run on major holidays (call first) or, usually, in January. The city also sponsors **Special Interest Tours,** which generally run about 4 to 6 hours and include lunch ($50 adults, $45 seniors and students). Regular topics include Literary Chicago, the Great Chicago Fire, Cemeteries and Monuments, the White City, Taste of the Neighborhoods, Polish Chicago, Greek Chicago, and others. Tours run throughout the year on Saturday mornings, departing from the **Chicago Cultural Center** at 10am.

The **Chicago History Museum** offers 2-hour walking tours of the neighborhoods surrounding the museum: the **Gold Coast, Old Town,** and **Sheffield,** and **Graceland Cemetery.** Led by museum docents, they average about four per month June through August. Day and evening tours are available, and a few specialty walking tours are usually offered as well. Tours are $20 per person, and registration is recommended but not required. Tours depart from the museum at Clark Street and North Avenue, and light refreshments are served afterward. The museum also offers stroller tours, El tours, running tours, and a pub crawl. Call © 312/642-4600, or visit the museum's website (www.chicagohistory.org) for schedules and to order tickets online.

Groups interested in African-American history should visit **Bronzeville** (also known as the "Black Metropolis"), the South Side neighborhood where immigrants from the South created a flourishing business and artistic community in the 1930s and '40s. Walking and bus tours of the area can be arranged through the **Bronzeville Visitor Information Center** (3501 S. Martin Luther King Dr.; www.bviconline.info; © 773/819-2054). A locally based company that specializes in black heritage tours, **Black CouTours** (www.blackcoutours.com; © 773/233-8907) offers a "Soul Side of the Windy City" tour, which includes Oprah and Obama-related sites.

CEMETERY TOURS

Don't be scared away by the creepy connotations. Some of Chicago's cemeteries are as pretty as parks, and they offer a variety of intriguing monuments that are a virtual road into the city's history.

One of the most impressive cemeteries is **Graceland,** stretching along Clark Street in the Uptown neighborhood, where you can view the tombs and monuments of many

Chicago notables. When Graceland was laid out in 1860, public parks were rare. The elaborate burial grounds that were constructed in many large American cities around that time had the dual purpose of relieving the congestion of the municipal cemeteries closer to town and providing pastoral recreational settings for the Sunday outings of the living. Indeed, cemeteries like Graceland were the precursors of such great municipal green spaces as Lincoln Park. If you're interested in a self-guided tour, you can purchase a 1922 historical road map from the office for $5.

The **Chicago Architecture Foundation** (www.architecture.org; ✆ **312/922-TOUR** [8687]) offers walking tours of Graceland on select Sundays during August, September, and October. The tour costs $15 and lasts about two hours. Among the points of interest in these 121 beautifully landscaped acres are the Ryerson and Getty tombs, famous architectural monuments designed by Louis Sullivan. Sullivan himself rests here in the company of several of his distinguished colleagues: Daniel Burnham, Ludwig Mies van der Rohe, and Howard Van Doren Shaw. Chicago giants of industry and commerce buried at Graceland include Potter Palmer, Marshall Field, and George Pullman. The Chicago Architecture Foundation offers tours of other cemeteries, including Rosehill Cemetery, suburban Lake Forest Cemetery, and Oak Woods Cemetery, the final resting place for many famous African-American figures, including Jesse Owens, Ida B. Wells, and Mayor Harold Washington.

STAYING ACTIVE

Because winters can be brutal, Chicagoans take their summers seriously. In the warmer months, with the wide blue lake, bright green parks, and 26 miles of beach, the city transforms into one big grown-up playground. Whether you prefer your activity in the water or on dry ground, you'll probably find it here. For information, contact the city's **park district** (www.chicagoparkdistrict.com; ✆ **312/742-PLAY** [7529]).

Beaches

Public beaches line Lake Michigan all the way up north into the suburbs and Wisconsin, and southeast through Indiana and into Michigan. The best known is **Oak Street Beach.** Its location, at the northern tip of the Magnificent Mile, creates some interesting sights as sun worshippers sporting swimsuits and carting coolers make their way down Michigan Avenue. Lincoln Park singles come to ogle one another at **North Avenue Beach,** about six blocks farther north. Here, you'll find the sand filled with rows of sun bathers and beach volleyball players, while kids build sand castles near the lake and mom and dad seek refuge at the vintage steamship-shaped beach house. **Hollywood-Ardmore Beach** (officially Kathy Osterman Beach), at the northern end of Lake Shore Drive, is a lovely crescent that's less congested and has steadily become more popular with gays who've moved up the lakefront from the Belmont Rocks, a longtime hangout. For more seclusion, try **Ohio Street Beach,** an intimate sliver of sand in tiny Olive Park, just north of Navy Pier, which, incredibly enough, remains largely ignored despite its central location. If you have a car, head up to **Montrose Beach,** a beautiful unsung treasure about midway between North Avenue Beach and Hollywood-Ardmore Beach (with plenty of free parking). It has an expanse of beach mostly uninterrupted by piers or jetties, and a huge adjacent park with soccer fields, one big hill that's great for kite flying, and even a small bait shop where anglers can go before heading to a nearby long pier designated for fishing.

BIKE safely

Aside from the popular lake path, Chicago has more than 200 miles of designated bike lanes, and it's often faster to get around the city by bike than it is by car or public transportation. With that said, urban cycling has its risks, and if you're planning on doing it, there are a few things you should know.

1. **Wear a helmet.** This is a bustling city, and cyclists share the streets with cars, buses, pedestrians, and aggressive cab drivers. You should always wear a helmet here.

2. **Stay off the sidewalks.** It's illegal to ride on the sidewalk in Chicago, and you can and will get a ticket, along with dirty looks from pedestrians. If you're uncomfortable riding in the street because of traffic or other conditions, walk your bike along the sidewalk.

3. **Watch out for parked cars.** It seems counterintuitive, but parked cars to your right can be more dangerous than those moving on your left. That's because careless drivers will often park and then, without checking the mirror, open the driver-side door directly into the path of a biker. "Dooring," as it's known, actually happens quite frequently. Be sure and ride a couple of feet away from parked cars and be vigilant about what's happening around you.

4. **Follow traffic laws.** Stop at stop signs and stop lights, use hand signals for stopping and turning, and head in the same direction as vehicle traffic. Be aware that there are many cyclists in Chicago, and many bike lanes have a steady flow. If you stop or turn suddenly, you risk being hit by the cyclist behind you. (It's happened to me.) Also, pedestrians have the right of way, so stop for them as needed.

5. **Lock your bike.** And not with one of those chain-link locks, which can be cut through in a heartbeat. Use a hefty U-lock. Bike theft is a huge problem in Chicago. I've actually had the seat stolen off of my bike, in a perfectly nice part of town.

If you've brought the pooch along, you might want to take him for a dip at the **doggie beach** south of Addison Street, at about Hawthorne and Lake Shore Drive. *Warning:* This minute spot aggravates some dog owners because it's in a harbor where the water is somewhat fouled by gas and oil from nearby boats. A better choice might be the south end of North Avenue Beach in early morning, before it opens to the public for the day. Keep in mind that in the off-season, all beaches are fair game for dogs.

The beach season runs from late May through early September (go to www.cpdbeaches.com for more info). Only the bravest souls venture into the water before July, and even then the water runs chilly. Please take note that the entire lakefront is not beach, and diving off the rocks is a bad idea. There are some pretty rough waves out there!

Biking

In 2013, the City of Chicago launched its new bike share program, called **Divvy** (www.divvybikes.com). Today, there are hundreds of Divvy stations across town, and to rent one, you can just swipe your credit or debit card, pay $7, and it's yours for the day (for longer-term use, an annual membership is $75). But there are limits. Divvy is aimed at people who are looking to take a quick trip from spot A to B, not tour the entire city.

Every 30 minutes, you have to return your bike to a station, and, if you wish to continue riding, check out a new bike.

That said, biking is a great way to see the city, particularly along the 18-mile lakefront path. The stretch between Navy Pier and North Avenue Beach gets extremely crowded in the summer (you're jostling for space with in-line skaters, joggers, and dawdling pedestrians), so if you're looking to pick up some speed, bike south. Once you're past the Museum Campus, the trail is relatively wide open, and you can zip all the way to Hyde Park. If you want a more leisurely tour with people-watching potential, head north, through the crowds. After you pass Belmont Harbor, the traffic lets up a bit. Ride all the way to Hollywood Beach, where the lakefront trail ends, for a good but not exhausting workout.

If you're interested in truly touring the city by bike, and don't want to deal with the hassle of checking your cruiser back in every half hour, it's best to rent one from **Bike and Roll Chicago** (www.bikechicago.com; ☎ **312/729-1000**), which has locations at Navy Pier, along the River Walk (at Wacker Dr. and Wabash Ave.), and at Millennium Park. This cycling outfit stocks mountain and touring bikes, kids' bikes, and even bike strollers. Rates for bikes start at $10 an hour, $35 a day, with helmets, pads, and locks included. If you'd like to cycle your way past some Chicago landmarks, guided tours are also available.

Both the park district (☎ **312/742-PLAY** [7529]) and the **Active Transportation Alliance** (www.activetrans.org; ☎ **312/427-3325**) offer free maps that detail popular biking routes. The latter, which is the preeminent organization for cyclists in Chicago, sells a much larger, more extensive map ($10) that shows routes within a seven-county area. The federation sponsors a number of bike rides throughout the year, so check the calendar for details.

One of Chicago's most popular rides is **Critical Mass**, www.chicagocriticalmass. org, held the last Friday of every month, rain or shine. Hundreds and often thousands of riders meet at 5:30pm at Daley Plaza, at Dearborn and Washington streets, and embark on a group ride, filling the rush-hour roads and, effectively, shutting down traffic wherever they go. The rides generally last a few hours, but you can pop in and out along the way and do as much or as little as you care to do. Some bring flasks, others bring kids, and you never quite know what you're going to get in this parade on wheels.

Golfing

For a major metropolis, Chicago has an impressive number of golf options within the city limits (not to mention many plush and pricey suburban courses). The Chicago Park District runs eight golf courses in the city. One of the most beautiful is the **Diversey Driving Range,** 141 W. Diversey Pkwy., in Lincoln Park just north of Diversey Harbor. This two-level range attracts all levels—from show-off heavy hitters to beginners—and is very popular on weekends with young singles who live in the surrounding apartment buildings. The price is right ($16 for a bucket of 100 balls), and the setting is pretty much perfect.

Another popular range is the 9-hole **Sydney Marovitz Course,** 3600 N. Lake Shore Dr. (at Waveland Ave.), which many Chicagoans simply call Waveland. Thanks to its picturesque lakefront location, it's always full on weekends, so make a reservation well in advance (and don't expect a quick game—this is where beginners come to practice). Another good bet—and usually less crowded—is the 18-hole course in **Jackson Park** on the South Side (63rd St. and Stoney Island Ave.). These city-run courses are open from mid-April through November; for information on greens fees, location, and hours, call the **Chicago Park District** golf office (② **312/245-0909;** www.cpdgolf.com).

For information about suburban golf courses, visit the website of the **Chicago District Golf Association** (www.cdga.org).

Ice Skating

The city's premier skating destination is the **McCormick-Tribune Ice Rink** at Millennium Park, 55 N. Michigan Ave. (www.millenniumpark.org; ② **312/742-1168**). The location is pretty much perfect: You're skating in the shadows of grand skyscrapers and within view of the lake on 16,000 square feet of well-groomed ice. The rink is open November through March, Monday through Thursday noon to 8pm; Friday noon to 10pm, Saturday 10am to 10pm; Sunday 10am to 9pm (be sure to call ahead; hours are subject to change). Admission is free, and skate rentals are $10.

The park district runs dozens of other skating surfaces throughout the city, along the lakefront and in neighborhood parks. Call ② **312/742-PLAY** [7529] for locations. There's also a relatively small rink at **Navy Pier,** 600 E. Grand Ave. (② **312/595-PIER** [7437]).

In-Line Skating

The wheeled ones have been battling bikers over control of Chicago's lakefront paths since the early 1990s. If you want to join in the competition, **Bike and Roll Chicago,** which has multiple locations, including at Millennium Park, 239 E. Randolph Street; and Navy Pier, 600 E. Grand Ave. (www.bikechicago.com; ② **312/729-1000**), rents blades for $10 an hour or $35 a day. The best route to skate is the lakefront trail. Beware, though, that those same miles of trail are claimed by avid cyclists, runners, walkers, and strollers, and collisions between distracted 'bladers and all of the above have been known to happen. On busy summer days, approach Chicago lakefront traffic as carefully as you would a major expressway.

Sailing

It seems a shame just to sit on the beach and watch all those beautiful sailboats gliding across the lake, so go on, get out there. **Chicago Sailing,** in Belmont Harbor (www. chicagosailing.com; ② **773/871-SAIL** [7245]), rents a variety of sail boats from 8am to sunset, weather permitting, May through October. A J-22, which holds four or five adults, rents for $55 to $75 an hour; a J-30, which accommodates up to 10 people, costs $90 to $110 per hour. New renters are required to submit a sailing résumé, and you'll need to prove to staff that you have the skills to sail. If you'd rather sit back and relax, you can charter a boat. Reservations are recommended.

Swimming

The Chicago Park District maintains dozens of indoor pools for lap swimming and general splashing around, but none is particularly convenient to downtown. The lakefront is open for swimming until 9:30pm Memorial Day to Labor Day in areas watched over by lifeguards (no swimming off the rocks, please). *But be forewarned:* The water is usually freezing. If you're willing to take a dip anyway, a good place for lake swimming is the water along the wall beginning at Ohio Street Beach, slightly northwest of Navy Pier. The Chicago Triathlon Club marks a course here each summer with a buoy at both the quarter- and half-mile distances. This popular swimming route follows the shoreline in a straight line. The water is fairly shallow. For more information, call the park district's beach and pool office (☎ **312/742-PLAY** [7529]).

Yoga/Fitness Classes

The yoga craze is running strong in Chicago, and there are some beautiful spots to bring your mat. Year-round, you can commune with the butterflies during Butterfly Haven Yoga at **Peggy Notebaert Nature Museum** (2430 N. Cannon Dr., at Fullerton Pkwy.; www.naturemuseum.org; ☎ **773/755-5100;** see p. 135), offered Saturdays, 8:30–9:45am, for $15. **Millennium Park** offers free workouts, including yoga, tai chi, pilates, and Zumba on the Great Lawn 7am to 11am every Saturday morning, June through September. Visit www.millenniumpark.org for the schedule. **Lincoln Park Zoo** offers yoga classes for adults, as well as parents and toddlers, at the Nature Park Boardwalk June through August. Check www.lpzoo.org for times.

SPORTS

Baseball

Baseball is imprinted on the national consciousness as part of Chicago, not because of victorious dynasties, but because of the opposite—the Black Sox scandal of 1919 and the perennially losing Cubs.

The **Chicago Cubs** haven't made a World Series appearance since 1945 and haven't been world champs since 1908, but that doesn't stop people from catching games at historic **Wrigley Field** ★★, 1060 W. Addison St. (www.cubs.mlb.com; ☎ **773/404-CUBS** [2827]), with its ivy-covered outfield walls, its hand-operated scoreboard, its view of the shimmering lake from the upper deck, and its "W" or "L" flag announcing the outcome of the game to the unfortunates who couldn't attend. After all the strikes, temper tantrums, and other nonsense, Wrigley has managed to hold on to something like purity. Yes, Wrigley finally installed lights (it was the last major-league park to do so), but by agreement with the residential neighborhood, the Cubs still play most games in the daylight, as they should. Because Wrigley is small, just about every seat is decent.

No matter how the Cubs are doing, tickets go fast; most weekend and night games sell out by Memorial Day. Your best bet is to hit a weekday game, or try your luck buying a ticket on game day outside the park, when you'll often find some season ticket holders looking to unload a few seats.

Wrigley's easy to reach by El; take the Red Line to the Addison stop, and you're there. Call ☎ **800/THE-CUBS** [843-2827] for tickets through **Tickets.com** (☎ **866/652-2827** outside Illinois); you can also order online through the team website.

Despite their stunning World Series win in 2005, the **Chicago White Sox** still struggle to attract the same kind of loyalty (despite the fact that they regularly win more games than the Cubs). Longtime fans rue the day owner Jerry Reinsdorf replaced admittedly dilapidated Comiskey Park with a concrete behemoth that lacks the yesteryear charm of its predecessor. That said, the current stadium, **U.S. Cellular Field,** 333 W. 35th St. (www.whitesox.mlb.com; ☎ **312/674-1000**), in the South Side neighborhood of Bridgeport, has spectacular sightlines from every seat (if you avoid the vertigo-inducing upper deck), and the park has every conceivable amenity, including above-average food concessions, shops, and plentiful restrooms. The White Sox's endearing quality is the blue-collar aura with which so many Cubs-loathing southsiders identify. Games rarely sell out—an effect, presumably, of Reinsdorf's sterile

Built in 1914, Wrigley Field is the second-oldest major-league ballpark, after Boston's Fenway Park, and remains one of the only surviving old-time baseball stadiums in the country (no luxury boxes here!). Known as the "friendly confines," Wrigley Field was the site of Babe Ruth's "called shot," when Ruth allegedly pointed to a bleacher location in the 1932 World Series and then hit a home run to that exact spot. For an intimate look at the historic ballpark, take one of the behind-the-scenes tours offered almost daily throughout the summer. Tours last 75 minutes to an hour and a half, and stops include the visitors' and home team locker rooms, press box, security headquarters, and yes, a walk around the field itself (be sure to check out the original scoreboard, built in 1937). Some dates do sell out, so buy tickets ($25) in advance online, if possible. Keep in mind that if you take a tour on a game day, some areas (such as the locker rooms) will be off-limits. Call ✆ 773/404-CUBS [2827], or stop by the box office at 1060 W. Addison St.; you can also buy tickets online through the Cubs website (www.mlb.com/chc/ballpark/wrigley_field_tours.jsp).

stadium and the blighted neighborhood that surrounds it. All of this makes it a bargain for bona fide baseball fans.

To get Sox tickets, call **Ticketmaster** (✆ **866/SOX-GAME** [769-4263]), or visit the ticket office, open Monday through Friday from 10am to 6pm, Saturday and Sunday from 10am to 4pm, with extended hours on game days. To get to the ballpark by El, take the Red Line to Sox/35th Street.

Basketball

When it comes to basketball, Chicagoans still live in the past, associating the **Chicago Bulls** (www.nba.com/bulls; ✆ **312/455-4000**) with the glory days of Michael Jordan and the never-ending championships of the 1990s. The fact that Jordan chose to remain in town after his playing days were over—a decision almost unheard of in professional sports—has only burnished his image here, and locals are still wowed by occasional Jordan sightings. The downside is that he's a constant reminder of our ever-more-distant winning past.

Although the current players don't inspire the same city-wide fervor, the Bulls have rebounded somewhat from the dismal seasons following Jordan's departure and even made some respectable showings in post-season play. The Bulls don't consistently sell out, which means you might be able to catch a game at the cavernous **United Center,** 1901 W. Madison St. (www.unitedcenter.com; ✆ **312/455-4500**). Yes, the space is massive and impersonal, but the pre-game buildup, with flashing lights and thumping music, is undeniably dramatic. You can get tickets through **Ticketmaster** (✆ **312/559-1212**). Be aware that the cheap seats are practically in the rafters. If money is no object, you can usually score good seats through local ticket brokers without much advance notice.

Football

The **Chicago Bears** play at **Soldier Field,** Lake Shore Drive and 16th Street (www.chicagobears.com; ✆ **847/295-6600**), site of a controversial renovation that added what looks like a giant space ship on top of the original stadium's elegant colonnade. Architecturally, it's a disaster, but from a comfort perspective, the place is much improved—although that doesn't impress longtime fans who prided themselves on surviving blistering-cold game days and horrifying bathrooms. The Bears themselves have been inspiring high hopes—most recently, winning a trip to the Super Bowl in 2007. But even during losing seasons, tickets are hard to come by. (Most are snapped up by season ticket holders long before the season starts.)

The **Northwestern Wildcats** play Big Ten college ball at **Ryan Field,** 1501 Central St., in nearby Evanston (℃ **847/491-CATS** [2287]). Unfortunately, Northwestern grads are not particularly loyal to their long-suffering team. In fact, fans of the visiting team often outnumber NU supporters in the stands.

Hockey

The **Chicago Blackhawks** have devoted, impassioned fans who work themselves into a frenzy with the first note of "The Star-Spangled Banner," but for years, they had to put up with mediocre play and less-than-stellar management. Over the past few seasons, though, the team that once boasted legends such as Bobby Hull and Tony Esposito has made a comeback, winning the Stanley Cup in 2010. Going to a Hawks games has once again become a rousing—and sometimes rowdy—experience. The Blackhawks play at the **United Center,** 1901 W. Madison St. (http://blackhawks.nhl. com; ℃ **312/455-7000**).

For a more affordable and family-friendly outing, catch the semipro **Chicago Wolves** at Allstate Arena, 6920 N. Mannheim Rd., Rosemont (www.chicagowolves. com; ℃ **847/724-GOAL** [4625]). The team has been consistently excellent over the past few years, and the games are geared toward all ages, with fireworks beforehand and plenty of on- and off-ice entertainment.

Soccer

Chicago's Major League Soccer team, the **Chicago Fire,** plays at its own 20,000-seat stadium in suburban Bridgeview (about 12 miles southwest of downtown). The season runs from late May through October (www.chicago-fire.com; ℃ **888/MLS-FIRE** [657-3473]). Games have a family feel, with plenty of activities for kids and affordable ticket prices.

SHOPPING

I f you're coming to Chicago to shop, you may want to pack an extra suitcase. Here, finding great stores is a given—they're everywhere. The hard part is narrowing down what you're looking for and where. In this chapter, I'll introduce you to some of Chicago's unique, stand-out shops that you won't find back home, while also giving brief descriptions of the "shopping personality" of different districts.

The big names in fashion—from Prada to Louis Vuitton—are all represented here, but you don't have to be a big spender to enjoy a Chicago shopping spree. The city's commercial success comes from offering something for everyone, and it's all about location, location, location. Here's my round up of the city's best shopping areas, followed by some favorite, must-see stores.

The Basics

Shopping Hours As a general rule, store hours are 10 or 11am to 6 or 7pm Monday through Saturday, and noon to 6pm Sunday. Stores along Michigan Avenue tend to keep later hours, because they cater to after-work shoppers as well as tourists. Almost all stores have extended hours during the holiday season. Nearly all of the stores in the Loop are open for daytime shopping only, generally from 9 or 10am to no later than 6pm Monday through Saturday. (The few remaining big downtown department stores have some selected evening hours.) Many Loop stores not on State Street are closed Saturday; on Sunday, the Loop—except for a few restaurants, theaters, and cultural attractions—shuts down.

Sales Tax You might do a double-take after checking the total on your purchase: At 9.25%, the local sales tax on nonfood items is one of the steepest in the country.

SHOPPING BY AREA

The Magnificent Mile

The overall area, which runs about eight blocks on Michigan Avenue, from the Chicago River north to Oak Street, is a little like New York's Fifth Avenue and Beverly Hills's Rodeo Drive rolled into one. The big name brands are all accounted for here, and whether your passion is Bulgari jewelry, Prada bags, or Salvatore Ferragamo footwear, you'll find it packed densely into this stretch of concrete. This is also home to the city's highest concentration of malls. The **900 North Michigan Shops** (900 N. Michigan Ave., btw. Walton St. and Delaware Place; www.shop900.com; © **312/915-3916**) is the higher end among them, with Bloomingdale's as its anchor tenant. **Water Tower Place** (835 N. Michigan Ave., btw. Pearson and

Chestnut sts.; www.shopwatertower.com; ℂ **312/440-3166**) is the most boisterous, with seven floors of shops, each of which can get shockingly packed with suburban teens in the summer time. Macy's and American Girl Place are two of the most popular places to peruse here. And **The Shops at North Bridge** (520 N. Michigan Ave., btw. Grand Ave. and Illinois St.; www.theshopsatnorthbridge.com; ℂ **312/327-2300**) are rather tranquil for a mall, with Nordstrom serving as anchor. For the most part, those malls are home to many of the types of chain stores you'll find across the country, so rather than going into painstaking mall detail, I've included shop highlights in the listings below.

Oak Street

Oak Street has long been a symbol of designer-label shopping; if a store has an Oak Street address, you can count on it being expensive. This shopping district itself is actually quite limited, taking up only one block at the northern tip of the Magnificent Mile (where Michigan Ave. ends and Lake Shore Dr. begins). While big-name designer showcases such as Giorgio Armani and Louis Vuitton pride themselves on having a Michigan Avenue address, Oak Street features smaller, more personal shops, like Tod's, and Hermès of Paris.

State Street & the Loop

State Street has a no-frills aura compared to Michigan Avenue—but it stays busy thanks to the thousands of office workers who stroll around during their lunch hour or after work. On weekends, the street is considerably more subdued. The main attraction here is **Macy's at State Street** (formerly Marshall Field's, see p. 176), but a number of chain stores (Nordstrom Rack, T.J.Maxx, Old Navy, H&M) also draw in penny pinchers.

River North

In the area west of the Magnificent Mile and north of the Chicago River, the mod home design shops, including **Bloomingdale's Medinah Home Store** (p. 175), will have you wishing for a home makeover. On the southwestern end of River North, **Merchandise Mart,** the world's largest commercial building, looms above the Chicago River. Unless it's December, when the **One of a Kind Show** (www.oneofakindshowchicago. com) brings in artists and jewelers to display their wares, keep on walking. The market for Merchandise Mart is professional designers, not the general public.

If the quick change from north to south in the Loop confuses you, keep in mind that in Chicago, "Point Zero" for the purpose of address numbering is the intersection of State and Madison streets.

Armitage Avenue

Hovering between the North Side neighborhoods of Old Town and Lincoln Park, Armitage Avenue has emerged as a shopping destination in its own right, thanks to an influx of wealthy young professionals who have settled into historic town homes on the neighboring tree-lined streets. Sophisticated boutiques aimed at well-heeled female shoppers line the streets here, and there are even catnip cigars and doggie "sushi" for their animals at the boutique pet shop. Second-hand shops, like **Millionaire Rejects** (p. 181), are a great lure for those of us up for bargain hunting. Start at the Armitage El stop on the Brown Line, and work your way east to Halsted Street, and then wander a few blocks north to Webster Street.

Lincoln Park & Lakeview

Radiating from the intersection of Belmont Avenue and Clark Street, you've arrived in the Boystown vicinity. Shops here are what high school boys' fantasies are made of: sex shops, records, leather jackets, bongs, comics, clothing stores with DJs, and more. Further west, wander along Southport from Belmont north to Addison, where women will be relieved to find a shoe store and boutique or two that they, too, can browse, and try on flirty dresses from **Cerato** (p. 173).

Wicker Park/Bucktown

Mixed in with old neighborhood businesses, such as discount furniture stores and religious icon purveyors, is a proliferation of antique furniture shops, edgy clothing boutiques, and eclectic galleries and gift emporiums. Despite the hefty price tags in many of these shops, the neighborhood is still just gritty enough to feel like an urban fix. Start at the Damen El stop on the Blue Line and walk north southeast along Milwaukee Ave., where you'll find a wealth of used books at **Myopic Books** (p. 171), records at **Reckless Records** (p. 180) and tempting trinkets at **Rudy's Roundup** (p. 179).

RECOMMENDED STORES

Antiques

Antiquers on the hunt head to **Chicago Antique Market** at the **Randolph Street Market** (1340 W. Washington; ✆ **312/666-1200**)—which takes place one weekend a month, in the West Loop—to browse vintage furnishings, housewares, watches, jewelry, clothing, and other finds from more than 200 vendors. Although it's open year-round, the market is far more fun in the summer, when the outdoor areas take on a street fest atmosphere, with live music, food, and drinks.

If you prefer to sort through piles of junk in brick and mortar stores, head to **Belmont Avenue west of Southport Avenue,** where a cluster of independently owned

It's not quite as impressive as the Big Apple's diamond district, but Chicago's own "Jewelers' Row" is certainly worth a detour for rock hunters. Half a dozen high-rises along the Wabash Avenue El tracks in the heart of the Loop service the wholesale trade, but the **Mallers Building** at 5 S. Wabash Avenue opens its doors to customers off the street.

There's a mall-like retail space on the ground floor crammed with tiny booths manned by smooth-talking reps hawking their wares. It's quite an experience—many of the booths are cubbyholes with hunched-over geezers who look as if they've been eyeballing solitaire and marquise cuts since the Roosevelt administration—Teddy, that is.

antique stores, such as **Lazy Dog Antiques** ★ (1903 W. Belmont, at Wolcott Ave.; www.lazydogantiques.com; ✆ 773/281-3644), are filled with well-maintained home furnishings and jewelry, and will keep you busy for the day.

For those less interested in urban antique spelunking, **Architectural Artifacts** ★★ (4325 N. Ravenswood Ave., east of Damen Ave. and south of Montrose Ave.; www.architecturalartifacts.com; ✆ 773/348-0622) is kind of like a museum gift shop, only the items for sale are the real deal—like a $45,000 medallion designed by famous architect Louis Sullivan, a $5,900 Japanese tea pot from the Edo period, or a $2,200 stained glass panel from a Lakeshore Drive penthouse. Even if it's entirely out of your price range, it's worth the short, 30-minute commute to the Ravenswood neighborhood to explore (take the Brown Line to Montrose).

Beauty

Merz Apothecary ★★★ Tinctures, salves, ointments: They're all here, at this old-timey beauty shop. A pharmacist opened Merz in 1875, selling herbal medicines and treatments that would, today, be classified as "alternative." The shelves are stocked with all-natural soaps, lotions, perfumes, creams, balms and other skin-care items that smell so good, they will make you want to immediately switch brands from whatever you last bought at Target. A second location in Lincoln Square (4617 N. Lincoln Ave., near Giddings Plaza; ✆ 773/989-0900) even has a pharmacist on hand to answer questions. 17 East Monroe (in the Palmer House Hotel). www.merzapothecary.com. ✆ 312/781-6900. Subway/El: Red Line to Monroe or Brown, Pink, Green, Purple, or Orange line to Adams/Wabash.

Mojo Spa ★ If you were to glance too quickly around this small Wicker Park store/spa, you might think you were in a bakery. That's because many of the soaps look like delectable cupcakes, layer cakes, and bundt cakes. The store's owner, a personal chef, created many of these items herself, using food ingredients, after struggling to find the natural skin care products she loved. There are also bath salts, perfumes, lotions, balms, scrubs, and oils, all locally made, and a spa in back does manis, pedis, scrubs, and soaks. 1468 N. Milwaukee (btw. Evergreen Ave. and Honore St.). www.mojospa.com. ✆ 773/235-6656. Subway/El: Blue Line to Damen.

Ruby Room ★ The fresh, floral scent is immediately soothing, and the ladies who work here are smiley and helpful. This one-stop-beauty shop offers a little bit of everything, from the usual—scrubs, balms, and lotions, along with a spa and salon—to the woo-woo—energy healing, colon hydrotherapy, and an "infrared amethyst biomat" (I didn't ask). The spa gets extra points for feeling so normal and comfortable, even to

Since the 1960s, when the Chicago Imagists (painters Ed Paschke, Jim Nutt, and Roger Brown among them) attracted international attention with their shows at the Hyde Park Art Center, the city has been a fertile breeding ground for emerging artists and innovative art dealers. Today, the primary art gallery district is concentrated in the River North neighborhood—the area west of the Magnificent Mile and north of the Chicago River—where century-old redbrick warehouses have been converted into lofty exhibition spaces. More recently, a new generation of gallery owners has set up shop in the West Loop neighborhood, where you'll tend to find more cutting-edge work.

A great time to visit the district is from mid-July through August, when the Chicago Art Dealers Association presents **Vision,** an annual lineup of programs tailored to the public. The *Chicago Reader,* a free weekly newspaper available at many stores, taverns, and cafes on the North Side, publishes a comprehensive listing of current gallery exhibitions, as does the quarterly *Chicago Gallery News* (www.chicago gallerynews.com), which is available free at the city's visitor information centers. Another good resource is the Chicago Art Dealers Association, www.chicago artdealers.org; the group's website has descriptions of all member galleries.

those who aren't quite sure what all of the service names mean. There's also a lovely inn upstairs (See p. 47). 1743-45 W. Division St. (btw. Hermitage Ave. and Wood St.). www.ruby-room.com. ☎ **773/235-5678.** Subway/El: Blue Line to Division.

Books

Abraham Lincoln Book Shop ★   Abraham Lincoln's had quite a resurgence in the last few years, from the blockbuster movie to his role as a vampire hunter. If you're hungry for more Lincoln lore, you'll find a veritable museum at this antique reading room, which is filled with memorabilia and, of course, books, from rare and out of print editions to new. 357 W. Chicago Ave. (btw. Orleans and Sedgwick sts.). www.alincolnbook shop.com. ☎ **312/944-3085.** Subway/El: Brown Line to Chicago.

Barnes & Noble ★   This national chain ensures easy access to hundreds of thousands of books at its two-story Gold Coast outfit, and also hosts story time for kids, author signings, and other events. There are a number of other stores in town, including the DePaul Center, 1 E. Jackson, at State Street (☎ **312/362-8792**) and one at 1441 W. Webster Avenue, at Clybourn Avenue (☎ **773/871-3610**). 1130 N. State St. (at Elm St.). www.barnesandnoble.com. ☎ **312/280-8155.** Subway/El: Red Line to Clark/Division

The Book Cellar ★★★   A visit to the book cellar is as cozy as having tea with an old friend. Small but remarkably stocked, the shelves are lined with illustrative hand-written recommendations by staff, and a significant portion of the inventory is dedicated to Chicago authors. The little cafe is a great stop for a latte, a sandwich, or a glass of wine, and a steady stream of book club meetings and author readings have a way of reminding you why it feels so good to shop locally. 4736-4738 N. Lincoln Ave. (btw. Lawrence Ave. and Leland Ave), www.bookcellarinc.com. ☎ **773/293-2665.** Subway/El: Brown Line to Western.

Myopic Books ★★   This used book store is one of Chicago's largest, and packs in as many tomes as it can, from the floor to the ceiling (well, almost) of three floors,

Chocolate and Chicago go hand in sticky hand, even if some of the most iconic chocolate producers have moved to browner pastures. **Fannie May** ★ (343 N. Michigan Ave., at Upper Wacker Dr.; www.fanniemay.com; ℂ **312/453-0010**), which is now owned by 1-800-Flowers, wasn't always the Pixie-wielding giant it is today. The chocolatier opened its first store downtown in 1920, and there are now more than a dozen locations around Chicago (and six other states and Canada), although the factory is based in Ohio. The famous **Frango** ★ mints, conceived in Seattle, rose to national acclaim when Chicago's Marshall Field's began making the delectables in the flagship State Street store (which is now Macy's). While you can still buy them there, the mints are now actually made in Pennsylvania. Which leaves **Vosges Haut-Chocolat** ★★ as today's home-town big-name confection. Far more exotic than the chocolates that have left Chicago behind, Vosges, which has a factory in the Logan Square neighborhood, embeds its truffles with flavors like violet, curry, chile, and bacon. Factory tours aren't an option, but there are multiple shops in Chicago, including a Mag Mile one at 520 N. Michigan, at Grand Ave. (www.vosgeschocolate.com; ℂ **312/644-9450**).

Looking for a more local sugar fix? Turn loose your inner sweet tooth in Lincoln Square at **Amy's Candy Bar** ★ (4704 N. Damen Ave., btw. Leland Ave. and Giddings St.; www.amyscandybar.com; ℂ **773/942-6386**), where you'll find a lifetime supply of gummies, licorice, malted milk balls, and melt-in-your-mouth house-made sea salt caramels. On a hot summer night, you'll wait in line at **Margie's Candies** ★★★ (www.margiesfinecandies.com; two locations: in Logan Square at 1906 N. Western Ave. at Armitage Ave., ℂ **773/384-1035;** and in Ravenswood at 1813 Montrose, btw. Honore St. and Ravenswood Ave., ℂ **773/348-0400**), where gargantuan sundaes are served in photogenic clamshell bowls. And don't forget a stop at **Garrett Popcorn** ★★★ (multiple locations, including 625 N. Michigan, btw. Ohio and Ontario streets; www.garrettpopcorn.com; ℂ **312/944-2630**), where you may just double-fist the best popcorn you've ever had. Particularly if you suspend disbelief and order the Chicago mix, a sweet-and-savory combo of cheese and caramel (trust us on this one.) Better eat it quick, because when the bag starts to color from the grease, you can no longer deny the calories you've just consumed in one sitting.

with more than 80,000 books. You'll find everything from new bestsellers to obscure, yellowed relics. The staff is usually chatty and knowledgeable, and it's a great place to lose yourself on a rainy or wintery day. 1564 N. Milwaukee Ave. (just southeast of Damen/Milwaukee/North aves. intersection). www.myopicbookstore.com. ℂ **773/862-4882.** Subway/El: Blue Line to Damen.

Powell's Bookstore ★   No, it's not as big as the Powell's in Portland (nor are the two related) but Chicago's own little used book store is packed to the gills with titles and has ladders at the ready if you see something you can't reach. Powell's now has two additional stores, one in Hyde Park, at 1501 E. 57th Street (ℂ **773/955-7780**) and one in University Village at 1218 S. Halsted between Roosevelt Road and Maxwell Street (ℂ **312/243-9070**). 2850 N. Lincoln Ave. (btw. Diversey Pkwy. and George St.). www.powellschicago.com. ℂ **773/248-1444.** Subway/El: Brown Line to Diversey.

Seminary Co-op Bookstore ★ Not everyone can nab the SAT scores required to get accepted into the prestigious University of Chicago, but that won't stop you from visiting the campus bookstore. *Warning:* it's maze-like, and you might wish for a GPS to get through it, but you may rub elbows with one of U of C's Nobel Prize laureates as you try to find your way out. 5751 S. Woodlawn Ave. (btw. 57th and 58th sts.). www.semcoop.com. ℰ **773/752-4381.** Bus: 172

Women & Children First ★ The name is a little hokey, but don't let that stop you from visiting this charming Andersonville bookstore. The mid-sized, feminist shop stocks more than 30,000 titles by women (along with titles by men), a colorful kids' section, and is well known for its impressive selection of gay and lesbian titles, fiction and non-fiction. It's an easy place to make new discoveries, based on the staff picks, and the weekly Wednesday story time (10:30–11am) fills the shop with giggles and songs. 5233 N. Clark St. (btw. Foster and Bryn Mawr aves.). www.womenandchildrenfirst.com. ℰ **773/769-9299.** Subway/El: Red Line to Berwyn.

Clothing & Shoes

In the not-so-distant past, local fashion addicts had to head for the coasts when they wanted to shop for cutting-edge designer duds. Those days are over. Although over-the-top outrageousness doesn't sell here—this is still the practical Midwest—stylish Chicagoans now turn to local independent boutiques when they want to stay on top of the latest trends without looking like fashion victims. Here are some unique places to start.

Alcala's ★ Here's a fun little Chicago surprise: a store dedicated to Western wear, and lots of it. While the surrounding Ukrainian Village has changed over the years, Alcala's hasn't, and thank goodness for that: The vintage horse statues out front are a hoot. Choose from thousands of boots, hats, shirts, and other yee-haw-worthy fashion. 733 W. Chicago (just east of Halsted St.). www.alcalas.com. ℰ **312/226-0152.** Bus: 66, 8, or 132.

AllSaints Spitalfields ★ This heavy, dark, industrial-like space feels, at first, a strange fit for the Mag Mile. Above you, a series of sewing machines fills the air, and industrial chunks of heavy, scary metal abound. Leather, zippers, and chunky spikey jewelry seem to dominate. But get past that and the U.K.-based store reveals an edgy collection of fashion basics for men and women, mostly in grey and black, along with a small section of shoes that could kill (literally, their heels are quite sharp). 700 N. Michigan Ave. (at Huron St.). www.us.allsaints.com. ℰ **312/283-0400.** Subway/El: Red Line to Chicago.

Balani ★★ Balani is the choose-your-own-adventure shop of menswear. Here, the clothiers (yes, clothiers) will consult with you on what you're looking for in a suit and let you select the fabrics (wool, cotton, silk, cashmere), patterns, and colors, right down to the buttonhole. After you're poked and prodded with a tape measurer, your own personal clothing masterpiece will be done in 6 to 8 weeks. If you don't recognize it by the colors you chose, you will by your name, which is inscribed inside. Sure, it's a splurge, but what a souvenir. 55 W. Monroe St. (btw. Clark and Dearborn sts.). www.balanicustom.com. ℰ **312/263-9003.** Subway/El: Blue Line to Monroe.

Cerato ★ This Chicago-centric shop embraces its hometown designers, while also keeping an eye out for flair from afar. You'll find everything on the fashion spectrum here, from the latest pair of boyfriend jeans to a new gown for the Goodman. Located on Southport Avenue, in Lakeview, this shop will lure you to a favorite locals shopping district, where you're surrounded by boutique and dining options (and not too far from

Wrigley). 3451 N. Southport Ave. (btw. Newport and Cornelia sts.). www.ceratoboutique.com. ℂ **773/248-8604.** Subway/El: Brown Line to Southport.

Haberdash ★   It sounds a bit British, and the classic clothes look a bit British, but Haberdash is all Chicago. I don't want to scare men off by calling this a boutique for the testosterone set, but that's really what it is, carried out in the most masculine of ways. Clothes here tend toward classic style, and the staff is always happy to help guys mix and match and make new outfits, and other, er, dapper ensembles. There's also a barbershop, so guys can get a shave and a haircut and look extra snazzy while shopping. Haberdash also has an outpost in the South Loop, 150 W. Roosevelt Rd. (in The Roosevelt Collection, ℂ **312/357-5134**).611 N. State St. (btw. Ontario and Ohio sts.). www.haberdashmen.com. ℂ **312/646-7870.** Subway/El: Red Line to Grand.

Hazel ★★★   Whether you're looking for a Mad Men–style dress, a pair of jeans, or an ironic Jesus t-shirt, Hazel has it. This affordable Ravenswood clothing boutique, just north of Lakeview, carries both men's and women's lines, and is run by a fashionable staff that is always happy to help you play dress up and suggest new looks. It also happens to be my favorite shop in the whole world. To accessorize, head to the jewelry/gift shop by the same name (and same owners) just a few stores east at 1902 W. Montrose. 1926 W. Montrose Ave. (btw. Winchester and Wolcott aves). www.hazelchicago.com. ℂ **773/904-7779.** Subway/El: Brown Line to Montrose.

Ikram ★   If you're not a fashionista, you may wonder, when stepping into the very red Ikram building, if you'll be allowed to leave in the dowdy duds in which you entered. That's because you've just penetrated a hallowed *Vogue*-style space in River North, filled with couture du jour, thanks to owner Ikram Goldman, one of the best-known names in fashion in the Midwest. Her shop doesn't just follow the trends, it actually sets them, as one of her clients, a woman named Michelle Obama, can attest. 15 E. Huron. (btw. Wabash Ave. and State St.). www.ikram.com. ℂ **312/587-1000.** Subway/El: Red Line to Chicago.

John Fluevog ★   Blend a little bit of funky, a little bit of sexy, and a whole lot of comfort, and you've got a pair of shoes by John Fluevog. One of just a handful of its kind of shops in the U.S., Fluevog feels like an especially good fit in Wicker Park, which is a similar mix of funky/sexy/comfort. Both men's and women's pairs all have a little bit of elf style to them, and the potential to totally make an outfit. 1539-41 N. Milwaukee Ave. (btw. Damen Ave. and Honore St.). www.fluevog.com. ℂ **773/772-1983.** Subway/El: Blue Line to Damen.

Robin Richman ★★   This sophisticated Bucktown boutique specializes in dresses, tops, and skirts that are a little bit flowy with just enough edge, thanks to the owner, who is a knitter with quite a unique sense of style herself. Robin Richman is frequently at the store, and she's incredibly welcoming and helpful, as are the rest of the staff. Whatever you're looking at, there's a story behind it, and it seems as though the staff has met all of the designers represented here. This is the kind of store where you might pay high dollar for fashion, but you know no one else at the party will be wearing the same thing. 2108 N. Damen Ave. (at Dickens St.). www.robinrichman.com. ℂ **773/278-6150.** Subway/El: Blue Line to Damen, and then a long walk (10 blocks) or a short cab ride.

Topshop and Topman ★   Usually found in Nordstrom, Chicago has one of just four London-based Topshop shops in the U.S. You'll find everything at this Mag Mile outpost, from jeans, t-shirts, and semi-conservative little black dresses to eyebrow-raising, animal-print club wear for a night out in River North. 830 N. Michigan Ave. (at Pearson St.). www.topshop.com. ℂ **312/280-6834.** Subway/El: Red Line to Chicago.

The T-Shirt Deli ★★ T-shirts hang in the windows like ham and salami and fill butcher display cases at the irresistibly shticky T-Shirt Deli. Shirts here are displayed like meat, and, if purchased, wrapped in butcher paper and served with a bag of chips. Your job is to come up with the perfect fashion statement and put it on a T-shirt. Mind blank? Look around the store and you'll find slogan and graphic inspiration in the shop's design binders, or bring in your own custom design, and voila, within minutes you'll be wearing it out the door. There's now a second location in Andersonville, 1482 W. Berwyn (at Clark St.), ℂ **773/571-7410.** 1739 N. Damen Ave. (btw. Willow St. and St. Paul Ave.). www.tshirtdeli.com. ℂ **773/276-6266.** Subway/El: Blue Line to Damen.

Department Stores

Barney's New York ★ The building alone, constructed in 2008, is beautiful. From outside, on the tony corner of Oak and Rush, you can watch the oh-so-fashionable shoppers wander up the stairs, which wind like urban switchbacks in front of the floor-to-ceiling windows. Inside, the beauty continues in true Barney's fashion. This hallowed ground of style is a little bit fashion museum and a lot retail, with every item, from accessories to gowns, arranged just so. Sure, staff will look down noses—through their designer glasses—at you if you're not dressed the part, but that's all part of the Barney's experience. If you want to see how the ladies who lunch do what they do, head up to Fred's, a cafe on the top floor. 15 E. Oak St. (at Rush St.). www.barneys.com. ℂ **312/587-1700.** Subway/El: Red Line to Chicago.

Bloomingdale's There are two options for Bloomingdale's in the downtown area: **Bloomingdale's Medinah Home Store ★★** and **Bloomingdale's ★**. The home store is located in River North in what used to be the Medinah Temple, an Arabic-style domed building, with dark brown bricks and gorgeous stained glass. You'll find a huge selection of bedding and home furnishings, along with a new department devoted entirely to Nespresso. Time it right in any department, and you could hit some great sales here. About nine blocks away is the more traditional Bloomingdale's, a six-level version of it, with cosmetics and accessories and apparel for men, women, and children, located in the 900 North Michigan Shops. The store always seems to be hosting a great sale, so look around for savings. www.bloomingdales.com. Bloomingdale's Medinah Home: 600 N. Wabash (at Ohio St.). ℂ **312/324-7500.** Subway/El: Red Line to Grand. Bloomingdale's: 900 N. Michigan Ave. (at Walton St.). ℂ **312/440-4460.** Subway/El: Red Line to Chicago.

Macy's ★★★ The sign outsides says Marshall Field and Company, because this was the former flagship of Field's, which originated in Chicago, before a buyout that forced a name change in 2006 (see sidebar for more on the history of Marshall Field's). Aside from being the most ornate and historic department store in Chicago, at Macy's you'll find all of the Macy's staples—fashions for men, women, and children; jewelry; cookware; bedding; gifts; and furniture—along with a wine shop, fur vault, salon, and celebrity-chef-dominated food court (see p. 95). Throughout the year, Macy's maintains a long-time Marshall Field's tradition: lavishly decorating the store windows. In fact, when Marshall Field was ruling the roost here, he was the first person to hire an actual theater designer to create enticing window displays like consumers had never seen. They're particularly popular during the holidays and for the annual Macy's flower show every spring (late Mar/early Apr). Another holiday tradition: Visit the Walnut Room, where the floor-to-raised-ceiling tree is a beloved Christmas destination.

When you know the history of Marshall Field and Company—now Macy's—shopping in the stately State Street building feels like an afterthought to its history and architecture. The 12-story neo-Renaissance building, built in 1892, occupies an entire city block. When you enter between the towering granite pillars on State Street, consider this: These were the largest columns in the country at the time Marshall Field's was built—and, yes, they belonged to a department store. You'll find more of them inside, bright, white and looming throughout the cosmetics department. Stand in the middle of that department and look up. Above you is the largest Tiffany glass mosaic dome in the U.S., and suspended from it are two beautiful Tiffany globe lamps.

Back in its day, Marshall Field's wasn't simply about shopping. It became a place where a man felt comfortable allowing his wife to stroll, unescorted, and unafraid for her safety—a rarity in Chicago. Marshall Field hired women to work at the counters and operate the elevators, and all of the employees went to charm school in order to provide the best possible service to shoppers. The slogan here, coined by Marshall Field himself, was, "Give the lady what she wants."

There's another, smaller Macy's downtown in Water Tower Place (835 N. Michigan Ave.; ℂ **312/335-7700**). It's seven very narrow floors tall, so you just might get dizzy riding the elevator to the top. 111 N. State St. (at Randolph St.). www.visitmacyschicago.com. ℂ **312/781-4483.** Subway/El: Red Line to Washington.

Neiman Marcus ★   Attentiveness is an understatement here. In fact, it's not unusual for three different women to try and "sample" you with cosmetics and perfume as you leap on the escalator from the first floor. Those greetings continue to the second and third levels—also women-centric, with clothes, jewelry, fur, shoes—and to the fourth, where the men's department sits, appropriately close to the bar. All of the clothing here is neatly arranged, with no cross-contamination of brands, and nary a hanger out of place. Glimpse at a price tag and you'll be reminded that you're helping fund that attention to detail. 737 N. Michigan Ave. (btw. Superior St. and Chicago Ave.). www.neimanmarcus.com. ℂ **312/642-5900.** Subway/El: Red Line to Chicago.

Nordstrom ★★   Located in The Shops at North Bridge, you won't find the stunning architecture here that you see at Macy's on State and Bloomingdale's Medinah Home Store. Instead, the city's only Nordstrom feels like a mall, albeit a refined one. Escalators lead to four floors of fashion. A small portion of the store revolves around men and kids and the rest is women's apparel, cosmetics, and the shoe department for which Nordstrom is famous. The cafe is a popular spot for women on the prowl for a good salad, and the neighboring spa is tempting after a day of Mag Mile marathon shopping. Need style help? Nordstrom offers complimentary personal stylist services, who will have a dressing room stocked for you before you even arrive (book online). 55 E. Grand Ave., inside The Shops at Northbridge, 520 N. Michigan Ave. www.nordstrom.com. ℂ **312/464-1515.** Subway/El: Red Line to Grand.

Saks Fifth Avenue ★   I tend to get a little nervous when I enter Saks. Am I stylish enough to get their attention, or will I feel snubbed? So far, so good, at least at Chicago's Magnificent Mile outpost. Despite the luxury appeal of the store, in my experience, the sales associates are actually quite outgoing and personable, even if you're just

Chicago's got a huge variety of ethnic grocery stores, where you can sample authentic specialties from around the world and stock up on unusual cooking-related gifts. Because most of the shops are in residential neighborhoods far from the usual tourist haunts, the best way to get an overview of them is by taking a culinary tour, led by a guide who knows the cuisine (and, best of all, can organize tastings along the way). Chef Rebecca Wheeler takes visitors to Southeast Asian and Indian stores, restaurants, and bakeries for during her **Chicago Food Tours** (www.rebecca wheeler.com; © **773/368-1336**). She'll even share cooking tips so you can arrive home with a few new recipes to try out. **Chicago Food Planet** (chicago foodplanet.com; © **312/818-2170**) also leads energetic tasting tours throughout Chicago, exploring ethnic shops and restaurants in Chinatown, the Gold Coast, Lincoln Park, and other areas.

browsing. The seven-level store is filled with luxury name brands, each in their own designated section: Prada, Gucci, Alexander McQueen, and on and on and on. Women's items fill floors one through five—cosmetics, accessories, shoes, fashion—while men get the top two floors. More than anything, Saks is known for its personalized service, so if you have a question or you're looking for an opinion, don't be afraid to ask. 700 N. Michigan Ave. (at Superior St.). www.saksfifthavenue.com. © **312/944-6500**. Subway/El: Red Line to Chicago.

Edibles

Chicago French Market ★ This airy market, located in the Metra's Ogilvie Transportation Center, has upped the ante on quality and diversity of lunch offerings near the Loop. Despite its name, it doesn't limit itself to Franco-food—although there's no shortage of bread and pastries—with more than 30 vendors representing a number of favorite Chicago restaurants, and peddling sushi, Kosher, Italian, Belgian, Vietnamese, soup, barbecue, and more. The prices ain't cheap, but you'd be paying much more at sit-down spots, and it's a great starting spot to fill your picnic basket and head to the lake. 131 N. Clinton St. (btw. Washington and Randolph sts.). www.frenchmarket chicago.com. © **312/575-0306**. Subway/El: Pink or Green Line to Clinton.

Eataly ★★★ I am absolutely in love with this Mario Batali grocer, as is every guest I bring here for an afternoon. In addition to an incredible stockade of specialty foods imported from Italy (which include truffles in any form you can imagine), Eataly, located in River North, has a pasta-by-the-pound counter, butcher, baker, seafood, cheese, wine, beer, lotions, potions, and more, along with 23 eateries—including a Nutella/crepe station. The two-level Italian market/eatery extravaganza opened in late 2013, and is only the second Eataly in the U.S. (brag: Although it may not have opened first, the Chicago store trumps the city-block-sized New York Eataly by about 13,000 square feet.) It's a great stop for stocking up on picnic items. 43 E. Ohio St. (at Wabash Ave.) www.eataly.com/chicago. © **312/521-8700**. Subway/El: Red Line to Grand.

Gene's Sausage Shop & Delicatessen ★★ If you find yourself in the Lincoln Square neighborhood with a hankering for sausage, Gene's has you covered. This window-lined, two-level, family-owned shop employs European-trained sausage makers to create more than 40 types of sausage. Check out the delicatessen, with its Eastern European specialties—such as Hungarian goulash, cabbage rolls, stuffed duck, and schnitzel—and the extensive selection of imported chocolates and sweets. Then, head up to the roof-top beer garden when the weather's nice for a bratwurst and a brew. 4750 N. Lincoln Ave. (btw. Lawrence and Leland aves. www.genessausageshop.com. ℭ **773/728-7243.** Subway/El: Brown Line to Western.

Old Town Oil ★★ Shoppers sip oil and vinegar as though they're at a wine tasting at this tiny specialty store in Old Town. The friendly staff will greet you at the door and lead you over to the oil dispensers, and then share with you a pretty fascinating lesson on what distinguishes one olive oil from the other as you sample different types from around the world. Then they'll walk you over to the vinegar section, where your mind will be blown by the selection: chocolate, cinnamon pear, peach, kiwi vinegars—who knew? 1520 N. Wells St. (btw. North Ave. and Schiller St.). www.oldtownoil.com. ℭ **312/787-9595.** Subway/El: Brown Line to Sedgwick.

Pastoral ★★★ This wine and cheese shop would be a stand-out in any neighborhood, but it's a true find in the 7-Eleven and sub-sandwich dominated Loop. Stop in and build your own picnic or grab a fancy-pants sandwich (with prosciutto, Jamón Serrano, or country pâté, among other options), salad, and a six-pack for the evening. You won't be the only one in Millennium Park who had this brilliant idea. 53 E. Lake St. (at Wabash Ave.). www.pastoralartisan.com. ℭ **312/658-1250.** Subway/El: Brown, Green, Orange, or Purple Line to Randolph, or Red Line to Washington.

The Spice House ★★ I sure never knew how tempting a spice shop could be until I saw—and smelled—The Spice House in Old Town. Gift/souvenir alert: Here, spice mixes are named after different Chicago neighborhoods, like Pilsen Latino Seasoning, Back of the Yards Garlic Pepper Butcher's Rub and Greektown "Billygoat" Seasoning. 1512 N. Wells St. (btw. North Ave. and Schiller St.). www.thespicehouse.com. ℭ **312/274-0378.** Subway/El: Brown Line to Sedgwick.

Electronics

Apple Store ★ It's as though Apple constructed a giant magnet to lure passersby into this perennially busy store. Apple Store now takes online appointments, so plan ahead, and the shop should have you and your iProduct in and out in a jiffy. You can also hop the train to the Lincoln Park location, which is right smack-dab in front of the North Avenue Red Line stop (801 W. North Ave.; ℭ **312/777-4200**), and less than a 10-minute ride away. 878 N. Michigan Ave. (at Huron St.). www.apple.com/retail/northmichiganavenue. ℭ **312/529-9500.** Subway/El: Red Line to Chicago.

Micro Center ★★ Friends stare at me blankly when I proclaim, time and again, "I love Micro Center." This place has just about everything that has anything to do with electronics: computer and even Mac spare parts, software, toys, stylish computer bags, "As Seen on TV" gadgets, and even a grumpy computer tech for when you need help. You might have to chase someone down if you have a question, but once you've got them, they'll give you the time you need. Located close to Bucktown, this big-box, no-frills store is about a half hour from the Loop by train and bus. If you have a car, it's easier to drive here. 2645 Elston Ave. (btw. Logan Blvd. and Leavitt St.). www.microcenter. com. ℭ **773/292-1700.** Subway/El: Blue Line to Western and then bus 49.

Home Decor, Gifts & Accessories

Galleria ★★★ If malls were small, navigable, friendly, and consisted of handmade items from local artists and artisans, they'd be like Andersonville's Galleria. It's about a 30-minute train ride from downtown to see the 90+ tiny shops/stalls of art, clothes, gourmet food, gifts, jewelry, antiques, and whatever else they have in store. What I love most about this place is that the artists aren't actually present, so, unlike a craft fair, you don't feel any guilt for less-than-pleasant facial expressions certain styles might inspire. What? It happens. 5247 N. Clark St. (btw. Berwyn and Farragut aves.). www.andersonvillegalleria.com. © **773/878-8570.** Subway/El: Red Line to Berwyn.

Rotofugi ★ It's hard to call Rotofugi a toy store, because, really, the toys are figurines that double as art, and the store feels more like a museum gift shop, except there's no museum in sight. This Lincoln Park/Lakeview store brings in artworks and toy creations from Eastern and Western designers, and many of those include small, angry looking animals with cigarettes hanging out of their mouths. Despite the lighthearted inventory, there's a rather odd seriousness and quiet to the store. 2780 N. Lincoln Ave. (at Racine Ave.). www.rotofugi.com. © **773/868-3308.** Subway/El: Brown Line to Diversey.

Rudy's Roundup ★★ I can't walk out of this kitschy, cutesy Wicker Park store without buying something. Most recently, it was a studded hedgehog purse and a pair of sloth socks. This is a total hodgepodge gift shop, filled with everything you want and nothing you need, at prices you can afford. Glassware, clothes, jewelry, accessories, stationary, cards: They've got a little bit of everything packed into a tiny space. 1410 N. Milwaukee Ave. (at Wolcott Ave.). www.rudysroundup.com. © **773/486-6400.** Subway/El: Blue Line to Damen.

Wolfbait & B-girls ★ Local is the theme at this trendy Logan Square gift boutique, where the wares come from 150-plus local designers, artists, and seamstresses. From flirty dresses, Chicago-centric t-shirts, Intelligentsia coffee, and artsy mobiles to locally made, non-toxic deodorant, this spot is as Chicago as it gets. 3131 W. Logan Blvd. (btw. Kedzie and Milwaukee aves.). www.wolfbaitchicago.com. © **312/698-8685.** Subway/El: Blue Line to Logan.

Kids & Toys

American Girl Place ★ If the giggles seem to hit a crescendo near Water Tower Place, this is why. Unless you're a parent of a young girl (and really, even then) don't expect to understand the excitement that builds around this pink palace, where dolls can visit the salon, photo studio, doll hospital, or join their owners for lunch, afternoon tea, dinner, or even a river cruise. Many of the dolls are modeled after historical figures, and despite the opinion I have about the high prices ($110 for a doll and a book, are you kidding me?), at least American Girl moves us away from the dysmorphic Barbie doll. 835 N. Michigan Ave. (in Water Tower Place). www.americangirl.com. © **877/247-5223.** Subway/El: Red Line to Chicago.

KS Psycho Baby ★ This is what happens when the cool, creative kids grow up and become parents. They open cool, creative shops, like this baby-store-with-a-sense of humor, which proves that kids' stores can be just as trendy as their moms' boutiques. The small, Ukrainian Village (south of Wicker Park) boutique is filled with clothes, toys, books, bags, and more. It's pricey enough that wouldn't want to buy your kids' entire wardrobe here, but an accent piece or two, like the onesie that says "I only cry when ugly people hold me," is well worth a gander. 1630 W. Division St. (at Paulina St.). www.psychobabyonline.com. © **773/772-2815.** Subway/El: Blue Line to Division.

Marbles the Brain Store ★★ It's hard to say who's having more fun in this brainiac game store: the employees who are demonstrating the games, the kids who are playing them, or the parents who are (usually) patiently waiting their turn. Marbles, which sells unique puzzles, games, software, and other items to tease and exercise your synapses, is aimed at everyone from kids just starting to flex those lobes to seniors battling to keep the gears turning. Although the store has a number of locations across the country, including one in the Lincoln Square neighborhood (4745 N. Lincoln Ave, btw. Lawrence and Leland aves.; *𝒞* **773/784-7991**), it all began right here, in Chicago. 845 Michigan Ave. (in Water Tower Place, level 4). www.marblesthebrainstore.com. *𝒞* **312/255-1201.** Subway/El: Red Line to Chicago.

Museum Shops

Chicago Architecture Foundation ★★★   I dare you to try to get out of this shop without getting out A. your wallet or B. your phone to take a photo of something you're barely resisting buying, like a ninja samurai sword umbrella or a Frank Lloyd Wright Millard House votive candle holder. I've certainly never succeeded at it. Everything here—toys, neck ties, scarves, games, gifts, books, purses—is design-centric, but in the most playful of ways. 224 S. Michigan Ave. (at Jackson St.). www.architecture.org. *𝒞* **312/922-3432,** ext. 241. Subway/El: Red Line to Jackson.

Museum of Contemporary Art Gift Shop★★   I admit, in my visits to the MCA, I often feel like I'm missing something, or that the art is over my head. At the gift shop, however, I feel right at home. The shop is small but loaded with clever little finds, like blinking jewelry, a book that pops up with 3D floral bouquets, and a vase made of a six-pack. This is how museum gift shops should be. 220 E. Chicago Ave. (1 block east of Michigan Ave.). www.mcachicago.org. *𝒞* **312/280-2660.** Subway/El: Red Line to Chicago.

Museum of Science and Industry Gift Shop ★   If FAO Schwartz invented a nerd toyshop, this would be it. Some of the gifts here are exhibit-centric, while others are just plain fun, like the spy handbook, pet tornado, and mugs/shirts/magnets with periodic table humor. With all the focus on science, technology, engineering and math (STEM) these days, this is a natural place to stock up on science fun while the kids are still amped from the MSI. 57th St. and Lake Shore Dr. www.msichicago.org. *𝒞* **800/468-6674** outside the Chicago area, 773/684-1414, or TTY 773/684-3323. Bus: 2, 6, or 10 or Metra Electric train to 57th St. and Lake Park Ave.

Music

Logan Hardware ★   This is your passageway to the '90s, where you can still buy Garbage Pail Kids cards, California Raisin keychains, CDs, DVDs, and records, in one place. More modern/less grungy than most record stores, the real highlight here is the semi-secret arcade in back. Make a purchase and the cashier will give you a code to punch into the door lock. Enter the dark back room and you're in arcade heaven, surrounded by pinball and vintage video games, all of which are free. 2542 W. Fullerton (at Maplewood Ave.). www.logan-hardware.com. *𝒞* **773/235-5030.** Subway/El: Take the Blue Line to California. Walk a few blocks north to Fullerton and catch the 74 bus heading east.

Reckless Records ★   John Cusack fans won't have much luck finding Championship Vinyl, the record store from *High Fidelity,* because the store never actually existed. But just a few storefronts away from the Wicker Park location of Championship is a hipster-filled find called Reckless Records, where vinyl lovers can spend hours flipping through records (along with CDs, DVDs, t-shirts, and more) and swapping music trivia with the record-store-cool staff. The store also has a small shop in the Loop (26 E. Madison St., at Wabash Ave.; *𝒞* **312/795-0878**) and another in Lakeview

(3126 N. Broadway, at Briar Pl.; ℭ **773/404-5080**). 1532 N. Milwaukee (btw. North Ave. and Honore St.). www.reckless.com. ℭ **773/235-3727**. Subway/El: Blue Line to Damen.

Vintage/Resale Shops

Millionaire Rejects ★★ You won't find clothing at this Lincoln Park consignment shop, but you will find just about everything else, from cowhide chairs to Oriental rugs decorated with seahorses and whatever else came in that day. The two-level store is warehouse-like and cluttered, which adds to the treasure hunt. The owner is chatty and friendly, and, in my experience, happy to haggle, if you ask nicely. 1131 W. Armitage Ave. (at Clifton Ave.). ℭ **773/857-3105**. Subway/El: Brown Line to Armitage.

Shangri-La Vintage ★ When I had to stock up on '70s-style cruise wear for a New Year's Eve Poseidon Adventure party, I came here and left fully styled. With the concentration of bellbottoms and butterfly collars at Shangri-La, you'd think you'd just walked onto the set of The Brady Bunch. This tiny Roscoe Village shop is truly vintage—not just filled with old, used clothes—and each piece is carefully cleaned and displayed, so you don't feel the need to shower off upon leaving. The store's hippie owner is so nice, you won't want to leave without buying at least a rhinestone brooch. 1952 W. Roscoe (btw. Damen and Wolcott Aves.). ℭ **773/348-5090**. Subway/El: Brown Line to Paulina.

Vintage Underground ★★ When a store has an entire category dedicated to "ocean liner memorabilia," you know you've swum into vintage waters. Here, you'll find the gloves, jewels, hats, and furs that call to mind Hollywood stars of years gone by. Located below the street level of Wicker Park, this dusty relic is so packed that getting around is like wandering a vintage maze. You just keep discovering sections you haven't explored. 1834 W. North Ave. (at Honore St.). www.chicagovintageunderground.com. ℭ **773/252-4559**. Subway/El: Blue Line to Damen.

Everything Else

American Science and Surplus ★★★ Need a giant cloth frog splayed out, dissection-style, on your wall? Head to this huge science-centric surplus store that moonlights as a fun shop and lab depot. Here, science experiment kits and lasers may fill one aisle, while furry robotic hamsters, inflatable rubber chickens, and UFO solar balloons are on the next. Oh, and then there's military equipment, dental and doctor tools, and so much more. The items are all surplus, so when they sell out, they're gone. You never know what you're going to get, but I, personally, have never been disappointed in the adventure. Located in Jefferson Park, it's about 40 minutes by train or 20 by car. 5316 N. Milwaukee Ave. (at Parkside Ave.). www.sciplus.com. ℭ **773/763-0313**. Subway/El: Blue Line to Jefferson Park.

The Boring Store ★ The Boring Store is, of course, anything but. It calls itself an "undercover secret agent spy store." And it does, indeed, have a rack of ex-agent's former trench coats, which sell for $20 each. But mostly, this eccentric little shop has trinkets, t-shirts, and books, a fair number of which are by Dave Eggers, who co-founded The Boring Store. You have to ask to learn about it, but the shop doubles as a front (and fundraising arm) for 826CHI, a non-profit that provides tutoring and creative writing workshops for kids ages 6 to 18. So if you want to buy a light that clips on to your glasses or a taco shaped wallet and benefit an admirable cause, this is where to go. 1331 N. Milwaukee Ave. (at Hermitage Ave.). www.notasecretagentstore.com. © **773/772-8108.** Subway/El: Blue Line to Damen.

Heritage Bicycles ★★ My first visit, I immediately fell in love with Heritage Bicycles, a coffee shop/bicycle maker/bike repair shop/bike apparel store in Lakeview. I still get that same warm and fuzzy feeling whenever I come back. First, the staff is so friendly, I can't imagine them existing outside of the Midwest. Second, the concept of a bike shop (where they make their own Chicago-specific bikes) and coffee shop seems a bit crazy, but it works, and happy people fill the long, communal table all day long, sipping lattes. Third, this shop proves that not all biker clothing has to be ugly spandex. It can be fashionable and comfortable while also hiding your awkward bits. 2959 N. Lincoln Ave. (btw. Wellington and Racine aves.). www.heritagebicycles.com. © **773/245-3005.** Subway/El: Brown Line to Wellington.

Recommended Stores

SHOPPING

CHICAGO STROLLS

Pack your most comfortable shoes, because above just about anything, Chicago is a walking city. A number of reasons make it that way. First, it's relatively compact and easy to get around. Second, walking is often faster than waiting for the train or bus, and less of a hassle than driving. Third, there is just so much to see. I've put together the following three tours to give a true taste of Chicago's diversity, highlighting the architecture of the bustling downtown business center, grandiose homes of the Gold Coast, and the pleasantly weird style of Wicker Park. These are all very safe areas, so while you're wandering, I encourage you to take a wrong turn or two and see what you discover. That's all part of the charm of a walkable city.

WALKING TOUR 1: THE LOOP

START:	**Willis Tower.**
FINISH:	**Harold Washington Library Center.**
TIME:	**2½ hours.**
BEST TIME:	**Daytime, particularly weekdays when downtown businesses are open.**
WORST TIME:	**Late evening, after shops and offices have closed.**

Walk through the Loop's densely packed canyon of buildings, and you'll feel the buzzing pulse of downtown. While you'll pass plenty of modern high-rises, you'll also get a mini lesson in architectural history as you survey the progression of the city's skyscrapers.

Start the tour at 233 S. Wacker at:

1 The Willis Tower

If you haven't made it to the top yet, now's your chance! Okay, so this 110-story megatower is no longer the world's tallest building. It's not even the Sears Tower anymore, since the naming rights were bought by the London-based insurance broker Willis Group in early 2009. But the towering structure remains a bold symbol of the city. If it's a clear day (and you've got the time), take a trip up to the **Skydeck** ★★★ (p. 113) before heading off on your tour. Stand on the Ledge and you'll know exactly how high up you are—you can see straight down through the glass to the ground. Once you catch your breath, look to the east and you'll look out over the lake, to the northwest you can watch planes take off from O'Hare Airport, and to the north you'll be able to see all the way to Wisconsin.

Walk north along Wacker Drive until you arrive at:

2 333 W. Wacker Dr.

Proof that Chicago inspires architectural creativity, this 1983 office building was designed to fit a rather awkward triangular plot (previously thought suitable only for a parking lot). But architectural firm Kohn Pedersen Fox came up with a brilliant solution, designing a curved facade that echoes the bend of the Chicago River. Walk out to the Franklin Street Bridge to get the full effect of the building's mirrored surface, which reflects the surrounding cityscape in ever-changing shades of blue, green, and gray.

Across the river you'll see 222 W. Merchandise Mart Plaza and:

3 The Merchandise Mart

Touted as the world's largest commercial building, the Mart is a Chicago landmark as much for its place in the history of American merchandising as for its hulking institutional look. Completed in 1931, it's occupied mostly by furniture and interior-design businesses. Perched on top of the pillars that run the length of the building are oversized busts of American retail icons, including Julius Rosenwald (Sears), Frank W. Woolworth, and Aaron Montgomery Ward.

Walk two blocks east along Wacker Drive. At LaSalle Street, turn right, and continue two blocks to Randolph Street. Turn left (east), go half a block, and you'll be standing in front of 100 W. Randolph St. and the:

4 The James R. Thompson Center

This postmodern cascade of glass and steel is—depending on your point of view—the pinnacle or the low point of architect Helmut Jahn's career. Home to offices of the Illinois state bureaucracy, it was designed to promote the idea of open government: The transparent glass walls inside allow citizens to see their tax dollars at work. Step into the atrium to check out the beehivelike atmosphere; you can even ride a glass elevator up to the 17th floor if you're not afraid of heights.

Cross Randolph Street and head south along Clark Street. On the left you'll come to the Richard J. Daley Center at 50 W. Washington St., an open space known as:

5 Daley Plaza

Shadowed by the looming tower of the Richard J. Daley Center—a blocky dark monolith of government offices—this square was named for the legendary mayor and longtime czar of Cook County politics. While you're here, go ahead and do what tourists do: Take a picture in front of the Picasso sculpture (p. 116).

Walk back up to Randolph Street and head east. At the corner of Randolph and State streets, you'll see two local landmarks: the marquee of the Chicago Theatre to your north and the block-long Macy's (previously Marshall Field's) to the south. Continue south along State Street until you reach 1 W. Washington St.:

6 The Reliance Building

Now known as the Hotel Burnham ★ (p. 52), this building may not look impressive, but it's famous in the world of architecture. Completed in 1895, it had a

Walking Tour 1: The Loop

1 Willis Tower
2 333 W. Wacker Dr.
3 The Merchandise Mart
4 The James R. Thompson Center
5 Daley Plaza
6 The Reliance Building
7 The Berghoff ☕
8 The Rookery
9 Chicago Board of Trade
10 Monadnock Building
11 Manhattan Building
12 Harold Washington Library Center

☕ Take a Break

W Kinzie St.

RIVER NORTH

Merchandise Mart ③

Chicago River

W Wacker Dr.

W Lake St. ②

W Randolph Dr. ④

⑤

THE LOOP ⑥

E Madison St.

W Washington St.

W Monroe St.

W Adams St.

Union Station

Willis Tower ①
start here

W Jackson Blvd.

90 94

Eisenhower Expwy. 290

⑧ ⑦

E Adams St.

⑨ ⑩

W Van Buren St.

⑪ ⑫ ★finish here

W Congress Pkwy.

SOUTH LOOP

W Harrison St.

E Harrison St.

South Branch Chicago River

0 1/4 mi
0 1/4 km

remarkably lighter look than its bulky predecessors, thanks to steel framing that allowed for the extensive use of glass on the facade. It also marked the first use of the "Chicago window": a large central pane of glass flanked by two smaller, double-hung windows used for ventilation. To get a glimpse of what it looked like when it was an office building, take one of the hotel elevators up to one of the guest room floors, which still have the original tile flooring and glass-windowed office doors.

Continue south along State Street until you reach Adams Street. Ready to pause for a bite or a drink? Then turn right (west), go half a block, and stop at:

7 The Berghoff ☕

In a world of chain coffee shops and fast-food joints, the Berghoff ★ (17 W. Adams St.; www.theberghoff.com; (𝒞 **312/427-3170;** p. 94), feels like a flashback to Old Chicago. The bar of this 100-year-old restaurant serves several different house brews on tap, along with sandwiches and appetizers. (For a nonalcoholic treat, try the homemade root beer.) If it's lunchtime, grab a table in the main dining room; although the menu has been modified for modern, lighter tastes, the Wiener schnitzel and spaetzle are house classics.

Go two blocks west along Adams Street until you reach LaSalle Street. Turn left (south) and you'll be at 209 S. LaSalle St.:

8 The Rookery

Built between 1885 and 1888, the Rookery represents a dramatic transition in Chicago architecture. (It's also one of the only surviving buildings designed by noted architect Daniel Burnham, along with the Reliance Building, above.) The name refers to the previous building that sat on this site, Chicago's original City Hall, which was a favorite spot for nesting birds; today it's an office building. The imposing Romanesque exterior has thick masonry walls, but the inside is surprisingly open and airy, thanks to an innovative use of iron framing. The building is essentially a square built around an open interior court that rises the full height of the building's 11 stories. Walk upstairs and follow the staircase to get a glimpse of the Rookery's interior courtyard and the sublime stairway spiraling upward.

Continue south along LaSalle Street. At Jackson Boulevard, the street appears to dead-end at 141 W. Jackson Blvd. at the:

9 Chicago Board of Trade

A temple to high finance, this building houses the city's commodities exchange, an echo of the days when corn and wheat from the prairie passed through Chicago on its way east. Opened in 1930, the setbacks on the upper stories are typical of the Art Deco styling of the era, as are the geometric decorative elements over the entrance. Along the building's rear (southern) wall, a 24-story postmodern addition by Helmut Jahn repeats the original's pyramid-shaped roof, maintaining the symmetry between old and new. When it was built, the 45-story Board of Trade was considered so tall that the aluminum sculpture of Ceres, the Roman goddess of architecture who adorns the building's peak, was left faceless, because the builders figured no one in neighboring buildings would ever be high enough to see it.

Head two blocks east along Jackson Boulevard to the southwest corner of Dearborn Street and Jackson Boulevard. At 53 W. Jackson Blvd. is the:

10 Monadnock Building

This mass of stonework forms two office buildings that occupy an entire narrow block all the way to Van Buren Street. Only 2 years separate the construction of these architectural twins, but they are light-years apart in design and engineering. (You'll need to step across Dearborn Street to fully appreciate the differences.)

Monadnock I, on the northern end, was built by the architectural firm of Burnham and Root between 1889 and 1891. To support a building of this size at the time, the masonry walls had to be built 6 to 8 feet thick (note the deeply recessed windows at street level). Monadnock II, on the southern wing, was built by Holabird & Roche in 1893. Here steel framing was used, allowing the lower walls to be significantly narrower. The second building may have been an engineering marvel at the time, but the original Monadnock has a certain gravitas that the later addition lacks.

Walk south along Dearborn Street until you reach Congress Parkway. At 431 S. Dearborn St., you'll find the:

11 Manhattan Building

Constructed in 1891 by William LeBaron Jenny, this broad structure was viewed as an architectural wonder by many who visited Chicago during the Columbian Exposition two years later. To some, the eclectic use of materials and varied design of the facade give the Manhattan Building an appearance of complete chaos; others see a dynamic rhythm in the architect's choices. Today, this former office building has been converted into condos.

From the corner of Dearborn and Van Buren streets, look a few blocks west along Van Buren until you spot a triangular tower, carved with slivers of window. That building is the Metropolitan Correctional Center, a 27-story jail for defendants preparing for trial in federal court downtown. The building's three-sided design derives from an attempt by the U.S. Bureau of Prisons to reform prison conditions: Cells were built along the edges surrounding a central lounge area. But it's still not a great place to hang out: To foil jailbreaks, the windows are only 5 inches wide (and have bars, to boot); although there's a recreation yard on the roof, it's enclosed on the sides and topped with wire mesh.

Walk two blocks east along Congress Parkway until you reach State Street. Turn left (north) to reach 400 S. State St. and the entrance of the:

12 Harold Washington Library Center

This block-long behemoth, named for the city's first African-American mayor, is the world's largest municipal library (p. 124). Designed by a firm led by Thomas H. Beeby, then dean of Yale University's School of Architecture, and completed in 1991, it self-consciously echoes the city's original grand buildings, such as the Auditorium Theater a few blocks east. Many Chicagoans think the place looks more like a fortress than a welcoming library, but judge for yourself. The Winter Garden on the ninth floor—a lovely retreat drenched with natural light—is a good place to relax at the end of your walking tour.

WALKING TOUR 2: **THE GOLD COAST**

START:	**Oak Street Beach.**
FINISH:	**Bellevue Place and Michigan Avenue.**
TIME:	**2 to 2½ hours, including break.**
BEST TIME:	**Weekends are ideal for this walk at any time of the year. On weekdays, wait until after the morning rush before setting out.**
WORST TIME:	**After dusk, when it's too dark to appreciate the buildings' decorative elements.**

The Gold Coast, as its name implies, is Chicago's ritziest neighborhood, site of its most expensive and exclusive houses. Its reputation dates back to 1882, when Potter Palmer, one of the city's richest businessmen, built a lakeshore castle here, in what was then a relative wilderness north of the city. The mere presence of the Palmers served as an instant magnet, drawing other social climbers in their wake (and Palmer, who owned vast parcels of North Side land, saw his holdings shoot up in value). This itinerary begins with a walk overlooking Lake Michigan before heading down charming tree-lined residential streets.

Begin the tour at:

1 Oak Street Beach

This confluence of city and lakeshore epitomizes what Chicagoans love about the city: Facing downtown, you've got the ultimate urban vista; stare at the shoreline, and the seemingly endless expanse of water makes you feel like you've escaped the city completely. You can stroll along the sand or keep to the concrete path (but beware of speeding bikes and rollerbladers). As you head north, look across Lake Shore Drive to see a few remaining historic mansions scattered among the more modern high-rises.

The first mansion you'll pass, just north of Scott Street, is:

2 The Carl C. Heissen House

Both the Heissen House (1250 N. Lake Shore Dr.), built in 1890, and its neighbor, the Starring House (1254 N. Lake Shore Dr.), built in 1889, show the popularity of the sturdy Romanesque style among wealthy Chicagoans.

A second cluster of former private mansions, all vaguely neoclassical in outline, faces Lake Michigan north of Burton Place. The first of these is:

3 1516 N. Lake Shore Dr.

This building is home to the International College of Surgeons; its neighbor at 1524 N. Lake Shore Dr. is a museum belonging to the same institution. **The International Museum of Surgical Science** ★ (p. 145) houses a fascinating collection of exhibits and artifacts that portray the evolution of medical surgery, but it's worth visiting for its elegant interior as well, designed by Chicago architect Howard Van Doren Shaw in 1917 as a private mansion (highlights include a massive stone staircase and the second-floor library, with fine wood paneling). A third structure, 1530 N. Lake Shore Dr., is today the Polish Consulate.

Follow the lakefront path to the Chess Pavilion on your left, and continue past the patch of green where the jetty leads out to a harbor light and into the parking lot. Straight ahead is:

4 Residence of the Roman Catholic Archbishop of Chicago

Catholicism has strong roots in Chicago, thanks to generations of German, Irish, and Polish immigrants who brought their faith along with them; the city's current archbishop, Cardinal Francis George, is a well-known local figure who receives regular press coverage. This Queen Anne–style mansion was built in 1885 for the first archbishop of Chicago, Patrick Feehan; it sits on the site of what used to be a cemetery that stretched between present-day North Avenue and Schiller Street. Of the 19 chimneys that march across the roofline, only three are still in use.

Across the street on the opposite corner of North Avenue is:

5 1550 N. State Pkwy.

Each apartment in this 1912 vintage luxury high-rise, known as the Benjamin Marshall Building, originally occupied a single floor and contained 15 rooms spread over 9,000 square feet. The architects were Marshall & Fox, highly regarded in their day as builders of fine hotels. There was once a garden entryway at the ground-floor level. Among the noteworthy architectural features adorning

Walking Tour 2: The Gold Coast

1 Oak Street Beach
2 The Carl C. Heissen House
3 1516 N. Lake Shore Dr.
4 Residence of the Roman
   Catholic Archbishop
   of Chicago
5 1550 N. State Pkwy.
6 Bullock Folsom House
7 4 W. Burton Place
8 Cyrus McCormick Mansion
9 1525 N. Astor St.
10 1451 & 1449 N. Astor St.
11 1444 N. Astor St.
12 Thomas W. Hinde House
13 Joseph T. Ryerson House
14 Charnley-Persky House
15 Playboy Mansion
16 1301 & 1260 N. Astor St.
17 Public Hotel
18 East Cedar St.
19 Bryan Lathrop House

the exterior of this Beaux Arts classic are the many small balconies and the bowed windows at the corners of the building.

Continue west for one block on North Avenue and turn left, following Dearborn Street to Burton Place and the:

6 Bullock Folsom House

As its mansard roof reveals, this 1877 landmark, at 1454 N. Dearborn St. on the southwest corner, takes its inspiration from the French Second Empire style. (That roof, incidentally, is shingled in slate, not asphalt.) Neighboring houses at nos. 1450 and 1434 have some of the same French-influenced ornamentation and styling. Across Burton Place just to the north, at 1500 N. Dearborn St., is another example of a rival architectural fashion of the day, the Richardsonian or Romanesque Revival.

Return to the east along Burton, but before crossing North State Parkway, stop at:

7 4 W. Burton Place

Built as a private residence in 1902 by Richard E. Schmidt for a family named Madlener, this striking building today houses the Graham Foundation for

Advanced Studies in the Fine Arts. There is something very modern about its appearance: The structure's clean lines and the ornamentation around the entrance were inspired by the work of architects Louis Sullivan and Frank Lloyd Wright. The Society of Architectural Historians offers tours of the home on Saturdays, along with the Charnley-Persky house (see stop no. 14, below).

Continue one block farther east to Astor Street. On the northwest corner, at 1500 N. Astor St., is the former:

8 Cyrus McCormick Mansion

New York architect Stanford White designed this building, which was constructed for the Patterson family in 1893. Cyrus McCormick, Jr., bought it in 1914, and David Adler's north addition doubled the size of the building in 1927. The senior McCormick made his fortune by inventing the mechanical reaper, which made it possible to farm vast tracts of wheat on the prairie without depending on seasonal labor at harvest time. Cyrus Sr.'s heirs shared in the wealth, and eventually so many members of the family owned homes near Rush and Erie streets, just south of the Gold Coast, that the neighborhood was known as "McCormicksville."

Like the Fifth Avenue mansions White and his contemporaries built in New York, the McCormick palazzo is an essay in neoclassical detailing. Square and grand, like a temple of antiquity, the construction combines Roman bricks of burnt yellow with touches of terra-cotta trim. The building now is divided into condominiums.

Head north briefly on Astor Street to check out a home with a connection to presidential history:

9 1525 N. Astor St.

This attractive town house was once the residence of Robert Todd Lincoln, the only surviving child of Abraham and Mary Todd Lincoln. The younger Lincoln started a private law practice after the Civil War. He remained in Chicago for much of his life, leaving twice during the 1880s and 1890s to serve under presidents James Garfield and Chester Arthur as Secretary of War, and later under Benjamin Harrison as Ambassador to Britain. On the death of George Pullman, one of his major corporate clients, Lincoln became president of the Pullman Palace Car Company in 1897 (for more about the Pullman Company, see "Exploring Chicago," p. 144).

Reversing direction, walk south along Astor Street. Notice the houses at:

10 1451 & 1449 N. Astor St.

The former, occupying the corner lot, is the work of Howard Van Doren Shaw, built in 1910 according to the so-called "Jacobethan" fashion; a combination of Jacobean and Elizabethan, it revives certain 16th- and 17th-century English architectural features, including narrow, elongated windows, split-level roofs, and multiple chimney stacks. The house at no. 1449 was built around the turn of the century, but the architect of this glorious chateau remains a mystery. Guarding the home's entrance is a somewhat intimidating stone porch, seemingly out of scale. Among the home's other unique characteristics are the big front bay and frieze below the cornice, a scroll decorated with a pattern of shells.

Another neighboring home of interest across the street is:

11 1444 N. Astor St.

While most of the homes in this area were built in the late 1800s and early decades of the 1900s—and most took their cues from architectural fashions from centuries before—this house was on the cutting edge of style when it was built in 1929. An Art Deco masterpiece, it was designed by Holabird & Roche, the same firm that designed Soldier Field football stadium a few years earlier.

Next, walk to 1412 N. Astor St., site of the:

12 Thomas W. Hinde House

This 1892 home, designed by Douglas S. Pentecost, is an homage to the Flemish architecture of the late Middle Ages. The facade has been altered, but some of the original stone ornamentation remains, as do such dominant features as the multipaned, diamond-shaped windows.

On the same side of the street, at 1406 N. Astor St., is the:

13 Joseph T. Ryerson House

David Adler designed this 1922 landmark home in the manner of a Parisian hotel. Adler himself supervised the 1931 addition of the top floor and the mansard roof. Woven into the wrought-iron grillwork above the entrance are the initials of the original owners.

Walk to 1365 N. Astor St. to see the landmark:

14 Charnley-Persky House

Shortly before he left the firm of Adler & Sullivan, a then-obscure draftsman, Frank Lloyd Wright, played a major role in designing this 1892 home. The house's streamlined structure gives it a far more contemporary look than its neighbors, making the case that there is something timeless in Wright's ideas. The building—appropriately enough—is now the headquarters of the **Society of Architectural Historians,** which gives tours of the house on Wednesday and more extensive tours including the surrounding area on Saturday. (Visit www.sah.org or call ✆ **312/915-0105** for details.)

Walk back to Schiller Street. Cross the street and turn left on North State Parkway, continuing south until the middle of the block to 1340 N. State Pkwy., the original:

15 Playboy Mansion

Little did the original owner of this building, an upright Calvinist named George S. Isham, know how his house would be transformed a mere half-century after it was built in 1899. Playboy founder Hugh Hefner lived here from 1959 to 1974, romping with his Bunnies and celebrities in the indoor pool and lounging in silk pajamas while perusing page layouts in his bedroom. Today that hedonistic past has been erased, and the building has been converted into high-priced condos.

Continue south on State Parkway, then swing east on Goethe Street, back to Astor Street. On opposite corners diagonally across Goethe Street are apartment towers that represent the trend toward high-rise living that began in the 1930s:

16 1301 & 1260 N. Astor St.

Constructed by architect Philip B. Maher in 1932 and 1931, respectively, these apartment buildings are classics of the sleek modernism that characterized

American commercial architecture after World War I. Contrast their timeless style with the 1960s apartment tower at 1300 N. Astor St., by architect Bertrand Goldberg; avant-garde at the time, it has not aged as well.

If you're ready for a snack, turn back north to Goethe Street and head west a block and a half west to Public Hotel, 1301 N. State Pkwy.

17 Public Hotel 🍴

Since we're taking a stroll through history, there's no better place to take a break than the Gold Coast's own Public Hotel. Inside, the Pump Room ★★ (p. 84) used to be the gathering spot for celebs and politicians. It's casual by day, so if you're hungry, request a table and order the delicious flatbreads, soups, salads, and sandwiches on the menu by famous Chef Jean Georges Vongerichten. If you prefer something simpler, the hotel's Library and Coffee Bar serves beverages, pastries, and salads throughout the day. Rest your weary feet by the cozy fireplace before hitting the street again.

Head south on Dearborn Street to Division Street. Walk one block east to State Street, then turn right (south), staying on the east side of the street where State and Rush streets merge, and proceed two blocks south to:

18 East Cedar Street

This long block between Rush Street and Lake Shore Drive deserves a look because much of its turn-of-the-century scale has been so well preserved, in particular the two clusters of "cottages," nos. 42 to 48 (built in 1896 by businessman Potter Palmer) and 50 to 54 (built in 1892).

Return to Rush Street, walk to the next block south, and turn left on Bellevue Place. At 120 E. Bellevue Place stands the:

19 Bryan Lathrop House

New York architect Charles F. McKim, partner of Stanford White, built this mansion for a local real estate agent and civic leader while staying in Chicago as a lead designer of the World's Columbian Exposition. It helped introduce the Georgian fashion in architecture, which replaced the Romanesque Revival throughout the Gold Coast.

WALKING TOUR 3: WICKER PARK

START AND FINISH: **The Damen El stop (Blue Line).**

TIME: **1 hour for neighborhood tour, plus additional time for food/ shopping.**

BEST TIME: **Any time during the day.**

WORST TIME: **After dark, when you'll have trouble seeing homes' decorative details.**

Wicker Park, along with adjacent Bucktown, is a great destination to shop for sassy duds you won't find elsewhere, followed by drinks and dinner at any of the popular area bars and eateries. This tour takes you along the residential side streets, overlooked by many tourists and even locals, and it will introduce you to the rich history of this neighborhood. Middle-class artisans, mostly Germans and Scandinavians, began settling here around 1870. In the following decades, wealthy families, whose foreign roots made them unwelcome along the Gold Coast, built luxurious homes here as well.

Walking Tour 3: Wicker Park

1 Wicker Park
2 1959-1961 W. Schiller St.
3 1941 W. Schiller St.
4 1958 W. Evergreen Ave.
5 1407 N. Hoyne Ave.
6 Wicker Park Lutheran Church
7 1558 N. Hoyne Ave.
8 2137 W. Pierce Ave.
9 2138 W. Pierce Ave.
10 Caton Street
11 Luxor Baths
12 Big Star
13 Piece Pizza

In the 20th century, the neighborhood's respectability gradually declined, and many of the grandest homes were converted into rooming houses. It wasn't until the 1980s that these distinctive homes were rediscovered and renovated, just as the gritty main streets of Milwaukee and Damen avenues began sprouting new shops and cafes.

Walk south along Damen Avenue to 1425 N. Damen Ave.:

1 Wicker Park

Two brothers, Charles and Joel Wicker, who were beginning to develop their extensive real estate holdings in the area, donated this land to the city in 1870, hoping the green space would make the surrounding area more attractive to prospective builders. Their timing was good. The area became quite popular following the Great Chicago Fire of 1871, as residents began to rebuild. Unfortunately, little remains of the 19th-century landscaping, which once included a pond spanned by a rustic bridge. Today, the 4-acre park is home to a field house and gym, a large centerpiece of a fountain, a sprinkling of historic statues, and a number of picnic tables, benches, and green space, if you care to sit a spell.

Cross the park to the corner of Damen Avenue and Schiller Street. Follow Schiller east, along the park, stopping first at:

2 1959–1961 W. Schiller St.

Built in 1886 for a ship's captain and a medical doctor, this double home reflects the fashionable Second Empire style. The building became a rooming house in the 1920s but has been restored to its original style. Note the Victorian colors of the cornices, tower, and trim. Other distinctive features are the large mansard roof and the decorative saw-toothed pattern in the brickwork.

Next move to:

3 1941 W. Schiller St.

Built for clothing manufacturer Harris Cohn in 1888, this home is also known as the Wicker Park Castle. Essentially Queen Anne in design, its limestone facade made it pricier and more luxurious than its neighbors. Granite columns were polished to look like marble, and a turret rests on a shell-shaped base.

At the end of the block, turn right on Evergreen Avenue until you come to:

4 1958 W. Evergreen Ave.

Novelist Nelson Algren (1909–1981) lived in a third-floor apartment here from 1959 to 1975. After he was caught stealing a typewriter in 1933, Algren spent 3 months in jail. This experience, which brought him in contact with criminals, outsiders, drug addicts, and prostitutes, was a strong influence on his work. Algren is best remembered for his two dark novels of the urban semi-underworld, *A Walk on the Wild Side* and *The Man with the Golden Arm* (which was set near here, around Division St. and Milwaukee Ave.), and for his tough but lyrical prose poem Chicago: "City on the Make."

Continue to Damen Avenue, then turn right (north) back to Schiller Street. Turn left on Schiller and head west one block to Hoyne Avenue, then turn right (north), where you'll see:

5 1407 N. Hoyne Ave.

Built by German wine and beer merchant John H. Rapp in 1880, this was the largest single-family estate in Wicker Park at the time. The original coach house, behind the mansion, is now a separate residence. This was not a happy home. Mrs. Rapp went insane, a son was convicted of embezzlement, and Rapp was murdered by his female bookkeeper. The home itself is of Second Empire style, with a large, curved mansard roof. The original wrought-iron fence defines the boundaries of the original grounds. Hoyne Avenue was at one time referred to as "Beer Baron Row," because Rapp wasn't the only brewer who took up residence here.

Heading north, you'll pass other late 19th-century mansions and, at 1426 N. Hoyne Ave., an example of a worker's cottage, a reminder that in these immigrant neighborhoods, artisans and their patrons often lived side by side. On the next corner, 1500 N. Hoyne Ave. at Le Moyne Street is the:

6 Wicker Park Lutheran Church

The city's oldest Lutheran church, it was modeled from plans of Holy Trinity Church in Caen, France, dating from the 12th century. The stone for this

Romanesque structure was recycled from a demolished brothel. When one of the scandalized parishioners protested, the pastor remarked that the building material "has served the devil long enough; now let it serve the Lord."

Walk on to:

7 1558 N. Hoyne Ave.

The building permit for this Queen Anne–style home was issued in 1877, making it one of the oldest homes in the area. It was built for C. Hermann Plautz, founder of the Chicago Drug and Chemical Company. Ever-conscious of the Great Chicago Fire, the builders created all the decorative trim on both towers, the cornices, and the conservatory of the south side from ornamental pressed metal. The seemingly misplaced cannon in the front yard is a relic of the years (1927–1972) when the building housed the local American Legion.

Turn back the way you came and walk one block to Pierce Avenue. On Pierce, walk west to:

8 2137 W. Pierce Ave.

This well-preserved gem is one of the highlights of historic Wicker Park. Built for the German businessman Hermann Weinhardt in 1888, it's a fanciful combination of elements that defies categorization. Notable details include the elaborate carved-wood balcony and the unusual juxtaposition of green stone and redbrick limestone around the large front window. The large lot used to be flooded in the winter for ice-skating.

Across the street is another notable home:

9 2138 W. Pierce Ave.

The original owner of this home, Hans D. Runge, was treasurer of a wood milling company, so it's no surprise that elaborate wood carvings characterize the home inside and out; among the unique designs are the Masonic symbols flanking the pair of dragon heads under the rounded arch. A well-heeled local banker and politician, John F. Smulski, acquired the house in 1902, about the time many Poles were moving into the neighborhood. Smulski committed suicide here after the stock market crash in 1929, and the house served for a time as the Polish consulate.

Continue west until you reach Leavitt Street. Turn right (north) and walk three blocks until you reach:

10 Caton Street

Many of the houses on this street were built in the early 1890s by the same architectural firm, each with its own style, including German Burgher (no. 2156) and Renaissance (no. 2152). The Classical Revival home at 2147 W. Caton St. was built by the owner of a metal company, hence the extensive metal ornamentation on the exterior. (If you peek at the porch, you'll see it has a tin ceiling.)

Retrace your steps along Caton Street and Leavitt Street to North Avenue, and turn left (east). As you pass Hoyne Avenue, take a quick look at 1617–1619 N. Hoyne Ave.; the building used to house the neighborhood livery stables, where local families kept their horses and carriages. (It's now condos.) The final stop on the tour is at 2039 W. North Ave., an address that used to house the:

11 Luxor Baths

These public baths were built in the 1920s and were reportedly once a hangout for local politicians and wheeler-dealers. Today the building has been transformed into—what else?—condos. Still, it's a fitting end to the tour, a reminder of the days when this was a neighborhood of European immigrants trading news from home in the Luxor Baths steam room.

Head east to the three-way intersection of Milwaukee, Damen, and North avenues.

12/13 Piece Pizza ☕ ★★ or Big Star ☕ ★★★

You have your choices of all kinds of wonderful food in Wicker Park, and two of them are right here, within steps of the giant intersection. I recommend Piece Pizza ★★ (p. 106) for a pie and a brew, or Big Star ★★★ (p. 106) for fancy tacos and a margarita. From there, continue walking southeast on Milwaukee, where you can shop the afternoon away, perusing records, books, trinkets, shoes, and more (see the Wicker Park itinerary, p. 34). When you're done, hop on the Blue Line and head back to wherever you need to go.

CHICAGO AFTER DARK

For many Chicago visitors (and residents), the daytime touring/ shopping/eating is just a way of making time pass until dark, when the city really comes to life. Theater, classical music, rock concerts, dance, improv, cocktail lounges, dive bars—you name it, Chicago has it. Although the city harbors its share of see-and-be-seen nightspots, Chicagoans in general are not obsessed with getting into the latest hot club. For the most part, chilling out with friends at a neighborhood bar is the evening activity of choice. To join the locals, you only have to pick a residential area and wander—it won't be long before you'll come across a tavern filled with neighborhood regulars and friendly bartenders.

PERFORMING ARTS

Theater

Over the years, as Broadway produced bloated, big-budget musicals with plenty of special effects but little soul, Chicago theater troupes gained respect for their risk-taking and no-holds-barred emotional style. With more than 200 theaters, Chicago might have dozens of productions playing on any given weekend.

The city's theaters have produced a number of legendary comedic actors, including comic-turned-director Mike Nichols *(The Graduate, Postcards from the Edge, Primary Colors),* as well as fine dramatic actors and playwrights. David Mamet, one of America's greatest playwrights and an acclaimed film director and screenwriter, grew up in Chicago's South Shore steel-mill neighborhood and honed his craft with the former St. Nicholas Players, including actor William H. Macy *(Fargo, Boogie Nights).*

The thespian soil here must be fertile. Tinseltown and TV have lured away such talents as John Malkovich, Joan Allen, Dennis Franz, Gary Sinise, George Wendt, and John Cusack. But even as emerging talents leave for bigger paychecks, a new pool of fresh faces is always waiting to take over. This constant renewal keeps the city's theatrical scene invigorated with new ideas and energy.

The listings below highlight the troupes that consistently present high-quality work, but they represent only a fraction of Chicago's theater scene. For a complete listing of productions that are playing while you're in town, check the comprehensive listings in the *Chicago Reader* (www.chicago reader.com), which reviews just about every show in town, and the digital entertainment magazine, *Time Out Chicago* (www.timeout.com/Chicago), or the Friday sections of the two daily newspapers. The website of the **League of Chicago Theatres** (www.chicagoplays.com) also lists all theater productions playing in the area.

A national standout and queen of Chicago's theater scene, **The Goodman Theatre** ★★★ (170 N. Dearborn St.; www.goodmantheatre.org; ℂ **312/443-3800**) is the oldest (and largest) non-profit theater in Chicago. Since 1925, Chicagoans have been donning their finest furs to come here, and you can count on seeing a flawless show with impeccable acting. The Goodman hosts everything from original productions to Broadway shows (*Venus in Fur* was there recently) and does its share of old standbys, like the remarkably popular annual production of *A Christmas Carol*. The Goodman actually consists of two theaters in the Loop, the Albert Theater, where the main stage is, and the smaller and less formal Owen Theater.

In its heyday, the **Steppenwolf Theatre Company** ★★★ (1650 N. Halsted St., at North Ave.); www.steppenwolf.org; ℂ **312/335-1650**) really put Chicago on the map as a theater town. Co-founded by a young Gary Sinise, Terry Kinney, and Jeff Perry in the 1970s, the theater bloomed from a handful of dedicated actors in a school basement to become one of the premiere theaters in Chicago. Today, the Steppenwolf puts on more than 700 performances a year in its three theaters, and most often, you can count on anchor-weight dramas. **Chicago Shakespeare Theatre** ★★ (800 E. Grand Ave.; www.chicagoshakes.com; ℂ **312/595-5600**) has the talent and staying power to lure tourist trap–wary locals to its beautiful roost on Navy Pier, and that's saying something. The two theater spaces—the larger of which is Globe-style—live in a gorgeous building that resembles a translucent gem, and put on up to 16 plays a year. The talent here is the main draw. Chicago Shakespeare Theatre hosts actors so grand that even William Shakespeare himself would have been impressed. As with many performing arts venues in town, the audience is invited to participate in lectures, meet-and-greets, and discussions before and after the show.

A number of the city's great historic theaters are concentrated in the North Loop. The **Ford Center for the Performing Arts/Oriental Theatre** ★★, 24 W. Randolph St., and the **Cadillac Palace Theater** ★★★, 151 W. Randolph St., book major touring shows and are quite a draw for arts buffs. The Oriental's fantastical Asian look includes elaborate carvings almost everywhere you look; dragons, elephants, and griffins peer down at the audience from the gilded ceiling. The Palace features a profusion of Italian marble surfaces and columns, gold-leaf accents a la Versailles, huge decorative mirrors, and crystal chandeliers. (If you'd like to get a look at these historic theaters for a fraction of the standard ticket price, guided tours of both start at 11am Sat and cost $10 per person; meet in the Oriental lobby.) The **Bank of America Theatre** ★ (formerly the Schubert Theatre), 18 W. Monroe St., was built in 1906 as a home for vaudeville shows; today it books mostly well-known musicals and sometimes comedy performers. For show schedules at all three theaters, call ℂ **312/977-1700** or visit www.broadwayinchicago.com.

The **Chicago Theatre** ★★ (175 N. State St., at Lake St.; www.thechicagotheatre.com; ℂ **312/462-6300**) is a 1920s music palace reborn as an all-purpose entertainment venue, playing host to pop acts, magicians, stand-up comedians, and more. Both the Chicago Theatre and the Bank of America Theatre, above, are quite large, so be forewarned that the cheaper seats are in nosebleed territory.

Classical Music & Opera

The world-class talent of the Chicago Symphony Orchestra—considered one of the best in the world—dominates the classical music calendar. Led by charismatic music director Riccardo Muti, who recently extended his contract until 2020, the CSO has been working to make classical music more approachable and accessible to the masses, whether that means backing a headliner, like Mavis Staples, in concert or playing the complete score to *Lord of the Rings.* You'll usually find the CSO at **Symphony Center ★★★,** 220 S. Michigan Ave., between Adams Street and Jackson Boulevard (© **312/294-3000**), home to a six-story sky-lit arcade and recital spaces. While the CSO is the main attraction, the Symphony Center schedules a series of piano recitals, classical and chamber music concerts, a family matinee series, and the occasional jazz or pop artists, and you can catch a free show by Civic Orchestra of Chicago, the farm team for the big leagues. In the summer, the CSO performs regular outdoor concerts at **Ravinia ★★★** (© **847/266-5100**), p. 152.

In addition to the CSO, many orchestra members play in smaller ensembles around town on a semi-regular basis; a few independent musical groups have also built loyal followings with eclectic programming. To find out what's playing when you're in town, check out the **Chicago Classical Music** website (www.chicagoclassicalmusic. org), maintained by a consortium of the city's leading music groups.

Chicago is actually home to two different operas. The most famous is the **Lyric Opera of Chicago ★★★,** Civic Opera House (Madison St. and Wacker Dr.; www. lyricopera.org; © **312/332-2244**), one of the most grandiose operas in the country, producing both classic masterpieces and modern works. Recent performances have included The *Barber of Seville, Don Pasquale,* and *A Streetcar Named Desire,* and opera fans are excited for the 2015/2016 world premiere of *Bel Canto,* based on the best-selling novel of the same name by Ann Patchett, in which opera-goers are taken hostage by a group of terrorists. The building where the opera lives, the Civic Opera House, is a star itself. A combination of Art Nouveau and Art Deco, the massive 3,563-seat theater ranks as the country's second largest opera house, standing 45 stories tall, in a regal, throne-like pose along the Chicago River. The sweeping interior is awash in rich gold, bronze, pinks, and greens, along with intricate architectural details that make it one of the most beautiful interiors in the city. *Tip:* If you end up in the nosebleed section, you might want to bring binoculars. Opera newbies and regulars will appreciate the pre-opera lectures, which give a quick primer on the performance. The Lyric's season runs September through March.

You won't have quite the same opulent opera experience at **Chicago Opera Theater ★** (205 E. Randolph Dr.; www.chicagooperatheater.org; © **312/704-8414**), which plays in the far more mundane and smaller theater, Harris Theater for Music and

FREE YOUR musical MIND

During the warmer months, the **Jay Pritzker Pavilion,** which is the ribbon-like, Frank Gehry-designed stage in Millennium Park, is *the* place to be for the best deal in town. June through August, the pavilion and great lawn fill with Loop workers, families, couples, and tourists, all excited to sprawl on the grass, gaze at the skyline, and listen to the free tunes. Here are some of the most popular events (to see an updated schedule go to www.millenniumpark.org).

The Grant Park Symphony and Chorus take the stage June through August most Wednesday, Friday, and Saturday nights as part of the **Grant Park Music Festival ★★★** (www.grantparkmusic festival.com; ✆ **312/742-7638**). The music fest is the only free, outdoor musical concert of its kind in the country, and it's been running for more than 80 seasons. The Grant Park Orchestra brings together musicians from near and far,

with "day jobs" in the Lyric Opera, the Metropolitan Opera, and symphonies in San Antonio, Seattle, Utah, and beyond, and the Grant Park Chorus is made up of talented pros who mostly hail from Illinois.

Downtown Sound ★★★ runs Mondays at 6:30pm, and features two new and up-and-coming bands per night, with sounds that are usually folk and acoustic, hip hop, or alt rock, drawing in a younger demographic, and **Loops and Variations ★★** is the name for the Thursday night concerts in the early part of the summer (through about mid-June), which showcase new music mixed with electronica, also drawing a younger crowd. Later in the summer, that Thursday night show morphs into **World Class Jazz ★★,** with flavors of Latin, African and American music. Grab a blanket and a picnic and head to the park!

Dance, but you can count on strong performances from this scrappy, 40-year-old-and-going-strong company. Plus, less expensive tickets make it a boon for a novice or regular opera-goer. While the Lyric is putting on the more familiar productions, Chicago Opera Theater is more of a community arts organization, with the goal of drawing in more diverse audiences. Because of that, the director is willing to take risks and pull some avant-garde operatic experiments.

ADDITIONAL OFFERINGS

The oldest all-volunteer civic chorus in the country, **Apollo Chorus of Chicago ★** (www.apollochorus.org; ✆ **312/427-5620**), was founded in 1872, just one year after the Great Chicago Fire. Today, it's best known for its annual holiday-season performances of Handel's *Messiah* at Orchestra Hall. The group also presents concerts during the year at various neighborhood venues, with choral styles that touch on gospel, jazz, folk, Broadway, and more.

The **Chicago Chamber Musicians ★** (CCM; www.chicagochambermusic.org; ✆ **312/819-5800**), a 13-member ensemble drawn from performers from the CSO, the Lyric Opera of Chicago Orchestra, and Northwestern University, presents chamber music concerts at various locations around the city. The season runs September through May, and you can always find the CCM performing free noontime concerts on the first Monday of the month (except September and March) on the second floor of the Chicago Cultural Center, p. 120.

The **Chicago Sinfonietta ★★** (www.chicagosinfonietta.org; ✆ **312/236-3681**), with its racially diverse orchestra and a wide-ranging repertoire, seeks to broaden

tippling TOURS

Chicago is a big drinking town—just ask the ghost of bootlegger Al Capone. But we don't just like to sample our own wares, we also love learning about them, drink firmly in hand. A number of distilleries and breweries are here to support us in that by offering tours and tastings. The most convenient to downtown is the West Loop's **CH Distillery** ★★ (564 W. Randolph St., at Jefferson St.); www.chdistillery.com; ℂ **312/707-8780**), which makes its own vodka, gin, limoncello, whiskey, and rum, and the alcohol alchemists will tell you all about it every Saturday and every other Tuesday at the 5:30pm tour. The $15 price of admission includes a tasting of three different types of high-octane sauce, plus rye bread and pickles. Hang out at the swanky bar if you want to keep the party going. At **Koval Distillery** ★ (5121 N. Ravenswood Ave.; www.koval-distillery.com; ℂ **312/878-7988;** Weds, Sat, and Sun, check site for times, $10), tours give you insight into the distilling process and teach you the difference between a white whiskey and an aged one. Located in Andersonville, Koval is about a 30-minute El ride from downtown (take the Brown Line to Damen Ave.), and also offers classes on making cocktails and even whiskey workshops.

And then there's beer. Chicago has a bustling craft brew scene, and most of the spots making beer offer tours. **Half Acre** ★★★ (4257 Lincoln Ave., at Cullom Ave.; www.halfacrebeer.com; ℂ **773/248-4038**), located just north of the Lincoln Square neighborhood, is a small but feisty brewery and offers tours that pretty much always sell out on Saturday at 11am ($10, Brown Line to Montrose). They're first-come, first served, so get there early. If you can't get on a tour, the nice guys who run the place are usually happy to give you a peek into the garage-like brewery. If you can get past the fact that **Goose Island** ★ (p. 216; 1800 N. Clybourn Ave., at Willow St.; www.gooseisland.com; ℂ **312/915-0071**) is now owned by Anheuser-Busch (many locals can't), the brewery offers a popular tour Saturdays at 12:30, 2, and 3:30pm and Sundays at 1 and 2:30pm, which fills up quickly ($10, Red Line to North/Clybourn). **Revolution Brewery** ★★ (p. 219; 3340 N. Kedzie; ℂ **773/588-2267**), which brews the not-quite-revolutionary-but-darn-good beers served at **Revolution Brewpub** (2323 N. Milwaukee Ave., btw. Humboldt Blvd. and California Ave; www.revbrew.com; ℂ **773/227-2739**), offers complimentary tours Wednesday to Saturday at 6pm, with additional tours Saturday at 4 and 5pm and Sunday tours at 3pm at its brewery, which is about a mile and a half from the restaurant and brewpub (Blue Line to Belmont). Lincoln Park's **Atlas Brewery** ★, which has seven stainless steel barrels and doubles as a restaurant with gastropub fare (2747 N. Lincoln Ave., btw. Diversey Pkwy. and Schubert Ave.); www.atlasbeercompany.com; ℂ **773/295-1270**), gives free Wednesday night tours at 7pm (Brown Line to Diversey).

the audience for classical music, throwing lighthearted events, like global dance parties. Concerts combine works by masters such as Beethoven and Mendelssohn with music from Latin America, Asia, and others. The group plays throughout the year at Orchestra Hall and other venues, and often takes a multimedia approach to its multicultural mission, collaborating with dance troupes, visual artists, museums, rock bands, and gospel choirs.

Music of the Baroque ★ (www.baroque.org; ℂ 312/551-1414) is a small, 60-member orchestra and chorus that pulls members from both the CSO and the Lyric Opera orchestra, and features professional singers from across the country. The ensemble performs the music of the 16th, 17th, and 18th centuries, in appropriately Gothic church settings in various neighborhoods. The group has made several recordings and has introduced lesser-known works by composers such as Mozart and Monteverdi to Chicago audiences.

Dance

Dance lovers should schedule their visit for October and November, when the annual **"Dance Chicago"** ★★ festival (www.dancechicago.com; ℂ 773/989-0698) takes place at various locations around town, or in August, when the free **Chicago Dancing Festival** (www.chicagodancingfestival.com; ℂ 773/609-2335) brings together more than 60 companies from across the world to Millennium Park and a handful of stages around town. Featuring performances and workshops from the city's best-known dance companies and countless smaller groups, it's a great chance to check out the range of local dance talent. Another phenomenon that has put a new move on the local scene is the **Chicago Human Rhythm Project** ★ (www.chicagotap.org; ℂ 773/542-2477), a non-profit group that brings together tap and percussive dancers from around the world for a series of workshops and performances throughout the year.

To find out what's going on at other times of the year, visit the website for the non-profit group **See Chicago Dance** (www.seechicagodance.com), which gives a comprehensive roundup of local performances. Another good reason to check out the site: You can often find links to discounted tickets.

Unless otherwise noted, the major Chicago dance troupes listed below perform at the **Harris Theater for Music and Dance,** 205 E. Randolph St. (www.harristheater-chicago.org; ℂ 312/334-7777) in Millennium Park.

The Dance Center–Columbia College Chicago ★ As an arts school, Columbia's performances are reliably fresh, and the styles from troupes from around the world (and from the college) may include West African, break dancing, tap, jazz, Bollywood, and more. The setting is a 275-seat theater housed in an Art Deco building from the '30s, and every seat is a winner. The Dance Center, located at 1306 S. Michigan Ave. (www.colum.edu/dance_center; ℂ 312/369-8330), also hosts dance lectures and family-friendly workshops, like FamilyDance, where families can learn to bust a move from the pros.

Hubbard Street Dance Chicago★★★ If you don't think dancers are athletes, check out a performance by Hubbard Street (www.hubbardstreetdance.com; ℂ 312/850-9744), and then come talk to me. The muscular performances, which are as diverse as they come, make you feel alive, and even the rhythmless get the wiggles. Every season, this Chicago favorite outdoes itself in originality, putting on shows for all ages. Particularly clever recent productions have included everything from a collaboration with Second City to a performance inspired by Marc Chagall's *American Windows.*

Joffrey Ballet of Chicago★★★ Its name, The Joffrey (www.joffrey.com; ℂ 312/386-8905), is uttered around Chicago with an air of reverence. It's been the subject of books and movies. Part rock ballet, part classic ballet, there are times that dancers are rocking out to Prince and other days, Romeo and Juliet. Every year, The Joffrey performs The Nutcracker to sold-out audiences in December. Another perk to

Performing Arts | CHICAGO AFTER DARK

HALF-PRICE theater TICKETS

For half-price tickets on the day of the show, drop by one of the **Hot Tix** ticket centers (www.hottix.org; ℂ **312/977-1755**), located in the Loop at 72 E. Randolph St. (btw. Wabash and Michigan aves.; Tues–Sat 10am–6pm, Sun 11am–4pm); the Water Works Visitor Center (163 E. Pearson St., Tues–Sat 10am–6pm, Sun 11am–4pm); and the new Block 37 location (108 N. State St., btw. Randolph and Washington sts.; daily 10am–6pm.) The website lists what's on sale for that day, and updates occur frequently. You can buy tickets to most shows online, but you'll have to pay Ticketmaster's irritating "convenience" charge.

A couple of other discount websites will also occasionally feature theater discounts. Visit Broadway in Chicago to look for specials, www.broadwayin chicago.com/specialoffers.php, and visit www.goldstar.com/chicago for great theater deals.

In addition, a few theaters offer last-minute discounts on leftover seats. **Steppenwolf Theatre Company** often has $20 tickets available beginning at 11am on the day of a performance Monday to Saturday and 1pm Sunday, and they go quickly. Stop by Audience Services at the theater. Also, half-price tickets become available in person, 1 hour before the show at the box office, or visit www.step penwolf.org. At the **Goodman Theatre,** "Mezztix" are half-price mezzanine tickets that are up for sale if a show doesn't sell out. Same-day performances are available starting at noon at the box office or at 10am online at www.good-mantheatre.org, with the promo code MEZZTIX.

seeing the Joffrey is a visit to its resident theater, the **Auditorium Theatre** (50 E. Congress Pkwy., btw. Michigan and Wabash aves; www.auditoriumtheatre.org; ℂ **312/341-2310**), which is among the most beautiful theaters in Chicago—and it's also a certified national landmark. Built in 1889 by Louis Sullivan and Dankmar Adler, this grand hall schedules mostly musicals, concerts, and dance performances. Even if you don't catch a show here, you can stop by for a tour (for more details, see p. 121).

Muntu Dance Theatre of Chicago ★ The brilliantly colorful costumes and booming drums transport you from the Harris Theater across Africa and into the Caribbean with Muntu (www.muntu.com; ℂ **773/241-6080**), a traditional African dance company that's been operating longer than any other of its kind. The barefoot moves pay homage to both tribal and modern dance, and the company prides itself in honoring historical moves, not just riffing off of them. Care to join? Muntu offers Wednesday night dance classes at the South Shore Cultural Center, 7059 South Shore Dr., from 6 to 7pm for $12.

Comedy & Improv

Chicago and comedy go together like "spit" and "take." In the mid-1970s, Chicago's own brand of comedy gave a big how-do-ya-do to the nation through the skit-comedy show *Saturday Night Live.* Back then, John Belushi and Bill Murray were among the latest to hatch from the number-one incubator of Chicago-style humor: Second City. Generations of American comics, from Mike Nichols and Robert Klein to Mike Myers and Tina Fey, cut their comedic teeth in Chicago before bringing the nation to tears of laughter. Visit one of our many comedy clubs, and who knows? You could be guffawing at a rising star.

ComedySportz ★ Comedy without the F-bomb? Okay, so occasionally one slips out, but at this family-friendly club, the perp is given a "Brown Bag Foul" by the ref. Yes, ref. Teams compete in this laugh-a-thon for audience applause, and the one that earns the most laughs wins. Most of the improv is based on audience suggestions, so leave your shyness at home. 929 W. Belmont Ave. www.comedysportzchicago.com.© **773/549-8080.** Subway/El: Red or Brown Line to Belmont.

Second City ★★★ Ah, the crown jewel of comedy in Chicago, and well deserved, at that. Second City launched the careers of hundreds of famous side splitters. If you're going to hit one comedy show in Chicago, make it this one. There's a reason that there's a comedy school here and comedy scouts are frequent visitors. It's just that good.

A word of warning: The website is confusing. You're going to see a whole bunch of shows to choose from and multiple theaters. The resident theaters are the Mainstage and E.T.C. (which stands for nothing, from what I can surmise). The Main Stage is the larger venue, with more broad-based improv, where you'll see a revue or a "best of" style show, versus the more intimate E.T.C., which hosts more topical and satirical shows, like, say, *A Clown Car Named Desire*. At both venues, expect to share tables and rub elbows with your neighbors; seating is quite tight. UP Comedy Club, located on the third floor of the complex, is a third option. Operating in a more traditional comedy club manner, it brings in a rotation of stand-up and improv. If you can't score a ticket to any of the above, you're still in luck. Every night except Friday, Second City puts on a free improv show following its last performance. (It usually starts around 10:30pm, but check the schedule to see when the last show runs, and plan on the freebie starting 2½ hours later). *Note:* Kids 10 and up are allowed at Second City, but keep in mind it's a nightclub atmosphere and the language and topics aren't exactly kid-friendly. 1616 N. Wells St. (in the Pipers Alley complex at North Ave.). www.secondcity.com.© **312/337-3992.** Subway/El: Brown Line to Sedgwick.

Zanies Comedy Club ★ Yes, it's not-so-coincidentally located about a block from Second City, but don't be too quick to assume you'll get sloppy seconds at Zanies. This comedy club holds its own, bringing in national headliners (Ari Shaffir of Comedy Central's *This is Not Happening* was recently there) as well as hilarious locals. Plus, theme nights dedicated to female, queer, and amateur comedians mix things up. Tickets generally run around $25 (plus two item purchase requirement), but check local sites like Groupon.com and Goldstar.com for half-off specials. 1548 N. Wells St. (btw. North Ave. and Schiller St.). www.chicago.zanies.com.© **312/337-4027.** Tickets $20–$25, plus 2-item food or drink minimum. Subway/El: Brown Line to Sedgwick.

THE LIVE MUSIC SCENE

Jazz

In the first great wave of black migration from the South just after World War I, jazz journeyed from the Storyville section of New Orleans to Chicago. Jelly Roll Morton and Louis Armstrong made Chicago a jazz hot spot in the 1920s, and their music lives on in a whole new generation of talent. Chicago jazz is known for its collaborative spirit and a certain degree of risk-taking—which you can experience at a number of lively clubs.

Andy's Jazz Club ★ The windows are aglow with neon signs advertising "live music" at this little brick storefront in River North. Its location, close to The Loop, is

AN ESCAPE FROM THE multiplex

Chicago has a fine selection of movie theaters, and three local movie houses, in particular, cater to cinema nerds. The **Gene Siskel Film Center,** 164 N. State St. (www.siskelfilmcenter.org; © 312/846-2600; subway/El: Red Line to Washington or Brown Line to Randolph), named after the well-known *Chicago Tribune* film critic who died in 1999, is part of the School of the Art Institute of Chicago. The center schedules a selection of films in two theaters, including lectures and discussions with filmmakers, and I've seen some incredible documentaries here. It's not uncommon to find foreign films playing here that haven't been released commercially in the U.S.

The **Music Box Theatre,** 3733 N. Southport Ave. (www.musicboxtheatre. com; © 773/871-6604; subway/El: Brown Line to Southport), is a movie palace on a human scale. Opened in 1929, it was meant to re-create the feeling of an Italian courtyard; a faux-marble loggia and towers cover the walls and electric "stars" sparkle in the painted sky overhead, while an organist plays live music on weekends and during certain festivals. The Music Box books a pretty fantastic array of foreign and independent American films, and will even host sing-alongs to *The Sound of Music* or pipe in a running commentary during *Poseidon Adventure.* Writers and directors make frequent appearances, and Wes Anderson hosted a Q & A in 2014 during an advance screening of *The Grand Budapest Hotel.*

Facets MultiMedia, 1517 W. Fullerton Ave. (www.facets.org; © 773/281-4114; subway/El: Red or Brown Line to Fullerton), is a nonprofit group that screens independent films, international films, and Chicago works. Die-hard cinemaphiles love Facets, while the average Chicagoan doesn't even know it exists. The group mounts an annual Children's Film Festival (Oct–Nov) and the Chicago Latino Film Festival (Apr–May), and screens films throughout the year. It also maintains a library of 65,000 titles, available for online rental through the company's mail subscription service.

a draw for tourists, but you'll find plenty of jazz-loving locals here, too—including, often times, those on the stage, who play two sets nightly. Peer at the "Wall of Fame," a photographic walk through time since the place opened in the early '50s. To guarantee a table, make a dinner reservation (food is decent—burgers, flatbreads, fish, proteins). The club allows diners to reserve in advance, but tables are first-come, first-served for others (there's a two-drink minimum). 11 E. Hubbard St. (btw. State St. and Wabash Ave.). www.andysjazzclub.com. © 312/642-6805. Cover $10–$15. Subway/El: Red Line to Grand.

Green Mill ★★★ The Green Mill is the most authentic jazz club in the city, hands down. People don't come here to socialize (and if they do, they may get hushed), they come for good, solid jazz. The sultry but bare-bones jazz club, which started as a roadhouse in 1907, used to be an Al Capone hangout, and remains a living museum of 1930s Chicago. Arrive early (8pm) or late (midnight) if you hope to nab a barstool or booth. The place gets elbow-to-elbow packed during its nightly shows, which range from traditional jazz to more challenging tunes. Because the music goes until the wee hours (4am during the week, 5am on Sat), you can often catch touring musicians stopping in to jam here after finishing up their own shows across town. 4802 N. Broadway Ave. (at Lawrence Ave.). www.greenmilljazz.com. © 773/878-5552. Cover $4–$15. Subway/El: Red Line to Lawrence.

Jazz Showcase ★★ Octogenarian Joe Segal will greet you as you enter Jazz Showcase, just as he's done since founding the joint in 1947. This is the oldest jazz club in town, and it's hosted a who's who of jazz greats: Count Basie, Dizzy Gillespie, Stu Katz, and the list goes on. It also may be the most tidy of jazz clubs in town, putting on shows that feel like concerts, rather than bar sets. The place is huge, so you can usually count on scoring a seat (tickets are available to purchase online or at the door), and the well-coifed bartenders know how to mix a good cocktail. The club puts on a family-friendly 4pm Sunday matinee, and kids younger than 12 get in free. 806 S. Plymouth Court (at Polk St.). www.jazzshowcase.com. ℂ **312/360-0234.** Most tickets $20–$45. Subway/El: Red Line to Harrison.

Blues & Reggae

If there's any music that epitomizes Chicago, it's the blues. As African-Americans migrated northward in the years following World War II, they brought their mournful, guitar-and-harmonica-based Delta blues. Once in Chicago, the addition of electric guitar gave the old blues a new jolt of life, and local musicians such as Howlin' Wolf, Muddy Waters, and Willie Dixon became the poster children of the Chicago blues genre. Today, blues clubs remain a staple of the cultural scene. Some spots cater to out-of-towners looking for an "authentic" blues experience, while others keep a relatively low profile, surviving thanks to the loyalty of die-hard blues aficionados. Jamaican reggae has also made the long migration to Chicago, and is now frequently heard at several area clubs.

Blue Chicago ★ Because of its location in River North, Blue Chicago has a big tourist draw, but holds its own with the locals too. What really distinguishes this club is its dedication to promoting the women of the blues, and man, can they sing. Talent is booked nightly, and the intimate club really packs them in on weekends. 536 N. Clark St. (btw. Grand Ave. and Ohio St.). www.bluechicago.com. ℂ **312/661-0100.** Cover $8–$10. Subway/El: Red Line to Grand.

B.L.U.E.S. ★★ Located just a few steps from always-rocking Kingston Mines, this tiny spot is a bit more mellow and neighborhoody, since it lacks the national reputation and tourist draw. Because it's so teeny, you can get eye to eye with the performers—and packed like sardines with audience members. Performers range from legends to locals on their way up. Shows start at 9:30pm nightly. 2519 N. Halsted St. (btw. Wrightwood and Fullerton aves.). www.chicagobluesbar.com. ℂ **773/528-1012.** Cover $5–$10. Subway/El: Red or Brown Line to Fullerton.

Buddy Guy's Legends ★ The best time to come here is in January, when Buddy Guy himself performs, and has been known to draw in other famous musicians. That, of course, is also the most difficult time to get in. Not to worry, year round, Buddy Guy's is worth a visit. The club itself is like a museum of Guy's own blues gear, filled with photos of blues greats, Grammy's and guitars signed by B.B. King, Carlos Santana, Eric Clapton, and Stevie Ray Vaughn. Performers here range from local to international acclaim, and take the stage seven nights a week. Of all the clubs listed, this is the best one to plan a meal around. The kitchen serves up New Orleans–inspired favorites, like gumbo, Jambalaya, blackened burgers, and other Cajun favorites. 700 S. Wabash Ave. (btw. Balbo Dr. and Eighth St.). www.buddyguys.com. ℂ **312/427-1190.** Cover $10–$20. Subway/El: Red Line to Harrison.

Exedus II ★ Ya mon! Exedus II is Chicago's oldest Jamaican-owned club, and it's as mellow as rum punch. In addition to the requisite Bob Marley, expect the DJs to

For up-to-date entertainment listings, check the local newspapers and magazines, particularly the Friday editions of the *Chicago Tribune* (www.chicagotribune.com), and the Trib's entertainment site, www.chicago.metromix.com, along with the *Chicago Sun-Times*, www.

chicagosuntimes.com. The digital magazine *Time Out Chicago*, www.timeout.com/chicago, has excellent comprehensive listings, as does *Chicago Reader*, www.chicagoreader.com, an alternative weekly.

introduce you to some lesser-known jams from hip hop and reggae. Because of its proximity to Wrigley Field, you'll see some frat boy infiltration during the free live reggae parties that follow Cubs' games. Either avoid going that night, if you can't take it, or have another rum punch and everything will be irie. Closed Mondays and Tuesdays. 3477 N. Clark St. (at Cornelia Ave.). www.exeduslounge.com. (℟ **773/348-3998.** Cover usually $4 to $10. Subway/El: Red Line to Addison.

Kingston Mines ★ Open since 1968, Kingston Mines was the first blues joint to open on the North Side of racially segregated Chicago. The crowd here changes, depending on who's playing, but with its proximity to DePaul University, you can count on an exuberant youthful crowd on the prowl for Bacardi bombs, Jäger shots, and cheap buckets of beer (all of which fill the "specials" board). The boozy juke joint has live music 7 nights a week on two separate stages, and you can hop from room to room, and take your pick of a seat (if you can find one) at long, old, thin wooden tables. Musicians here are reliably great, playing all forms of blues and hailing from Chicago or around the country. A touch of grit, combined with murals on the walls depicting the Mississippi Delta, really make it feel as though you've stepped into a little piece of New Orleans. 2548 N. Halsted St. (btw. Wrightwood and Fullerton aves.). www.kingstonmines.com. (℟ **773/477-4647.** Cover $12–$15 or $10 with student ID. Subway/El: Red or Brown Line to Fullerton.

Rosa's Lounge ★ It's a bit of a hike to this Logan Square blues dive, but if you're already in the area, stop in and see what a hipster-filled blues bar looks like. This hole-in-the-wall, which is not much more than a long, skinny room, has been here for more than 3 decades, and a photo on the wall of Barack Obama, who held fundraisers here before he was president, is a reminder of just how hip our Commander-in-Chief is to have discovered this out-of-the-way boozy blues spot. Shows usually start between 8 and 10pm Tuesday through Saturday; check website for exact times. 3420 W. Armitage Ave. (at Kimball Ave.). www.rosaslounge.com. (℟ **773/342-0452.** Cover $7–$15. Subway/El: Blue Line to Western or Logan, and then a short cab ride.

Underground Wonder Bar ★ This place springs to life when owner/trippy blues rocker Lonie Walker is at the helm—and that happens at least four nights a week. A little bit divey, this long, narrow bar has remarkably friendly staff, smiling even into the wee hours when the fans are really feeling the music. Underground Wonder Bar hasn't had a quiet night since it opened in 1989, and it wins the "eclectic" award for bringing in funk, soul, reggae, rock, comedy, and even burlesque. 710 N. Clark St. (btw. Huron and Superior sts.). www.undergroundwonderbar.com. (℟ **312/266-7761.** Cover $5–$15. Subway/El: Red Line to Chicago.

9

CHICAGO AFTER DARK

The Live Music Scene

Come summertime, Chicago's parks spring to life with three distinct music festivals. Every August, **Lollapalooza** (www.lollapalooza.com) takes over a prime section of Grant Park for 3 days of performances by big-name artists and rising stars. Popular Chicago chefs get in on the action, too, putting together vendor booths that rival most food festivals. Hipster music connoisseurs prefer the **Pitchfork Music Festival** (www.pitchforkmusicfestival.com) in July, which brings mostly alt rock bands and hip hop artists to play a series of shows at Union Park on the near west side. Much to the chagrin of the most hardcore hipsters, many of the headliners at Pitchfork are actually quite mainstream these days, although there are still a fair number of bands that most of us have never heard of. Then, in September, men and women trying to relive the mosh pits of their youth head to Humboldt Park for **Riot Fest** (www.riotfest.org). It actually isn't nearly as riotous as it sounds, mixing a fair amount of estrogen-charged alt rockers with its more hardcore acts. If it's anything like last year, keep your eyes peeled for a John Stamos sculpture carved out of butter.

Rock & More

We never quite hit the Seattle level of grunge fame, but the early 1990s were prime rock times in Chicago, as the burgeoning alternative rock scene churned out national hits from the Smashing Pumpkins, Liz Phair, Veruca Salt, Urge Overkill, and Material Issue. The moment of "it-ness" may have faded (as did most of the aforementioned artists), but the live music scene holds its own, and then some. Wilco, Andrew Bird, and Fall Out Boy all spring to mind when it comes to home-grown talent. But truth be told, most Chicago bands concentrate on keeping it real, happy to perform at small local clubs and not obsessing (at least openly) about getting a record contract. The city is also a regular stop for touring bands, from big stadium acts to smaller up-and-coming groups. Scan the *Reader* to see who's playing where.

The biggest rock acts tend to play at the local stadiums: the **United Center** ★ (1901 W. Madison St. at Damen Ave.; www.unitedcenter.com; ✆ 312/455-4500), home of the Bulls and Blackhawks; **Wrigley Field** ★★, home of the Cubs (1060 W. Addison at Clark St., www.chicago.cubs.mlb.com/chc/ballpark, and **Allstate Arena** ★ (6920 N. Manheim Rd.; www.allstatearena.com; ✆ 800/745-3000), in Rosemont near O'Hare Airport. These venues are about what you expect: The overpriced seats nearest the stage are fine, but you'd better bring binoculars if you're stuck in the more affordable upper decks. During the summer, you'll also find the big names at the outdoor **FirstMerit Bank Pavilion at Northerly Island** ★, formerly the Charter One Pavilion at Northerly Island (1300 S. Lynn White Dr.; www.livenation.com/venues/14638/firstmerit-bank-pavilion-at-northerly-island; ✆ 312/540-2668). With its convenient Museum Campus location and incredible views of the lake and skyline, I wish I could recommend this spot more, but the debut in 2013 of the expanded lawn seat space left concert-goers soggy from the muddy grounds and annoyed by the terrible sound system and shoddy concessions service. A suburban option is **First Midwest Bank Amphitheatre** ★ (19100 S. Ridgeland Ave.; www.firstmidwest.com/fmba; ✆ 708/614-1616), inconveniently located in the suburb of Tinley Park, about an hour outside the city, and also cursed with pretty bad acoustics.

Picture it: You're sitting in a pew, the moonlight streaming through the stained glass above the altar, heavy, medieval-looking chandeliers looming above, and the concert begins. The acoustics are incredible, as music fills **Fourth Presbyterian Church** ★★★ (126 E. Chestnut, at Michigan Ave.; www.fourthchurch.org; ℭ **312/787-4570**) and you know that, having seen a concert in a gothic, stone-carved temple built in the early 1900s, no other venue will compare. Concerts here are rare, and the music has to be of a certain mellow, non-sacrilegious quality to be a fit, but if you can see a concert here, I highly recommend it. In recent years, Josh Ritter and Andrew Bird have played at Fourth Presbyterian. Shows aren't well advertised (I found out about Josh Ritter through his site), so check the church calendar and see if anything is going on during your visit. It's not quite the same, but you can also stop in at 4pm Sundays to see a jazz quartet play during the church service.

The good news: You can catch midlevel rock acts at local venues with a lot more character. The **Riviera Theatre** ★ (4746 N. Racine Ave.; www.jamusa.com/Venues/Riviera/Concerts.aspx; ℭ **773/275-6800**), is a relic of the Uptown neighborhood's swinging days in the 1920s, '30s, and '40s. A former movie palace, it retains the original ornate ceiling, balcony, and lighting fixtures, but it has definitely gotten grimy with age, and the acoustics could use some help. (Head upstairs to the balcony seats if you'd rather avoid the crowd that rushes toward the stage during shows.) The **Aragon Ballroom** ★, a few blocks away, at 1106 W. Lawrence Ave. (www.aragon.com; ℭ **773/561-9500**), was once an elegant big-band dance hall; the worn Moorish-castle decor and twinkling-star ceiling now give the place a seedy charm despite its less-than-ideal acoustics. A former vaudeville house is now the **Vic Theatre** ★★ (3145 N. Sheffield Ave.; www.victheatre.com; ℭ **773/472-0449**) a midsize venue that's as open to up-and-coming acts as big names. (Get there early to snag one of the lower balcony rows.)

More sedate audiences love the **Park West** ★★ (322 W. Armitage Ave.; www.parkwestchicago.com; ℭ **773/929-5959**), both for its excellent sound system and its cabaret-style seating (no mosh pit here). And we can't complete the mid-level spots without including the **House of Blues** ★★ (329 N. Dearborn St., at Kinzie St.; www.houseofblues.com; ℭ **312/923-2000**). Yes, it's a chain, but this Southern-style spot brings in acts of all levels of fame and fortune, and the sound here rivals the best in town. Plus, the wavy, toadstool-like exterior, located in the cone-like Marina Towers complex, is a site to see.

For tickets to most shows at all these venues, you're stuck going through the service-fee-grabbing **Ticketmaster** (ℭ **312/559-1212**).

Here are some bars and clubs that book live music most nights of the week:

City Winery ★ This West Loop restaurant, winery, and concert venue burst onto the music scene in 2012, bringing in night after night of acts that critics—and fans—absolutely love, from blues and jazz to folk and hip hop, rock, country, and more. Prince, Sinead O'Connor, Lucinda Williams, Billy Bragg: They've all already played here, along with some lesser known talents. You'll hear few complaints about the bookings; rather, the grumbling is about the so-so food, which is actually served during the performance at long, communal, assigned tables, and the house-blended wine,

Chicago attracts artists from a wide range of genres, and while the big-name country music stars tend to play at stadium-sized arenas, "alt country" and folk groups are a staple of the local music scene, mixing traditional American tunes with more experimental sounds. For a piece of that action, head to **The Old Town School of Folk Music** ★★★ (4544 N. Lincoln Ave., btw. Wilson and Montrose aves.; www.oldtownschool.org; ℂ **773/728-6000;** Subway/El: Brown Line to Western) a flourishing center that regularly hosts well-known singer-songwriters, bluegrass groups, Celtic fiddlers, and other traditional musicians from around the world, who play concerts in the two-level concert hall. Famous musicians, including Pete Seeger, Alison Krauss, Steve Goodman, and John Prine have all graced the stage at Old Town, and lesser knowns are always eager to play a concert hall with such a storied history, dating back to 1957. Aside from concerts, the venue hosts regular events like World Music Wednesdays, which are dedicated to sounds from afar, and every Friday is a Global Dance Party, as live bands or DJs play and visitors get their groove on. Old Town also has concerts for kids, teen open mics, and a summer music fest. Way more than just a concert venue, it's also a school that offers musical lessons to adults and kids, which you'll see in the constant flow of traffic in and out of the school carrying accordions, banjos, harmonicas, and other instruments. The school also operates a store where you can purchase or rent instruments.

which doesn't measure up to the price tag. 1200 W. Randolph St. (at Racine Ave.). www.citywinery.com/chicago. ℂ **312/733-9463.** Subway/El: Green or Pink Line to Morgan.

The Empty Bottle ★ Remember the first live show you ever saw in a bar? The Empty Bottle, located in Ukrainian Village, a bit south of Wicker Park, will take you back to that. A tad grungy, with Christmas lights above the bar and weird, doll head art on the walls, this place brings in alt rock and alt country performers 7 nights a week. Try and get in to see the Hoyle Brothers, who fill the bar with some hardcore twang every Friday at 5:30pm. 1035 N. Western Ave. (btw. Division St. and Augusta Blvd.). www.emptybottle.com. ℂ **773/276-3600.** Subway/El: Blue Line to Western, and then bus no. 49.

The Hideout ★★ Located in an old house, in a just out-of-the-way enough industrial area, The Hideout draws in crowds nightly. If there's no music playing at the small venue in this friendly dive bar, something will be going on, whether it's storytelling during the regular "The Write Club" or locals breaking bread over soup during the weekly soup and bread dinner that benefits local food pantries. If you're in town in September, try to nab a ticket to the popular Hideout Block Party, a family-friendly 2-day event that, in the past, has featured Neko Case, Mavis Staples, Superchunk, The Both, and other indie favorites. 1354 W. Wabansia Ave. (btw. Elston Ave. and Throop St.). www.hideoutchicago.com. ℂ **773/227-4433.** Bus 73.

Lincoln Hall ★★★ You know how some concert venues just make you feel old, in contrast to the grunge-loving youth? Lincoln Hall is a place where you'll never feel that way. This two-level Lincoln Park hall brings in some mid-level names in rock, hip hop, folk, alternative, and alt country, and has first-come, first-served seats upstairs—complete with cocktail service—and a large floor downstairs for the moshers (or just those who want to stand). Sister venue Schubas (see below) offers a similar vibe. 2424 N. Lincoln Ave. (at Fullerton Ave.). www.lincolnhallchicago.com. ✆ **773/525-2501.** Tickets usually run $12–$25. Subway/El: Red Line to Fullerton.

Schubas Tavern ★★★ This small, neighborhood concert venue is a favorite for indie rock, country, and folk fans. In an intimate hall, with room for just 165 concert-goers, every single seat is a winner here, and acts fill the stage 7 nights a week, with tickets usually going for less than $20. Some are big names, like Train and Neko Case, while others have gotten discovered by Chicagoans here. The on-site restaurant, Harmony Grill, is packed before and after each show, serving up way better-than-average bar food and a solid Midwest-centric beer list. 3159 N. Southport Ave. (at Belmont Ave.). www.schubas.com. ✆ **773/525-2508.** Subway/El: Red or Brown Line to Belmont.

Cabarets & Piano Bars

Chicago's relatively low-key cabaret scene is concentrated in River North and tends to attract a relaxed—but well-dressed—clientele.

The Baton Show Lounge ★ A taste of Vegas in Chicago? Sure, why not. You might want to wear a little extra lipstick tonight if you hope to outshine the drag queens here. The Baton Show Lounge has been staging raucous performances for more than 45 years now, and bachelorettes go crazy for it. Expect large estrogen-filled groups hooting and hollering at the stage and service that's fairly disinterested. Shows are Wednesday through Sunday at 8:30 and 10:30pm, and 12:30am (the later you go, the rowdier it'll be). Reservations are accepted and recommended on weekends. 436 N. Clark St. (btw. Hubbard and Illinois sts.). www.thebatonshowlounge.com. ✆ **312/644-5269.** Cover $15–$20 plus 2-drink minimum. Subway/El: Red Line to Grand or Brown Line to Merchandise Mart.

Coq d'Or ★ This 80-year-old bar was serving classic cocktails long before the word "classic" was added to them, and the martini, today, is as perfectly shaken as ever. Enter this old-school piano bar, with its dark woods and deep leather booths, and you know you're seeing the same scene you're grandparents did, when this was one of Chicago's hot spots. Try to come on a Friday or Saturday night, when the piano player gets going and romance fills the air. The Drake Hotel, 140 E. Walton St. (at Michigan Ave.). www.thedrakehotel.com. ✆ **312/787-2200.** No cover or drink minimum. Subway/El: Red Line to Chicago.

Gorilla Tango Theatre ★ Perhaps this listing belongs in comedy, but because it's burlesque, I'm going with the cabaret section. Gorilla Tango is one of the most creative spots in town when it comes to cabaret, and, while the schedules change, the theater continues to put on hilarious, culture-poking burlesque shows aimed at the nerdy crowd, with themes that include *Star Wars,* Super Mario Bros., Batman, Indiana Jones, The Oregon Trail, and more. If you take your cabaret with a dose of humor, check out this small Bucktown haunt. 1919 N. Milwaukee Ave. (at Western Ave.). www.gorillatango.com. ✆ **773/598-4549.** Tickets: $35. Subway/El: Blue Line to Western.

Redhead Piano Bar ★★ Men and women, usually 40 and up, dress to the nines at this old-school piano bar, where those wearing sneakers and hats are turned away. Expect to sing along to lots of Elton John and Billy Joel, and plan on getting to know your neighbors. Seats are close together and the crowd is quite extroverted. 16 W. Ontario St. www.redheadpianobar.com. ✆ **312/640-1000.** No cover or drink minimum. Subway/El: Red Line to Grand.

THE CLUB SCENE

Chicago is the hallowed ground where house music was hatched in the 1980s, so it's no surprise to find that it's also home to several vast, industrial-style dance clubs with pounding music and an under-30 crowd. Some spots specialize in a single type of music, while others offer an ever-changing mix of rhythms and beats that follow the latest DJ-driven trend. I'm going to give a brief overview of the hot spots du jour, but I recommend you visit Time Out Chicago (www.timeout.com/chicago) to keep tabs on the latest parties.

Those looking for a dance floor filled with a, shall we say, colorful crowd (you'll see a fair share of tattoos and transgender types at this Boystown favorite) will find something to love at **Berlin** ★★ (954 W. Belmont Ave., at Sheffield Ave.; www.berlin chicago.com; ✆ 773/348-4975), a Chicago institution that was cutting edge when it opened in the '80s and, as times changed and the club didn't, became retro. Come for the palindrome theme (yes, palindrome can actually be a theme!) at **EvilOlive** ★ (1551 W. Division St., at Ashland Ave.; www.evil-olive.com; ✆ 773/235-9100), and stay for the late night weekend rock and hip hop dance parties, brimming with the cool kids from surrounding neighborhoods. Wrigleyville's **Smart Bar** ★★★ (3730 N. Clark St., at Racine Ave.; www.smartbarchicago.com; ✆ 773/549-4140), has one of the best sound systems in town, which acts as a magnet to bring in top DJs from across the world playing house and techno. The beautiful River North set flocks to **Spybar** ★ (646 N. Franklin St., at Ontario St.; www.spybarchicago.com; ✆ 312/337-2191), dancing 'til the sun comes up to top DJs at this basement club/lounge, located 4,500 feet below street level. **Transit** ★, situated in a 10,000 square-foot warehouse in the West Loop (1431 W. Lake St.; www.transitnightclubchicago.com; ✆ 312/491-8600), is a no-nonsense dance destination with five bars and three music rooms playing hip hop, house, and reggae, and a favorite with the college crowd. **The Underground** ★ (56 W. Illinois St., btw. Dearborn and Clark sts.; www.theundergroundchicago.com; ✆ 312/943-7600), is a magnet for Chicago's most fashionable 20- and 30-somethings, who spend hours on prepping hair and makeup to spend the night in a bomb shelter-themed club blasting hip hop and house.

THE BAR SCENE

Much of Chicago nightlife centers around the ol' watering hole. We've got every kind of bar you could ask for here: sports bars, bro bars, gay bars, lesbian bars, trendy bars, dive bars, speakeasies, craft cocktail lounges, neighborhood bars. All you have to do is pick a location and there's bound to be a beer within stumbling distance. One word of advice: For a true neighborhood tavern, it's best to venture beyond the Loop and River North (it's also cheaper). Hop on the El and take a quick ride to Lincoln Park, Wrigleyville, Bucktown, Wicker Park, or any of the other neighborhood spots listed below. On Friday and Saturday nights, the train is filled with others who are bar hopping or heading out to a night on the town. It's a totally different scene from the sober weekday commute, and it can be pretty amusing to watch as the night wears on.

Bars

THE LOOP & VICINITY

Aviary ★★★ Talk about an only-in-Chicago experience. Attached to Next restaurant (p. 97) in the West Loop and co-owned by renowned Chicago chef Grant Achatz,

TRUE story

Good, old-fashioned storytelling has washed over Chicago, as residents take to the mic and bare all, usually with a courage-filled beverage in hand. Visiting one of these narrative nights is a great way to be a Chicago voyeur, while mixing with locals at a neighborhood bar.

If you're a fan of **The Moth Radio Hour** (www.themoth.org), presented by the Public Radio Exchange (PRX), now is your chance to hear the raw version of those stories at **The Moth StorySlam** ★★★. Each StorySlam has a different theme (escape, pornography, fate, etc.) and attendees who want to tell a story put their name in a drawing. If they're selected, they have to tell a story that fits within the given theme, and judges select a winner. The Moth stands out from other local storytelling events listed because the participants aren't professional writers; they're everyday Chicagoans telling real-life tales, some heartbreaking, others hilarious, and, occasionally, awkward.

Two different bars host The Moth: it's at Martyr's, just south of Lincoln Square (3855 N. Lincoln Ave., at Byron St.; www.martyrslive.com; ℭ **773/404-9494**), the last Tuesday of the month, and in the West Loop at **Haymarket Pub & Brewery** (737 W. Randolph, at Halsted; www.haymarketbrewing.com; ℭ **312/638-0700**), the second Monday of the month.

Essay Fiesta ★★ (www.essayfiesta.com) turns the mic over to local Chicago writers each month at Lincoln Square's **Book Cellar** (p. 171; 4736 N. Lincoln Ave.; www.bookcellarinc.com; ℭ **773/293-2665**) to share their latest works. **Write Club** ★ (www.writeclubrules.com) at **The Hideout** (p. 210; 1354 W. Wabansia Ave., at Ada St.; ℭ **773/227-4433**), the third Tuesday of the month, is a flashback to debate club. There, writers duke it out, sharing essays they've written about the same ideas, but on opposing sides. **The Paper Machete** ★, a weekly salon hosted by the storied **Green Mill** (p. 205; 4802 N. Broadway Ave., at Lawrence; www.greenmilljazz.com; ℭ **773/878-5552**), brings together journalists, authors, musicians, and comedians to put on an energy-filled show of readings and rants Saturdays 3 to 5pm.

Aviary is a libations laboratory that puts a touch of molecular gastronomy into every drink. When you enter, you'll get a glimpse of the chemists at work, inside what looks like a large, gated-off cage, as the staff pours the time, energy, and thought into each drink that you'd expect in crafting a fine-dining course. One beverage may be served in a scented bag that you have to pop to get inside, while another is in a mini-aquarium-like container, filled with fruits and herbs. My personal favorite, the "In the Rocks," is an old fashioned that's served inside of an egg-shaped sphere of ice. You use a tiny sling shot to crack the ice and let the drink spill out. You'll pay close to $20 for a beverage here, but, if you ask me, it's worth its weight in stories to take home. 955 W. Fulton St. (at Morgan St.). www.theaviary.com. ℭ **312/226-0868.** Subway/El: Green or Pink Line to Morgan.

Lone Wolf ★★ Seems every block in just about every neighborhood in Chicago has a dive bar that could pass as any dive bar. Outside, there's red brick and frosted windows, along with a generic beer sign. Lone Wolf is a new, playful take on that neighborhood bar, capturing each of those elements, but in an intentional way. Its generic beer sign, for example, isn't from Pabst or Schlitz, it's from Indiana microbrewery and local favorite, Three Floyds. There's nothing divey about the inside, either, with its deep black booths and clean lines. Located in the trendy West Loop, where the restaurant scene is booming, there are surprisingly few non-restaurant bars, and Lone Wolf fills that void. 806 W. Randolph St. (at Halsted St.) © **312/600-9391.** Subway/El: Green or Pink Line to Morgan.

Miller's Pub ★ It's not easy to find a welcoming spot filled with regulars inside the Loop, where restaurants and bars often struggle to draw a nighttime crowd after workers go home. Miller's has done just that—and kept its beer prices low—since it opened in 1935. It's the closest thing you'll find to a neighborhood pub in a neighborhood-free zone. 134 S. Wabash Ave. (btw. Jackson Blvd. and Adams St.). www.millerspub.com. © **312/263-4988.** Subway/El: Red Line to Monroe, or Brown, Green, Orange, Pink, or Purple Line to Madison/Wabash.

RIVER NORTH & VICINITY

The Berkshire Room ★★ Tucked inside the super hip Acme Hotel (p. 67), The Berkshire Room is one of the more mellow bars in the River North area. Dim and casual, but not dive-ish in the slightest, you can get just about any libation you can think of, from inexpensive beers, including a section designated to "Blue Collar Lagers," like Miller Lite, to "Dealer's Choice" cocktails, wherein you select the spirit (mezcal, sake, blended Scotch, wheated bourbon, and many more) the flavor profile (sweet and sour, fruity, herbaceous, strong and stirred, spicy, smoky), and even the glassware. Although new to the scene, the bar is drawing in large numbers of locals, which is quite a feat for a River North hotel bar. 15 E. Ohio St. (inside Acme Hotel). www.theberkshireroom.com. © **312/894-0800.** Subway/El: Red Line to Grand.

Billy Goat Tavern ★ A *Saturday Night Live* sketch, along with Billy Goat's proximity to the city's scribes at the *Chicago Tribune,* have made this dive bar, located under Michigan Avenue, world famous. The walls are lined with historic photos, not to mention about 80 years of hamburger fumes. Today, Billy Goat remains a popular spot for journalists and locals looking to have an after-work cocktail—and none of those fancy craft cocktails or craft beers, mind you. Known for its surly service, the bartenders here are actually quite nice. 430 N. Michigan Ave. www.billygoattavern.com. © **312/222-1525.** Subway/El: Red Line to Grand/State.

Rockit Bar & Grill ★ The warehouse-chic saloon was styled by celebri-designer Nate Berkus, and it draws in the 20-something crowd with its lengthy beer/wine/cocktail list and scenester cred. Its late night menu is a particular draw for the beautiful bar crowd, and includes one of the best burgers ever created. 22 W. Hubbard St. (btw. State and Dearborn sts.). www.rockitbarandgrill.com. © **312/645-6000.** Subway/El: Red Line to Grand.

The Terrace at Trump ★★ A cocktail here will run you at least $20 and a beer about $12 or so, but the views from the 16th floor terrace, which include the Wrigley Clock Tower, Tribune Tower, and the neighboring Chicago skyline, are totally worth the price of admission. Expect long waits Wednesday and Saturday nights, when locals and visitors know they can get a top-notch view of the fireworks at Navy Pier. 401 N. Wabash Ave. (at the Chicago River). www.trumpchicagohotel.com. © **312/588-8000.** Subway/El: Red Line to Grand.

Three Dots and a Dash ★★★ You have to be in the know to find this hidden tiki bar. The actual address listed will take you to a more typical River North bar, called Bub City. Instead, head to the alley between Hubbard and Illinois streets. You'll see a blue light cast on a brick building and a Three Dots and a Dash sign. Inside, down a dark, blue-lit, skull-lined stairway, is an exotic tiki bar, covered with a grass awning and filled with shrunken skulls and a perennially packed house. Each drink comes in some sort of unique vessel, like a coconut shell or tiki head, filled with fresh fruit and in-your-face-strong cocktails, like the bar's namesake beverage, Three Dots and a Dash. 435 N. Clark St. (in the alley behind Clark, btw. Hubbard and Illinois sts.). www.threedots chicago.com. ℂ **312/610-4220.** Subway/El: Red Line to Grand or Brown Line to Merchandise Mart.

Travelle Bar and Lounge ★★   This mid-century modern style lounge, located on the second floor of the Langham, has cozy, curvy couches, comfortable lounge chairs, dim lighting, and an air of sexy chic. Nestled in the former IBM building, a landmark designed by architect Ludwig Mies van der Rohe, the lounge is surrounded by floor-to-ceiling windows that look out at the neighboring Marina Towers and the Chicago River. The Langham opened quietly in 2013, and many locals have yet to discover this beautiful bar, and, selfishly, I hope it stays that way so I can reliably score a seat. Stop in Thursday through Saturday for live music. 330 N. Wabash (at Illinois St.). www.chicago.langhamhotels.com. ℂ **312/923-9988.** Subway/El: Red Line to Grand.

RUSH & DIVISION STREETS

Around Rush Street are what a bygone era once called "singles bars"—although the only singles that tend to head here now are suburbanites, out-of-towners, and barely legal partiers. Rush Street's glory days may be long gone, but there are still a few vestiges of the old times on nearby Division Street, which overflows with party-hearty spots that attract a loud, frat-party element to an area of town that locals refer to as the Viagra Triangle. They include **She-nannigan's House of Beer** 16 W. Division St. (www.rushanddivision.com/she-nannigans-house-of-beer; ℂ **312/642-2344**); **Butch McGuire's,** 20 W. Division St. (www.butchmcguires.com ℂ **312/787-4318**); the **Lodge,** 21 W. Division St. (www.rushanddivision.com/the-lodge; ℂ **312/642-4406**); and **Mother's,** 26 W. Division St. (www.rushanddivision.com/the-original-mothers; ℂ **312/642-7251**). Many of these bars offer discounts for women, as loud pitchmen in front of each establishment will be happy to tell any attractive ladies who pass by.

OLD TOWN

The center of nightlife in Old Town is **Wells Street,** home to Second City and Zanies Comedy Club, as well as a string of reliable restaurants and bars, many of which have been in business for decades. You're not going to find many trendy spots in Old Town; the nightlife here tends toward neighborhood pubs and casual restaurants, filled mostly with a late-20s and 30-something crowd.

Benchmark ★   Technically, Benchmark is a sports bar, so it's popular with the bros (read: former frat boys turned adult), and has more flatscreens than I care to count. But there's also a see-and-be-seen quality to the space, and at night, the heels go on and everyone from college kids to cougars seem to be on the prowl. Plus, there are the perks: better-than-the-average-bar food (tuna tostadas, lamb burgers, flatbreads, and a ridiculously good skillet cookie) and a retractable roof, which draws a more mellow, less sporty crowd to the second level. 1510 N. Wells St. (btw. North Ave. and Schiller St.). www.benchmarkchicago.com. ℂ **312/649-9640.** Subway/El: Brown Line to Sedgwick.

Corcoran's ★   Irish pubs are a dime a dozen in Chicago, where Irish pride runs strong. But Corcoran's manages to stand out in the crowd, thanks to a daily beer specials, a hugely popular beer garden during the warm months, and its proximity to Second City, which is across the street. You'll find a good mix of folks here, with all ages and income brackets accounted for, coming together for a cold Guinness. 1615 N. Wells St. (at North Ave.). www.vaughanhospitality.com. ℂ **312/440-0885.** Subway/El: Brown Line to Sedgwick.

Old Town Ale House ★★ First, the art. The primary eye-catcher is a portrait of a nude Sarah Palin, toting a machine gun, standing on a bear rug. Then there's former Illinois governor turned federal prisoner number 40892-424, Rod Blagojevich, stripping down in his orange jumpsuit for a cavity search. And that's just the start of the lewd collection, painted by the husband of the bar's owner, at this divey but beloved watering hole. Open since the '50s, the small mainstay bar draws in everyone from young hipsters to old barflies who look like they haven't been home in years. 219 W. North Ave. (at Wells St.). www.theoldtownalehouse.com. ℂ **312/944-7020.** Subway/El: Brown Line to Sedgwick.

LINCOLN PARK

Lincoln Park, with its high concentration of apartment-dwelling singles, is one of the busiest nightlife destinations in Chicago. Real estate is at a premium in this residential neighborhood, so you won't find many warehouse-size dance clubs here; most of the action is at pubs and bars. Concentrations of hot-spots run along Halsted Street and Lincoln Avenue.

Barrelhouse Flat ★ Craft cocktails have even infiltrated the neighborhood bars, and Barrelhouse Flat is a Lincoln Park favorite for high-octane mixes. The menu, which includes curiosities like the Dirty Streisand and Corn and Oil, along with all the classics, is organized by hooch—gin, rum, whiskey, etc.—and reads like a book. The downstairs area is comfortable and filled with booths, but the opulent upstairs speakeasy is where you really want to be to kick back. If you're visiting on a weekend, come early or expect to wait in line. 2624 N. Lincoln (btw. Wrightwood and Kenwood aves.). www.barrelhouseflat.com. ℂ **773/477-1741.** Subway/El: Brown Line to Diversey.

Goose Island Brewing Company ★ Even though Anheuser-Busch purchased Chicago's hometown brewer in 2011, some locals still claim the brewpub as their own. This large, well-lit bar has 20 beers on tap daily, so you can try old favorites, such as the popular Honker's Ale, or something more obscure, like the Identity Crisis barrel-aged porter. The bar draws in a steady stream of bubbly locals and tourists, and brewery tours (see p. 201) fill quickly. Goose Island also has a bar in Wrigleyville, at 3535 N. Clark St. (ℂ **773/832-9040**). 1800 N. Clybourn Ave. (at Willow St.). www.gooseisland.com. ℂ **312/915-0071.** Subway/El: Brown Line to Armitage.

The J. Parker ★★ If you're lucky enough to be in Chicago during the warm months, hie thee to the rooftop of Hotel Lincoln (p. 72), stat. Grab a chair or couch and a glass of rosé and gaze out on Lake Michigan to the east, or the lights of the city all around you. I'll warn you that service here is less than amazing, the wine glasses are plastic, and the crowd can border on pretentious, particularly after dark. But even with that, I'm still giving it two stars, all for the view. (*Note:* an enclosed portion of the rooftop is open year round, but the main reason to go is when it's warm enough to stand or sit outside). 1816 N. Clark St. (at Wells St.). www.jparkerchicago.com. ℂ **312/254-4747.** Bus: 22, 36, 73.

WRIGLEYVILLE, LAKEVIEW & THE NORTH SIDE

Real estate in Wrigleyville and Lakeview is a tad less expensive than in Lincoln Park, so the nightlife scene here skews a little younger, but still has a sheen of post-fraternity/sorority party life, especially on Clark Street across from Wrigley Field. But head away from the ball field, and you'll discover some more exotic choices.

Carol's Pub ★★ This weird little Uptown honkytonk, just north of Wrigleyville, appeals to the young and hip, the old and broken-hipped, and everyone in between who

SOMETHING TO wine ABOUT

Chicago has always been a big beer city, but that's not to say we don't love our reds, whites and rosés, too. The following wine and Champagne bars are all worth toasting.

The closest wine bar to the Loop, **Bin 36** ★ (339 N. Dearborn St.; www.bin36.com; ✆ **312/755-9463**), fills with the after-work crowd, dates, and girls-night-out gatherings, and is a large, welcoming spot, with vibrant wine descriptions for wine novices and oenophiles alike. If you're feeling the thirst along the Magnificent Mile, **Eno** ★★ (505 Michigan Ave., at Illinois St.; www.enowinerooms.com; ✆ **312/321-8738**), located in the InterContinental Chicago, looks right out on Michigan Avenue and is a comfortable spot to help recharge your shopping muscles. For fancy bubbles, head to **Pops for Champagne** ★★ (601 N. State St., at Ohio St.; www.popsfor champagne.com; ✆ **312/266-7677**). This popular River North spot carries more than 200 choices, plus live jazz fills the air Sunday through Tuesday starting at 9pm. Hidden off a cobblestone alley in the West Loop, **RM Champagne Salon** ★★ (116 N. Green St., btw. Randolph St and Washington Blvd.; www.rmchampagnesalon.com; ✆ **312/243-1199**) feels more like a European parlor, with a cozy fireplace and five pages of bubbles from which to choose.

In the charming Roscoe Village neighborhood, located west of Lakeview, **Volo** ★★ (2008 W. Roscoe, btw. Damen and Seeley aves.; www.volorestaurant.com; ✆ **773/348-4600**) seems like a tiny spot, with just a few chairs and booths, until you discover the lush backyard garden, which fills on warm evenings. Grapes from France, Greece, Germany, Italy, and Spain are all accounted for at **Webster's Wine Bar** ★ (1480 W. Webster Ave., btw. Clybourn and Ashland aves.; www.websterwinebar.com; ✆ **773/868-0608**), a romantic spot in Lincoln Park.

can take a little grit with their MGD. A classic roadhouse, Carol's comes to life on weekends, when live bands take the stage crooning country tunes, and the dance floor fills with two-steppers, one-steppers, or even an occasional wheelchair dancing queen. Want to publicly cry into your own beer—and mic? Stop in Thursday at 9pm for country karaoke. Talk about hillbilly heaven. 4659 N. Clark (at Leland Ave.). ✆ **773/334-2402.** Subway/El: Red Line to Wilson.

The Cubby Bear ★ Located across from Wrigley Field, the party following a Cubs game spills into the enormous Cubby Bear. It's not for everyone, and if you do go, get your elbows ready to fend for space from drunken baseball fans. Still, throwing one back at the Cubby Bear is practically a rite of passage in Chicago. Everyone should do it once. The Cubby Bear doubles as a concert venue and is popular with the white-t-shirted college crowd. 1059 W. Addison St. (at Clark St.). www.cubbybear.com. ✆ **773/327-1662.** Subway/El: Red Line to Addison.

Hopleaf ★★★ There are so many neighborhood bars in Chicago that it takes something special for a tavern's name to carry beyond the zip code. Andersonville's Hopleaf has that something special. You're likely to find as many people who walked here as you are to see commuters, interested in checking out what's new on the 200-plus mostly Belgian beer menu and stuffing themselves with the bar's famous mussels in the process. If you're coming on a weekend, expect it to be packed with a boisterous, welcoming crowd. 5148 N. Clark St. (btw. Foster Ave. and Winona St.). www.hopleaf.com. ✆ **773/334-9851.** Subway/El: Red Line to Berwyn.

As kids, we loved arcades. As adults, we fell in love with bars. Along the way, some genius decided to meld the two worlds and create a barcade (also known as a beercade).

Chicago has a number of barcades to choose from. Location-wise, my favorite is Wicker Park's **Emporium Arcade Bar**, 1366 N. Milwaukee Ave., just northwest of Wood St. (www.emporiumchicago.com; C **773/697-7922**), which has dozens of vintage machines, like Donkey Kong, Dig Dug, and Centipede, along with pinball machines and other games. The drawback: The games cost a token (tokens are 25¢), and it's pretty amazing how quickly you burn through them when the beer is flowing. With that said, its location is close to lots of other bars and restaurants and it's incredibly walkable.

Headquarters Beercade (2833 N. Sheffield Ave., at Wolfram St.; www.hqbeercade.com; C **773/665-5660**), is a little further out of the way, but the games here are actually free, and the same holds for **Logan Hardware** (2410 W. Fullerton, www.logan-hardware.com; C **773/235-5030**), the latest beercade on the scene (it's just up the street from a record store of the same name, see p. 180), located in Logan Square. **Replay** (3439 N. Halsted St.; C **773/975-9244**), which is in Boystown, is another fun option (p. 221). It's a smaller spot, but games are free and so is popcorn.

Northdown Taproom ★★
The quintessential neighborhood bar, Northdown has an impressive revolving beer list, displays local artists work, and is as welcoming as they come, despite the long facial hair and tattoos adorning servers. Grab a can of Schlitz or try something you probably won't find back home, like a Gumballhead wheat bear, brewed by Three Floyds in Munster, Indiana, and chat with your bar mates, who, most likely, can share some other great tips about where to go in their neighborhood. If you're hungry, the kitchen makes awesome burgers and incredible vegan fare. Weird, right? 3244 N. Lincoln St. (btw. School and Melrose sts). www.northdownchicago.com. C **773/697-7578.** Subway/El: Brown Line to Paulina.

Uncommon Ground ★★
This bar and restaurant is a reminder that not all of Wrigelyville is Cubs crazy, and, in fact, it's possible to enjoy a nice glass of wine while listening to self-contained musicians on weekends. Grab a seat in the living-room-like interior, or, if you still want one hand in the screaming drunk fest of Wrigleyville and one holding your Pinot noir, request to sit on the patio when the weather is nice. There, you can take a deep breath and smell the fresh scent of basil, mint, and other herbs from the restaurant's own "sidewalk farm," part of its green initiatives and cocktail program (there's also a rooftop garden). There's also a second location further north in the Edgewater neighborhood, 1401 W. Devon Ave. (C **773/465-9801**). 3800 N. Clark St. (at Grace St.). www.uncommonground.com. C **773/929-3680.** Subway/El: Red Line to Addison.

WICKER PARK, BUCKTOWN & LOGAN SQUARE
In Wicker Park and Bucktown, both slackers and adventurous suburbanites populate bars dotting the streets leading out from the intersection of North, Damen, and Milwaukee avenues. Don't dress up if you want to blend in: A casually bohemian getup and low-key attitude are all you need. Logan Square still has the grit that Wicker Park and Bucktown have mostly lost. In this up-and-coming neighborhood,

you'll find yourself in front of some of Chicago's most popular bars one second, and the next walking past a sprawling, warehouse-like flea-market with no windows to peer inside. The dress here ranges from smart casual to ripped casual, depending on where you go.

Big Star ★★   By day, the skinny jeans–wearing masses come for the tacos (p. 106). By night, they comb their ironic (I think?) mustaches and come for the whiskey. Every night of the week, Big Star has a $3 whiskey special, or if you're willing to pay more, peruse their deep single-barrel bourbon list, and admire the extensive variety of tequila and mescal. Big Star is hopping year-round, but it's at its best when the giant patio looking out on Damen Avenue opens, and regulars wait in long lines for a table to enjoy Chicago's too-brief summer. 1531 N. Damen (btw. Milwaukee and Wicker Park aves.). www.bigstarchicago.com. ℭ **773/235-4039.** Subway/El: Blue Line to Damen Ave.

Billy Sunday ★★★   You'll need a dictionary to understand the drink menu, but don't let that stop you from ordering one of the house-made tonics, which are full of booze, pumped with carbonation, and served on tap at Billy Sunday, a speakeasy-style bar named for teetotaling evangelist Billy Sunday. Or stick with an Old Fashioned or other classic, prepared with a variety of beakers and tinctures and styles of ice (we counted four different types of cubes in as many drinks). Sit at the bar so you can watch the alchemy happen. 3143 W. Logan Blvd. (btw. Kedzie Blvd. and Milwaukee Ave). www.billy-sunday.com. ℭ **773/661-2485.** Subway/El: Blue Line to Logan.

Longman & Eagle ★   Confession: I never feel quite cool enough to fit in at Longman & Eagle, where the young and beautiful staff all seem to wear oversized hipster glasses and have a slightly detached air. Whiskey, of course, helps alleviate that out-of-place sense, and Longman & Eagle offers nearly 150 different types, a fifth of which are available for just $3 a shot. This bar is notoriously crowded in winter, when the disaffected artsy crowd is waiting to get seated at the gastropub. During warm months, a patio opens up, giving you more breathing room. If you want to make a night of it, reserve one of the rooms upstairs at the Longman & Eagle Inn (p. 47), which will also score you a rare reservation at the popular farm-to-table restaurant. Only hotel guests are granted such a thing. 2657 N. Kedzie Ave. (at Schubert Ave.). www.longmanandeagle.com. ℭ **773-276-7110.** No reservations accepted. Subway/El: Blue Line to Logan.

The Map Room ★   Travel is the key theme at The Map Room, a Bucktown favorite that's been around since the early '90s. You'll see it in the maps that line the walls and the flags that hang from the ceiling. More importantly, you'll taste it in the 200-plus beers that the bar offers, with far-flung options, including a Sinebrychoff Porter from Finland. This casual, comfortable spot is a great place to strike up a conversation about your travels with the friendly imbibers, or get an education on beer from the manager, who is also a *cicerone* (that's like a sommelier of beer). Bring cash; no credit cards allowed. 1949 N. Hoyne Ave. (at Armitage Ave.). www.maproom.com. ℭ **773/252-7636.** Subway/El: Blue Line to Damen Ave.

Revolution Brewpub ★★   One of Logan Square's largest and most popular spots, the bar here gets packed with artsy neighbors, even during mid-week lunch hour, and you can pretty much forget getting in in under an hour Friday or Saturday. The loud brewpub is filled with raised fists—the symbol of revolution—and cycles through about 20 different types of beer in a year. The Anti-Hero IPA is a local favorite, and patrons here are just as crazy about the food as they are the brews. Try the bacon fat popcorn, burger, or fish and chips and you'll understand why. 2323 N. Milwaukee Ave. (btw. Humboldt Blvd. and California Ave). www.revbrew.com. ℭ 773/227-2739. Subway/El: Blue Line to California.

The Violet Hour ★★★ Yes, it's another speakeasy-style bar, but Violet Hour was one of the early ones to explore the Prohibition-era theme, and it takes it so seriously that newcomers might struggle to find the door, which isn't marked with a sign. Have no fear, though, you'll know the Violet Hour by the line of snazzy dressers waiting to get in on Damen Avenue. They only let in as many people as there are seats, so once you're in, you're in. Violet Hour wears its snobbishness with pride, publishing a set of rules for all to see, which ban cellphone use in the lounge, along with the types of drinks you'd find at a place like the Cubby Bear (p. 217). "No O-Bombs. No Jäger-Bombs. No bombs of any kind. No Budweiser. No light beer. No Grey Goose. No cosmopolitans." Drinks, many of which are made with fresh fruit and house made bitters, run lethal, but after you get a coveted seat, you'll want to try at least one more. 1520 N. Damen Ave. (at Pierce St.). www.theviolethour.com. ℭ 773/252-1500. Subway/El: Blue Line to Damen Ave.

THE GAY & LESBIAN SCENE

Most of Chicago's gay bars are clustered on a stretch of North Halsted Street in Lakeview, in what's known as Boystown. Men's bars predominate—few places in town cater exclusively to lesbians—but a few gay bars get a mix of both genders. As with other clubs, what's hot and what's not changes frequently, so I've given my best to point out some mainstays. For up-to-the-minute info and listings, check out the weekly entertainment guide *Nightspots*.

Berlin ★★ Get your freak on at Berlin, a favorite dance spot among all clubgoers, gay or straight. With a history of 3 decades, there's a decidedly retro sense to Berlin, with Depeche Mode/New Order Nights and Björk Showcases on the calendar. In true gay bar fashion, almost every night has some kind of theme (Madonna-rama, Drag matinee, and so forth). This is the place to be for the Boystown afterhours crowd looking to work up a disco sweat until the sun rises. Fueled by an eclectic cast of rotating DJs, Berlin stays open 'til 4am on Fridays and 5am Saturdays. 954 W. Belmont Ave. (east of Sheffield Ave.). www.berlinchicago.com. ℭ 773/348-4975. Cover after midnight Fri–Sat $5–$8. Subway/El: Red or Brown Line to Belmont.

Big Chicks ★★ Men and women tired of the fashion-show vibe of Boystown head to Big Chicks, a casual Uptown bar with funky decor, including the lady-filled art collection of owner Michelle Fire, aka the original Big Chick. Regulars include a smart, artsy crowd of gays, lesbians, and heteros who love this attitude-free bar for its free Sunday buffet (4–6pm) and the new geeky Wednesday night trivia. A DJ rolls in on weekends and the dance floor gets packed Friday and Saturday nights. **Tweet,** 5020 N. Sheridan Rd. (ℭ 773/728-5576), a vegetarian-friendly bunch spot next door, is also popular with the gay and lesbian set. Whether you're going to Big Chicks or Tweet, bring cash; neither business accepts credit cards. 5024 N. Sheridan Rd. (btw. Argyle St. and Foster Ave.). www.bigchicks.com. ℭ 773/728-5511. No credit cards. Subway/El: Red Line to Argyle.

The Closet ★ The "Cheers" of the neighborhood, this tiny but comfortable neighborhood dive bar has been a lesbian (and gay and hetero) favorite since owners

Judi and Rose opened it in 1978. Grab a bucket of beers, some darts, and settle in for an evening with friendly regulars. If the bartender doesn't know your name when you arrive, she will by the time you leave. The Closet is an estrogen-rich change of scenery from the boy-sterous bars nearby, and the tiny dance floor here really gets going on weekends. The bar is open until 4am nightly and 5am Saturdays. Bring cash; bartenders will frown at your credit card. 3325 N. Broadway Ave. (at Buckingham St.). www.theclosetchicago.com ℂ **773/477-8533.** No credit cards. Subway/El: Red or Brown Line to Belmont.

Downtown ★ You could be walking into just about any River North bar when you enter Downtown, with its flatscreen TVs, low lighting and sophisticated sensibility. You may or may not realize that you've just walked into the closest gay bar to the Loop. Expect an older, professional, male-dominated clientele to gather here for a drink after work. But they don't stay quite so buttoned up as the drinks start flowing, especially during the underwear parties on the second and fourth Friday of each month. 440 N. State St. (at Illinois St.). www.downtownbarandlounge.com. ℂ **312/464-1400.** Subway/El: Red Line to Grand.

Elixir ★★ You won't find a shower competition or show tune sing along here. Instead, you'll discover something that is all too often missing on the gummy-bear-shot-filled Chicago gay bar circuit: craft cocktails, which have made Elixir a welcome newcomer to the scene. This tiny Boystown lounge never seems to have enough seating for its well-heeled, mostly male patrons, so if you see an available white barstool, grab it, and request a black maple margarita or nutty Old Fashioned, stat. 3452 N. Halsted St. (at Cornelia Ave.). www.elixirchicago.com. ℂ **773/975-9244.** Subway/El: Red Line to Addison.

Replay ★★ Grab a brew from one of the cute, scruffy bartenders and get your quarters ready. Replay is home to about a dozen classic games, like Frogger, Centipede, Super Mario Bros., and a couple of pinball machines, and many of them are even free. The young, energetic crowd alternates between being social, playing video games and staring at the flatscreen TVs that line the bar. A deep beer and bourbon list are a reminder that this is a serious bar, even with all the bleeping and blooping going on. 3439 N. Halsted (at Newport Ave.). www.replaylakeview.com. ℂ **773/975-9244.** Subway/El: Red Line to Addison.

Roscoe's Tavern ★ A mainstay in the gay and lesbian community since it opened in 1987, Roscoe's, which is located in the heart of Boystown, is a casual spot for a weekday beer or a rollicking weekend party that gets more crowded as the clock ticks on. Despite the crowds, which span the generations and genders, the friendly staff does a good job of running two bars and multiple rooms (including a dance floor, pool table, and large patio). Grab a barstool by one of the large windows and watch the Boystown crowds pass on Halsted, or choose a quiet nook to sit in. Just be sure and go to the bathroom before you get here, if you can. They're dingy and dirty. 3356 N. Halsted St. (at Roscoe St.). www.roscoes.com. ℂ **773/281-3355.** Cover after 10pm Sat $5. Subway/El: Red or Brown Line to Belmont.

Sidetrack ★ Slushies and show tunes are the name of the game here. Sidetrack is a huge bar filling eight storefronts and a rooftop deck, where flirty patrons (and flirty bartenders) sip on super sweet frozen drinks (Midori melon ball, Bacardi Pineapple Mai Tai, Effen Black Cherry Buzz, you get the picture) and bust out "Summer Nights" (everyone sings along). If you're not here on a Show Tune Night, which are Sunday, Monday and Friday, you're bound to be here for another theme. Expect a colorful crowd any night of the week. 3349 N. Halsted St. (at Roscoe St.). www. sidetrackchicago.com. ℂ **773/477-9189.** Subway/El: Red or Brown Line to Belmont.

Spin ★ Topless bartenders (male), shower contests, Dragzilla drag competitions—what more could you ask for? Well, maybe a strong drink, and while they tend to be a bit watered down here, on Wednesday they're only $1. Music is thumping on the two dance floors, and with five bars, a number of lounge areas, and a patio, be sure to keep your companions close or you'll risk losing them in this clubby maze. 800 W. Belmont (at Halsted St.). www.spin-nightclub.com. ℂ **773/327-7711.** Subway/El: Red or Brown Line to Belmont.

PLANNING YOUR TRIP TO CHICAGO

As with any trip, a little advance preparation will pay off once you arrive in Chicago. This chapter provides a variety of planning tools, including information on how to get here, local visitor resources, and tips on getting around. In the last section of this chapter, Fast Facts, we offer dozens of miscellaneous resources and organizations that you can turn to for help.

GETTING THERE

By Plane

Two major airports serve Chicago: **O'Hare International Airport** (www. flychicago.com; © **773/686-2200;** online airport code ORD), about 15 miles northwest of downtown Chicago (driving time can take about 30 minutes to an hour, depending on traffic); and **Midway International Airport** (www.flychicago.com; © **773/838-0600;** about 11 miles from the Loop (it takes about 20 to 45 minutes driving, depending on traffic). Almost every domestic airline is represented at both airports, although Southwest only flies into Midway.

GETTING INTO TOWN FROM THE AIRPORT

Taxis are plentiful at both O'Hare and Midway, but you can get downtown relatively easily by public transportation as well. Follow the "taxi" or "ground transportation" signs and you'll find a person at the front of the cab line directing passengers to get into available cars. The base fare is $3.25, the first additional passenger is $1, and each passenger thereafter is 50¢. Each additional mile costs $1.80, and there's an airport arrival/departure tax of $2, and tolls are charged to the passenger. Tips aren't included on the meter, so it's up to you to add that (15–20% is customary). A cab ride into the city will cost a little less than $40 from O'Hare and around $30 from Midway. *One warning:* Rush-hour traffic can be horrendous, especially around O'Hare, and the longer you sit in the traffic, the higher the fare will be.

RIDING THE EL   If you're not carting a lot of luggage and want to save money, I highly recommend taking public transportation, which is convenient from both airports. For $2.25 from Midway or $5 from O'Hare, you can take the El (elevated train) straight into downtown. By riding the rails, you'll also miss freeway traffic, which can hit you from either airport.

O'Hare is on the Blue Line; a trip to downtown takes about 40 minutes. If you're staying on or near Michigan Avenue, you'll want to switch to the Red Line, which will add another 10 or 15 minutes to your trip. Trains leave every 3 to 10 minutes during the day and early evening, and every half-hour at night. The Blue Line runs 24 hours a day.

Getting downtown from Midway is much faster. The ride on the Orange Line takes 20 to 30 minutes. Trains leave the station every 3 to 12 minutes. The train station is a fair walk from the terminal—without the benefit of O'Hare's moving sidewalks—so be prepared if you have heavy bags. From either airport, allow extra time if you're traveling during rush hour or on holidays. The Orange Line stops operating each night at about 1am and resumes service by 5am.

Though you can see all the major sights in the city without a car, both airports have outposts for every major car-rental company.

EXPRESS VAN SERVICE   GO Airport Express (www.airportexpress.com; ℂ 888/2-THEVAN [284-3826]) serves most first-class hotels in Chicago with its green-and-white vans; ticket counters are at both airports near baggage claim (outside Customs at the international terminal at O'Hare). For transportation to the airport, reserve a spot through one of the hotels (check with the bell captain). The cost is $32 one-way ($58 round-trip) to or from O'Hare, and $27 one-way ($48 round-trip) to or from Midway. Add more people in the mix and you save significantly. Group rates for two or more people traveling together are less expensive than sharing a cab. The shuttles operate from 4am to 10:30pm (Midway) and 11:30pm (O'Hare).

PRIVATE CAR AND LIMO SERVICE   Reserving a private car (livery) or limo service from O'Hare or Midway is another option. While limos will cost about $100 to $150 from Midway and $150 to $200 from O'Hare (not counting gratuity and tax), livery services are often quite reasonable. The drivers don't charge much more than a cab, but they'll meet you at baggage claim and make you feel just a bit like a celebrity. For this service, I recommend downloading the app for **Uber** (p. 230), which will fill you in on what cars (or cabs) are in the area by reading the GPS on your phone. Another limo/livery service with a great reputation is **Home James Chicago** (www.homejameschicago.com; ℂ 773/709-5419).

By Car

Interstate highways from all major points on the compass serve Chicago. I-80 and I-90 approach from the east, crossing the northern sector of Illinois, with I-90 splitting off and emptying into Chicago on the Skyway and the Dan Ryan Expressway. From here, I-90 runs through Wisconsin, following a northern route to Seattle. I-55 snakes up the Mississippi Valley from the vicinity of New Orleans and enters Chicago from the west along the Stevenson Expressway; in the opposite direction, it provides an outlet to the Southwest. I-57 originates in southern Illinois and forms part of the interstate linkage to Florida and the South, connecting within Chicago on the west leg of the Dan Ryan. I-94 links Detroit with Chicago, arriving on the Calumet Expressway and leaving the city on the Kennedy Expressway en route to the Northwest.

Here are approximate driving distances in miles to Chicago: From **Milwaukee,** 92; from **St. Louis,** 297; from **Detroit,** 286; from **Denver,** 1,011; from **Atlanta,** 716; from **Washington, D.C.,** 715; from **New York City,** 821; and from **Los Angeles,** 2,034.

For information on car rentals and gasoline (petrol) in Chicago, see "Getting Around by Car," p. 230.

By Train

Chicago's central train station is **Union Station,** 210 S. Canal St., between Adams and Jackson streets. A hub for both national train routes operated by Amtrak and local commuter lines that run to the Chicago suburbs, it's located just across the river from the Loop. Although Union Station is relatively convenient to downtown, the nearest El stop is at Adams and Wells streets (Brown Line), a four-block walk, so you may want to take a taxi or bus to your hotel if you have a lot of luggage.

For train tickets to Chicago from other cities in the U.S., consult your travel agent or call **Amtrak** (www.amtrak.com; ✆ **800/USA-RAIL** [872-7245] in the U.S. or Canada; ✆ **001/215-856-7953** outside the U.S.). Ask the reservations agent to send you Amtrak's travel planner, with useful information on train accommodations and package tours.

International visitors can buy a **USA Rail Pass,** good for 15, 30, or 45 days of unlimited travel. The pass is available online or through many overseas travel agents. See Amtrak's website for the cost of travel within the western, eastern, or northwestern United States. Reservations are generally required and should be made as early as possible. Regional rail passes are also available.

By Bus

Bus travel is often the most economical form of public transit for short hops between U.S. cities. **Greyhound** (www.greyhound.com; ✆ **800/231-2222**) is the sole nationwide bus line. Chicago's Greyhound station is at 630 W. Harrison St. (✆ **312/408-5821**), just southwest of downtown.

If you're planning on traveling elsewhere in the Midwest, **Megabus** (www.megabus.com; ✆ **877/GO2-MEGA** [462-6342]) offers low-cost trips to cities such as Milwaukee, Minneapolis, and St. Louis. The well-kept buses are equipped with Wi-Fi and electrical outlets, and are a popular option for students and car-free penny pinchers. Buses leave from the city's main train station, Union Station.

GETTING AROUND
Finding an Address

Chicago is laid out in a **grid system,** with the streets neatly lined up as if on a giant piece of graph paper. Because the city itself isn't rectangular (it's rather elongated), the shape is a bit irregular, but the perpendicular pattern remains. A half-dozen or so major diagonal thoroughfares make moving through the city relatively easy, but can also confuse you if you're relying on the grid (Lincoln Ave., Milwaukee Ave., Elston Ave., Clark St., and Clybourn Ave. are a few of those pesky but convenient diagonals).

Point zero is located at the downtown intersection of State and Madison streets. **State Street** divides east and west addresses, and **Madison Street** divides north and south addresses. From here, Chicago's highly predictable addressing system begins. With this grid in mind, it's easy to plot the distance in miles between any two points in the city.

Virtually all of Chicago's principal north–south and east–west arteries are spaced by increments of 400 in the addressing system—regardless of the number of smaller streets nestled between them—and each addition or subtraction of the number 400 to an address is equivalent to a half-mile. Thus, starting at point zero on Madison Street and traveling north along State Street for 1 mile, you will come to 800 N. State St., which intersects Chicago Avenue. Continue uptown for another half-mile and you arrive at the 1200 block of North State Street at Division Street. And so it goes, right to the city line, with suburban Evanston located at the 7600 block north, 9½ miles from point zero.

The same rule applies when you're traveling south, or east to west. Thus, starting at point zero and heading west from State Street along Madison and Halsted streets, the address of 800 W. Madison St. would be the distance of 1 mile, while Racine Avenue, at the intersection of the 1200 block of West Madison Street, is 1½ miles from point zero. Madison Street then continues westward to Chicago's boundary with the nearby suburb of Oak Park along Austin Avenue, which, at 6000 W. Madison, is approximately 7½ miles from point zero.

Once you've got the grid figured out, you can look at a map and estimate about how long it will take to walk around any given neighborhood. The other convenient aspect of the grid is that every major road uses the same numerical system. In other words, the cross street (Division St.) at 1200 N. Lake Shore Dr. is the same as at 1200 N. Clark St. and 1200 N. LaSalle St.

Street Maps

The boundaries of Chicago neighborhoods are notoriously blurry (neighbors get in fights about such parameters regularly). Regardless, free maps are available at the city's official visitor information centers at the Chicago Cultural Center and the Chicago Water Works Visitor Center (see "Visitor Information," p. 245). You can also print out maps before your trip by visiting the Chicago Convention and Tourism Bureau's website, www.choosechicago.com.

By Train (the El)

The **Chicago Transit Authority,** better known as the **CTA** (www.transitchicago.com; ℭ 312/836-7000 or TTY 312/836-4949), operates an extensive system of trains throughout the city of Chicago; both the below-ground subway lines and aboveground elevated trains are know collectively as the El. The system is generally safe and reliable, although I'd avoid long rides through unfamiliar neighborhoods late at night.

Fares are $2.25 per ride, regardless of how far you go. For an additional 25¢, you can transfer to the bus or take a different El ride within 2 hours. Children 6 and under ride free, and those between the ages of 7 and 11 pay $1.10. Seniors can also receive the reduced fare if they have the appropriate reduced-fare permit (call ℭ 312/836-7000 for details on how to obtain one, although this is probably not a realistic option for a short-term visitor).

The CTA uses credit card–size fare cards called "Ventra" that automatically deduct the exact fare each time you take a ride. You can purchase the cards at vending machines located at all CTA train stations using cash or a credit card. You'll have a few choices: a single-ride ticket, a reusable/refillable card, or a 1-day pass. The single-ride ticket costs $3 (that's $2.25 to cover the ride plus a transfer plus a fee); the reusable card comes with a $5 surcharge (which will be refunded to you if you register the card online) and then charges the exact fare, $2.25, per ride; and the 1-day Unlimited Ride Pass costs $10 and gets you unlimited use for 24 hours (3-, 7-, and 30-day passes are also available). To use the card, you simply touch it to the Ventra reader, located above the turnstiles, and the reader will tell you to proceed. If within 2 hours of your first ride you transfer to a bus or the El, the turnstiles at the El stations and the fare boxes on

The El Around the Loop

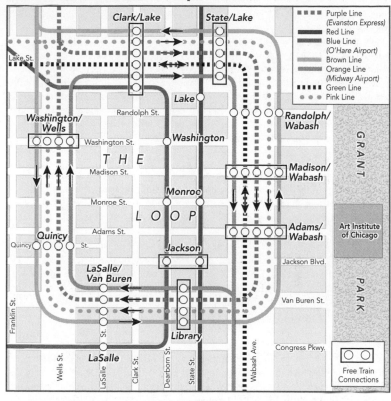

Legend:
- Purple Line (Evanston Express)
- Red Line
- Blue Line (O'Hare Airport)
- Brown Line
- Orange Line (Midway Airport)
- Green Line
- Pink Line

Clark/Lake · State/Lake · Lake St. · Lake · Randolph St. · Randolph/Wabash · Washington/Wells · Washington St. · Washington · T H E · Madison St. · Madison/Wabash · Monroe · Monroe St. · L O O P · Quincy · Adams St. · Adams/Wabash · Quincy St. · Jackson · Art Institute of Chicago · LaSalle/Van Buren · Jackson Blvd. · Franklin St. · Van Buren St. · Library · Wells St. · LaSalle St. · Clark St. · Dearborn St. · State St. · LaSalle · Wabash Ave. · Congress Pkwy. · GRANT PARK

Free Train Connections

buses will automatically deduct from your card just the cost of a transfer (25¢). If you make a second transfer within 2 hours, it's free.

The CTA operates seven major train lines, identified by color: The **Red Line,** which runs north–south, is most likely the only one you'll need, because it runs parallel to the lakefront and past many tourist attractions. The **Green Line** runs west–south; the **Blue Line** runs through Wicker Park/Bucktown west–northwest to O'Hare Airport; the **Pink Line** branches off from the Blue Line and serves the southwest side of the city; the **Brown Line** runs in a northern zigzag route; and the **Orange Line** runs southwest, serving Midway airport. The **Purple Line,** which runs on the same Loop elevated tracks as the Orange and Green lines, serves north-suburban Evanston and runs only during rush hour.

I highly recommend taking at least one El ride while you're here—you'll get a whole different perspective on the city (not to mention fascinating views inside downtown office buildings and North Side homes as you zip past their windows). Although the Red Line is the most efficient for traveling between the Magnificent Mile and points south, your only views along this underground stretch will be of dingy stations. Sightseers are better off taking the aboveground Brown Line, which runs around the

Visitors who plan on taking a lot of train or bus trips should consider buying an **Unlimited Ride Pass,** which works like a fare card and allows individual users unlimited rides on the El and CTA buses over a prescribed period. The cards are available for 1 ($10), 3 ($20), 7 ($28), and 30 ($100) days. The passes are available at any Ventra vending machine, or you can buy them online at www.transitchicago.com or by calling ℂ **888/YOUR-CTA** [968-7282]). Although the passes save you the trouble of feeding the fare machines yourself, they're economical only if you plan to make at least four distinct trips at least 2 or more hours apart (remember that you get two additional transfers within 2 hr. for an additional 25¢ on a regular fare).

---

downtown Loop and then north through residential neighborhoods. You can ride all the way to the end of the line at Kimball (about a 45-min. ride from downtown), or hop off at Belmont to wander the Lakeview neighborhood. Avoid this scenic ride during rush hour (before about 9am and 3:30–6:30pm), when your only view will be of tired commuters.

Study your CTA map carefully (there's one printed on the inside front cover of this guide) before boarding any train. Most trains run every 5 to 20 minutes, decreasing in frequency in the off-peak and overnight hours. The Orange Line train does not operate from about 1am to 5am, the Brown Line operates only until about 2am (1am on Sundays), and the Purple Line operates only during the morning and afternoon rush hours on weekdays. The Red Line and Blue Line run 24 hours.

By Bus

The best way to get around neighborhoods along the lakefront—where the trains don't run—is by public bus. The buses are operated by the Chicago Transit Authority, the same department that oversees trains, and the website is www.transitchicago.com. Look for the **blue-and-white signs to locate bus stops,** which are spaced about two blocks apart. Each bus route is identified by a number and the name of the main street it runs along; the bus that follows Grand Avenue, for example, is the no. 65 Grand.

Buses accept the same fare cards used for the El, but you can't buy a card onboard. That means you have to stop by a train station to buy a card in advance, or pay $2.25 cash when you board. The bus drivers cannot make change, so make sure that you've got the right amount in coins and dollar bills before hopping on.

A few buses that are particularly handy for visitors are the **no. 146 Inner Drive/ Michigan,** an express bus from Belmont Avenue on the North Side that cruises down North Lake Shore Drive (and through Lincoln Park during nonpeak times) to North Michigan Avenue, State Street, and the Grant Park Museum Campus; the **no. 151 Sheridan,** which passes through Lincoln Park en route to inner Lake Shore Drive and then travels along Michigan Avenue as far south as Adams Street, where it turns west into the Loop (and stops at Union Station); and the **no. 156 LaSalle,** which goes through Lincoln Park and then into the Loop's financial district on LaSalle Street.

PACE buses (www.pacebus.com; ℂ **847/364-7223**) cover the suburban zones that surround Chicago. They run every 20 to 30 minutes during rush hour, operating until midevening Monday through Friday and early evening on weekends. Suburban bus

10

Getting Around

PLANNING YOUR TRIP TO CHICAGO

routes are marked with nos. 208 and above, and vehicles may be flagged down at intersections where stops aren't marked. In 2014, the bus payment system switched over, so you can now use the Ventra card, which is the same card accepted on the El and city buses, to ride PACE. Standard fare is $1.75, or $4 for express buses and buses going to popular destinations, such as Wrigley Field, U.S. Cellular Field, Soldier Field, and Six Flags Great America.

By Commuter Train

The **Metra** commuter railroad (www.metrarail.com; © **312/322-6777** or TTY 312/322-6774; Mon–Fri 8am–5pm; at other times, call the **Transit Information Center** at © **312/836-7000** or TTY 312/836-4949) serves the six-county suburban area around Chicago with 12 train lines. Several terminals are located downtown, including **Union Station** at Adams and Canal streets, **LaSalle Street Station** at LaSalle and Van Buren streets, the **Ogilvie Transportation Center** at Madison and Canal streets, and **Randolph Street Station** at Randolph Street and Michigan Avenue.

To view the leafy streets of Chicago's northern suburbs, take the **Union Pacific North Line,** which departs from the Ogilvie Transportation Center, and get off at one of the following scenic towns: Kenilworth, Winnetka, Glencoe, Highland Park, or Lake Forest.

The **Metra Electric** (once known as the Illinois Central–Gulf Railroad, or the IC), running close to Lake Michigan on a track that occupies some of the most valuable real estate in Chicago, will take you to Hyde Park. (See "Exploring Hyde Park" in chapter 6, p. 135.) You can catch the Metra Electric in the Loop at the Randolph Street Station and at the Van Buren Street Station at Van Buren Street and Michigan Avenue. (Both of these stations are underground, so they're not immediately obvious to visitors.)

Commuter trains have graduated fare schedules based on the distance you ride. On weekends, on holidays, and during the summer, Metra offers a family discount that allows up to three children 11 and under to ride free when accompanying a paid adult. The commuter railroad also offers a $7 weekend pass for unlimited rides on Saturday and Sunday. Fares range from $2.75 to $9.25, depending on the distance you're traveling, and you can purchase a ticket in a vending machine or from a ticket agent. You can also purchase tickets on the train from a conductor, but if a vending machine or ticket agent was available, you'll be charged an additional $3.

By Taxi

Taxis are a convenient way to get around the Loop and to reach restaurants and theaters beyond downtown, in residential neighborhoods such as Old Town, Lincoln Park, Bucktown, and Wicker Park.

Taxis are easy to hail in the Loop, on the Magnificent Mile and the Gold Coast, in River North, in Lincoln Park, and along the main drags of most neighborhoods highlighted in this book. But if you end up in an area and can't find a cab, you might need to call. Cab companies include **Flash Cab** (© **773/561-4444**), **Yellow Cab** (© **312/ TAXI-CAB** [829-4222]), and **Checker Cab** (© **312/CHECKER** [243-2537]).

The meter in Chicago cabs currently starts at $3.25 for the first mile and costs $1.80 for each additional mile, with a $1 surcharge for the first additional rider and 50¢ for each person after that. Those who plan on hitting the bars hard should also know that there is a $50 "vomit clean-up fee" in every cab. I don't speak from experience, but I can't help giggle every time I see that posted in a cab.

A Taxi Alternative

It's no longer necessary to stand on a corner and wave like a crazy person to get a cab in Chicago, thanks to **Uber, www.uber.com**. Download this app on your smartphone, and you can input your location and see exactly how many drivers (some are cab drivers, others are independent contractors) are within your radius. The app allows you to estimate your fare and the time it'll take the car to get to your doorstep. Plus, you save your credit card in your account and won't have to exchange any cash. A word of warning: Uber relies on "surge" pricing, which means the cost can go up during inclement weather or busy holidays, like New Year's Eve. The app will inform you when surge pricing is in effect.

By Car

One of the great things about visiting Chicago is that you don't need to rent a car to get around: Most of the main tourist attractions are within walking distance of downtown hotels or public transportation. If you do drive here, Chicago is laid out so logically that it's relatively easy for visitors to find their way around. Although rush-hour traffic jams are just as frustrating as they are in other large cities, traffic runs fairly smoothly at most times of the day. Chicagoans have learned to be prepared for unexpected delays; it seems that at least one major highway and several downtown streets are under repair throughout the spring and summer months. (Some say we have two seasons: winter and construction.)

Great diagonal corridors—such as Lincoln Avenue, Clark Street, and Milwaukee Avenue—slice through the grid pattern at key points in the city and shorten many a trip that would otherwise be tedious on the checkerboard surface of the Chicago streets. On scenic **Lake Shore Drive** (also known as Outer Dr.), you can travel the length of the city (and beyond), never far from the great lake that is Chicago's most awesome natural feature. If you're driving here, make sure you take one spin along what we call LSD; the stretch between the Museum Campus and North Avenue is especially stunning.

DRIVING RULES   Unless otherwise posted, a right turn on red is allowed after stopping and signaling. As in any big city with its share of frustrating rush-hour traffic, be prepared for aggressive drivers and the occasional taxi to cut in front of you or make sudden, unexpected turns without signaling. Chicago drivers almost universally speed up at the sight of a yellow light; you'll most likely hear some honking if you don't make that mad dash before the light turns red.

GASOLINE (PETROL)   Over the past few years, the price of gas in Chicago has fluctuated between $3.50 and $4.50 per gallon. Taxes are already included in the printed price. One U.S. gallon equals 3.8 liters or .85 imperial gallons. In general, you pay more within the Chicago city limits than you will in the suburbs (the city adds an extra tax into the price), so if you're planning a day trip, it pays to fill up once you're out of town.

PARKING   As in most large cities, parking is at a premium in Chicago, so be prepared to pay up. Throughout downtown, street parking is limited to 2 hours (if you can find a spot); you must purchase a receipt from a designated pay box and display it on your dashboard. When that ticket expires, you must move your car. You can get a ticket, still, if you simply pay the meter again. Rates change depending on the neighborhood, but you can count on exorbitant prices, particularly downtown, where meters score $4 to $6.50 per hour. Meters continue to work all night in some areas downtown, so read carefully before leaving your car anywhere.

Read signs carefully, too, because parking regulations are vigorously enforced throughout the city. Many streets around Michigan Avenue forbid parking during rush hour—and I know from bitter firsthand experience that if you violate such a sign your car will be towed immediately. If you're visiting in the winter, make note of curbside warnings regarding snow plowing. Many neighborhoods also have adopted resident-only parking that prohibits others from parking on their streets after 6pm each day (even all day in a few areas, such as Old Town). The neighborhood around Wrigley Field is off-limits during Cubs night games, so look for yellow sidewalk signs alerting drivers about the dozen-and-a-half times the Cubs play under lights. You can park in permit zones if you're visiting a friend who can provide you with a pass to stick on your windshield.

The best deals I've found for parking come through the site **Park Whiz** (**www. parkwhiz.com**). You can enter an address into the site and view all of the parking options around you. I've scored valet parking at hotels near my destination for $10 a day—a steal in the Loop. Garages are also prevalent downtown, at Navy Pier and at the Museum Campus, if you want to wing it. Expect to pay in the $15 to $30 range.

CAR RENTAL   All the major car-rental companies have offices at O'Hare and Midway, as well as locations downtown.

If you're visiting from abroad and plan to rent a car in the United States, keep in mind that foreign driver's licenses are usually recognized in the U.S., but you may want to consider obtaining an international driver's license. International visitors also should note that insurance and taxes are almost never included in quoted rental car rates in the U.S. Be sure to ask your rental agency about additional fees for these. They can add a significant cost to your car rental.

By Bicycle

The city of Chicago has earned kudos for its efforts to improve conditions for bicycling, installing hundreds of miles of bike lanes (some are protected from the streets, others are simply painted lanes). In 2013, the city unveiled its bike share program, called **Divvy** (p. 161; divvybikes.com; *©* **1/855-55-DIVVY** [3-4889]). For $7, you get a 24-hour pass to ride these powder blue cruisers all across town. Just pick one up at any of the hundreds of stations, swipe your credit card, and start pedaling. You'll likely get to your destination quicker by bike than you would by train or car. Because the Divvy program is intended to get cyclists from point A to point B, you'll need to switch the bike out at another station within 30 minutes of your start time. One word of warning: Every cyclist in Chicago should wear a helmet, for safety purposes. Chicago's bike trails fill up with families who aren't necessarily looking out for a cyclist, so you must ride with extreme caution. Then there's the other extreme: Drivers, pedestrians and cabbies on the roads aren't necessarily looking out for you either, so please be on the defensive at all times (see p. 161 for safety tips).

The **Active Transportation Alliance** (www.activetrans.org; *©* **312/427-3325**), a nonprofit advocacy group, has been at the forefront of efforts to make the city more bike-friendly. Their website lists upcoming bike-focused events, including the annual "Bike the Drive," when Lake Shore Drive is closed to cars.

Bike and Roll Chicago rents all sorts of bikes, including tandems and four-seater "quadcycles," as well as in-line skates, from three locations: Millennium Park, Navy Pier, and along the River Walk (www.bikechicago.com; © **888/BIKE-WAY** [245-3929]). Bike rentals start at $10 an hour or $35 a day. Helmets, pads, and locks are provided free of charge.

WHEN TO GO

You'll see Chicago at its best if you visit during the summer or fall. Summer offers a nonstop selection of special events and outdoor activities; the downside is that you'll be dealing with the biggest crowds and periods of hot, muggy weather. Autumn days are generally sunny, and the crowds at major tourist attractions grow thinner—you don't have to worry about snow until late November at the earliest. Spring is extremely unpredictable, with dramatic fluctuations of cold and warm weather, and usually fair amounts of rain (as I write this, it's almost April and it's just barely above freezing). If your top priority is indoor cultural sights, winter's not such a bad time to visit: no lines at museums, the cheapest rates at hotels, and the pride that comes from slogging through the slush with the natives.

When planning your trip, book a hotel as early as possible, especially if you're coming during the busy summer tourist season. The more affordable a hotel, the more likely it is to be sold out in June, July, and August, especially on weekends. It's also worth checking if a major convention will be in town during the dates you hope to travel. It's not unusual for every major downtown hotel to be sold out during the Housewares Show in late March or the Restaurant Show in mid-May.

Weather

With steamy summers and frigid winters, Chicagoans live for the in-between days, where the sun is shining, the lake breeze hits just right, and everyone seems even friendlier than their normal Midwestern selves. In spring and autumn, be prepared for a wide range of temperatures; you may be shivering in a coat and gloves in the morning, only to be fine in a T-shirt by mid-afternoon. Although Chicago winters get a bad rap, they're no worse than in other northern American cities. January isn't exactly prime tourist season, but the city doesn't shut down; as long as you've got the proper cold-weather gear and sturdy boots, you should be fine. Summers are generally warm and sunny, with temperatures that range from pleasant to steamy. The closer you are to the lake, the more you'll benefit from the cool breezes that float off the water.

As close to your departure as possible, check the local weather forecast at the websites of the *Chicago Tribune* newspaper (www.chicagotribune.com) or the **Weather Channel** (www.weather.com). You'll find packing a lot easier if you know whether to expect snow, rain, or sweltering heat. (That said, bring a range of clothes and an umbrella if you're going to be in town for awhile—you should be prepared for anything!)

Chicago's Average Temperatures & Precipitation

	JAN	FEB	MAR	APR	MAY	JUNE	JULY	AUG	SEPT	OCT	NOV	DEC
High °F	32	38	47	59	70	80	84	83	76	64	49	37
Low °F	18	24	32	42	51	61	66	65	57	46	35	24
High °C	0	3	8	15	21	27	29	28	24	18	9	3
Low °C	-8	-4	0	6	11	16	19	18	14	8	2	-4
Inches of precipitation	2.2	1.9	3	3.7	3.7	4.3	3.7	3.7	3.2	2.7	3.3	2.6

Chicago Calendar of Events

The best way to stay on top of the city's current crop of special events is to check in with website of Choose Chicago, aka the Chicago Convention & Tourism Bureau, www.choosechicago.com. The site maintains updated listings on conventions, music, museum exhibitions, nightlife, festivals, and other Chicago goings on. Another great resource is Time Out Chicago, www.timeout.com/chicago, a former magazine that's now all digital, and keeps updated reviews and listings of all that is Chicago centric.

JANUARY

Chicago Boat, Sports & RV Show. Just as we're getting stir-crazy from winter, the boat show comes along and reminds us of how much we love every other season but this one. Well, a city can dream, especially while looking at all the latest boats and recreational vehicles or splashing in a SCUBA pool, watching paddling demos, and spotting big-time entertainment. At McCormick Place; www.chicagoboatshow.com; (✆ **312/946-6200.** Mid-January.

Chicago Restaurant Week. For 2 weeks every year, Chicago gourmands can sample multi-course meals from some of the city's best restaurant for unbeatable rates. Prix fixe menus start at $22 for lunch and $33 or $44 for dinner. Restaurant week takes place in late January/early February. Visit www.choosechicago.com for details on who's participating and make reservations early. Spots at the hottest restaurants fill quickly.

FEBRUARY

Chinese New Year Parade. The sacred dragon whirls down the boulevard and restaurateurs pass out small envelopes of money to their regular customers as Chinatown celebrates 2015, the Year of the Sheep. Call to learn the date of the parade, held at Wentworth and Cermak streets; www.chicagochinatown.org; (✆ **312/326-5320.**

Chicago Auto Show. First, the irony. I'm willing to bet that the majority of the people at the country's largest auto show got here via public transportation. Once here, it's easy to get swept away in car fever, whether you're driving home or not. With more nearly 1,000 vehicles on display—many of which you can climb in, some you can even drive on an obstacle course—it's car porn for car lovers. Held at McCormick Place, 23rd Street and Lake Shore Drive (www.

chicagoautoshow.com; (✆ **630/495-2282**). Date varies.

MARCH

St. Patrick's Day Parade. Die-hards start drinking around 7am the day of the St. Paddy's Day Parade—that is, if they're not still feeling it from the night before. That said, it gets messy. But if you don't mind crazy drunken crowds, Chicago is one of the country's best spots for celebrating Irish heritage. We dye the river green and go all out the Saturday before the holiday. The parade route is along Columbus Drive from Balbo Drive to Monroe Street. Don't expect to get quick service at any of the packed-to-the-O'gills bars in the hours preceding or following the parade. A second, more neighborhood-like parade is held on the South Side the day after the downtown parade, on Western Avenue from 103rd to 115th streets. Visit www.southsideirishparade.org for information. Both parades are held the weekend before St. Paddy's Day, which is March 17.

APRIL

Chicago Improv Festival. We're a funny people here in Chicago, and our improv scene is known as a training ground for performers who have gone on to greater comedic pastures, such as *Saturday Night Live* or *MADtv*. That tradition makes the Chicago Improv Festival a huge draw for big names and lesser-known comedians, who converge for a celebration of silliness, with large mainstage shows and smaller, more experimental pieces. Check website for details; performances occur at theaters all across town (www.chicagoimprovfestival.org; (✆ **773/472-3492**). Early April (sometimes starts in late March).

MAY

Chicago Humanities Festival. Chicago is a force to be reckoned with when it comes to the humanities. Authors, storytellers, actors, and others flex their poetic muscles for more than two weeks during this annual festival, taking over locations in libraries and concert halls throughout downtown to stage cultural performances, readings, and symposiums tied to an annual theme (recent themes included "What Makes Us Human?" and "Stages, Sights & Sounds"). Expect appearances by major authors, scholars, and policymakers, all at a very reasonable cost (usually $5–$15 per event). www.chfestival.org; ✆ 312/661-1028. Early November.

All Wright Housewalk. Sneak a rare peek inside Frank Lloyd Wright–designed private homes and public buildings in Oak Park (www.wrightplus.org; ✆ 708/848-1976). For 40 years, this walk has drawn Wright fans from around the world to get a glance, first-hand, at the Prairie and Victorian styles that surround the architect's former hometown. Tickets sell out quickly, so buy them well in advance when they go on sale in March. Third Saturday in May.

Navy Pier Fireworks. The twice-weekly fireworks shows begin Wednesday nights at 9:30pm and Saturday nights at 10:15pm. You can see the show all across town (and from crowded Navy Pier), but I recommend taking a blanket and a late-night picnic to North Beach or Oak Street Beach for the full Chicago experience. www.navypier.com; ✆ 312/595-PIER [7437]; Memorial Day through Labor Day.

Bike the Drive. One morning a year, cyclists are given access to ride on beautiful Lakeshore Drive—a highway that parallels Lake Michigan. The road is closed to motor vehicles for 5 hours, so bikers have their pick of distance, whether it's just a couple of miles or the whole 30-mile loop. Start at 5:30am or a bit later at any of the open entrances along Lakeshore Drive, from the Museum of Science and Industry to the south to Bryn Mawr Avenue to the north. Sponsored by the Active Transit Alliance; www.activetrans.org; ✆ 312/427-3325. The ride happens Sunday during Memorial Day Weekend.

JUNE

Ravinia Festival. Ravinia means summer to Chicagoans. This suburban, open-air venue is the summer home of the Chicago Symphony Orchestra and the stage for a range of top-rate talent, from pop artists to chamber ensembles. The venue is quite casual, but you wouldn't know it by the candelabras, fine china, wine goblets, and full on gourmet meals that people pack into Ravinia Park in Highland Park. www.ravinia.com. ✆ 847/266-5100. See also "Exploring the 'Burbs," in chapter 5. June through September.

Printers Row Lit Fest. One of the largest free outdoor book fairs in the country, this weekend event fills five city blocks with everything from readings and signings by big-name authors to panel discussions on penning your first novel. Located within walking distance of the Loop, the fair also features more than 200 booksellers with new, used, and antiquarian books; a poetry tent; and special activities for children. One Dearborn Street from Congress Parkway to Polk Street; www.printersrowlitfest.org; ✆ 312/222-3986. First weekend in June.

Chicago Blues Festival. Muddy Waters would scratch his noggin over the sea of suburbanites who flood into Grant Park every summer to quaff Budweisers and accompany local legends Buddy Guy and Lonnie Brooks on air guitar. All concerts at the Blues Fest are free, with dozens of acts performing over 3 days, but get there in the afternoon to get a good spot on the lawn for the evening show. Millennium Park and Grant Park (www.choosechicago.com; ✆ 312/744-3316). Second weekend in June.

World Naked Bike Ride. Ready to bear all on your fixie? Join masses of other hipsters willing to do the same, and who have done so for more than a decade. Some wear body paint, others don costumes, and many wear nothing at all. It's held late in the evening to be less offensive to sensitive eyes. The rules: "Burn fat not oil! Nude not crude!" www.chicago nakedride.org. (Location isn't disclosed until days before to minimize creep factor.) Mid-June.

Old Town Art Fair. For more than 60 years, this juried fine arts fair has drawn scads of art lovers—40,000 and counting—to Old Town. (There's even another art festival that sprung up the same weekend 40 years ago to add to the mix, see below). They're here to see more than 250 painters, sculptors, and jewelry designers from the Midwest and around the country on display. The festival also features an art auction, garden walk, concessions, and children's art activities. It tends to get crowded, but the overall vibe is low-key festive rather than rowdy. Main gate is Lincoln Avenue and Wisconsin Street (www.oldtowntriangle.com; ✆ 312/337-1938). Second weekend in June.

Wells Street Art Festival. Held on the same weekend as the more prestigious Old Town Art Fair, this event has been going on for more than 40 years, in the same neighborhood, and also draws in hundreds of juried artists, along with arts and crafts vendors, food, music, and carnival rides. Wells Street from North Avenue to Division Street; www.chicagoevents.com. Second weekend in June.

Puerto Rican Fest. One of the city's countless summer festivals, the Puerto Rican Fest ranks as one of the largest of its kind, and is filled with 4 days of live music, theater, games, food, and beverages, peaking with a parade that winds its way from Wacker Drive and Dearborn Street to the West Side Puerto Rican enclave of Humboldt Park. Humboldt Park is located at Division Street and Sacramento Boulevard. www.prpcchicago.org. Mid-June.

Grant Park Music Festival. Have I mentioned how many amazing free musical offerings beckon in the summer? This classical music series is one of the best-regarded, and presents free concerts in picture-perfect Millennium Park. Many of the musicians are members of the Chicago Symphony Orchestra, and the shows often feature internationally known singers and performers. Bring a picnic and enjoy dinner beforehand with a view of the skyline. Pritzker Music Pavilion at Randolph Street and Columbus Drive, in Millennium Park; www.grantparkmusicfestival.com; ✆ 312/742-7638. Concerts begin the last week in June and continue through August.

Taste of Chicago. The city claims that this is the largest free outdoor food fest in the nation. Three and a half million rib and pizza lovers feeding at this colossal alfresco trough say they're right. Over 5 days of feasting in the streets, scores of Chicago restaurants cart their fare to food stands set up throughout the park. To avoid the heaviest crowds, try going on weekdays earlier in the day. Grant Park (www.choosechicago.com; ✆ 312/744-3315). Admission is free; you pay for the sampling and music. Early July.

Chicago Pride. This parade has really outgrown its Boystown route in the 40 years it's been going on, drawing nearly 750,000 people to the neighborhood streets. For some, that makes it more fun, while those who hate crowds (and drunken unpredictability) know to keep a safe distance. Pride is the colorful culmination of a weekend Pride fest put on by Chicago's gay and lesbian communities. Halsted Street is usually mobbed; pick a spot on Broadway for a better view. Parade kicks off at Montrose and Broadway aves. and ends near Diversey Pkwy and Sheridan Rd. in Lincoln Park. www.chicagopride.gopride.com. Late June.

Chicago Gospel Festival. Blues may be the city's most famous musical export, but Chicago is also the birthplace of gospel music: Thomas Dorsey, the "father of gospel," and the greatest gospel singer, Mahalia Jackson, hailed from the city's South Side. This 3-day festival—the largest outdoor, free-admission event of its kind—offers music on three stages with dozens of performances at Pritzker Music Pavilion in Millennium Park, Chicago Cultural Center, and Ellis Park. www.choosechicago.com; ✆ 312/744-3316. Late June.

Old St. Pat's World's Largest Block Party. This hugely popular blowout is hosted by the city's oldest church, an Irish Catholic landmark in the West Loop area. It can get pretty crowded, and for good reason: Old

St. Pat's always lands some major acts. Multiple bands perform over two nights on two stages and attract a young, lively crowd. 700 W. Adams St., at Des Plaines Avenue; www.oldstpats.org. Late June/early July.

JULY

Independence Day Celebration. For a traditional Fourth of July, Chicago celebrates the holiday with a free classical music concert in Grant Park in the evening, followed by fireworks over the lake. Expect huge crowds at the main event. Although that's the city's "sanctioned" fireworks show, my favorite way to spend the holiday is to head to the nearest neighborhood park and watch the home-grown explosives light up the sky. Chicagoans are notorious for their love of this holiday, and begin lighting Roman candles and other pyrotechnics in late June. www.choosechicago.org. (C) **312/744-3315.** July 4.

Chicago Yacht Club's Race to Mackinac Island. This 3-day competition is the grandest of the inland water races, as more than 300 boats set sail across Lake Michigan, heading to Mackinac Island. The race has been going on intermittently since 1898. On Saturday, the public alternates between jockeying for a good place to watch the boats set sail toward northern Michigan and enjoying the live music, cocktails, and family fun at a Navy Pier party. Starting line at the Monroe Street Harbor; www.chicagoyachtclub.org; (C) **312/861-7777.** Mid-July.

Sheffield Garden Walk & Music Festival. More than 80 Lincoln Park homeowners open their backyards to visitors at this annual event, giving you a chance to snoop around these normally hidden retreats. The walk isn't just for garden nuts; it has also grown into a lively street festival, with live bands, children's activities, and food and drink tents. It's a popular destination for a wide cross-section of Chicagoans, from singles to young families to retirees. Walk start at Sheffield and Webster aves., www.sheffieldgardenwalk.com. Third weekend in July.

Dearborn Garden Walk & Heritage Festival. A more upscale affair than the Sheffield Garden Walk, this event allows regular folks to peer into lavish private gardens on the Gold Coast, one of the most expensive and exclusive neighborhoods in the city. As you'd expect, many yards are the work of the best landscape architects, designers, and art world luminaries that old money can buy. There's also live music, a marketplace, and a few architectural tours. At North Dearborn and Astor streets (www.dearborngardenwalk.com; (C) **312/632-1241**). Third Sunday in July.

Chicago SummerDance. Feeling footloose? From July through late August, the city's Department of Cultural Affairs transforms a patch of Grant Park into a lighted outdoor dance venue on Thursday, Friday, and Saturday from 7:30 to 9:30pm, and Sunday from 5 to 7pm. The 4,600-square-foot dance floor provides ample room for throwing down moves while live bands play music—from ballroom and klezmer to samba and zydeco. One-hour lessons are offered from 6 to 7pm. East side of South Michigan Avenue between Balbo and Harrison streets (www.choosechicago.com; (C) **312/744-3316**). Free admission.

Pitchfork Music Festival. It may feel more grassroots than Lollapalooza, but the headliners are just as big for this annual music festival, which also brings in its fair share of esoteric alt rock acts. At Union Park on the Near West side, tickets available online at www.pitchfork.com. Late July.

Newberry Library Book Fair & Bughouse Square Debates. Over 4 days, the esteemed Newberry Library invites the masses to rifle through bins stuffed with more than 100,000 books, most of which go for a few dollars. Better than the book fair is what happens across the street in Washington Square Park: soapbox orators re-creating the days when left-wing agitators came here to exercise their First Amendment rights during a re-creation of the Bughouse Square Debates. At 60 W. Walton (at Dearborn St.); www.newberry.org; (C) **312/255-3501.** Late July.

AUGUST

Lollapalooza The city is awash in skinny jeans as the hipster masses arrive for one of the country's most popular music festivals, drawing in top-rate bands and celebrities. Chicago's star chefs also turn out for the event, cooking up concessions that rival what you'll get at a food-centric festival here. At Grant Park; www.lollapalooza.com. Early August.

Northalsted Market Days. A huge street fest, held in the heart of the North Side's gay-friendly neighborhood, Northalsted Market Days, or Market Days, as it's known, draws more than 100,000 people to shimmy to oldie-but-goodie music on three stages (Wilson Philips, 10,000 Maniacs, Olivia Newton-John, The Pointer Sisters, and Sheena Easton have performed in recent years), nosh on neighborhood bites, and gaze upon some of the best people-watching of the summer. Halsted Street between Belmont Avenue and Addison Street (www.northalsted.com; ✆ 773/883-0500;). Early August.

Bud Billiken Parade and Picnic. This annual African-American celebration, which has been held for more than 80 years, is one of the oldest parades of its kind in the nation, and signals the end of the summer and the start of the school year. It's named for the mythical figure Bud Billiken, reputedly the patron saint of "the little guy," and features the standard floats, bands, marching and military units, drill teams, and glad-handing politicians. Starting at 39th Street and King Drive and ending at 55th Street and Washington Park; www.budbillikenparade.com; ✆ 773/536-3710. Second Saturday in August.

Chicago Air & Water Show. Even if you don't plan to watch it, you can't help but experience it with jets screaming overhead all weekend. This 2-day, free event has been a tradition for more than 50 years, and draws a crowd of 2 million folks interested in watching the civilian and military air and watercraft, and even parachute teams (oooh!). Arrive early at North Avenue Beach if you want a spot along the water, or park yourself on the grass along the east edge of Lincoln Park Zoo, where you'll get good views (and some elbow room) www.choosechicago.com. Free admission. Mid-to-late August.

Riot Fest. Punk and rock bands fill the weekend at this popular music fest. There's also a hint of bizarre carnival fun, with rides, Lucha Libre wrestlers and, in recent years, a John Stamos butter sculpture. Takes place outdoors in Humboldt Park, on the west side. Buy tickets online at www.riotfest.org. Early September.

Chicago Jazz Festival. This steamy, Labor Day weekend festival draws in hundreds of thousands of jazz lovers to see national headliners at the largest free event of its kind. Jazz Fest dates back to 1974, when it started as a tribute to Duke Ellington. Now, it serves as a bookend to a summer of free music festivals held at Millennium Park (some concerts are at Chicago Cultural Center, as well.) www.choosechicago.com. Labor Day weekend.

South Chicago Mexican Independence Day Parade. Flamenco dancers, mariachi bands, and families from all over come to Chicago's Little Village for this 2-day festival and Mexican Independence Day parade. It's the largest celebration of its kind in the Midwest. At 26th St. and Kostner Ave, www.chicagoevents.com. Early to mid-September.

Chicago Gourmet. Presented by *Bon Appétit*, this food festival is everything that Taste of Chicago isn't: Civilized and pleasant. It's also packed with celebrity chefs, cooking demonstrations, and food and wine tastings, and I think of it as Taste of Chicago for the 1%. The price of admission is steep (around $170), but once you're inside, you won't have to open your wallet. Just eat and drink your weight for 6 hours. At Millennium Park; www.chicagogourmet.org; ✆ 312/380-4129. Late September

Chicago International Film Festival. With 50 years under its celluloid belt, the oldest U.S. festival of its kind remains fertile ground for discovering new talent. Do names like Martin Scorsese, John Carpenter, Taylor Hackford, and Susan Seidelman ring a bell? They've all been a part of the festival in the past. Every year, the 2-week festival screens films from around the world, as well as a few high-profile American independent films, many of which are world or U.S. premieres. If you don't see the films here, you may not have a chance to see a fair number of them elsewhere in the country. Most screenings are held at downtown movie theaters that are easily accessible to visitors. www.chicago filmfestival.com; ✆ **312/683-0121.** Early October.

Chicago Bank of America Marathon. Chicago's marathon is a major event on the international long-distance running circuit. It brings in elite talent from across the world, along with newbies, for a heart-pumping tour of Chicago, and the streets fill with enthusiastic audiences cheering on the runners in an incredible show of support. The race begins and ends in Grant Park but can be viewed from any number of vantage points along the route. www.chicago marathon.com; ✆ **312/904-9800.** Second Sunday in October.

Dance Chicago. One of the largest dance festivals in the world, Dance Chicago showcases more than 5,000 choreographers and 50,000 performers over 6 weeks. From the city's best-known dance troupes (including Hubbard Street and Joffrey Ballet) to the lesser-known little guys, just about every form of dance is represented here, along with workshops, at the **Athenaeum Theatre,** 2936 N. Southport Ave., on the city's North Side. It's a great chance to check out the range of local dance talent. www.dance chicago.com; ✆ **773/935-6875.** Late October through November.

NOVEMBER/DECEMBER

Holiday happenings. Visitors know that Chicago is still relatively un-cold in November and December, making it bearable to visit to see the many holiday celebrations. Beginning at dusk the Saturday before Thanksgiving, a colorful parade of Disney characters makes its way south along Michigan Avenue, from Oak Street to the Chicago River for the **Magnificent Mile Lights Festival,** www.magnificentmilelights festival.com. Retailers offer hot chocolate and other treats as thousands of holiday lights are set aglow as the procession passes. Carolers, elves, and minstrels

appear with Santa along the avenue throughout the day and into the evening, followed by fireworks over the Chicago River. The arrival of the city's official tree in **Daley Plaza** signals the beginning of the Christmas season (even though it happens before Thanksgiving). Families gather for the festive **Christmas Tree Lighting Ceremony** (www.choosechicago.com) the Tuesday before Thanksgiving, and the plaza fills with lights and song, as the mayor flips the switch. On Thanksgiving Day, floats, marching bands, horses, and performers are front and center on State Street from Congress Parkway to Randolph Street during the **McDonald's Thanksgiving Parade,** www. chicagofestivals.org. **Christkindlmarket,** an open-air, mini–European village, springs up in downtown's Daley Plaza on Thanksgiving Day (www.christkindlmarket.com; ✆ **312/644-2662**), inspired by traditional German Christmas festivals. German-speaking vendors showcase handcrafted ornaments and other seasonal decorations, and of course, it wouldn't be a true celebration without German beer, sausages, and glogg (hot spiced wine). Admission is free and it remains open from Thanksgiving Day until Christmas. Following Thanksgiving, the **Lincoln Park Zoo** burns bright with **Zoo Lights,** which draws families in to meet with Santa inside the lion house, ice skate, and watch live ice carving through early January (see www.lpzoo.org for exact dates and times; ✆ **312/742-2000**). Tickets sell out well in advance for **A Christmas Carol,** a holiday mainstay for more than 2 decades at Goodman Theatre (170 N. Dearborn St.; www.goodman-theatre.org; ✆ **312/443-3800**), which runs from mid-November to the end of December. The same level of popularity surrounds **The Nutcracker Ballet,** which the esteemed Joffrey Ballet performs with a Victorian-American twist in one of the city's most gorgeous theaters, Auditorium Theatre. For tickets call ✆ **312/386-8905** (www.joffrey.com). Early to late December.

One of a Kind Show. For most of the year, the wares at Merchandise Mart are only accessible to interior designers and others in the home industry. The exception is early December, when more than 600 artists set up shop, selling their handmade wares over 4 days. Locals and visitors clamor to browse the jewelry, pottery, clothing, and accessories, in hopes of scoring the perfect holiday gift. At Merchandise Mart, www. oneofakindshow.com, © **312/527-4141.** Early December.

Holidays

Banks, government offices, post offices, and many stores, restaurants, and museums are closed on the following legal national holidays: January 1 (New Year's Day), the third Monday in January (Martin Luther King, Jr., Day), the third Monday in February (Presidents' Day), the last Monday in May (Memorial Day), July 4 (Independence Day), the first Monday in September (Labor Day), the second Monday in October (Columbus Day), November 11 (Veterans' Day/Armistice Day), the fourth Thursday in November (Thanksgiving Day), and December 25 (Christmas). The Tuesday after the first Monday in November is Election Day, a federal government holiday in presidential-election years (held every 4 years, and next in 2016).

FAST FACTS: CHICAGO

Area Codes The 312 area code applies to the central downtown business district and the surrounding neighborhoods, including River North, North Michigan Avenue, and the Gold Coast. The code for the rest of the city is 773. Suburban area codes are 847 (north), 708 (west and southwest), and 630 (far west). You must dial 1 plus the area code for all telephone numbers, even if you are making a call within the same area code.

Business Hours Shops generally keep regular American business hours, 10 or 11am to 6 or 7pm Monday through Saturday. Many stores in downtown Chicago stay open later at least one evening a week. Certain businesses, such as bookstores, are almost always open during the evening hours all week. Most shops are also open on Sundays, usually from 11am to 6pm, with the possible

exception of shops in the Loop. Malls are generally open until 7pm and on Sunday as well. Banking hours in Chicago are normally from 9am (8am in some cases) to 5pm Monday through Friday, with select banks remaining open later on specified afternoons and evenings.

Customs Every visitor more than 21 years of age may bring in, free of duty, the following: (1) one liter of wine or hard liquor; (2) 200 cigarettes, 100 cigars (but not from Cuba), or 4.4 pounds of smoking tobacco and (3) $100 worth of gifts. These exemptions are offered to travelers who spend at least 72 hours in the U.S. and who have not claimed them within the preceding 6 months. It is forbidden to bring into the country almost any meat products (including canned, fresh, and dried meat products such as bouillon, soup

mixes, and so forth). Generally, condiments including vinegars, oils, spices, coffee, tea, and some cheeses and baked goods are permitted. Avoid rice products, as rice can harbor insects. Fruits and vegetables are prohibited as well. Customs will allow produce depending on where you got it and where you're going after you arrive in the U.S. International visitors may carry in or out up to $10,000 in U.S. or foreign currency with no formalities; larger sums must be declared to U.S. Customs on entering or leaving, which includes filing form CM 4790. For details regarding U.S. Customs and Border Protection, consult your nearest U.S. Embassy or consulate, or **U.S. Customer and Border Protection (www.cbp.gov).**

What You Can Take Home from the U.S. If you're an international visitor, for information on what you're allowed to bring home, contact one of the following agencies:

U.S. Citizens: U.S. Customs & Border Protection (CBP), 1300 Pennsylvania Ave. NW, Washington, D.C. 20229 (www.cbp.gov; ℃ **877/227-5511**).

Canadian Citizens: Canada Border Services Agency, Ottawa, Ontario, K1A 0L8 (www.cbsa-asfc.gc.ca; ℃ **800/461-9999** in Canada, or 204/983-3500).

U.K. Citizens: HM Revenue and Customs, Crownhill Court, Tailyour Road, Plymouth, PL6 5BZ0 (www.hmrc.gov.uk; ℃ **300/200-3710**).

Australian Citizens: Australian Customs Service, Customs House, 5 Constitution Ave., Canberra City, ACT 2601 (www.customs.gov.au; ℃ **1300/363-263**; from outside Australia 612/9313-3010).

New Zealand Citizens: New Zealand Customs, 1 Hinemoa St., Harbour Quays Box 2218, Wellington, 6140 (www.customs.govt.nz; ℃ **0800/428-786**; from outside New Zealand, 649/927-8036).

Disabled Travelers

Almost all public establishments in Chicago, including restaurants, hotels, and museums, provide accessible entrances and other facilities for those with disabilities. All city buses are equipped to accommodate wheelchairs, but not all El stations are accessible (some can be reached only via stairs). Contact the

Chicago Transit Authority (CTA) at ℃ **312/836-7000** for a list of accessible stations. For more information on facilities for people with disabilities, contact the **Mayor's Office for People with Disabilities** (www.cityofchicago.org/disabilities; ℃ **312/744-7050** for voice, or 312/744-4964 for TTY). The office is staffed from 8:30am to 4:30pm Monday through Friday.

Horizons for the Blind, www.horizons-blind.org, ℃ **815/444-8800,** is a social service agency that provides information about local hotels equipped with Braille signage and cultural attractions that offer Braille signage and special tours. The **Illinois Relay Center** enables hearing- and speech-impaired TTY callers to call individuals or businesses without TTYs 24 hours a day by dialing 771. The city of Chicago operates a 24-hour information service for hearing-impaired callers with TTY equipment; call ℃ **312/744-8599**. At www.easyaccesschicago.org, you'll find a wealth of information on Chicago and accessibility, including information on transportation, airports, tours and more. For **accessible taxis,** call 800/281-4466, a dispatch service that connects to cab companies with wheelchair accessible vehicles.

Doctors Most hotels in Chicago keep a list of local doctors who are available to tend to guests; in case of health problems, your best bet is to contact your hotel's

concierge or manager. **Northwestern Memorial Hospital,** 251 E. Huron St., a well-regarded downtown hospital, also has a physician referral service (℃ **877/926-4664**), if you need to find a specialist. Also see "Hospitals," later in this section.

Drinking Laws The legal age for purchase and consumption of alcoholic beverages is 21; proof of age is required and often requested at bars, nightclubs, and restaurants, so it's always a good idea to bring ID when you go out. Do not carry open containers of alcohol in your car or in any public area that isn't zoned for alcohol consumption. The police can fine you on the spot. Don't even think about driving while intoxicated.

In Chicago, beer, wine, and other alcoholic beverages are sold at liquor stores and supermarkets. Bars may sell alcohol until 2am, although some nightclubs have special licenses that allow alcohol sales until 4 or 5am.

Driving Rules See "Getting Around," earlier in this chapter.

Electricity Like Canada, the United States uses 110 to 120 volts AC (60 cycles), compared to 220 to 240 volts AC (50 cycles) in most of Europe, Australia, and New Zealand. Downward converters that change 220 to 240 volts to 110 to 120 volts are difficult to find in the United States, so bring one with you.

Embassies & Consulates All embassies are in the nation's capital, Washington, D.C., and a number of consulates are in major U.S. cities, including Chicago, and you can find those at www.thechicagocouncil. org. If your country isn't listed below, call for directory information in Washington, D.C. (① **202/555-1212**) or check **www.embassy. org/embassies**.

The consul of **Australia** is at 123 N. Wacker Dr., #1330, www.usa.embassy. gov.au/whwh/ChicagoCG. html, ① **312/419-1480;** the consul of **Britain** is at 625 N. Michigan Ave. #2200, www.gov.uk, ① **312/970-3800;** the consul of **Canada** is at 180 N. Stetson Ave. #2400, can-am.gc.ca/Chicago, ① **312/616-1860.**

Emergencies For fire or police emergencies, call ① **911.** This is a free call. If it is a medical emergency, a city ambulance will take the patient to the nearest hospital emergency room. The nonemergency phone number for the Chicago Police Department is ① **311.**

Family Travel Chicago is full of sightseeing opportunities and special activities geared toward children. Chapter 4 includes a list of the popular hotels for families, and chapter 6 lists kid-friendly activities.

Gasoline Please see "Getting Around by Car," earlier in this chapter.

Hospitals The best hospital emergency room in downtown Chicago is at **Northwestern Memorial**

Hospital, 251 E. Huron St. (www.nmh.org; ① **877/926-4664**), a state-of-the-art medical center right off North Michigan Avenue. For an ambulance, dial ① **911,** which is a free call.

Insurance For information on traveler's insurance, trip cancelation insurance, and medical insurance while traveling, please visit www.frommers.com/planning.

Internet & Wi-Fi If you are traveling without your own computer, almost every hotel in Chicago has a business center with Internet access for guests (although you may have to pay extra to use it). The **Harold Washington Public Library** (p. 124) has computers available to the public for free. You can also pay per hour to use computers at **FedEx Offices,** which are located throughout Chicago. Find one through **local.fedex.com/il/Chicago** or call ① **800/463-3339.** To find public Wi-Fi hotspots in Chicago, go to **www.openwifispots.com**, which lists all of Chicago neighborhoods and free spots within.

Legal Aid While driving, if you are pulled over for a minor infraction (such as speeding), never attempt to pay the fine directly to a police officer; this could be construed as attempted bribery, a much more serious crime. Pay fines by mail, or directly into the hands of the clerk of the court. If accused of a more serious offense, say and do nothing before consulting a lawyer. In the U.S., the burden is on

the state to prove a person's guilt beyond a reasonable doubt, and everyone has the right to remain silent, whether he or she is suspected of a crime or actually arrested. Once arrested, a person can make one telephone call to a party of his or her choice. The international visitor should call his or her embassy or consulate.

LGBT Travelers Although it's not quite San Francisco, Chicago is a very gay-friendly city. The neighborhood commonly referred to as Boystown (roughly from Belmont Ave. north to Irving Park Ave., and from Halsted St. east to the lakefront) is the center of gay nightlife—and plenty of daytime action, too. There, you might also want to stop by **Unabridged Books,** 3251 N. Broadway (① **773/883-9119**), an excellent independent bookseller with a large lesbian and gay selection. Here, and elsewhere in the Lakeview neighborhood, you can pick up several gay publications, including the weekly **Windy City Times** (www.windycitytimes.com), which covers local news and entertainment.

Mail At press time, domestic postage rates were 34¢ for a postcard and 49¢ for a letter. For international mail, a first-class letter of up to 1 ounce and a first-class postcard costs $1.15. For more information go to **www.usps.com**.

If you aren't sure what your address will be in the

United States, mail can be sent to you, in your name, c/o General Delivery at the main post office of the city or region where you expect to be. (Call ✆ **800/275-8777** for information on the nearest post office.) The addressee must pick up mail in person and must produce proof of identity (such as a driver's license or passport). Most post offices will hold mail for up to 1 month, and are open Monday to Friday from 8am to 6pm, and Saturday from 9am to 3pm.

Medical Requirements

Unless you're arriving from an area known to be suffering from an epidemic (particularly cholera or yellow fever), inoculations or vaccinations are not required for entry into the United States.

Money & Costs

Although not as expensive as New York or London, Chicago's hotel and restaurant prices are near the high end compared to other American cities. In terms of how much to bring: not that much in cash. Credit cards are accepted just about everywhere, aside from a few hole-in-the-wall restaurants, and ATMs are easy to find throughout the city, especially downtown and near tourist attractions. Keep an eye out for fees, which can get hefty.

WHAT THINGS COST IN CHICAGO	US$
Taxi from O'Hare Airport to downtown	40.00
Single full fare on the El or bus	2.25
Seven-day unlimited El/bus pass	28.00
Day of bike riding on Divvy bike	7.00
Movie	12.00
Bottle of water	1.00–2.00
Craft beer	6.00–12.00
Non-craft macro-brewed beer	3.00–7.00
Café latte	4.00

Newspapers & Magazines The two dailies are the *Chicago Tribune* and the *Chicago Sun-Times*. The *Chicago Reader* is a free weekly that appears each Thursday, with all the current entertainment and cultural listings, and *Chicago* magazine comes out monthly. For entertainment listings, check out www.chicago.metromix.com and www.timeout.com/chicago, which I cite throughout the book. The *Windy City Times* publishes both news and feature articles about gay and lesbian issues.

Packing First and foremost, bring comfortable walking shoes. Beyond that, be prepared for anything. Rapid weather shifts are common in the spring and fall. Unless you'll be here in July or August, bring at least one jacket and warm sweater in case of a sudden cold front. The winds off the lake, in particular, can be frosty well into the spring. Your best bet is to bring a selection of long- and short-sleeved shirts that can be layered to adapt to changing temperatures (it's not unusual to start out the morning shivering only to be sweating by afternoon). If you're brave enough to venture to Chicago in the winter, make room for hats, gloves, scarves, and boots: You'll need them.

Chicago is a casual town, so standard tourist-wear is acceptable at all the city's museums and most of the restaurants and theaters. A few traditional fine-dining restaurants have a jacket requirement for men, but otherwise male travelers probably won't need to pack a suit.

Passports To enter the U.S. by air, international visitors must have a valid passport that expires at least 6 month later than the scheduled end of your visit. **Note:** U.S. and Canadian citizens entering the U.S. at land and sea ports of entry from within the Western Hemisphere must now also present a passport or other documents compliant with the Western Hemisphere Travel Initiative (WHTI; see www.getyouhome.gov for details). Children 15 and under may continue entering with only a U.S. birth certificate or other proof of U.S. citizenship.

Passport Offices Australia Australian Passport Information Service (www.passports.gov.au; 📞 **131-232**).

Canada Passport Office, Department of Foreign Affairs and International Trade, Ottawa, ON K1A 0G3 (www.ppt.gc.ca 📞 **800/567-6868**).

Ireland Passport Office, Setanta Centre, Molesworth Street, Dublin 2 (www.foreignaffairs.gov.ie; 📞 **01/671-1633**).

New Zealand Passports Office, Department of Internal Affairs, 109 Featherston St., Wellington, 6011 (www.passports.govt.nz; 📞 **0800/225-050** in New Zealand or 04/474-8100).

United Kingdom Visit your nearest passport office, major post office, or travel agency or contact the **HM Passport Service,** Peel Building, 2 Marsham St. 89 Eccleston Square, London, SW1P 4DF (www.gov.uk/government/organisations/

hm-passport-office; 📞 **0300/222-0000**).

United States To find your regional passport office, check the U.S. State Department website www.travel.state.gov) or call the **National Passport Information Center** (📞 **877/487-2778**) for automated information.

Police For emergencies, call 📞 **911.** This is a free call (no coins required). For non-emergencies, call 📞 **311.**

Safety Although Chicago has one of the highest murder rates in the United States, the vast majority of those crimes are tied to drug dealing or gang activity and take place in areas visitors are unlikely to be walking around. That said, Chicago has the same problems with theft and muggings as any other major American city, so use your common sense and stay cautious and alert. After dark, stick to well-lit streets and don't carry your cellphone as you walk, because personal electronics are frequent targets.

Senior Travel Traveling as a senior can definitely save you money in Chicago; people 60 and older qualify for reduced admission to most major cultural attractions and lower-priced theater tickets. At major museums such as the Art Institute and Field Museum of Natural History, the senior rate is about 30% less than the general admission price.

Smoking Smoking is banned in all public buildings in Chicago, including offices, restaurants, and bars. It's rare to even find a hotel that allows it, so ask before you light up.

Student Travel Most museums and many attractions offer student discounts, so don't leave your student ID at home.

Taxes Chicago sales tax is 9.25%—one of the highest in the nation—and that applies to meals, goods, and some services. Depending on where a restaurant is located (yes, we have special taxing districts in the high tourist areas) taxes can be even higher, at 10.5%. The hotel tax is a whopping 16.4%. The U.S. has no value-added tax (VAT) or other indirect tax at the national level. Every state, county, and city must levy its own local tax on all purchases, including restaurants, hotels, and plane tickets. These taxes will not appear on price tags.

Telephones Many convenience groceries and packaging services sell **prepaid calling cards** in denominations up to $50. While pay phones are increasingly difficult to find, the public pay phones at airports now accept American Express, MasterCard, and Visa. **Local calls** made from most pay phones cost either 25¢ or 50¢. Most long-distance and international calls can be dialed directly from any phone. **To make calls within the United States and to**

Canada, dial 1 followed by the area code and the seven-digit number. **For other international calls,** dial 011 followed by the country code, city code, and the number you are calling.

Calls to area codes **800, 855, 888, 877,** and **866** are toll-free. For **reversed-charge or collect calls,** and for person-to-person calls, dial the number 0 then the area code and number; an operator will come on the line, and you should specify whether you are calling collect, person-to-person, or both. If your operator-assisted call is international, ask for the overseas operator.

For **directory assistance** ("Information"), dial ✆ **411** for local numbers and national numbers in the U.S. and Canada. For dedicated long-distance information, dial 1, then the appropriate area code plus 555-1212.

Mobile Phones. Just because your phone works at home doesn't mean it'll work everywhere in the U.S., thanks to our nation's fragmented cellphone system. If you're traveling from elsewhere in the U.S., your phone should work here, but check your wireless company's coverage chart to be sure. There's also the option of using your smartphone's Skype app at Wi-Fi hotspots for free or cheap calling.

If you know your phone won't work, rent a phone from National Geographic Talk Abroad Services (www.cellularabroad.com;

✆ 800/287-5072), or a rental-car location, but be aware that those prices can be hefty. Companies such as **TracPhone** (www.tracfone.com; ✆ **800/867-7183**) offer cheap, pay-as-you-go options.

If you're not from the U.S., you'll be appalled at the poor reach of the **GSM (Global System for Mobile Communications) wireless network,** which is used by much of the rest of the world. Your phone should work in Chicago, but it definitely won't in many rural areas. To see where GSM phones work in the U.S., check out www.t-mobile.com/coverage. And you may or may not be able to send SMS (text messages) home.

Time The continental United States is divided into **four time zones:** Eastern Standard Time (EST), Central Standard Time (CST), Mountain Standard Time (MST), and Pacific Standard Time (PST); Chicago is in the Central time zone (CST). Alaska and Hawaii have their own zones. For example, when it's 9am in Los Angeles (PST), it's 7am in Honolulu (HST), 10am in Denver (MST), 11am in Chicago (CST), noon in New York City (EST), 5pm in London (GMT), and 2am the next day in Sydney.

Daylight saving time (summer time) is in effect from 1am on the second Sunday in March to 1am on the first Sunday in November, except in Arizona, Hawaii, the U.S. Virgin

Islands, and Puerto Rico. Daylight saving time moves the clock 1 hour ahead of standard time.

Tipping In hotels, tip **bellhops** at least $1 per bag ($2–$3 if you have a lot of luggage) and tip the **chamber staff** $1 to $2 per day (more if you've left a big mess for him or her to clean up). Tip the **doorman** or **concierge** only if he or she has provided you with some specific service (for example, calling a cab for you or obtaining difficult-to-get theater tickets). Tip the **valet-parking attendant** $1 every time you get your car.

In restaurants, bars, and nightclubs, tip **service staff** and **bartenders** 15 to 20% of the check, tip **checkroom attendants** $1 per garment, and tip **valet-parking attendants** $1 per vehicle.

As for other service personnel, tip **cab drivers** 15% of the fare; tip **skycaps** at airports at least $1 per bag ($2–$3 if you have a lot of luggage); and tip **hairdressers** and **barbers** 15 to 20%.

Toilets You won't find public toilets or "restrooms" on the streets in most U.S. cities, but they can be found in hotel lobbies, bars, restaurants, museums, department stores, railway and bus stations, and service stations. Large hotels and fast-food restaurants are often the best bet for clean facilities. Restaurants and bars in resorts or heavily visited areas may reserve their restrooms for patrons. Libraries are also a good, reliable option.

Visas The U.S. State Department has a **Visa Waiver Program (VWP)** allowing citizens of the following countries to enter the United States without a visa for stays of up to 90 days: Andorra, Australia, Austria, Belgium, Brunei, Czech Republic, Denmark, Estonia, Finland, France, Germany, Greece, Hungary, Iceland, Ireland, Italy, Japan, Latvia, Liechtenstein, Lithuania, Luxembourg, Malta, Monaco, the Netherlands, New Zealand, Norway, Portugal, San Marino, Singapore, Slovakia, Slovenia, South Korea, Spain, Sweden, Switzerland, and the United Kingdom. (**Note:** This list was accurate at press time; for the most up-to-date list of countries in the VWP, consult http://travel.state.gov/visa.)

Even though a visa isn't necessary, in an effort to help U.S. officials check travelers against terror watch lists before they arrive at U.S. borders, visitors from VWP countries must register online through the Electronic System for Travel Authorization (ESTA) before boarding a plane or a boat to the U.S. Travelers must complete an electronic application providing basic personal and travel eligibility information. The Department of Homeland Security recommends filling out the form at least 3 days before traveling. Authorizations will be valid for up to 2 years or until the traveler's passport expires, whichever comes first. Currently, there is a

US$14 fee for the online application. Existing ESTA registrations remain valid through their expiration dates. **Note:** Any passport issued on or after October 26, 2006, by a VWP country must be an **e-Passport** for VWP travelers to be eligible to enter the U.S. without a visa. Citizens of these nations also need to present a round-trip air or cruise ticket upon arrival. E-Passports contain computer chips capable of storing biometric information, such as the required digital photograph of the holder. If your passport doesn't have this feature, you can still travel without a visa if the valid passport was issued before October 26, 2005, and includes a machine-readable zone; or if the valid passport was issued between October 26, 2005 and October 25, 2006 and includes a digital photograph. For more information, go to **http://travel.state.gov/visa**. Canadian citizens may enter the United States without visas, but will need to show passports and proof of residence.

Citizens of all other countries must have (1) a valid passport that expires at least 6 months later than the scheduled end of their visit to the U.S.; and (2) a tourist visa.

For information about U.S. visas, go to **http://travel.state.gov** and click on "Visas." Or go to one of the following websites:

Australian citizens can obtain up-to-date visa

information from the **U.S. Embassy Canberra,** Moonah Place, Yarralumla, ACT 2600 ((℃ **02/6214-5600**) or by checking the U.S. Diplomatic Mission's website at **http://canberra.usembassy. gov/visas.html**.

British subjects can obtain up-to-date visa information by calling the **U.S. Embassy Visa Information Line** (℃ **09042-450-100** from within the U.K. at £1.23 per minute; or (℃ **866/382-3589** from within the U.S. at a flat rate of $20, payable by credit card only) or by visiting the "Visas to the U.S." section of the American Embassy London's website at **http://london.usembassy.gov/visas.html**.

Irish citizens can obtain up-to-date visa information through the **U.S. Embassy Dublin,** 42 Elgin Rd., Ballsbridge, Dublin 4 (℃ **1580-47-VISA** [8472] from within the Republic of Ireland at 2.44€ per minute; **http://dublin.usembassy.gov**).

Citizens of **New Zealand** can obtain up-to-date visa information by contacting the **U.S. Consulate General,** Citigroup Center, 23 Customs St., East Auckland CBD (**http://newzealand.usembassy.gov**; (℃ **649/887-5999**).

Visitor Information Before your trip, check in with the **Chicago Convention & Tourism Bureau, aka Choose Chicago** (www.choosechicago.com; (℃ **877/CHICAGO** [244-2246]) to find out about upcoming events and travel packages. (They'll also mail you a packet of materials, if you want.) They have an impressive, easy-to-navigate website, full of Chicago history, itineraries, and event guides, and you can even book hotels there. When you're here, stop by one of the city's two official visitors' centers, the **Chicago Cultural Center,** 77 E. Randolph St. (at Michigan Ave.) and the **Chicago Water Works Visitor Center** in the old pumping station at Michigan and Chicago, for more insider information and free maps.

Index

See also Accommodations and Restaurant indexes, below.

General Index

A

Abbott Oceanarium, 128
Abraham Lincoln Book Shop, 171
Accommodations, 43–73. *See also* Accommodations Index
  alternative, 44–47
  architectural icons, 64
  bed & breakfasts (B&Bs), 45–47
  best deals, 43–48
  best hotels, 6–7
  chains, 44
  discounts, 60
  excess charges and hidden costs, 44
  family-friendly, 66
  The Gold Coast, 69–71
  Green Hotels Initiative, 27
  in historic buildings, 68
  homes, apartments, and couches, 45
  hostels, 47–48
  Lincoln Park, 71–73
  The Loop, 48–56
  The Magnificent Mile, 56–64
  near McCormick Place, 73
  no-tell motels, 53
  off-season winter months, 44
  package bundles, 44
  parking, 50
  pet policies, 46, 62
  price alerts, 44
  price categories, 47
  price matches, 44
  rates, 48
  River North/Near North, 64–69
  smoking, 43
Active Transportation Alliance, 162, 231
Addresses, finding, 225–226
Adler After Dark, 126
Adler Planetarium, 125
African Americans, 18–19
AirBnB, 45
Air travel, 223–224
Alcala's, 173
AllSaints Spitalfields, 173
Allstate Arena, 208
All Wright House Walk (Oak Park), 148
American Girl Place, 179
American Science and Surplus, 181
Amy's Candy Bar, 172
Andy's Jazz Club, 204–205
Antiques, 169–170
Apollo Chorus of Chicago, 200
Apple Store, 178
Aragon Ballroom, 209
Architectural Artifacts, 170
Architecture, 2, 18–23, 122
Architecture River Cruise, 156

Area codes, 239
Arlington International Racecourse, 152–153
Armitage Avenue, shopping, 169
Art, 23, 235
Art Deco buildings, 22
Art Institute of Chicago, 22, 29, 112–113
Astor St.
  No. 1301 & 1260 N., 191–192
  No. 1444 N., 191
  No. 1451 & 1449 N., 190
  No. 1525 N., 190
Athenaeum Theatre, 238
Atlas Brewery, 201
Auditorium Theatre, 121–122, 203
Aviary, 212–213

B

Bahá'í House of Worship (Wilmette), 150–151
Balani, 173
Bank of America Theatre, 198
Barbecue restaurants, 101
Barcades (beercades), 218
Barnes & Noble, 171
Barney's New York, 175
Barrelhouse Flat, 216
Bars, 212–220
Baseball, 31, 164
Basketball, 165
The Baton Show Lounge, 211
Beaches, 5, 160–161
Beauty products, 170–171
Beaux Arts, 22
Bed & breakfasts (B&Bs), 45–47
Beercades, 5
Benchmark, 215
The Berkshire Room, 214
Berlin, 212, 220
Big Chicks, 220
Big Star, 219
Bike and Roll Chicago, 162, 163, 232
Bike the Drive, 234
Biking, 2, 161–162, 231–232, 234
  lake path, 30–31
  The Puppet Bike, 119
  safely, 161
  shop, 182
Billy Goat Tavern, 214
Billy Sunday, 35, 219
Bin 36, 217
Black CouTours, 159
Blagojevich, Rod, 10
Bloomingdale's, 175
Bloomingdale's Medinah Home Store, 168, 175
Blossom House, 141
Blue Chicago, 206
Blues, 7, 25–26, 206–207
B.L.U.E.S., 206
Bond Chapel, 142
Book Cellar, 213
The Book Cellar, 36, 171
Books, 23–25, 171–173
The Boring Store, 181–182
The Bowman and the Spearman (sculpture), 118

Bravco, 168
Breakfast and brunch restaurants, 92–93
Breweries, 201
Bronzeville, 159
Brookfield Zoo, 153
Brown Line elevated. *See* The El
Bryan Lathrop House, 192
Buckingham Fountain, 31, 118
Bucktown/Wicker Park, 40–41, 193–194, 218
  shopping, 169
  walking tour, 34, 192–196
Buddy Guy's Legends, 206
Bughouse Square debates, 132
Bullock Folsom House, 189
Burton Place, No. 4 W., 189–190
Business hours, 239
Bus travel, 225, 228–229
Butch McGuire's, 215

C

Cabarets and piano bars, 211
Cadillac Palace Theater, 198–199
Calendar of events, 233–239
Candies and chocolates, 172
Capone, Al, 16
The Carl C. Heissen House, 188
Carol's Pub, 216–217
Car travel, 224, 230–231
Caton Street, 195
Cedar Street, East, 192
Cellphones, 244
Cemetery tours, 159–160
Cerato, 173–174
Charnley-Persky House, 158, 191
Chase Building, food court, 95
CH Distillery, 201
Chicago Antique Market, 169
Chicago Architecture Foundation (CAF), 120–121, 155–157, 160
  River Cruise, 28–29, 156
  shop, 180
Chicago Bears, 165
Chicago Blackhawks, 166
Chicago Blues Festival, 234
Chicago Board of Trade, 22, 186
Chicago Botanic Garden (Glencoe), 151–152
Chicago Bulls, 165
Chicago Chamber Musicians, 200
Chicago Children's Museum, 6, 154
Chicago Classical Music, 199
Chicago Cubs, 164, 165
Chicago Cultural Center, 22, 120, 159
Chicago Dancing Festival, 202
Chicago Detours, 158
Chicago Federal Center, 23
Chicago Fed Money Museum, 124
Chicago Fire, 166
Chicago Food Planet, 177
Chicago Food Tours, 177
Chicago French Market, 177
Chicago Gospel Festival, 235
Chicago History Museum, 32, 133, 159
Chicago Human Rhythm Project, 202

Accommodations